Fine Meshwork

IRISH STUDIES
Kathleen Costello-Sullivan, *Series Editor*

Edna O'Brien and Philip Roth at the premier of O'Brien's play *Haunted* (2009). Courtesy Barry Gordin.

Fine Meshwork

Philip Roth, Edna O'Brien, and Jewish-Irish Literature

DAN O'BRIEN

SYRACUSE UNIVERSITY PRESS

Syracuse, New York 13244-5290

First Edition 2020

20 21 22 23 24 25 6 5 4 3 2 1

∞ The paper used in this publication meets the minimum requirements of the American National Standard for Information Sciences—Permanence of Paper for Printed Library Materials, ANSI Z39.48-1992.

For a listing of books published and distributed by Syracuse University Press, visit https://press.syr.edu.

ISBN: 978-0-8156-3621-2 (hardcover) 978-0-8156-3639-7 (paperback)
978-0-8156-5467-4 (e-book)

Library of Congress Control Number: 2019956081

Manufactured in the United States of America

For Jim and Joan

Contents

Acknowledgments

As this monograph bears out, a book is a symphony of voices. I would like to briefly thank some of those voices here. My first and greatest thanks to my supervisors, Lee Jenkins and Maureen O'Connor, for their patience, enthusiasm, and inspiration. Without them this book would not exist. I also sincerely appreciate the help and support of the School of English, University College Cork (UCC), especially that of Alan Gibbs, Claire Connolly, Anne Fitzgerald, Katie Ahern, and Eoin O'Callaghan. Ken O'Donoghue in the Department of Irish was also an invaluable friend throughout my studies.

I would like to thank the faculty of Keough-Naughton Institute for Irish Studies, particularly Chris Fox and Susan Canon Harris, for their kindness to me during my year at Notre Dame. My fellow graduate students Jessica Kim, Kevin Gallin, and César Soto all provided much-needed distraction. I owe a large debt to Aimee Pozorski, Debra Shostak, and David Brauner, as well as everyone involved in the Philip Roth Society and the *Philip Roth Studies Journal*, for offering me numerous opportunities to present and publish my work. Also, my thanks to the special collections librarians at Emory University, the University of Chicago, the Library of Congress, and University College Dublin, who afforded me every courtesy during my research. At University College Dublin, my adviser, John Brannigan, provided crucial guidance during my postdoctoral fellowship, as did the rest of the staff, particularly Margaret Kelleher, Danielle Clarke, Lucy Collins, Maria Stuart, P. J. Mathews, Pauline Slattery, and Karen Jackman. Thank you too to the Humanities Institute for giving me a home.

This venture would have been impossible without financial and professional support from a number of sources: the Irish Research Council Postgraduate Scholarship and Postdoctoral Fellowship, the Notre Dame Murphy Irish Exchange Fellowship, and the UCC School of English Studentship. Travel bursaries from the School of English, the College of Arts, Celtic Studies and Social Sciences, and the Irish Association of American Studies also greatly aided my ability to attend conferences and conduct archival research. Unprompted, the students of my second-year seminar Statue of Hybridity: Jewish American Literature frequently made associations between Jewish American culture and its Irish counterpart, allaying my fears over the potential arbitrariness of this study. I thank them for their engagement and ebullience.

My parents, Jim and Joan, and my siblings, Mary-Louise and James, have all in innumerable ways supported this work and sustained its author. Eoin McNally, Therese Kennedy, and Alan O'Gorman all read and improved chapters, while Bridie O'Brien edited the entire manuscript and immensely improved its flow and coherence. My examiners Patricia Coughlan and Tara Stubbs were also very encouraging in my thesis's final stages. Deborah Manion, Kate Costello-Sullivan, and all at Syracuse University Press have helped the transformation of that original thesis into this book. Thanks too to Stephen Watt and to the other readers for their constructive criticism and words of encouragement. Versions of chapters have appeared or will appear in *Philip Roth Studies* and *Irish Studies Review* as well as in Lee Jenkins and Mark Leone's edited collection *Atlantic Crossings* (2017) and the forthcoming *Roth in Context*, edited by Maggie McKinley for Cambridge's Literature in Context series. Thank you to all the editors and readers of those publications.

Edna O'Brien has generously answered questions and allowed me reproduce material from her archives. Erica Jong granted permission to quote from her letters to Edna O'Brien, as have the estates of Philip Roth, Isaac Bashevis Singer, and Bernard Malamud. The cover image is *Departure*, the 1983 painting by the Irish Jewish artist and Joycean scholar Gerald Davis. It appears with the kind permission of his family.

My final thanks go to Emilie, my best friend and guiding light.

Fine Meshwork

Introduction

"Gorgeous Strangers"

Fine Meshwork: Philip Roth, Edna O'Brien, and Jewish-Irish Literature looks at the intertwining lives and works of two giants of twentieth- and twenty-first-century literature: the Irish writer Edna O'Brien (1930–) and her American counterpart Philip Roth (1933–2018). Their long acquaintance was marked by early quarrels and later camaraderie, and the fiction of one bears the indelible prints of the other. This book investigates the striking biographical, textual, and stylistic symmetries between two writers from very different cultures and literary traditions, united in a shared endeavor to say always the unsayable thing. Through understanding the complex interrelations at play between the fiction of Roth and O'Brien, and between their work and that of a wider pantheon of Irish and American writers, this book repositions both as transnational authors. At the same time, it develops an account of the broader transatlantic literary relations between their respective countries.

In 1984 Roth interviewed O'Brien for the *New York Times*. Reflecting on the dualism of the Catholic society she grew up in, she tells him, "The body was as sacred as a tabernacle and everything a potential occasion of sin. It is funny now, but not that funny—the body contains the life story just as much as the brain." Though he makes no mention of it in the interview, Roth's own Jewish cultural upbringing made him familiar with the antagonistic divide between mind and body. He denotes this inherent tension in the epigraph to *Portnoy's Complaint* (1969), which seems to echo O'Brien's sentiment: "Strongly-felt ethical and altruistic impulses are perpetually warring with extreme sexual longings, often of a perverse nature." It is clear that O'Brien's words resonated with Roth, as seventeen years after the interview he reemployed them in the epigraph to another novel, *The Dying Animal* (2001): "The body contains the life story just as much as the brain." O'Brien's words expose the fallacy of isolating body from intellect, a line of argument with which Roth's novel (in fact, his entire career) is in agreement, and one that is furthered by the Yeatsian title of the book. Debra Shostak, one of only a handful of Roth scholars to mention O'Brien at all, sees the novel as proof of Roth's "continued preoccupation with how the self comes into consciousness of itself within and through its fleshly habitation, a point neatly captured in the epigraph."[1] Yet O'Brien's dictum as it appears in *The Dying Animal*—truncated and shorn of its original context—evokes several other binaries. Teasing out these contradictory positions will attest to the complexity of the works of Roth and O'Brien, explain the critical value of their pairing, and undermine simplistic notions of how each interacts with her or his own (and the other's) literary heritage.

Roth's O'Brien-derived epigraph queries the bisection of the pure mind from the sinful body, yet it also destabilizes the demarcation between two related concepts: autobiography and fiction. If the body represents lived experience or biography, then the mind symbolizes the realm of the imagination. To reviewers' frustration, since the start of their careers Roth and O'Brien have willfully blurred the boundaries of fact and fiction. Both inhabit the porous membrane between the two in a manner reminiscent of O'Brien's compatriot Oscar Wilde. Maureen O'Connor positions O'Brien in the Wildean tradition of the dandy, noting how both Irish authors "playfully encourage and abet critical and popular confusion between their gleefully marketed, self-consciously manipulated personae and their fictional productions . . . problematiz[ing] foundational ideas about identity, gender, social role and position, even 'race.'"[2] Roth's public persona is no less an illusion than O'Brien's, one he actively confuses with his fictional avatars: "Am I Lonoff? Am I Zuckerman? Am I Portnoy? I could be I suppose. I may be yet. But as of now I am nothing like so sharply delineated as a character in a book. I am still amorphous Roth."[3]

"For Roth, the self takes its form through experimentation," argues Timothy Parrish, "and should be perceived as a type of fiction." On this subject, Wilde famously claimed that "Life imitates Art far more than Art imitates Life," a direct contradiction of the Aristotelian tenet that art should reflect nature.[4] Like Wilde, then, Roth and O'Brien efface the lines that divide art and life and revel in self-contradictions.

These paradoxes are exemplified in the corollary appended to another of Wilde's famous essays, "The Truth of Masks": "Not that I agree with everything that I have said in this essay. There is much with which I entirely disagree. . . . For in art there is no such thing as a universal truth. A Truth in art is that whose contradictory is also true." For Roth and O'Brien, the slippage between man and manuscript, Wilde and words, is one element of a larger appeal. Principally, Wilde provides both means and permission to inhabit two (or three, or four, ad infinitum) sides of every argument, without the obligation to put forth a dialectical synthesis. Roth has spoken of his "increasing distrust of 'positions,' my own included." This is a (non)position he shares with O'Brien, who tells him, "Artists detest and suspect positions because they know that the minute you take a fixed position you are something else, you are a journalist or you are a politician."[5] Both are extremely wary of so-called universal truths, ideologies, and propaganda. They share with Jacques Derrida and other deconstructionist theorists a skepticism of "transcendental signifiers"—a concept more simply put by Stephen Dedalus of James Joyce's *Ulysses* (1922), who admits his fear of the "big words" like "History" and "Justice," "which make us so unhappy."[6] Both Roth and O'Brien, like Wilde, inhabit liminal positions in their respective societies, allowing their work to vigorously question the monolithic absolutes—morality, nationality, history, gender—of the majority narrative, without feeling compelled to respond with definitive answers of their own.

Wilde was not the only Irish artist to anticipate Roth's and O'Brien's unease with dogma. Their willingness to question their *own* works might also stem from their reading of the Wilde-influenced Yeats, a major figure for both authors. "Yeats's thought was profoundly dialectical," asserts Marjorie Howes, "for nearly every truth he made or found, he also embraced a counter-truth: a proposition that contradicted the first truth, was equally true, and did not negate it." Yeats's later poetry often repurposed the themes and ideas of his earlier corpus. Thus, not only do his poems contain arguments within themselves, but they also argue with one another. Roth's novels perform a similarly critical self-revision, as Parrish makes clear when he exhorts readers of Roth to "[understand] the trajectory of [his] later work as a rethinking of [his] familiar earlier fiction." Amanda Greenwood sees the same dynamic in O'Brien, arguing that in her later works she "*deliberately* comes full circle, not 'recycling' but linking her original perceptions to the rural Ireland of the millennium."[7] How does one critique the half-century careers of two authors who have spent much of that time reworking and self-criticizing their own work, often with more insight and élan than their academic and print-media counterparts? The answers lie in embracing the dialogic manner of inquiry of Roth and O'Brien (and Yeats and Wilde), in never positing a conclusion without the skepticism provided by a counterconclusion and in allowing later chapters to productively challenge what has come before.

Roth's novel *The Counterlife* (1986)—which O'Brien read in proofs—provides a useful model for seeking out and arguing these counterconclusions. The book eschews the linear and conclusive precepts of traditional narratives. The disparate sections contradict each other, and none is given ultimate authority. The novel celebrates life (and history) as "the accidental and the immutable, the elusive and the graspable, the bizarre and the predictable, the actual and the potential, all the multiplying realities, entangled, overlapping, colliding, conjoined." Though Roth and O'Brien are routinely criticized for their supposed overreliance on autobiography, for writing too much about *themselves*, as *The Counterlife* intimates they are just as engrossed in the idea of "multiplying realities" and "*counterselves*." That is, they often form their understanding of the self by imagining different lives and contrasting them with versions closer to their own experiences. For Roth, the female Irish Catholic O'Brien in many ways forms the antipode of his identity as a male American Jewish novelist—a multisided counterself. Likewise, Roth functions as O'Brien's uncanny double. In O'Brien's (and wider Irish) fiction, the Jew is often positioned as an exotic but dangerous "Other," while in the Jewish American canon, Irish Catholics are frequently depicted as both foils and objects of desire. Roth and O'Brien explode these ethnic, cultural, and racial binaries through their central theme of sexuality by rendering relationships that cross such boundaries. For Jacques Lacan, the desire for this radically dissimilar Other is never satisfied, as the Other is always an ideal. Thus, Roth's and O'Brien's focus on such sexual interactions uncovers the uncomfortable fact that Jews and Irish are (like all peoples) very similar and that trenchant divisions between the two are based on little more than what Sigmund Freud terms "the narcissism . . . of minor differences"—a disenchanting revelation for those individuals who see such relationships as a way of escaping the confines of their ethnic group. Further, by undermining the walls that stand between one group and another, they challenge the idea of fixed, cogent collectives. Rather, as their fiction repeatedly shows us, nations and ethnicities are—like the self—constructs. In this way, their work is consonant with the theories of Werner Sollors: "The forces of modern life embodied by such terms as 'ethnicity,' 'nationalism,' or 'race' can indeed be meaningfully discussed as 'inventions.'"[8]

There are three interrelated elements shared by the works of Roth and O'Brien that have motivated this comparative study: the self, the body, and a relentless attack on the concept of purity. To explain the critical importance of these subjects to the authors, I will turn to a clichéd comparison often made in reference to O'Brien and attempt to wrest fresh meaning from it. In his preface to her short-story anthology *A Fanatic Heart* (1984), Roth asserts that "there is a rawness and earthiness in Edna O'Brien that some critics have compared with Colette. But she is not like Colette, because the stories are darker and full of conflict." Here Roth ties O'Brien to Colette, albeit by negation, a comparison that, according to Kathryn Laing, Sinéad Mooney, and Maureen O'Connor, "suggests at once exoticism, foreignness, and a suspicion about authenticity and literariness."[9]

While there is undoubtedly an element of exoticism and foreignness in Roth's attraction to O'Brien's work (and vice versa), there is in no sense a "suspicion about authenticity and literariness." Roth rather holds Colette in the highest esteem, as is evident in his novel *The Professor of Desire*

(1977), where the central character, David Kepesh, ponders the lack of an American Colette:

> Leafing through a pile of [Colette's] books, I have been wondering if there has ever been in America a novelist with a point of view toward taking and giving of pleasure even vaguely resembling Colette's, an American writer, man or woman, stirred as deeply as she is by scent and warmth and color, someone as sympathetic to the range of the body's urgings, as attuned to the world's every sensual offering, a connoisseur of the finest graduations of amorous feeling, who is nonetheless immune to fanaticism of any sort, except, as with Colette, a fanatical devotion to the self's honorable survival. Hers seems to have been a nature exquisitely susceptible to all that desire longs for and promises—"these pleasures which are lightly called physical"—yet wholly untainted by puritan conscience, or murderous impulse, or megalomania, or sinister ambitions, or the score-settling rage of class or social grievance. One thinks of her as egotistic, in the sharpest, crispest sense of the word, the most pragmatic of sensualists, her capacity for protective self-scrutiny in perfect balance with the capacity to be carried away.[10]

Kepesh hazards an uncertain guess that John Updike might be a contender, but this book puts forward that it is Roth himself that Kepesh seeks: Roth is, in his own eyes, the American Colette. This sleight of hand will be observed again and again in this book's chapters, where it will be demonstrated that Roth and O'Brien use their biographies, fictions, and critical analyses of other authors as displaced commentaries on their own work. Colette's Roth-adduced qualities—her sympathy to the "body's urgings," her immunity from "puritan conscience," and her capacity for "self-scrutiny"—are all thus key components of *Roth's* fiction. These components he also sees and admires in O'Brien, reemphasized in an undated letter from him: "There is no American Colette, but there is an Irish one: you."[11]

One might contend that these characteristics are not the most important qualities in O'Brien's (or indeed Colette's) work; rather, it is the tireless disclosure and consequent subversion of structures of control, most especially patriarchy. Yet Roth's take does not dismiss such a reading. Rather, he sees these three elements, the body, the self, and the celebration of the impure, as starting points for any successful attack on Joyce's "big words" and the entrenched systems of power they represent: what Roth terms the "puritan conscience." For him, humans build all social systems, and therefore understanding the grasping, gasping human body in all its selfishness and material frailty is critical to understanding and confronting these systems. As a result, vast ideologies can be critiqued through the deconstruction of their most basic constituent, the individual self.

O'Brien and Roth are routinely maligned for their dogged excavation of the self. For many detractors, it demonstrates a tunnel vision that ignores history and society. As each of the following chapters will show (in their focus on censorship, war, race, and historical narratives), this is a straw-man argument. After all, viewing the world through the inevitably tendentious self is still a means of viewing the world—a means more productive, perhaps, than attempting to achieve an always-impossible objectivity. Hence, the concern with the self does not preclude a concern with the historical and the social; rather, it provides the most suitable vantage point from which to examine them. In the push to prove Roth and O'Brien are politically aware, there is a danger that the importance of the self might be downplayed. However, it is essential that the two be given parity. Their repeated return to their own biographies is not a failure of imagination, but rather a sign of their impressive artistic endeavor.

Considering their oeuvres as a whole, the ceaseless reimagining of the self gives the impression of a cubist painting, in which an object is viewed from all sides at once. Or perhaps a better analogy would be the art of Georgia O'Keeffe—for example, her obsessive repainting of the same door, in different light, at different times, or the equally plentiful renditions of what O'Brien describes as her "both spent and fertile" orchids.[12] Far from being reductive and repetitive, the recurring biographical elements in the works of O'Brien and Roth are each time shown in a fresh light, from complex stylistic, temporal, and spatial angles. It is through this process that Roth and O'Brien achieve their great longitudinal triumphs—what are to my mind some of literature's most comprehensive depictions of the self. Yet rather than capturing a stable, eternal totality, these depictions rather leave us with the deflationary fact that, ultimately, the self is contingent, transitory, and fragmented. A key corollary of this decades-long self-study is the dignity both writers afford the body (from which, as the epigraph to *The Dying Animal* relates, the self is inseparable), unsentimentally tracking its progress from birth to death and refusing to ignore it in either lustful prime or inevitable decline.

Finally, we turn to that great enemy of the body and the singular self, "puritanical conscience." As this book will testify, Roth and O'Brien have spent their considerable novelistic careers defying concepts of purity: religious purity, nationalist purity, racial purity, historical purity, and literary purity. In bringing together two authors so culturally disparate—Catholic and Jewish, Irish and American, male and female—this study hopes to do the same, most obviously in problematizing the purity of national canons. Jewish and female respectively, Roth and O'Brien were born into groupings at odds with the then conventional visions of American and Irish canonicity. Though this conceptual narrowness has now changed to varying degrees, these prior lacunae highlight the constructed, arbitrary, idealized, and exclusionary nature of literary traditions. This drive for purity will be seen as a guiding force behind the ruling governmental and communal structures that O'Brien and Roth rail against. This book is engaged in two tasks. First, it will show how Roth and O'Brien push back against the ruthless Manichaeanism of puritan conscience by emphasizing the hybridity of identity and the multiplicity of history. Second, it will demonstrate how the texts of these authors similarly reject national and literary purity through allusiveness that pays little heed to spatial or temporal boundaries.

Flirtatious Intertextuality

In his interview with O'Brien, Roth describes her work as akin to "a piece of fine meshwork, a net of perfectly observed sensuous details that enables you to contain all the longing and pain and remorse that surge through the fiction." Not only does the phrase "fine meshwork" describe O'Brien's writing, but it also illustrates the multiple connective threads that bind her books to other texts, not least to those works of Roth. The intertwined nature of their writing is symbolic of a far-ranging symbiosis between Irish literature and its American—particularly Jewish American—counterpart. It is also representative of parallels and crossings-over between Irish and

Jewish history and culture. Like Roth, Joyce is aware of the metaphorical potential of fabric, using it here to represent the merging of cultures and languages: "Our civilization is a vast fabric, in which the most diverse elements are mingled. . . . In such a fabric, it is useless to look for a thread that may have remained pure and virgin without having undergone the influence of a neighbouring thread. What race, or what language . . . can boast of being pure today?"[13] Joyce imagines literature and society as an interwoven patchwork that counteracts the dangerous fallacy of purity. How Roth and O'Brien critique this myth of ethnic and racial wholeness (often with reference to Joyce's work) will be explored in later chapters. This section will set out how their work subverts literary purity; yet the two issues are significantly interlinked. The intermixing of texts provides a metonym for the intermixing of cultures, peoples, and nations—the many-voiced text reflects the many-voiced nation.

The study of influence often looks to human relations to find metaphors for how texts interact with one another. Most famous, perhaps, is Harold Bloom's conception of the struggle between poet and precursor as a Freudian battle between father and son, as he sets out in *The Anxiety of Influence* (1973) and its sequel, *A Map of Misreading* (1975): "A poet, I argue . . . is not so much a man speaking to men as a man rebelling against being spoken to by a dead man (the precursor) outrageously more alive than himself."[14] As this statement makes clear, Bloom's vision of influence is highly gendered. Few literary critics would today invoke Bloom's model without significant disclaimers. However, as Asha Varadharajan warns, "Bloom's idiosyncratic myth [remains] a perdurable cultural force with implications for our present." Irish feminist critics are keenly aware of the myth's enduring legacy, most obviously in its perpetuation of exclusive literary canons—a concept made manifest in the first three volumes of *The Field Day Anthology of Irish Writing* (1991). As Patricia Coughlan notes, "Oedipal and masculinist models . . . still prevail . . . in the reception and transmission of Irish writing."[15] The fourth and fifth volumes of *The Field Day Anthology of Irish Writing: Irish Women's Writing and Traditions* (2002) provide a corrective to this tiered, male-centered structure, replacing it with a fluid network of texts that transcend limiting ideas of what qualifies as "Literature." Bloom's theory is most often criticized for its androcentrism and its static, hierarchical nature, yet its invocation of violent struggle also causes concern. Terms such as "agon" and concepts like "battle" and "domination" are increasingly tired metaphors for incredibly dense and complicated relationships between one author and another as played out through their textual interactions. The problem in relation to the fiction of Roth and O'Brien is that the Oedipal model is, superficially at least, a seductive one. The fictional worlds of both are teeming with overbearing fathers and father figures as well as mothers and mother figures. Reading these familial relationships into how Roth and O'Brien interact with other authors can thus be tempting. However, Irish feminist scholarship points out how ill-served women writers are by such a mode of inquiry, in which they are arbitrarily squeezed into a Freudian paradigm, or, more often, inserted as an afterthought.[16] Furthermore, this model fails to consider the relationship between contemporaneous authors, who do not simply write *back* toward another national or ethnic literary tradition but also write *out* toward others.

Gilles Deleuze and Félix Guattari's theory of the rhizome presents an inviting counterpoint to the Oedipal family tree. Deleuze and Guattari's work is concerned not with "pyramidal hierarchization" systems such as Bloom's, but rather with "notions of multiplicities, flows, arrangements, and connections . . . [with] proliferation, juxtaposition, and disjunction." "There are no points or positions in a rhizome such as those found in a structure, tree or root," as Deleuze and Guattari demonstrate, by contrasting the diverse and multiple growth system of the humble mushroom with that of the mighty oak.[17] Is there an equivalent to the rhizomatic mushroom in the traditional family structure? Father-son relationships have little novel to offer, and sibling and other consanguine relationships, though looser and relatively more manifold, can be similarly stifling. However, casting the net beyond the family captures an apposite metaphor: the act of flirting. Flirting is an activity that takes many diverse forms and can provide connections (both fleeting and sustained) between a near-infinite number of people. It is everything that a constraining, antagonistic parent-child relationship is not: playful, protean, assorted. Though one can have only a single biological father or mother, one can conceivably have a multitude of love relationships, dalliances, and flirtations.

As a metaphor for textual transmission, flirtation provides many benefits for a comparative project. It takes in direct references one author makes to another, but also more subtle correlations that may stem from their inhabiting similar literacy milieus, sharing common influences, and investigating connected themes. Rather than imagining authors in rebellion against a small number of aggressive core predecessors, their texts can instead be envisioned in flirtatious dialogue with a global literary network. It does not grant temporal or spatial privilege to canonical authors, but rather considers all writers democratically. Unlike its Oedipal counterpart, it is gender neutral and can be conducted and enjoyed for its own sake, without necessarily working toward a sexual or reproductive goal. It is nonviolent, yet at the same time sensitive enough to register contention between its participants. It also takes better account of the playfulness of association between such authors as Roth and O'Brien. Adam Phillips argues that flirting is the "calculated production of uncertainty" and "puts in disarray our sense of an ending," making it a useful metaphor for the fluidity of intertextuality as opposed to the more defined presumptions of Bloomian influence.[18] Intertextual traces are often indeterminate; their intended outcomes, if any, are debatable. Just as a flirtation is not as obvious or demarcated a relationship as a filial, marital, or parental bond, flirtatious intertextuality is not necessarily predicated on explicit allusion. Often the connections drawn will be tentative, contingent, and studied as sites of multiple rather than singular meaning.

In the spirit of this new metaphor, this book will not struggle with Bloom alone, but rather interact promiscuously with theorists of intertextuality such Julia Kristeva, Gerard Genette, and Roland Barthes. Kristeva's reading of Mikhail Bakhtin allowed her to reformulate his concept of dialogism into her own paradigm, namely, intertextuality: "Any text is constructed as a mosaic of quotations; any text is the absorption and transformation of another."[19] From such readings, it becomes apparent that seeing the text as flirtatious is not a wholly new concept. Barthes, for example, maintains that texts flirt with their audience: "Texts . . . contain within themselves, *if they want to be read*, that bit of neurosis necessary to the seduction of their readers: these terrible texts are *all the same* flirtatious texts." To imagine texts that flirt with one another is a more original approach, yet the seeds of it are also present in Barthes's argument. He imagines the text as an "anagram . . . of our erotic body."[20] Extrapolating from this point, the intertextual trace (where two texts meet) can be figured as flirtation. By discarding the vertical model of influence, this book embraces the horizontal delight of the intertextual mode. This method considers texts on an egalitarian level, not as subordinate to (or derivative from) a small number of precursor master texts. In addition, Genette's idea of the paratext helps this book handle those areas of text that stand in between the novel proper and the wider world: introductions, interviews, autobiographies, and archives. Considering the frequent quests by Roth and O'Brien to muddy the clear dividing lines of art and life, Genette's theories regarding these textual abutments are invaluable.

The "intertextuality as flirtation" metaphor is inspired by the personal relationship between Roth and O'Brien.[21] Their letters revel in ludic, bodily humor—for example, O'Brien sympathizing with Roth's depression, "I wish I could make you laugh but I've always been better at the inducing of the other glands! I mean tears," and congratulating him on his recovery from an operation, "I hope you're better—back, brain and all other zones."[22] Roth advises her to "fuck (though not actively) 'longing.'"[23] At Roth's eightieth birthday, O'Brien denied that they had been lovers. While refuting an actual relationship, however, she gave scope to a fictional one: "It has been assumed that we were lovers. I have to confess to you we were not. However, a zealous student of [Roth's] has pointed out to me that perhaps I am the prototype for a heroine Caesara O'Shea in his novel *Zuckerman Unbound*."[24] This book does not speculate on Roth and O'Brien's relationship, but rather takes their correspondence as a model of intertextual contact. The fictionalized liaison between Zuckerman and Caesara can lead the aware reader on an intertextual trail outside the bounds of *Zuckerman Unbound* and into the works of O'Brien. Thus, the flirtation within the text both points to and provides a theoretical metaphor for how the novel connects with other texts. It provides a counterweight to the critical fixation on the contentious relationship between Zuckerman and his father, which has always obscured a consideration of supposedly peripheral characters like Caesara in *Zuckerman Unbound* (as will be explored in chapter 4).

Flirting can have both a serious and a playful intent, often simultaneously, with flirtation's mischievous delivery often obscuring an earnest attraction. In an analogous manner, the frequently playful nature of Roth's and O'Brien's allusions can belie a weightier purpose. Serious references to influential texts and writers are often overlooked or disregarded because they are gloved in comic cloth. Yet by compounding the serious and the silly, the effect of the former is often heightened. The desirability, if not the necessity, of the frivolous mode in addressing the serious is another technique that both Roth and O'Brien share with Wilde, exemplified in his paradoxical dictum, "Life is far too important a thing to ever talk seriously about." This combination of the giggle inducing and the grave also recalls once more the epigraph of *The Dying Animal.* Body and mind might in this context refer to the division between "high" and "low" literary registers, in addition to the connotations of Cartesian duality and the art-life divide. In a 1973 interview impishly conducted with himself, Roth rejects the Jewish intellectual Philip Rahv's binary division of American writers into refined East Coast "palefaces" and lusty frontier "redskins."[25] Instead, he creates the neologism "redface" to describe his own work, a fusion of literary finesse and the boisterous bark of life. Roth and O'Brien thrive within the carnivalesque juxtaposition of these two assumed opposites, arguing against the purity of high literature.

Roth once told Joyce Carol Oates, "Sheer Playfulness and Deadly Seriousness are my closest friends."[26] It pays to keep this paradoxical pairing in mind when reviewing how Roth's texts communicate with one another and the vast world of literature. Flirting captures the playfulness and seriousness that are often bound up in direct allusions.[27] He is conscious of the frequently counterproductive nature of approaching serious subjects in a serious manner. Such attempts often suffer from debilitating overearnestness and myopic idealism and tend toward propaganda. He admits to encountering such problems when writing *The Ghost Writer* (1979), which he discusses in his 1984 "Art of Fiction" interview with Hermione Lee: "When I began, in the third person, I was somehow revering the material. I was taking a high elegiac tone in telling the story of Anne Frank surviving and coming to America. . . . Instead of Anne Frank gaining new meaning within the context of my story, I was trying to draw from the ready store of stock emotions that everybody is supposed to have about her."[28] Flirting, both within the text and without, comes to Roth's rescue. Within the text, Roth reshuffles the plot so that Anne Frank does not come to the United States, but does so only in the mind of the young, idealistic novelist Nathan Zuckerman. Zuckerman imagines a courtship (and eventual marriage) between himself and Anne, a means of atoning for the impropriety of his fiction. A revealing short story of his has led to accusations of anti-Semitism and self-hatred from the 1950s Jewish American community, still reeling from the Holocaust. As Zuckerman grandly fantasizes, "Who dares to accuse of such unthinking crimes the husband of Anne Frank!"[29] While Zuckerman flirts with his fictional Anne Frank *within* the novel, the book itself sets out on flirtatious assignations of its own, namely, with texts such as *A Portrait of the Artist as a Young Man* (1916), *The Diary of Anne Frank* (1952), and the works of Henry James, Saul Bellow, and Bernard Malamud. The romantic fancies of Zuckerman investigate the contentious issues surrounding, in Roth's words, "the difficulties of telling a Jewish story—How should it be told? In what tone? To whom should it be told? To what end? Should it be told at all?"[30] This novel has been mined from a Bloomian perspective, with the young Zuckerman falling out with his father over the short stories before seeking a new literary father figure in the reclusive writer I. E. Lonoff (a fictional composite of Malamud and Isaac Bashevis Singer). However, focusing on the relationship between Zuckerman and "Anne" offers exciting horizontal tangents for critical exploration.[31] Roth likes to approach his literary forebears through the intimate and revealing position of their imagined love lives. This playful method has the effect of stripping away any unhelpful urge to deification that Roth may feel for his predecessors (or, indeed, contemporaries) and permits him to view them as human. This approach allows him to treat so-called great texts not as holy, unchangeable objects, but as mortal works to be kvetched with, cajoled, charmed, and critically disassembled. The manifestation of other authors as characters in Roth's work can communicate to the reader some of Roth's thoughts and views on their work. As shown with Colette, however, Roth's speaking of other writers can also be read as a displaced commentary on himself.

By emphasizing the multitudinous, flirting provides a remedy to the binary lock of the parental model. In reference to *The Professor of Desire* (but indicative of Roth's oeuvre as a whole), David Parker Royal postulates, "By portraying Kepesh's textual indulgences and extensive name-dropping as he does, Roth may be suggesting that such efforts to forge links of legacy are inherently problematic."[32] Here lies a contradiction. While overburdening his novels with allusions as a means of undermining schematic notions of legacy and literary genealogy, Roth still wishes his reference points to promote texts that have mattered to him as a reader. He is, in effect, both undermining canons and providing the reader with his own created canon. It is not necessary to resolve this seeming incongruity; Roth, like Wilde and his friend Walt Whitman, can comfortably contain contradictions and multitudes. Roth's literary signposting leads to another, much older but nonetheless pertinent, definition of "flirt": "To give (a person) a sharp, sudden blow or knock; to rap, strike." It is a reaction Roth demands from the books he reads, as is evinced by Zuckerman's quoting of Kafka in *Zuckerman Unbound*: "I believe that we should read only those books that bite and sting us. If a book we are reading does not rouse us with a blow to the head, then why read it?"[33] Roth's allusions face two ways at once, looking within the text, to alter or emphasize internal themes, and without, to provide a guide for the reader, leading him or her to what are, in the author's opinion, literature's seminal texts.

Flirtatious Paratexts

Edna O'Brien shares Roth's thoughts on the power of great novels. In her memoir she restates the advice she gave to her American students: "I brought Kafka to read to them and told them how Kafka had said a book must be an axe to the frozen seas inside us." If a book must have such an effect simply to be read, what sort of formidable impact must a text possess to be referenced in a novel or short story? A powerful book is a blow, a knock, an attack to the system, and thus referring to such a text, despite the comic or playful way it might be set up, can be a very serious business. However, as with Roth, respecting a powerful text does not mean revering it. O'Brien is just as comfortable reworking formative literary texts as her American counterpart. For example, her early short story "Irish Revel" reimagines Joyce's "The Dead" from the perspective of a young woman. As Roth does with Anne Frank, O'Brien also brings her literary antecedents to life in both her fiction and her nonfiction. This point is particularly the case in her dedicated biographies *James Joyce* (1999) and *Byron in Love* (2009), in which she brings her role as a novelist to bear, as Michael Gillespie acknowledges: "*James Joyce* . . . appears to me to be every bit as artistic in its aims as any of O'Brien's writings." He continues, "In writing about Joyce, O'Brien offers useful guidelines for approaching her own work."[34]

As with Roth, then, O'Brien's disquisitions on her literary forerunners are valuable not only in themselves but also as a means of reading her oeuvre. The writings of Roth and O'Brien overflow the embankments that separate fiction from biography. This is a feat these authors achieve both through their own autobiographical fiction and through their equivocal autobiographies and memoirs.[35] By allowing these already vaguely defined generic modes to blend into one another, Roth and O'Brien emphasize the fundamentally fictional nature of the self. Whether it is fiction that closely adheres to biography or autobiography that knowingly points to its own fictionality, O'Brien and Roth continue their mission to prove that no objective truth exists in such narratives, or, indeed, in any narrative. The anger Roth and O'Brien inspire in their detractors stems in part from this biographical-fictional hybrid, the playful flirtation of life and art. It implicitly (and in their later work explicitly) confronts the idea that narrative, either on a personal or on a national level, provides singular and stable meaning.

If what Roth and O'Brien say about other authors can be mined for new means of understanding their own work, then special attention needs to be paid to phenomena such as the prefaces, interviews, and introductions they write for, or conduct with, fellow writers. Some examples of how Roth and O'Brien discuss different authors will be delineated below, so as to provide textual ballast to considerations of how they discuss each other in later chapters. Whereas the previous section focused most on Barthes and Kristeva, this section engages primarily with Genette, specifically his theories on the "paratext," namely, all the material not within the novel proper that helps the reader interpret and frame the text. It is divided into two segments, the peritext and the epitext. The former refers to everything that is on or within the covers of the book, but not within the text itself. It includes titles, prefaces, and epigraphs. Pertinently for this transnational study, Genette envisions the peritext as a type of liminal borderland: "Rather than with a limit or a sealed frontier, we are dealing in this case with a threshold . . . which offers to anyone and everyone the possibility either of entering or of turning back."[36] If the peritext can be likened to a frontier, the epitext covers the much larger space beyond. It is everything outside the covers of the book that nonetheless frames the text. Most prominently these include interviews with the author, letters written by the author, reviews, and draft manuscripts. Thus, the paratext is made up of the peritext and the epitext—the inside and out—forming a conceptual structure through which to study how the novels of Roth and O'Brien invoke, interact, and intertwine with the works of their precursors, of their contemporaries, and of each other.

The role of the peritext is a flirtatious one. The outer cover of a novel is, like a sharp suit or revealing dress, intended to attract an audience. The layers beneath that cover—prefaces, dedications, epigraphs, and biographical notes—are, like lingerie, a more intimate means of seduction.[37] All of them are intended to entice the reader into engaging with the body of the text.[38] For Genette, these auxiliary elements are a means of consolidating meaning and guiding the reader toward (and subsequently through) the text. However, as I suggested earlier, what an author writes about another author (here in the form of a preface or introduction) can often be a better guide to the author's own work than to his or her professed subject.

Roth and O'Brien expose the constructed nature of the self by comparing their lives and fictions with those of other authors, and in doing so set up implicit contrasts between their own nations and others and between their own historical eras and others. Therefore, prefaces written by Roth and O'Brien deserve careful consideration. In Roth's case, he has written both a preface and an afterword for his Czech coeval Milan Kundera. Roth's peritextual foray into Kundera's fiction, the afterword to *The Book of Laughter and Forgetting* (1981), emphasizes the divergence between American and Eastern European social liberty and takes a strong interest in the liminal condition that lies in between these two states: exile. Kundera escaped Czechoslovakia for France in 1975, and Roth candidly asks him, "How do you feel as an émigré?"[39] Though Roth does not mention it, or choose himself as a comparison, he too had at this time gone into semiexile, making London his residence for six months of every year between 1975 and 1989. The stress Roth puts on issues of exile in this afterword (and throughout his paratextual writings) may reflect his own anxieties about belonging and the effect of an author's distance from his or her homeland and subject matter. Roth was also preoccupied with writers who could *not* escape. This preoccupation was most especially the case regarding the Jewish authors of Eastern and Central Europe, for whom the twentieth century provided no means of flight; those writers who somehow avoided the gas chambers were often banned, oppressed, or deported to gulags by the new Soviet authorities.[40] In his prefaces, as in his fiction, Roth imagines counterlives to his own existence as a free, successful American Jewish novelist.

The prefaces that O'Brien writes for her compatriots can be viewed similarly. In her introduction to the Signet edition of J. M. Synge's *The Playboy of the Western World, and Other Plays* (1997), for example, she covertly touches on elements of Synge's life and work that correlate to and diverge from her own.[41] O'Brien's account of the reception of *The Playboy of the Western World* (1907) might just as well describe that which met the publication of her own first novel: "It was . . . booed by Irish zealots who believed it to be a travesty of Irish life." These zealots are, in O'Brien's words, the "Roman Catholic Irish men who . . . rose up in mutiny at this insult to their womankind." She and Synge are thereby united in their enemies. Chief among his denouncers was Arthur Griffith, who condemned Synge's play *In the Shadow of the Glen* (1903) as "a slur on Irish womanhood" for its offensive presumption that any Irishwoman would "go away with the Tramp." Griffith's wish to keep Ireland safe from the influence of foreign "strangers" also found expression in his fierce anti-Semitism, best displayed in his reaction to the 1904 Limerick Boycott of Jewish businesses, during which he railed against Jews as "usurers and parasites."[42]

O'Brien sees analogies not only between herself and Synge but also between herself and Synge's lover Molly Allgood (stage name Maire O'Neill).[43] This double affinity gives O'Brien's preface an exhilarating bifocal perspective. On the surface, it appears that O'Brien makes little of Allgood, describing her as "a mere shop assistant" whom Synge attempts to "educate." Yet to a reader with any knowledge of O'Brien's life, her sketch of Maire's biography is implicitly equated with her own, working as she did as a "mere shop assistant," before falling in love with an older intellectual who patronizingly promised to cultivate her. This double point of view is one Amanda Greenwood also acknowledges in her analysis of O'Brien's biography of Joyce: "*James Joyce*'s intertextualities conflate 'Nora' not only with O'Brien's fictional characters, but implicitly with O'Brien herself."[44]

The newly minted terms "flirtatious intertextuality" and "flirtatious paratextuality" form two sides of the same coin. The first considers the internal fictional world of the text; the second takes as its domain the external material world that frames the text. Yet as Roth and O'Brien have shown throughout their long literary careers, there is no clear demarcation between the fictive and the factual. Rather, both write fiction that appears tantalizingly close to fact, and fact that repeatedly draws attention to its own constructed nature. Intertextuality reminds the reader that all text is an amalgamation of previous texts, that no text is wholly pure, original, or unique, but is rather one thread in a transnational literary meshwork. Intertextuality consequently provides a valuable metaphor for modern society, a metaphor that defies nationalist and ethnic purists and instead rejoices in the densely interlaced cultural groups from which a nation is stitched. To study this mix, one must forgo crude binary judgments, instead relying on concepts of multiplicity to forge new perspectives. On Roth, Shostak argues, "The writer talks to himself, through a diverse population of fictive avatars, in order to pry out the many selves he inhabits and embraces and thus to sketch out a host of counterlives."[45] Yet it is not only through an *internal* dialogue that the writer produces these counterlives, but also through his or her external interactions with a mass of other writers and writings. The constant inward gaze that is the hallmark of Roth's and O'Brien's fiction is matched by an equally powerful outward vision, irrepressibly curious about the reality of others. This vision is not a glare into the past, as Bloomian readings would have it, but rather a panoramic wink.

Crossing the Fields: Review of Literature

Despite the fact that Roth has interviewed O'Brien, prefaced her work, quoted her in epigraph, and corresponded with her over more than three decades, and that she has dedicated a memoir to him—indeed, explicitly modeling it on *Patrimony* (1991), Roth's account of his father's life—and defended his fiction in print, there has yet been no comparative study of these two important authors. This dearth became apparent to me when I attended Roth@80 in 2013, a conference celebrating Roth's eightieth birthday and recent retirement. Arriving in Roth's hometown of Newark, New Jersey, on Saint Patrick's Day, I felt it a fitting time to put forward a reconsideration of Roth's Irish influences beyond Yeats and Joyce. My paper took Roth's use of Synge's work in *The Humbling* (2009) as its topic, while my discussions with other Roth scholars centered on Roth's literary connections with O'Brien.[46] Later we toured the Newark immortalized in Roth's fiction. The tour ended (a little bizarrely for the majority of academics, who were Jewish American) in Newark's Catholic Basilica. I, however, found it suitably symbolic of the growing recognition of the subtle parallels Roth draws between Jewish and Irish culture. The celebrations reached their peak with a series of speeches in the Newark Public Library. Jewish American author Jonathan Lethem warmed up the crowd with a hilarious discourse on the love-hate dichotomy through which any young author must view Roth's extensive oeuvre. *New Yorker* writer Claudia Roth Pierpont gave an important reassessment of Roth's female characters, rescuing them from criticisms of caricature. Then, unexpectedly (and to the bemusement of those academics I had yet to regale with my thesis), Edna O'Brien appeared onstage to introduce Roth. While the other speakers focused on Roth the writer, O'Brien gave a moving portrait of Roth the man: "feared and revered, plagiarized, envied, hermit and jester, lover and hater, foolish, yet formidable, too adorable for words, a true friend and undoubtedly one of Yeats's 'Olympians.'"[47]

Despite the growing recognition of their pioneering roles in twentieth-century fiction, no study of any length has yet considered Roth and O'Brien together. This work's unique temporal and geographical scope means that it utilizes and inflects a variety of different fields. In terms of Irish studies, this book owes much to the pivotal work of Declan Kiberd in *Inventing Ireland* (1998), most pertinently his thesis that "far from providing a basis for doctrines of racial purity, [Irish texts] seem to take pleasure in the fact that identity is seldom straightforward and given, more often a matter of negotiation and exchange." Also crucial is Elizabeth Butler Cullingford's *Ireland's Others* (2001), which focuses specifically on those groups—Ireland's "internal others"—that challenge this racial purity. Joe Cleary does much to complicate the stability of national canons in *The Cambridge Companion to Irish Modernism* (2014), continuing the field's global turn by making a claim for the consideration of Americans such as Eugene O'Neill and F. Scott Fitzgerald as part of an Irish modernism, a horizontal move that lessens the imposing and often blinding presence of Joyce and Yeats. Tara Stubbs draws on even bolder comparisons, looking at American authors with less obvious and traditional (read: Catholic and male) claims to "Irishness," such as John Steinbeck (of Scotch-Irish heritage) and Marianne Moore (whose multicultural genealogy would have confused even Leopold Bloom). This study takes another step outside of conventional Irish comparatives, using as a guide Scarlett Baron's exemplary two-author monograph, *"Strandentwining Cable": Joyce, Flaubert, and Intertextuality* (2011), in which she balances out a feeling that "to probe the relations between such towering geniuses is to do the obvious" with the opposing sense: "The very suggestion that [these authors] may have much in common has the power to mystify, for the differences between the contexts, textures, plots, structures, and tonalities of their various works, as well as between their lives in terms of places, time, and event—are substantial, and can make the existence of any significant intertextual connection between them seem unlikely."[48]

Such Irish/non-Irish critical juxtapositions are not new to O'Brien studies, the feminist roots of which have encouraged the study of O'Brien in relation to other female authors, as in Dawn Duncan's and Amanda Greenwood's analyses of O'Brien and Virginia Woolf as well as Eve

Stoddard's postcolonial exploration of O'Brien and Jamaica Kincaid. Literary criticism on O'Brien has been growing steadily since the publication of *The Field Day Anthology of Irish Writing: Irish Women's Writing and Traditions*, which formed not just a corrective to the near-complete absence of women writers in the first three volumes, but also a specific rebuke to the tokenism of O'Brien's position in previous anthologies.

This late acknowledgment of both her literary worth and her Irishness (however one might decide to define this slippery term) in some ways granted permission for the academic study of her texts as significantly informed by, and informing, Irish twentieth-century history and culture.[49] In the wake of this extraordinary piece of scholarship, two edited collections, *Edna O'Brien: New Critical Perspectives* and *Edna O'Brien: Wild Colonial Girl* (both 2006), further disprove O'Brien's marginal place within the Irish canon, while also querying any stable conceptions of canonicity. Full-length studies of O'Brien remain sadly sparse—Amanda Greenwood's 2003 *Edna O'Brien* is the most comprehensive so far, though Maureen O'Connor's forthcoming literary biography promises to be definitive—but since 2006 articles have appeared with regularity in a variety of Irish studies journals, many of them based outside Ireland, attesting to O'Brien's global appeal and encouraging comparisons with other, often marginalized, literary traditions. O'Brien's work is also central to many of the most recent studies in Irish literature. Michael Cronin's *Impure Thoughts: Sexuality, Catholicism and Literature in Twentieth Century Ireland* (2012) uses her novels to delve into the function of sexuality, history, and trauma in Ireland, drawing fascinating correspondences with the early writing of John McGahern, before setting both authors in dialogue with their predecessors Joyce and Kate O'Brien. Clair Wills's *The Best Are Leaving* (2015) employs O'Brien to probe the seeming disconnect between the social phenomenon of Irish emigration during the twentieth century—not always a negative experience for those individuals who wished to escape clericalism, poverty, and stagnant social advancement—and its nearly universally negative portrayal in literature. Tony Murray's *London Irish Fictions: Narrative, Diaspora and Identity* (2012) looks at O'Brien's lesser-studied mid-1960s fiction as a means of shifting the analytical focus from departing emigrants and the Ireland left behind to arriving immigrants and new lands found. The pairing of Roth and O'Brien continues the outward momentum of both O'Brien and Irish studies.

In Roth studies, Shostak acknowledges that Roth's original Jewish context "has been supplanted by a far richer texture of reference and intellectual history."[50] This push on critical boundaries is, however, only beginning. Velichka Ivanova's edited collection *Philip Roth and World Literature* (2013) has shifted the focus from America to Europe, especially probing Roth's myriad links to Eastern Europe. Roth has received exponentially more critical attention than O'Brien, with a peer-reviewed journal, *Philip Roth Studies*, dedicated to his work and a mass of monographs, to several of which this book is particularly indebted, including David Cooper's *Philip Roth and the Jews* (1996), Mark Shechner's *Up Society's Ass, Copper* (2003), Shostak's *Philip Roth: Countertexts, Counterlives* (2004), Ross Posnock's *Philip Roth's Rude Truth* (2006), David Brauner's *Philip Roth* (2007), David Gooblar's *The Major Phases of Philip Roth* (2011), and Aimee Pozorski's *Roth and Trauma* (2011). The expanding perspective of the critical literature on Roth, from early Jewish angles to fuller American considerations and to the eastward gaze back to Europe, mirrors a shifting paradigm in American studies more generally. The "transnational turn" (a term, like its linguistic, postcolonial, and multicultural predecessors, so overused as to be almost meaningless) situates America within a worldwide context. Still, when employed carefully it proves a useful tool in challenging national orthodoxies and reminding us that flows of peoples, passions, printed material, and prejudices over borders and seas are not only contemporary phenomena. Often, however, transnational theory has lagged behind these transnational practices and has thus proved inattentive to the complex interplay between nation, narration, and the transnational in the careers of authors such as Roth and O'Brien. Indeed, at its best, American transnational theory often turns to Roth's fiction—just as the transnational turn in Irish studies, as exemplified by Wills and Murray, looks to O'Brien—to address this complexity, as can be seen in Pease, Rowe, and Fluck's *Re-framing the Transnational Turn in American Studies* (2011) and Paul Giles's *The Global Remapping of American Literature* (2011).

In comparing Roth and O'Brien, this project can, as Paul Gilroy argues in *The Black Atlantic* (1993), "transcend both the structures of the nation state and the constraints of ethnicity and national particularity."[51] Along with Gilroy's influential work, this monograph also draws on black/Irish comparative works such as *The Harlem and Irish Renaissances* (1998) by Tracy Mishkin—who helpfully begins her argument by outlining how Jews relate to both her studied groups—and Peter D. O'Neill and David Lloyd's edited collection, *The Black and Green Atlantic* (2009), along with Irish/southern ones such as Kieran Quinlan's *Strange Kin: Ireland and the American South* (2005) and Kathryn Stelmach Artuso's *Transatlantic Renaissances: Literature of Ireland and the American South* (2013). The literary and personal relationship between Roth and O'Brien symbolizes myriad linkages between Jewish and Irish literature and culture, linkages lately scrutinized by critics such as Stephen Watt in *"Something Dreadful and Grand": American Literature and the Irish-Jewish Unconscious* (2015) and George Bornstein in *Colors of Zion: Blacks, Jews and Irish, from 1845 to 1945* (2011).[52] Watt rightly argues that the composite "Jewish-Irish studies, or Irish-Jewish studies . . . could produce a fresh purchase on cultural phenomena . . . which neither Jewish studies nor Irish studies could produce alone." He and Bornstein seek out a more balanced and critically productive vision of Irish-Jewish relations than found in current scholarship: "When our present historical memory includes contact at all, it usually stresses tension rather than cooperation."[53] Bornstein and Watt have not picked their subjects at random; rather, there is "an unusual relationship between these peoples that goes well beyond comparisons of their respective diasporas."[54]

As a means of explicating some of the most pertinent elements of this Jewish-Irish interrelationship, this book turns to Roth's fellow New Jersey Jewish poet Gerald Stern. In Stern's poem "Sixteen Minutes," the speaker observes the merging of two clouds—"One was Ireland and one was Long Island"—before falling into a reverie in which she or he tries to "unravel the history" of the Jews and Irish:

> Strange to think that they had different poets,
> so close they were together, and strange to think
> how it would be if ours were closer or theirs
> were closer to us or if they drifted together
> . . . .

> Odd to think of the Jews and Irish too,
> how we married each other,
> how my own children have pink faces,
> how we hated each other, Jews and Irish,
>
> and fought each other, how the Jews were horrified
> by one thing, how the Irish were enraged
> by another, how the Irgun on our side
> and the IRA on theirs both battled English
>
> . . . .
>
> the world in shreds. Language too we had
> together, I would call it subversive, and spoke we
>
> still another tongue and spoke we this tongue
> as gorgeous strangers.

In the poem, Stern sets forth the paradoxical relationship between the Irish and the Jews, raised in American ghettos to hate and fear the other, only for many to defiantly intermarry, an attraction bred out of the assumed radical difference of the Other. He then inflates this claustrophobic image of urban adjacency and considers the global picture, blending the Irish and Jewish experience together through their twentieth-century confrontations with British imperialism, in Ireland and in Israel, while elsewhere in the poem harking back to a shared history of oppression and mass death, captured in the pall of "livid chimneys and smoking hillsides."[55] He finally focuses on language, first dispensing with the truism of the shared love of talk, "blarney, / a Jewish characteristic," before delving deeper into the psychological effects of the traumatic transition from Yiddish and Irish to English, "we spoke / still another tongue," the stanza break emphasizing the rupture and loss of this sundering. Yet there are advantages too in this linguistic hybridity, evinced in Stern's compelling phrase, "spoke we this tongue as / gorgeous strangers," which echoes a declaration made by Oscar Wilde during his American tour: "The Saxon took our lands from us and left them desolate—we took their language and added new beauties to it."[56]

Drawn together (when not repelled) by this common outsider status, traditionally subjugated, bereft of homeland and home language, yet endowed with the outsider's ability to adapt, the Jews and Irish were indeed "gorgeous strangers" in America, not least to each other. It is these similarities that, in part, explain the allure of Irish authors such as Wilde, Joyce, Yeats, Synge, and O'Brien to Jewish American authors, a feeling that, in both Ireland and America, the Irish had mapped out a trail the Jews could (warily) follow. It is these literary correspondences that leads Stern's speaker to ponder, "Strange to think they had different poets, / so close they were together," an understandable confusion when one thinks of Joyce's Leopold Bloom, Ireland's most famous, though fictional, Jew, or indeed the pervasive intertextual presence of Joyce apparent in Henry Roth, Malamud, and Bellow. It is often in these imaginative landscapes where Jewish and Irish writers meet, a malleable space Stern portrays as the clashing, cleaving, and coming together of clouds, a flirtatious and hybrid space in which the "foggy city / called Irishaloyem" and its native creole "Judish" is to be found. Hence, Stern's poem conjures up some of the shared spheres of Irish and Jewish history, which have so influenced Jewish and Irish literature and political discourse, and all of which will be crucial to this thesis: the immigrant experience in America, the Jewish experience in Ireland, historical and mythical analogies between Irish and Jewish history, the shared love of—yet feelings of exclusion from—the English language, and finally the tenderness and terror of two heritages intimately wrapped around one another.[57]

Outline of Chapters

This introductory chapter has, through the concept of flirting, limned a nonhierarchical comparative framework that can best account for the interrelatedness of the fiction of Roth and O'Brien, without privileging either, and in doing so better address the fluid nature of transnational intertextual linkages. Though transnationalism has, in the past decade, given a new primacy to movement across borders, it is essential to remember that the reading practices of authors—and the resultant allusiveness of their work—have never taken much notice of national boundaries. Authors are "always already" transnational beings, often in actuality—living outside of their home country—and always in textuality. With this obvious (though frequently forgotten) point in mind, this introductory chapter has begun to unravel some of the knots that bind Roth's work to O'Brien's and vice versa, and in doing so it exposes the larger nodes of an Irish/Jewish American literary nexus. Following a biographical chapter that elaborates on the lives and works of these authors, the book proceeds in a broadly chronological fashion, with the second chapter focusing on Roth's and O'Brien's early careers in the 1960s, the third taking on their experimental 1970s work, the fourth looking at race in the early 1980s, the fifth chapter centering on nation in the 1990s, and the sixth and final chapter on displacement in the twenty-first century. In each of its chapters, the book demonstrates the ways in which Roth and O'Brien confute notions of purity.

Chapter 2 looks at how both authors challenge the moral purity of their communities, examining the controversy that greeted their bildungsroman debuts, O'Brien's *The Country Girls Trilogy* (1960–64) and Roth's *Goodbye, Columbus* (1959). O'Brien uses the figure of a Jew to scrutinize Ireland's repressive relationship with sexuality, while Roth conversely employs Irish Catholic writers and symbols to express his young protagonists' emerging sexual understanding during the conservative Eisenhower era. In both cases, this unknown or imagined community (Catholics in Roth, Jews in O'Brien) is portrayed as having sexual knowledge that is alternatively dangerous and enticing. Primarily focused on O'Brien, with comparative reference to Roth, this chapter examines how these young authors defy both conventional censorship and less official forms of silencing.

Chapter 3 investigates the authors' increasing concern with gendered identity, contrasting O'Brien's exploration of Irish femininity in *Night* (1972) with Roth's deconstruction of Jewish manhood in *Portnoy's Complaint* (1969). My argument considers these texts in the context of thc "Troubles" in Northern Ireland and the Six-Day War in Israel, events that challenged previously accepted conceptions of identity in Ireland and Jewish America. In doing so, it disputes contemporary criticism that attacked O'Brien and Roth for failing to address the major political upheavals of the 1960s and 1970s. Rather than avoiding these events, Roth and O'Brien refuse to take sides, denying the ideological purity demanded by nationalisms that reduce everything to "with us or against us" dichotomies. A prudish focus on these novels' representation of sex has obscured their subversive political content.

From nationalist purity to racial purity, chapter 4 looks at the extended intertextual ties between Roth's novel *Zuckerman Unbound* (1981) and O'Brien's *Mother Ireland* (1976), and in doing so continues to contradict schematic denunciations of their lack of concern with their political, social, and international milieus. Specifically, Roth's probing of Jewish America's social ascension into whiteness and his use of O'Brien to warn against the Irish American whitening model will be studied. Roth's novel, far from avoiding politics, is a potent castigation of the rise of white ethnicities and of the concomitant swing by (some) Jewish and Irish voters toward the film-fantasy version of American history embodied by Ronald Reagan.

At the center of chapter 5 lie the trilogies Roth and O'Brien wrote in the 1990s, which were received as epic close-of-century, country-capturing canvasses. These "national" trilogies ironically had international spurs, with decisive intertextual flirtations attesting to the inspiration O'Brien's triptych provided for Roth, and with both authors greatly affected by William Faulkner, particularly his contention that history is "never dead" but is rather constantly reinvented for present purposes. Through Faulkner, Roth and O'Brien repudiate the purity of state-approved narratives, promoting in its stead a polyvalent conception of history.

The final chapter, chapter 6, investigates the stylistic and thematic parallels between the late novels, exploring how, in their postmillennium fiction, Roth and O'Brien use literary displacement to consider the mass population displacements of the twentieth and twenty-first centuries. While their early work considered the relationship between the individual and the community, and their middle work the relationship between the artist and the nation, their late books use mythic methods to address contemporary—and at the same time perennial—global dilemmas. Throughout this chapter and *Fine Meshwork* as a whole, the flirtatious, the multiple, and the contradictory will be prescribed as antidotes to the pure, the linear, and the certain.

Just as this introduction began by explicating the intertextual flirtations between Roth and the Irish literary tradition of O'Brien, Yeats, and Wilde, it seems fitting here to close by mentioning O'Brien's personal and textual relationships with writers of the Jewish American tradition observed in her correspondence. O'Brien charmed and befriended J. D. Salinger, who praised her incomparable stories; Malamud, who commended her early fiction as "fresh, strong, full of human things"; Bellow, who felt a writer's affiliation with her, "There seems to be only one significant thing for me—for the likes of us—and it hasn't a great deal to do with parties"; Joseph Heller, who playfully schemed to bring her to New York for free, through dint of his "long experience trading on the literary Levant"; Norman Mailer, who "gave [her] a walking tour of the [New York] city" as she researched *Light in Evening*; Singer, who was particularly struck by *A Pagan Place* and its "love scene with the priest"; and Erica Jong, who saw her as a mentor figure, "I think you are the true inheritor of James Joyce's tradition."[58]

O'Brien's Atlantic-crossing letters offer a tangible symbol of the intertextual networks this book strives to chart. Roth and O'Brien make apt subjects in the study of the transnational flow of literary ideas, with Roth's work influenced by O'Brien's fiction in particular, and by the Irish literary tradition and Irish culture in general, and with O'Brien's inflected by an array of Jewish American and American writers. Their relationship began stormily but over time developed into an ever-deeper bond. Discussing her friendship with Roth, O'Brien told me, "We found that we liked or disliked the same works of fiction. . . . We didn't really go into discussions about [our own work]. But the sense of solidarity was always there." *Fine Meshwork* seeks to delineate that sense of solidarity as it came into being and as it played out over a forty-year literary friendship between two authors now central to, yet for many years set apart from, their respective national literary canons. In a letter to Roth, O'Brien admits that she is "fascinated by change in people, especially in artists where it is more traceable."[59] The change (and continuity) evident in these authors' half century–spanning careers will be traced through their fiction, exploring how both were seen in their own countries, within each other's communities, and, by one another, as "gorgeous strangers."

1

"The Body Contains the Life Story Just as Much as the Brain"

The Novelists' Biographies of Philip Roth and Edna O'Brien

Throughout their oeuvres Philip Roth and Edna O'Brien repeatedly warn of the danger of simply reading a novel through the life of the novelist—even while teasing their readers with cornucopias of embedded biographical detail. Roth affected exasperation at such readings: "If all these subtle readers can see in my fiction is my biography, then they are simply numb to fiction—numb to impersonation, to ventriloquism, to irony, . . . numb to all the delicate devices by which novels create the illusion of a reality more like the real than our own," while O'Brien wryly commented, "I'd be a goner now if I did everything I wrote."[1] It is thus with caution that this chapter outlines "the facts" of their lives and works.[2] Nevertheless, as the subsequent chapters deal primarily with literary texts, it is advantageous to present some relevant biographical and historical context here at the outset. In addition, this chapter also includes pertinent moments of cultural crossover, highlighting the allure of Irish (and Irish American) themes, characters, and writers for Roth and the pull of Jewish (and Jewish American) subjects, settings, and books for O'Brien. Finally, it sketches Roth and O'Brien's evolving friendship and its implications for their literature.

The Facts: The Life and Works of Philip Roth

In the fiction of Jewish American authors such as Henry Roth (1906–95) and Saul Bellow (1915–2005), and their Irish American counterparts like

James T. Farrell (1904–79), the relationship between Jews and Irish in the crowded urban spaces of early twentieth-century America ranges from animus to enchantment. In Henry Roth's modernist epic of 1900s New York tenement life, *Call It Sleep* (1934), the young, timid Jewish protagonist, David, and his braver Polish friend are attacked with sling shots by Irish "marauders": "Ya Irish mutts! Waid'll I git ya, I'll rap de piss odda ye!"[3] Yet at the same time, David is beguiled by the strange rituals of Catholicism and keeps a rosary hidden in his pocket.[4] In Bellow's tale of rocketing assimilation in 1920s and 1930s Chicago, *The Adventures of Augie March* (1953), the hero, Augie, listens as his brother tells him of a fight—later revealed to be an invention—with "two micks": "a couple of drunk jokers, ferocious Irishmen . . . [who] threw him down the stairs." Farrell, who mentored the younger Bellow, views the relationship from the other side in his story of interwar working-class Irish life, *Studs Lonigan* (1934), where Old Man O'Brien enumerates some ancient and modern tenets of Jew hatred among Irish Catholics: "There never was a white Jew, a Jew that wasn't yellow. . . . Why they even killed their own God . . . And now I'll be damned if they ain't comin' in spoiling our neighborhood." Yet throughout the story the antihero, Studs, seems to identify with Jews and even, in his own mind, looks like one: "His long nose was too large for his other features; almost a sheeny's nose."[5] E. L. Doctorow perfectly captures this interethnic tension in *Ragtime* (1975), and in doing so nods at the cognate patterns of Irish and Jewish acculturation in America: "[Jewish immigrants] were filthy and illiterate. . . . They had running sores. They had no honor and worked for next to nothing. . . . They killed each other casually. Among those who despised them the most were the second-generation Irish, whose fathers had been guilty of the same crimes."[6] The Jews and Irish loom frighteningly large in one another's imaginations, in part, because the differences between them are so slight. This vacillating relationship has a deep cultural resonance in America, evident in the plethora of Tin Pan Alley songs and early Hollywood films that draw on the theme of Irish/Jewish love affairs and the trouble they engender. Of particular interest in this regard is the perennially popular drama *Abie's Irish Rose*, "a comic treatment of cross-ethnic lovers, the Jewish Abraham Levy and the Irish Rosemary Murphy," which spawned films, books, other plays, and innumerable imitations throughout the twentieth century.[7]

This ambivalence between the Jews and Irish was still extant when Philip Roth was born in 1933 in Newark, New Jersey, to insurance salesman Herman (1901–89) and homemaker Bess (1904–81), as Roth writes in *The Facts: A Novelist's Autobiography* (1988): "At home the biggest threat came from the Americans who opposed or resisted us . . . because we were Jews. Though I knew that we were tolerated and accepted as well . . . and though I never doubted that this country was mine . . . I was not unaware of the power to intimidate that emanated from the highest and lowest reaches of gentile America."[8] At a national level, there was much antipathy among Irish Catholic figures toward the Jews, as Claudia Roth Pierpont explains in her biography of Roth, *Roth Unbound* (2013): "As for anti-Semitism, [the young Roth] knew about the larger hate-filled American figures such as Father Coughlin and Henry Ford." Coughlin was a famous radio demagogue in the 1930s, with an audience in the tens of millions, who used his broadcasts to attack President Roosevelt's New Deal and, as Timothy Meagher suggests, "helped convert some disaffected Irish and other Catholics into anti-Semitic crusaders."[9] Ford used his automobile wealth to sponsor the printing in America of a half-million copies of the anti-Semitic conspiracy pamphlet *The Protocols of the Elders of Zion*, thereby earning a favorable mention in *Mein Kampf* (1925–26).

At the street level, the adolescent Roth also "witnessed several attacks on Jewish kids by local toughs."[10] Newark was a city divided roughly into jostling Italian, African American, Irish, and Jewish enclaves. The domineering Herman, with whom Roth had a love-hate relationship that permeates his fiction, explains this urban rivalry to his son, when he speaks of the Jewish boxers of the interwar period: "You know how it was: these kids grew up, they had a tough life, the slums, no money, and they always had an adversary. The Christian religion was an adversary. They fought two battles. They fought because they were fighters, and they fought because they were Jews. They'd put two guys in a ring, an Italian and a Jew, an Irishman and a Jew, and they fought like they meant it, they fought to hurt. There was always a certain amount of hatred in it. Trying to show who was superior.” As a young man, Herman himself was not immune from such conflicts, and later tells his son of how he stood “up to [an] Irish ruffian from ‘down neck’ Newark.”[11]

Yet besides this enmity, there was allurement, too. Growing up in the Jewish quarter of Weequahic, the young Roth was spellbound by a Catholic orphanage across the road from his house, in which “he could observe the orphans playing—he never spoke to any of them—and felt how lucky he was to have a family.”[12] This orphanage had a powerful effect on the author and recurs throughout his fiction, from his earliest short stories through to the late novels. In Roth’s novel *Zuckerman Unbound* (1981), for example, the orphanage is described as the protagonist’s first encounter with “caste” (see chapter 4). This difference bred attraction, and Roth tells Pierpont of “the little Irish girl he loved when he was twelve. . . . He used to sing ‘Peg o’ My Heart’ to [her].”[13] Whether positive or negative, Irish Catholics were for the Jews always strange and Other. This point is comically seen in Roth’s 1959 short story “The Conversion of the Jews,” in which the young Jewish protagonist uses “Catholic” as an all-encompassing synonym for anyone non-Jewish, considering the term “in its broadest sense—to include the Protestants.”[14]

By the time Roth entered college in the late 1940s, these distinct ethnic boundaries were beginning to blur. He reflects on his time at Rutgers University: “[It was strange] to be seated alongside Italian and Irish kids from city high schools that had been foreign, unknowable, even unnervingly hostile to me when I was attending a neighborhood school whose student body was more than ninety percent Jewish.” America’s new public universities, rising prosperity, and the recently ended Second World War—in which Irish, Jews, and other ethnic groups had fought alongside one another, as is powerfully traced in Norman Mailer’s *The Naked and the Dead* (1948)—began to bridge the gulf between many of the country’s previously antagonistic groups. In Roth’s novel *Indignation* (2008), the protagonist celebrates this expanding late 1940s reality: “Some [of my class] were Jewish and from my high school, but most were not, and it first excited me to have lunch with them because they were Irish or Italian and to me a new category, not only of Newarker but of human being.

And I was excited to be taking college courses. . . . [S]omething was beginning to happen to my brain akin to what had happened when I first laid eyes on the alphabet."[15] Roth thus began to see beyond his Jewish upbringing through both his encounters with people and his engagement with literature: "I came upon books that I'd never heard of before. My brother had . . . *Portrait of the Artist as a Young Man*, *Ulysses*, and that changed everything. I had leaped forward into adult reading."[16]

However, at the staunchly traditional Bucknell University where Roth studied after Rutgers, literature still meant British literature.[17] The only American on the course was the Irish American Eugene O'Neill, in whose work Roth got a "glimpse . . . of [something] different."[18] It was at Bucknell that Roth began to write in earnest, and his satirical columns in the university journal earned him an Irish/Jewish nickname: "Swiftberg."[19] After Bucknell, Roth completed his two years of compulsory national service, before beginning graduate work—and his writing career—at the University of Chicago. Here Roth read "*The Adventures of Augie March*, Saul Bellow's book . . . that dazzled me," and later met Bellow himself, who advised him to drop the big concepts from his stories and focus on people: "I have a thing about *Ideas* in stories. . . . With you the *Idea* gains ground fast, easily. It conquers. What of [man]?"[20]

In 1959 Roth published his first book, *Goodbye, Columbus*, a novella that satirized postwar Jewish affluence—along with several short stories of Jewish adultery, religious questioning, and prejudice—to general acclaim and Jewish outrage. The book was attacked in synagogues throughout the country, with one rabbi asking, "What is being done to silence this man? Medieval Jews would have known what to do with him."[21] Roth appeared in a debate at Yeshiva University to defend his work, only to be pilloried as a self-hating Jew: "Mr. Roth, would you write the same stories you've written if you were living in Nazi Germany?"[22] This outcry did not prevent *Goodbye, Columbus* from winning the National Book Award in 1960, alongside Richard Ellmann's *James Joyce* (1959), which won in the nonfiction category.[23] The book had many other admirers, such as Bellow, who says in his review, "*Goodbye, Columbus* is a first book but it is not the book of a beginner. . . . Roth appears with nails, hair, and teeth, speaking coherently," and Farrell, who wrote directly to Roth: "There is something lacking in too many of your contemporaries . . .—saturation. . . . Not even Saul Bellows [*sic*] has saturation."[24] The year 1959 proved a consequential time for Roth not only in professional terms but in personal ones as well, as he married his (non-Jewish) girlfriend, Margaret Martinson, and moved from Chicago to New York City to pursue writing full-time.

Many early reviewers compared *Goodbye, Columbus* with Joyce's *Portrait of the Artist as a Young Man*, and it was fitting then that in 1960, on the way back from a Guggenheim year in Italy, Roth "stopped in Ireland . . . to walk around Joyce's Dublin."[25] He was joined there by his friend novelist William Styron, who humorously recalls the visit thirty years later:

> We were . . . out for some good clean fun, which I might add is the only kind of fun ever to be found in Dublin. . . . Philip was in fine form as we strolled the streets, dispensing good-natured cultural perceptions. . . . The Irish were really an incredibly repressed people. . . . [T]he public modesty was extravagant. . . . At Trinity College the great library . . . was covered in hideous scaffolding . . . the mythic riverrun of Joyce's stupendous vision . . . full of mud and garbage. [The day ended in a] shooting gallery, two adult American males with Bachelor of Arts degrees mugging in do-it-yourself photograph booths and bending over pinball machines. . . . This, I realized, was a chapter out of a novel by Philip Roth [who] convert[ed] these ghastly dead ends and moments of existential insult into an episode of both genuine gravity and high hilarity.[26]

Perhaps understandably, Roth never returned. Neither was his fiction welcome, as despite favorable reviews several of Roth's early books were banned there.

In 1962 Roth published his second novel, *Letting Go*—and also separated acrimoniously from Martinson, who would die in a car accident in 1968, though she would continue to haunt his fiction. This Jamesian book concerns how much a person should become involved in the life of another, following two young Jewish graduate students, Gabe Wallach and Paul Herz, as they grapple with the responsibilities of "manhood" in the 1950s. Paul marries a Catholic woman, Libby, and is thus ostracized by his family, with the father lamenting her unsuitability in Yiddish-inflected English: "A Catholic the girl is." The rabbi is similarly against the match:

"I marry Jew and Jew." Gabe visits Paul's parents in an attempt to solve the impasse. Spurned, he consults with Paul's old friends, who live next door. The neighbors—part of the rapidly advancing Jewish middle class—are no more liberal and see Paul's marriage as a betrayal of family and community: "It's just funny when a [Jewish] boy . . . marries a Gentile girl. . . . I don't think those things generally work out, do you? Most divorces are intermarried, you know."[27] There is hostility toward Gabe too, who has also broken from the Jewish fold:

> "You don't look Jewish, you know?"
> "No?"
> "You look Irish."[28]

Religious divisions continue to bedevil the Herzes, as they try to adopt a baby. Catholic orphanages will not accept their mixed-marriage status, while Jewish orphanages have a three-year waiting list. Paul and Libby thus find a young pregnant woman from rural Kentucky who wishes to give her child up for adoption. She agrees, but soon becomes suspicious of their religious otherness: "He's a Jew?" she asks Gabe about Paul, who affirms. She elaborates, "I want to go to a Catholic hospital, mister. . . . I ain't going by no Jewish hospital." She then proceeds to explain her deep misgivings of Jewish medical institutions: "There was a boy . . . he got hit by a car. . . . And then they take him in the ambulance to the Jewish hospital. . . . [H]e was knocked out good, and then counta he was a boy, they made a Jew out of him."[29] The book is full of such painful comedy, cataloging Catholic myths of Jewish depravity and vice versa, all of which underscore the continued wariness between these two groups in midcentury America. Roth's own marriage furnished him with insights into what happens when two communities are forced into contact with one another. He would frequently return to intermarriage as a literary device in his fiction. For instance, contemporaneous to *Letting Go*, Roth wrote an unpublished play titled "The Nice Jewish Boy," which he later described as "in its way a less comforting, more aggressive *Abie's Irish Rose*."[30] Around this time, Roth began corresponding with Bernard Malamud, whose short-story collection *The Magic Barrel* (1958) had won the National Book Award the year before *Goodbye, Columbus*. In 1965 Roth—then teaching at the University of Iowa—wrote to tell his elder Jewish counterpart that his students were studying Malamud's novel of crossethnic love and redemption, *The Assistant* (1957).

After *When She Was Good* was published in 1967—notable for being Roth's only book told entirely through a female narrator and containing no Jews—Roth revisited the ambivalent relationship between Gentiles and Jews in 1969's *Portnoy's Complaint* (discussed in chapter 3).[31] The book, a psychoanalytic narrative of a "nice Jewish boy's" unbridled sexual fantasies, was an explosive success and catapulted Roth from the position of highbrow literary author to notorious best-selling sensation: "A novel in the guise of a confession was received and judged by any number of readers as a confession in the guise of a novel."[32] If *Goodbye, Columbus* satirized the conformist complacency of 1950s America, *Portnoy's Complaint* epitomized the rebellious, individualist spirit of the 1960s. As Roth puts it, the period saw "the emergence of a counter-history, or counter-mythology, to challenge the mythic sense of itself the country had when the decade opened with General Eisenhower, our World War II hero, still presiding."[33] It was around this time that Roth first met Edna O'Brien, as she related to me in an interview—"I met Philip Roth in the late '60s through our publisher Jonathan Cape"—though it would be several years before they met again.[34]

The late 1960s were marked by a countercultural revolution in the United States and the country's increasing embroilment in the Vietnam War. In response, Roth wrote two heavily Swiftian satires, "Cambodia: A Modest Proposal" (1970) and *Our Gang* (1971), to voice his specific dismay over American policy in Southeast Asia and the Nixon presidency more generally. *Our Gang* viciously burlesques the doublespeak of the pre-Watergate Nixon administration and was widely condemned as crass, a charge Roth refuted: "[A book is] 'Swiftian' . . . if it's about what Englishmen were doing to Irishmen in 1729; if, however, you were to employ similar means to indict our country for what it has done to the Vietnamese now . . . you would find your satire unpublishable in most places because of bad taste."[35] The book infuriated Nixon, as is evident in his presidential tape transcripts, proving Roth's point that bizarre American truth trumps American fiction:

> NIXON: What is he? What is he? . . .
>
> [CHIEF OF STAFF H.R.] HALDEMAN: [Roth's] big thing is *Portnoy's Complaint*, which is the most obscene, pornographic book of all time.
>
> NIXON: That's what I mean. . . . Roth is of course a Jew. . . . A lot of this can be turned to our advantage. . . . I think the anti-Semitic thing can be, I hate to say it, but it can be very helpful to us.
>
> HALDEMAN: There are a lot more anti-Semites than there are Jews, and the anti-Semites are with us generally and the Jews sure aren't.[36]

There follows in quick succession several other experimental novels: *The Breast* (1972), a Kafkaesque exploration of desire; *The Great American Novel* (1973), an absurdist baseball tale; and *My Life as a Man* (1974), a metafictional portrayal of the life of a failed novelist. The hero of this book, Peter Tarnopol, finds his first and only novel in a secondhand bookstore, between "to one side Sterne, Styron and Swift, to the other Thackeray, Thurber, and Trollope."[37] The position of Tarnopol's book symbolizes the generic experimentation of Roth's fiction at this time, as it straddled the threshold between the realist tradition of Thackeray and the surrealist and self-referential style of Swift and Sterne. It was around this time that Roth became friends with the Irish American novelist Mary McCarthy, having flirted with her own iconoclastic work in his first novel and later declaring himself to have been "seduced by her early stories."[38]

In the 1970s, Roth became increasingly concerned with the plight of writers in communist Europe. He traveled frequently to Czechoslovakia, where he supported the work of writers by organizing covert financial aid and through his editing of the Penguin series "Writers from the Other Europe." The series published dissident and otherwise suppressed authors such as Milan Kundera, Tadeusz Borowski, Bruno Schulz, Danilo Kiš, and Witold Grombrowicz in English translation in the West—thereby circumventing communist censorship. His visits stopped in 1977 when he was denied entry to the country. His travel of these years is reflected in his fiction, with the critic Velichka Ivanova noting Roth's increasing "engage[ment with] the European literary tradition." *The Professor of Desire* (1977), which culminates with the protagonist visiting Prague and meeting, in a dream, Kafka's prostitute—who for a small fee tells him fabricated inanities about the great writer: "They were clean and they were gentlemen. As God is my witness, they never beat on my backside. Even in bed they had manners"—is surely a playful warning (unheeded by this chapter) against delving too deeply into the life of a novelist.[39] Alongside Kafka, Joyce is present, too, with the young repressed Kepesh wandering through London's red-light district in a chapter of sexual awakening that recalls the Nighttown scene of *A Portrait of the Artist as a Young Man*.[40]

In 1976 Roth began dating the English Jewish actor Claire Bloom and soon after began to live with her for several months a year in England—with the rest of the time divided between Connecticut and New York, an arrangement that continued until the 1990s (they would marry in 1990 and divorce in 1995). O'Brien had befriended Bloom on the set of the film *Three into Two Won't Go* (1969), on which they both worked, and thus became reacquainted with Roth.[41] O'Brien relates this renewed encounter in her introduction to Roth at his eightieth birthday: "It was not auspicious. There he sat, lean, watchful and scorchingly handsome. In those days, I was a gushing and eager cook. Suddenly, coming out of his reverie, he said, 'Do you do the soup and the soufflés in between writing your books.' It was in an Irish accent and a not very convincing Irish accent at that. I smarted somewhat, and swallowed it."[42]

A month later, having read O'Brien's book *Night* (1972), Roth called to apologize for his flippancy. As they continued to meet, she found that his "mask had slipped somewhat." By way of example, she relates another story: "One day there was a pounding on my door . . . and there was Mr. Roth in a lather of rage and self-righteousness. He had done a version of *The Cherry Orchard* [1981] . . . and rehearsals were not going to his liking. He was not being listened to, he was not consulted. . . . He was also hyperventilating. . . . He threw himself down on the grass . . . and railed against the injustices and stupidities of mankind. I urged him to get up, fearing headlines like—'Irish Woman Rescues Famous Author.'"[43] Following this scene, Roth and O'Brien's friendship grew steadily throughout the 1980s, with mutual friends including Richard and Maud Ellmann, Antonia Fraser and Harold Pinter, and Arthur Schlesinger Jr.[44]

Following *Portnoy's Complaint*, Roth was increasingly confused with his most outrageous character in the press and in the popular imagination—this fallacy would spur much of his fiction in the 1980s. In 1979 Roth wrote *The Ghost Writer*, which became the first of a trilogy concerning the position of the Jewish writer in America. The young Nathan Zuckerman publishes an unvarnished short story of Jewish life, which leads to a rift with his father and the wider Jewish community. The novel follows him as he seeks out a new father figure in the author E. I. Lonoff and a new lover in a woman he blasphemously imagines to be Anne Frank.[45] For not presenting the Jews in an idealized light, Nathan finds himself ostracized. He compares his lot with that of an Irish writer: "It wasn't . . . Joyce's father who had impugned me for my recklessness—it was my own. Nor was it the Irish he claimed I had maligned and misrepresented, but the Jews. Of which I was one. Of which, only some five thousand days past, there had been millions more. . . . Hadn't Joyce, hadn't Flaubert, hadn't Thomas Wolfe . . . all been condemned for disloyalty or treachery or immorality by those who saw themselves as slandered in their works?"[46] *Zuckerman Unbound*, which followed on two years later, bursts with Irish-Jewish parallels, as collated in chapter 4. The close of the trilogy, *The Anatomy Lesson* (1983), shifts tack from *The Ghost Writer*, with Zuckerman not lamenting the restrictions placed on the Jewish writer in America but attempting, rather, to celebrate the freedom this position confers: "Without an Old Country link and a strangling church like the Italians, or the Irish, or the Poles, without generations of American forebears to bind you to American life, or blind you by your loyalties to its deformities, you could read whatever you wanted and write however and whatever you pleased."[47]

Yet Jews did have an old country, or rather a new one: Israel. In 1986 Roth wrote what many critics regard as his masterpiece, *The Counterlife*, which won the National Book Critics Circle Award for Fiction. The novel sees Zuckerman crisscross the United States, England, Israel, and Palestine. It concerns Jewish identity in these places, while also interrogating the differences between the lived world and the written word. As Alan Cooper puts it: "Zuckerman . . . is suspended in a state of fictive uncertainty about his own identity: about how much he is the American, how much the Jew, how much the fiction writer." While Roth stages the final act of *Portnoy's Complaint* in Israel, *The Counterlife* presents a more in-depth exploration, with Zuckerman confronting the leader of an illegal Israeli settlement to which his brother has made aliyah. Roth juxtaposes the ultranationalist racism toward Palestinians—and disdain for diasporic Jews—here with the covert anti-Semitism of upper-middle-class England, into which Zuckerman has recently married. It is Roth's most postmodern book, having in place of a conclusive ending a series of conflicting chapters that elbow, contradict, and rewrite one another. His friend Mary McCarthy wrote to him praising the novel, but also setting out some qualms: "I bridle at your picture of Christianity. There's more to Christmas . . . than Jew-hatred. True, I've sometimes thought that all our Christmas-caroling must be offensive to non-sharers of that wondrous occasion. But perhaps non-sharers . . . can get the general idea or try to, as I hope I would try to get the idea of the Wailing Wall, repellent as it is to me, if I were taken to it." Roth responds, "Zuckerman behaves beautifully at the carol service and therefore looks at least as you might look at the Wailing Wall." He expands, "I didn't want all [Zuckerman's] skepticism focused on Jewish ritual and none of it on Christian. That would have had all the wrong implications and made him seem what he is not, and is a self-hating Jew who—to borrow a phrase—casts a cold eye only on his own."[48]

Here, as elsewhere, Roth turns to Yeats, whose complex overlapping identities as Irish Protestant poet provided inspiration for an American Jew living in London (McCarthy's own 1950 short-story collection was called *Cast a Cold Eye*). At this time, attitudes in the West were turning steadily against Israel as the occupation that followed the Third Arab-Israeli War in 1967 wore on into its second decade. Hermione Lee, who interviewed Roth in 1984, describes his views at this time: "Roth was feeling an increasing sense of cultural isolation in England. . . . Nobody—for instance—talked to him about Northern Ireland. They talked to him reprovingly, to his growing exasperation and bafflement, about American foreign policy in Nicaragua, the outrageousness of bombing Libya, and the evils of Israeli expansionism and militarism. He developed a distaste for what he saw as fashionable anti-American leftism; it felt to him unself-critical and biased."[49] By employing multiple, parallel, narrative frames, *The Counterlife* captures the ambivalence of Jewish identity, at once repelled by dangerous nationalisms in the diaspora—of which the Jews are often the first target—yet tribally drawn to Jewish nationalism in Israel. Powerful and complex, *The Counterlife* marked a pivotal moment for Roth; as Ross Posnock suggests, it "is a crucial transition in Roth's art."[50]

In 1988 Roth wrote *The Facts: A Novelist's Autobiography*, a memoir that played with the boundaries between biography and fiction, in which he detailed in a letter to his fictional character Zuckerman his very real mental breakdown: "In the spring of 1987, at the height of a ten-year period of creativity, what was to have been minor surgery turned into a prolonged physical ordeal that led to an extreme depression that carried me right to the edge of emotional . . . dissolution."[51] According to Roth, he wrote the book as a type of therapy to separate in his own mind a life of fact over works of fiction, "demythologizing to induce depathologizing." Zuckerman, however, challenges this notion: "With autobiography, there's always another text, a countertext, if you will, to the one presented. It's probably the most manipulative of all literary forms."[52] Roth followed *The Facts* with *Patrimony: A True Story* (1991), a moving yet unscrupulous account of his father's last year of life.[53] Following this overtly autobiographical turn, Roth made his most comprehensive foray into the relationship between the Jewish American author and Israel in his 1993 novel *Operation Shylock*.[54] The novel details the protagonist "Philip Roth" as he travels to Israel in 1988 to confront an impersonator who has usurped his identity to further Diasporism, a scheme that champions the return of Israeli Jews to Europe to prevent a Middle Eastern Holocaust. While in Israel, Philip attends the trial of John Demjanjuks, the suspected Nazi gas chamber operator; interviews the Israeli author and Holocaust survivor Aharon Appelfeld; and discourses with his former college roommate the Palestinian Christian George Ziad (based on literary critic Edward Said). Like *The Counterlife*, the novel uses the trope of the double to symbolize the position of Jews in America, loyal to Israel yet linked by oppressive history to the Palestinians, as Elaine B. Safer attests: "The duality of ideas and their resultant paradoxes are at the center of the Jewish experience in Roth's Israel, in the current events of Israel in the twentieth century, and in the region's history of warfare."[55]

The story becomes more bizarre and far-fetched as Israeli and Palestinian intelligence agents mistake Philip for his Diasporist counterpart and attempt to recruit him. All of it takes place against the backdrop of the First Intifada. While there are winks at Swift's *Gulliver's Travels* (1726) throughout, the novel most heavily flirts with Joyce. Roth afterward made this connection explicit: "In *Finnegans Wake*, there is the character Humphrey C. Earwicker, who sleeps with absolutely everything flowing through his mind, and Joyce uses the initials H.C.E. as 'Here Comes Everybody.' Well, in *Operation Shylock* you have 'Here Comes Everybody Jewish.' Leon Klinghoffer. Jonathan Pollard. Menachem Begin. Meir Kahane. All these names were passing through the collective Jewish brain at the time, and I wanted to get inside the Jewish mind." Pierpont concurs, describing the book as a "kind of Jewish *Finnegans Wake*: hallucinatory, folkloric, dense."[56]

While critics at this time began to commend Roth's fiction for moving outward from the self, Roth himself was turning inward. Following the collapse of his marriage to Bloom in the early 1990s, he cut himself off from friends and the world at large throughout much of rest of the decade.[57] O'Brien says of this time: "Domestic bliss as such, however, came to an end. And with the purposefulness of a samurai he entered a prolonged state of solitude. The cleared desk, what Robert Lowell has called, 'the poet's guillotine.' Tearing himself loose from any worshipping family or friends, from marriage, and from what he once called the moral propriety of his earlier work, he went underground. There he wrote . . . some great books." She describes their relationship at this time: "Friendships were either postponed, or mistrusted, or severed. I went once, during his hermitage, and I felt, I felt ostracized. It was as if I had somehow betrayed him. I never knew what, and of course, we survived it."[58]

In 1994 Roth published *Sabbath's Theater*, a book about a man, Mickey Sabbath, crippled by his childhood grief of losing his older brother during the Second World War. There are notes of *King Lear* in Sabbath's descent into madness, but Yeats is present too in his poem "Meru," which Sabbath recites:

> [man], despite his terror, cannot cease
> . . . Ravening, raging, and uprooting that he may come
> Into the desolation of reality.[59]

Roth then returned to Zuckerman to begin what became known as his American trilogy, beginning with the 1997 Pulitzer Prize–winning *American Pastoral*, a book that depicts the turmoil of 1960s America (tackled in chapter 5). *I Married a Communist* (1998) comes next, rendering the Senator McCarthy–led anticommunist witch hunts of the 1950s and the ruin of a Jewish communist radio actor, Ira Ringold.[60] The trilogy's close, *The Human Stain* (2000), explores race through the life of a young light-skinned African American Newarker named Coleman Silk, who passes for Jewish.[61] Like all Roth's novels, it sets its sights on dismantling what Zuckerman calls "the fantasy of purity."[62] In the wake of the trilogy, Roth became seen less as a "Jewish" writer and more as an "American" one. In recognition of this growing stature and vision, Bill Clinton awarded him the National Medal of Arts in 1998.

In 2001 Roth published *The Dying Animal*, another Kepesh novel, this one with a title from Yeats and an epigraph from O'Brien. In the same year, he brought out a collection of his interviews and discussions with other writers titled *Shop Talk*, which included exchanges with O'Brien, McCarthy, Appelfeld, Ivan Klima, Isaac Bashevis Singer, and Kundera as well as articles on Malamud and Bellow.[63] The range gives an idea of Roth's influences, from Europe, Israel, America, and Ireland. Of the collection John Burns says that "the conversation with O'Brien is the most illuminating, as 'Roth the Interviewer' is confronted with something several steps removed from himself—a writer of a different nationality and a different gender."

The Plot against America was published in 2004 and reimagines Roth's childhood, but through an alternative historical lens with fascist sympathizer aviation hero Charles Lindbergh winning the 1940 presidential election and, along with his secretary of state, Henry Ford, enacting anti-Semitic policies in America (see chapter 6). The year 2006's *Everyman* is the story of a Jewish ad executive reflecting on his life and contemplating his death, which John Banville describes as "a remarkably low-key performance by an artist who, in a number of recent works, has gone at the theme of aging and death with foul-mouthed ferocity." The book also reflects back on the interactions between Jews and Irish in America during the 1940s. The protagonist's father, a Jewish jeweler, hires Irish Catholic girls to make the store more welcoming for Christian customers: "Over the years our father sold wedding rings to Elizabeth's Irish and German and Slovaks and Italians and Poles, most of them young working-class stiffs." The next year's *Exit Ghost* explores American life and politics at the beginning of the second George W. Bush administration and caps off the Zuckerman books. It also looks back to the twentieth-century attraction between Jews and Irish, with intermarriage seen as a way of leaving Jewishness behind, as one of Zuckerman's elderly neighbors tells him, "I did not want to marry a Jewish girl. I did not want my children to be raised in the Jewish religion," but instead wanted someone "of Irish extraction."[64]

Banville describes *Indignation* (2008), Roth's excogitation on the moral exigencies of 1950s American life, as the "best novel since *The Counterlife*. . . . [It is] a late masterpiece." It follows a young university student as he balances his first encounters with sex with the closeness of death as the Korean War rages. *The Humbling* (2009) centers on an aging actor who has lost his ability to act. One of his most famous roles was in J. M. Synge's *Playboy of the Western World*, and, as in that play, Roth's novel toys with traditional gender roles. Roth's final novel, *Nemesis*, published in 2010, imagines a polio outbreak in 1940s Newark and is surveyed in chapter 6. That same year, Roth was awarded the National Humanities Medal by Barack Obama.[65]

In 2011 Carmen Callil, the founder of the feminist publisher Virago, resigned from the judging panel of the Man Booker Prize to protest the award going to Roth: "There are great moments in Roth's work. He is clever, harsh, comic, but his reach is narrow. Not in the Austen, Bellow or Updike sense, because they use a narrow canvas to convey the widest concepts and ideas. Roth digs brilliantly into himself, but little else is there. His self-involvement and self-regard restrict him as a novelist." There has always been a deep ambivalence among feminist writers and thinkers about Roth's work. For example, second-wave feminist writers like Erica Jong and Marilyn French were influenced by the confessional style of *Portnoy's Complaint*, while at the same time discomfited by its representation of women. Literary critic Elaine Showalter describes herself as a lifelong fan, despite some reservations: "He is just a great artist, and he is also a very compassionate writer. So despite the fact that there are passages that I skip over when I'm reading, I don't think that puts Roth beyond the pale in any sense." Roth has been frequently criticized for not using his considerable talents to write from a female perspective and for creating one-dimensional women characters. This charge ignores *Letting Go* and *When She Was Good*, both of which feature layered female narrators, and the many complex women found in the pages of his fiction, such as the libertine Drenka of *Sabbath's Theater*, as driven by desire as any of Roth's male characters and not chastised, but celebrated, for it. Elsewhere, Roth appears to acknowledge gaps in his own vision, as with Amy Belette of *The Ghost Writer*, Maria of *The Counterlife*, and Faunia Farley of *The Human Stain*, all of whom actively frustrate attempts by the male narrator to access their interiority. As Zadie Smith, who gave the inaugural lecture in the Philip Roth series at the Newark Public Library in 2016, said, "He had blind spots, prejudices, selves he could imagine only partially, or selves he mistook or mislaid. But, unlike many writers, he did not aspire to perfect vision. He knew that to be an impossibility."[66]

In 2012 Roth announced his retirement and the following year celebrated his eightieth birthday at the Newark Public Library—the setting for *Goodbye, Columbus*—in which he was introduced by Jonathan Lethem, Hermione Lee, Alain Finkielkraut, Claudia Roth Pierpont, and Edna O'Brien. In attendance were many of the next generation of Jewish American writers, such as Jonathan Safran Foer, Nicole Krauss, and Nathan Englander. After his retirement, Roth continued to make headlines as many of his books—long considered unfilmable since the disastrous adaptation of *Portnoy's Complaint* in 1972 and the badly received *Human Stain* in 2003—reached the screen, with 2008's *Elegy* (*The Dying Animal*), *The Humbling* (2014), *Indignation* (2016), and *American Pastoral* (2016), all recently released. Moreover, his entire oeuvre has been published by the Library of America over ten volumes. There is also a renewed interest in Roth's fiction, as for example with *The Plot against America*, which when published first in 2004 was taken as an attack on the Bush presidency, but since the election of Donald Trump has been read as a prophetic work in its depiction of populism, isolationism, and intolerance.[67] Consequently, even as Roth retreated from public view, his work continued to speak to American reality in the twenty-first century. When asked at the beginning of 2018 by journalist Charles McGrath what he does in his retirement, Roth replied simply, "Read." When pushed for an example he said, "Just in the past week, I read . . . Edna O'Brien's wise little biography of James Joyce."[68]

On the May 23, 2018, Roth died of heart failure at the age of eighty-five. Krauss, the leading light of twenty-first-century Jewish American literature, wrote in tribute to her friend and mentor: "In his books I found a peculiar, sustaining solace. . . . From him, [I learned] a great deal about what it is to wrestle, and to persevere. Not how to solve the argument but how to keep it alive. Not just to withstand the discomfort and the tension of questioning but to make a life there." But Roth's influence stretches beyond his Jewish American context, as evidenced by the wide-ranging accolades that flooded national newspapers and media outlets in the days after his passing. Irish author Kevin Powers celebrated Roth's ability to make "the experience of being Jewish in America the central narrative of twentieth century American literature. . . . Roth wrote about being a second generation Jewish immigrant in America and made it resonate so profoundly and powerfully with this muscular philosophical, funny voice, he made that experience a way of talking about the American experience in general." In the *Irish Times*, Colm Tóibín, who befriended Roth through their shared love of chamber music, wrote, "He had a great comic gift and a sense of adventure. He was serious about what he did. He was also brave and wrote the books he wanted to write. . . . He was a towering presence in American letters."[69]

At his memorial in September 2018, his old friends Romanian Jewish writer Norman Manea and Edna O'Brien both spoke. Manea eulogized:

> Philip Roth, the great writer, an acute observer of human existence, with all its cruel and burlesque conflicts and contradictions, has left us to face

> without him our explosive present and uncertain future. His forceful intelligence, his lucid and interrogative conscience, his unshaken devotion to the written page will not be forgotten; all the libraries of our tormented world will remind us of him in our fight for truth and beauty, for ardor and authenticity. Literature—America's and the world's—lost one of the most brilliant writers of modernity, an incomparable creative force. In the planetary crisis of our time, with so many aggressions against our spiritual environment, we will more than ever miss his intensity, his code of work and honesty, his humor and humanness.[70]

O'Brien praised Roth's ability to paint "a portrait of the artist in all his ingenuity, anxiety, isolation, dissatisfaction, restlessness, secretiveness, self-addiction" and at the same time to create "the magic matter of a great story arising from all that human mess." She recounts his last words to her: "'You're valiant, kid.' It was not said in flattery, but rather as an incentive to keep going, to harden the walls of the burrow."[71]

Country Girl: The Life and Works of Edna O'Brien

Since its inception as a written form, Irish literature has been bound up with its Jewish counterpart. The monks of Middle Ages Ireland assiduously copied down the native legends with biblical texts in mind. The twelfth-century the *Book of Invasions*, which traces Irish history from the Flood, even suggests that Ireland was first inhabited by the progeny of Noah. This trend continued, as Abby Bender explains in her book *Israelites in Erin* (2015): "From the seventeenth century through the twentieth, a common strain of Irish lament involved analogy with the Jews."[72] Often regarded as the first Irish novel, Maria Edgeworth's *Castle Rackrent* (1800) explores the fluidity of identity through what would become a common Irish literary instrument: Jewish/Irish intermarriage.[73] In political terms, Daniel O'Connell—"the most notable nineteenth-century nationalist to express sympathy for the Jewish people"—promoted the dismantling of anti-Jewish laws in the British Empire alongside his advocacy of Catholic Emancipation.[74]

Jewish numbers in Ireland (rarely above the low hundreds in previous centuries) grew rapidly in the 1880s as a result of pogroms in the Russian

Empire, reaching four thousand at the turn of the twentieth century—with the majority situated in Dublin. This growth provoked instances of aggression, such as Arthur Griffith's anti-Semitic broadsides during the Limerick Pogrom of 1904, alongside ones of affiliation. Joyce populates his fictional universe with Jews, from the fantasies of "rich Jewesses" found in his early story fiction, through Stephen Dedalus's confusion of Dublin's red-light district with the "quarter of the Jews" in *Portrait of the Artist*, to *Ulysses*'s Jewish Irish Leopold Bloom.[75] Joyce says of his choice to make Bloom Jewish: "Yes. Only a foreigner would do. The Jews were foreigners in Dublin at that time. There was no hostility towards them. But contempt, the contempt that people always show towards the unknown." For Bryan Cheyette, "It is . . . the instability of 'the Jew' as a racial and cultural signifier that Joyce . . . exploits to undermine any dominant discourse whether it be religion [or] nationalism." Like Joyce, Edna O'Brien uses her Jewish characters to confront Irish myths of racial and cultural homogeneity. Jews and other outsiders appear throughout her fiction, often aligned with her more overtly Irish protagonists who are themselves critics of, and thus cast out from, conservative Irish society.[76]

O'Brien was born in 1930 in between the villages of Scariff and Tuamgraney, County Clare, to farmers Lena and Michael O'Brien; she had a difficult relationship with both. As she tells Roth, "My father liked horses and liked leisure. He inherited a great deal of land and a beautiful stone house but he was profligate and the land got given away or squandered in archetypal Irish fashion." In her memoir *Mother Ireland* (1976), O'Brien compares her family's decline to that of Edgeworth's Rackrents, with her father (like the final lord of the Rackrent manor) so drunken and impecunious that "at last he was deposed to the gate-lodge." She grew up in a community distrustful of anything considered foreign, later recalling in her 2012 memoir *Country Girl* "the ingrained memories of a suspicion of the stranger." This suspiciousness was directed against those persons who existed outside the Catholic hub of Irish life: "The eight neighbouring Protestants would never reach [heaven] and neither would the black doctor or the travelling Jew man." The existence of such interlopers challenged Irish monoculture, and thus their marginalization was required to reinforce it. Yet alongside this distrust came a yearning for the foreign and the exotic. In *Some Irish Loving* (1978), her anthology of Irish writing, O'Brien includes an extract from Synge's *Playboy of the Western World*, in which Pegeen Mike speaks of her desire to run away with a "Jewman, with ten kegs of gold."[77] In the Ireland of O'Brien's youth, outsiders were at once sites of difference and at the same time potential means of flight.

America held a particular attraction for the adolescent O'Brien, something she inherited from her mother, who worked as a maid in Brooklyn in the early 1920s: "Important visitors were few, except for Yanks who came in the summer and talked with a twang and brought us necklaces and bone bracelets as gifts. Afterwards, when they had gone, my mother hankered for her times in America and the style she had."[78] O'Brien explains to Roth, "Our greatest excitement was these visits, these gifts of trinkets and things, these signals of an outside, cosmopolitan world, a world I longed to enter."[79] Driving this ambition was a desire to escape her abusive father. O'Brien was born into a strongly nationalist household in a newly independent state, but from an early age she saw the oppressive reality behind the liberating rhetoric of Irish freedom, which did not seem to extend to the lives of Irishwomen.[80] In *Country Girl*, she recalls how her father burned down his own house so that the British could not use it as a base during the War of Independence (1919–22): "another notch of victory over the invader."[81] In this image, which she returns to frequently in her fiction, O'Brien finds an apt metaphor for the self-defeating nature of Irish nationalism.

After convent schooling, O'Brien moved to Dublin to study as a pharmacist. There she met Irish writer Ernest Gébler, author of *He Had My Heart Scalded* (1946) and *The Voyage of the Mayflower* (1950). O'Brien describes Gébler's complex heritage as of "Armenian, Jewish, Czech and German and Irish stock." Though born in Ireland to an Irish mother and Czech father, he was regarded with hostility by O'Brien's family, not only for his lineage but for his politics as well (he was a socialist). Despite multiple attempts by her family to pry her loose from this older, "alien," sophisticate, O'Brien eloped with Gébler in 1952 and had two children with him, Sasha (b. 1952) and Carlo (b. 1954). In 1958 the Géblers emigrated to England, joining a wave of Irish escaping a deep recession and stultifying culture. Speaking of this generation, Clair Wills says, "The migrants themselves . . . stayed oddly silent about the iniquitous social system which had forced them out. . . . [T]he emigrants carried with them pride in a nation that had failed to provide for them."[82]

For O'Brien, however, leaving Ireland did not still her voice, but rather liberated it. In 1960 she published her first novel, *The Country Girls*, which was greeted with acclaim in Britain and America—and condemnation in Ireland, where it was banned by the state and burned by a local priest. As O'Brien said of it, "I had offended several fashions. I offended the Catholic Church. I betrayed Irish womanhood. . . . I betrayed my own community by writing about their world."[83] Irish novelist Anne Enright concurs: "Censorship was a measure to protect the ordinary public from foreign, corrupting material. As it turned out, particular ire would be saved for Irish writers: when you are trying to keep 'indecent' and 'obscene' material from entering the country, it is a great betrayal to discover it bubbling up from within."[84] *The Lonely Girl* (1962) and *Girls in Their Married Bliss* (1964) were published in quick succession and together make up a trilogy that skewered the misogyny, isolationism, and xenophobia prevalent in Irish society.[85] They are also profoundly funny books, though the humor has a whetted edge. O'Brien would later say of her friend Samuel Beckett, in words that might be just as readily applied to her own writing: "He jokes, of course, but the jokes are excruciating as if in laughter he wishes on the reader some kind of fit."[86] The trilogy and O'Brien's next two books were banned by the Irish Censorship Board. Neither was she immediately welcomed by the great Irish writers of the time—themselves victims of censorship—such as Frank O'Connor, who said that *The Country Girls* merely displayed the author's "poor taste in men."[87] Meanwhile, O'Brien earned plaudits for her novels in Britain and the United States, where her short stories started to appear in the *New Yorker*, beginning with 1962's "Irish Revel," a rural rewriting of Joyce's "The Dead" from the perspective of the maid (who, despairing of the local drunken suitors, falls in love with a "Jewish" sightseer).[88]

As her marriage to the controlling Gébler fell apart in the 1960s, O'Brien began to travel frequently to America to publicize her novels.

There she befriended many of the great Jewish American writers of the twentieth century. *Catch-22* (1961) author Joseph Heller wrote to O'Brien's American publishers about *The Lonely Girl*, "It is a beautiful, sincere, refreshing novel, and I enjoyed its candor and humorous vitality from beginning to end," before corresponding with O'Brien herself for several years. At the same time, O'Brien wrote to Bernard Malamud to say how much she admired his work: "I've just finished reading *The Assistant* and *The Magic Barrel* and both are absolutely wonderful." He responded to tell her that everyone in his writing class had read *The Lonely Girl* and that he was now reading it himself: "My feeling throughout was one of constant pleasure in the people you have created." O'Brien and Malamud met in New York in 1963 and later in London. His biographer describes one of these later meetings: "On one of his London stays in the early sixties, Malamud, preparing to visit . . . Edna O'Brien . . . gallantly sent on ahead of himself a full dozen red roses. When he arrived, however, he carefully counted only nine—the rest it turned out, were given away to the girl next door. Disappointed, he went away again, three roses down." The next year, this scene found its way into O'Brien's *Girls in Their Married Bliss*, in which one character attempts to sell the flowers sent by an admirer, only to be caught. The pair remained friends until Malamud's death in 1983.[89]

In 1965 O'Brien wrote to Saul Bellow to praise his just-published novel: "I derive such sustenance from *Herzog* [1964] that I can't understand how I managed (life wise) before I read it. . . . Every time I buy myself a copy I find I'm giving it away because I want other people to read it and so I buy another."[90] After meeting her later that year, Bellow wrote to say, "I took a great liking to you. I think you are a lovely woman." They would meet in subsequent years at parties thrown by Roth in England and America, and O'Brien would continue to read and reflect on Bellow's fiction—for example, speaking in her memoir *Country Girl* of her admiration for the "aggrandizement and delusion" of his novel *Seize the Day* (1956). The year 1965 also saw the publication of O'Brien's *August Is a Wicked Month*, which the *New York Times*' Eliot Fremont-Smith described as "a serious and moving piece of work," drawing parallels between the protagonist and Martha Reganhart of Roth's *Letting Go*. O'Brien's 1966 book *Casualties of Peace* is a novel of desire that crosses racial borders in postwar

England and is dense with traces of Bellow's epistolary *Herzog*, particularly in its closing use of a series of unanswered letters: "The letters saved her. They were at once her consolation and her nourishment, through the letters she pleaded her cause and though never posted they absorbed the juice of sorrow. Delirium, strange outpourings and the drunkening smell of yellow roses."[91]

Like Roth, who had to defend his work before angry Jewish crowds, O'Brien faced incensed Irish audiences. The questions at one such meeting in Limerick in 1966 are telling: "Why do you live and write in England? . . . Isn't there enough experience here? Is it because we are a Christian society?" She responded, "[Ireland] is rooted in me. . . . It is becoming increasingly clear to me that the country of the mind is what is important. Love of country is not nationalism or patriotism." Others at the meeting charged O'Brien with obscenity and "vulgarity."[92] According to Julia Carlson, as the 1960s progressed, O'Brien (like Roth) became more and more "identified with the characters in her fiction," and "her fiction made her a scapegoat and reflected how far the foundations of Irish society were threatened by sexual permissiveness for women." The overwhelming influence of the church in Irish life began to wane slightly in the mid-1960s (though Ireland would remain one of the most outwardly devout Catholic countries in Europe until the 1990s). One outcome of this decline was change to the censorship regime in 1967, adjustments for which O'Brien, according to historian Diarmaid Ferriter, acted as a catalyst: "[She] protested strongly against censorship, speaking at public meetings, [and] bringing her books into the South across the border from Northern Ireland."[93] As a result, *Casualties of Peace* would be the last novel of O'Brien's to be banned in Ireland.

It was around this time that O'Brien met J. D. Salinger (who was himself of Jewish and Irish Catholic extraction), as she was in her own words "emerging from the dungeons" of her relationship with Gébler: "We went on the wheel at Battersea fun fair, and we had lots of dinners together. I was very naïve. I gave him an Irish linen tablecloth—that's how naïve. But he was terribly pleased with it. I liked him very much. He was quite suspicious of people, even then; he had a kind of test—he wouldn't tell you what it was—but you had to pass it. But he was very funny, very alive. We only lost touch when he started to withdraw completely."[94] In 1968 O'Brien published her first collection of short stories, *The Love Object* (1968), which was greeted with widespread acclaim, not least of all by Salinger, who was particularly impressed by the title story and "Paradise."

The year 1969 saw the publication of *A Pagan Place*, which returned O'Brien's fiction to Ireland after three novels set in England and Europe with a strikingly experimental second-person narrative.[95] It also saw the beginning of the period known as the Troubles, where the Catholic civil rights movement in Northern Ireland was met by ever-increasing violence from the Protestant state and paramilitary groups, which in turn encouraged the formation or revival of Irish nationalist groups such as the Irish Republican Army (IRA). As an Irishwoman deeply critical of Irish nationalism, yet sympathetic to the plight of disenfranchised Catholics in Northern Ireland, O'Brien found that her nuanced attitudes toward the situation stood in contrast to the polarized environment in Britain at that time, as an interviewer asked her in 1972: "'[Do you] have difficulty expressing [your] point of view to English colleagues and neighbours?' 'Oh yes, huge trouble.'"[96]

In 1972 O'Brien brought out her experimental novel *Night* (examined in chapter 3). That same year, Isaac Bashevis Singer wrote to her from America as "one of the many admirers you have in this country." Her short-story collections *A Scandalous Woman* and *Mrs Reinhardt* appeared in 1974 and 1978, respectively, while the novel *Johnny, I Hardly Knew You* was published in 1977. O'Brien continued to visit the United States during these years, for book promotions and to teach at institutions such as the City College of New York, New York University, and Bard College. In 1979 she published *Some Irish Loving*, an anthology of Irish love writing, with extracts from, among others, Beckett, Elizabeth Bowen, Edgeworth, Flann O'Brien, Lady Gregory, Joyce, Patrick Kavanagh, John McGahern, James Clarence Mangan, Brian Merriman, John Montague, Sean O'Casey, Frank O'Connor, Sean O'Faolain, Somerville and Ross, George Bernard Shaw, Laurence Sterne, Swift, Synge, Wilde, and Yeats, giving a sense of some of her important Irish antecedents. It was around this time that she began to correspond with the young Jewish American writer Erica Jong, author of the Portnoy-esque confessional novel *Fear of Flying* (1973), who in a letter to O'Brien recognizes their shared literary endeavor: "There is no doubt . . . that you and I, and certain other women writers, are daring to write about the female experience from a perspective that has never been used before."[97]

In the early 1980s, O'Brien wrote to Norman Mailer, with whom she had become acquainted during her New York visits in the 1960s and 1970s, to seek information, perhaps surprisingly, on Joan of Arc (Mailer had tried, unsuccessfully, to write a novel on the French heroine). He wrote back, "I fear she's much too good and great for me. So even if I were madly generous, and sometimes I hope I am, I can't help you any more and feel sad about that. I'll make it up when you come to America again by taking you on that promenade through Brooklyn. We'll have fun that day." Mailer was himself deeply influenced by Joyce's *Portrait of the Artist*, Farrell's *Studs Lonigan Trilogy*, and Irish and Irish American culture more generally. In her memoir, O'Brien says of him: "There were many Mailers, Mailer the artist, Mailer the bruiser, Mailer the intellectual, forever trying to shrug it off with fights and confrontation, and Mailer the boyish man who shyly kissed me in St John the Evangelist Catholic church in Brooklyn, where we had gone to shelter from a shower of rain. He gave me a walking tour of [New York], as I was researching the novel I was intending to write about my mother [later to become *The Light of Evening*]."[98]

O'Brien also met Russian Jewish poet Joseph Brodsky in these years, then in exile in America. Of him she says, "Brodsky was a brilliant, bristling man. . . . He has a liking for the ballad 'The Night Before Larry was Stretched' which Brendan Behan had sung to him."[99] Behan (a friend of O'Brien's through Gébler) sang and drank not only with Brodsky but with a whole coterie of Jewish artists in New York, as delineated by Stephen Watt, who explores Behan's "uncanny familiarity with and enjoyment of Jewish culture."[100] Of this affiliation, the writer would famously quip, "Other people have a nationality. The Irish and Jews have a psychosis."

In 1984 O'Brien brought out a short-story anthology titled *A Fanatic Heart*—which takes its name from Yeats's "Remorse for Intemperate Speech":

Out of Ireland have we come.
Great hatred, little room,
maimed us at the start.
I carry from my mother's womb
A fanatic heart.

Roth offered to write the introduction and in it highlights O'Brien's scope as an author: "The worlds depicted are not just those of small farms full of lovelorn women and inebriate men, but also the larger world of cities . . . of estrangement." He also praises their complexity: "The sensibility is on two levels and shuttles back and forth, combining the innocence of childhood with the scars of maturity. It is what gives these stories their wounded vigor. The words themselves are chiseled. The welter of emotion is rendered so sparsely that the effect is merciless, like an autopsy."[101] O'Brien wrote to thank Roth for the preface to *A Fanatic Heart*, which was her most successful book since her *Country Girls* trilogy and was immediately republished in a signed edition by Franklin Library: "[The book has] been taken by the Franklin Library (15,000 copies). And I am sure your name was what induced them to read."[102] She playfully continues, "I think that not only do you befriend the Czechs but hah, you also befriend the Irish and you will be crowned king of the tortured minorities."[103]

In the same year, Roth interviewed O'Brien for the *New York Times*, "cajoling," as O'Brien describes it, book-review editor Mike Levinas into it after seeing her get "an ongoing roasting from the critics." Clair Wills describes the interview as "rather flirty . . . (he's the flirt)." Roth's questions in the interview do appear teasing, in that they could just as easily be directed at himself. For example, he asks O'Brien, "Here you are, a woman of experience, talking about forgiving your mother and father. Do you think that still worrying [about] those problems has largely to do with your being a writer?" O'Brien replies, "Absolutely. It's the price of being a writer. One is dogged by the past—pain, sensations, rejections, all of it. I do believe that this clinging to the past is a zealous, albeit hopeless desire to reinvent it so that one could change it." Roth impishly pushes the point, "But not all writers feast on their childhood as much as you have"—surely a moment of self-satire considering his own devouring (and, according to critics, regurgitation) of his life in his fiction. This parallel proves to be the case, as for Roth this verisimilar re-creation of a disappeared world, far from being a flaw, is a quality to be lauded: "I'm struck . . . by the vastness and precision of your powers of recall. You seem to remember the shape, texture, color and dimensions of every object your eye may have landed upon while you were growing up—not to mention the human significance of all you saw, heard, smelled, tasted and touched."[104]

At his eightieth birthday, Roth cites this re-creative power as one of the greatest qualities a writer can possess. Sitting in the Newark Public Library, he reminisces about cycling home as a child with a basket full of books. He wryly adds, "But I've told that story already, and, probably, you are thinking, in more than one book." Yet he continues:

> In my defense, however, I should insert here that remembering objects as mundane as a bicycle basket was a not insignificant part of my vocation. . . . Unlikely as it may seem, a passion for local specificity—the expansive engagement, something close to fascination, with a seemingly familiar, even innocuous, object like a lady's kid glove or a butcher shop chicken or a gold-star flag or a Hamilton wristwatch. . . . [T]his passion for specificity, for the hypnotic materiality of the world one is in, is all but at the heart of the task to which every American novelist has been enjoined since Herman Melville and his whale and Mark Twain and his river: to discover the most arresting, evocative verbal depiction for every last American thing. Without strong representation of the thing—animate or inanimate—without the crucial representation of what is real, there is nothing. Its concreteness, its unabashed focus on all the particulars, a fervor for the singular and a profound aversion to generalities is fiction's lifeblood. It is from a scrupulous fidelity to the blizzard of specific data that is a personal life, it is from the force of its uncompromising particularity, from its *physicalness*, that the realistic novel, the insatiable realistic novel with its multitude of realities, derives its ruthless intimacy.[105]

Roth's questions for O'Brien, along with his observations about her work, seem always to be directed at once at her and at himself. He asks her, "If ever there was a case for a writer staying within earshot of the old neighborhood, it's been provided by . . . Faulkner . . . and Bellow. . . . [N]either Beckett nor Joyce seemed to want or to need a base in Ireland . . . but do *you* ever feel that leaving Ireland as a very young woman and coming to London to make a life has cost you anything as a writer?" O'Brien, then denizen of London for more than a quarter of a century, responded by quoting Joyce: "Ireland is the sow that eats its farrow."[106] Roth's persistent inquiries suggest that he too was interrogating his position as a writer adrift from his own country, living as he was at that time large portions of the year in London.[107] O'Brien wrote to thank Roth for the interview: "Fiction is a hell of a lot easier to write! Above all I want to thank you for doing it and I am sure it will bring a few new readers. Next time I will interview you." To thank him, she encloses "the Synge that I promised you."[108]

The year 1984 marked a turning point for O'Brien in terms of critical attention. Peggy O'Brien, one of the first scholars to discuss O'Brien's work, said in 1987: "She is receiving a great deal of attention now in America, where two collections of her work have been published within the last three years," referring to *A Fanatic Heart* and the republication of *The Country Girls* trilogy (with a new epilogue) in 1987—for which Roth provided the blurb: "O'Brien is the most gifted woman now writing fiction in English." Since 1984 Roth had been an effective and persuasive advocate of O'Brien's work, as O'Brien publicly acknowledged in 2013, thanking him for his "great and subtle generosity."[109] However, it would be the 2000s before O'Brien received sustained critical scrutiny, driven by feminist reappraisals of the Irish literary canon.

As one might expect, Roth and O'Brien frequently discussed writing and the travails of life as an author. O'Brien writes, "It's a little miracle really to write well and we both know that the penalties are high life-wise! In many ways only writers understand writers—I think of my dear Flaubert as someone I know and love. Knowing you is one of the nicest things in my life as I feel I have a friend." Both wrote at various times of depressions and difficulties in writing. But they also continued to buoy each other up, with Roth writing to O'Brien as she came close to finishing her first novel in ten years: "Glad to hear you're feeling your writing power. You've got it, my girl—keep punchin'." Some years later, O'Brien wrote,

"Sometimes, indeed most times I wonder why we do it. The excruciation of doing, then the exposure and crass misunderstandings that attends publication and then having to start all over again. Suffice to say we are not all there. Was Sisyphus?"[110]

In 1988 O'Brien published *The High Road*, her first novel in a decade. It was followed by the well-received short-story collection *Lantern Slides* in 1990. In the same year, she taught Roth's *Anatomy Lesson*—through the lens of its immigrant Polish American character Jaga—at the City College of New York: "So painful, so heavenful and so haunting. Anything good (lit-wise) stays in the mind forever."[111] Her novel *Time and Tide* came out in 1992.[112] In 1994 O'Brien published what would be the first of her Irish trilogy *House of Splendid Isolation* (discussed in chapter 5).[113] This novel was followed by *Down by the River* (1997), an excoriation of Irish societal hypocrisy surrounding abortion, and *Wild Decembers* (2000), an exploration of land hunger and violence—which Roth deemed Faulknerian.[114] Around this time, while researching her biography of Joyce at New York University, O'Brien received a visit from Roth, as she tells Northern Irish novelist Glenn Patterson: "Philip . . . comes in . . . and I'm not feeling my best and all these books . . . including Richard Ellmann's massive and great biography of Joyce [surround me]. Philip sees all these books along the floor and . . . he gave me a little dig—he's very mischievous—and said, 'I bet you think the made-up stuff is easier.'"[115]

In 2002 O'Brien published *In the Forest*, a fictionalization of a 1994 murder in County Clare that traverses the themes of madness, institutionalization, and repression. Reviewing the novel, Irish writer Ronan Bennett looks back on O'Brien's life and compares it with Roth's: "[Beyond] a shared emphasis on the centrality of the sexual . . . [O'Brien's and Roth's] careers have followed a similar trajectory: dazzling, flamboyant, turbulent beginnings followed by restless middle periods in which the writer takes time (and books) to reconsider and recast, to work through what he has seen, what he has learned, and then arresting returns to form in which experience, style and subject successfully cohere." While Roth's place in the American literary canon was ensured by the 1980s, O'Brien's position became certain in (and central to) the Irish canon only after the corrective publication of the fourth and fifth volumes of *The Field Day Anthology of Irish Writing* in 2002. Since then, O'Brien has received a series of literary accolades on the Irish and international stage that before eluded her, including an Irish PEN Award, University College Dublin's Ulysses Medal, the Frank O'Connor International Short Story Award, and the PEN/Nabokov Award, while Dublin City Council chose *The Country Girls* trilogy for its "One City, One Book" initiative in 2019. Kathleen Costello-Sullivan neatly sums up her significance: "From the 1960s to the 2010s, O'Brien has been a consistent voice speaking out against the worst abuses that have plagued Irish society." Despite all this recognition, O'Brien's place within Irish literature remains contested by some, with lingering accusations about her authenticity, Irishness, and persona. As Sinéad Mooney writes in a chapter dedicated to O'Brien in *A History of Modern Irish Women's Literature* (2018), "It is difficult to think of another major Irish writer whose work still provokes so much unease, whose reputation is so unsettled and unsettling."[116]

In the 2000s, O'Brien continued to teach in America at places such as Bard College and wrote to Roth about an upcoming trip to New York to research a new novel: "I'd love to see you . . . both for its own sake and [for] some guidance with the teaching." The resulting novel, *The Light of Evening* (2006), is a book of transatlantic migration (and is discussed in chapter 6). In 2009 O'Brien complemented her critical study *James Joyce* by publishing a book on Lord Byron called *Byron in Love*.[117] The same year, O'Brien's play *Haunted* was performed off Broadway. Roth attended, telling his fellow novelist Andrew O'Hagan, "She's just one of the best." At a party after the performance, Roth came along to offer further praise. O'Brien writes of the scene in her memoir *Country Girl*: "Known to be a hermit, he sometimes comes out and is invariably the magus in any gathering. Unyieldingly scrupulous about the written word, and with a knife-edge intelligence, he is also, when in jocular mood, the funniest person on earth."[118]

In 2011 O'Brien published a book of short stories titled *Saints and Sinners*—Roth particularly liked her story of a foundering love affair, "Manhattan Medley." This collection was followed by her autobiography *Country Girl* in 2012. In an email to me, O'Brien said that Roth wrote her "a wonderful letter about my memoir, a few lines of which my publishers have used on the front cover as an enticement": "Only Colette is her equal as a student of the ardors of an independent woman who is also on her own as a writer."[119] In 2013 her short-story anthology *The Love Object* (2013) was dedicated to Roth, "in long friendship." That same year, she attended his eightieth birthday and said of her friend:

> He's paralyzingly funny, he's morally rigorous . . . and he is the most perfect tuning fork of the written word of any period. He loves good and great writing and by association good and great writers, even the ones he can't abide to be with. Yes, he's at the top table of the literary Escalon, but he's not of it: too unpredictable, too aesthetically honed, and too viscerally honest. To hear him list the literary gentlemen and gentlewomen Vaselined from head to toe in hypocrisy as they greet their peers in the hope of advancement is to be treated to a modern restoration comedy. He is a frugal man, but he's also capable of great and subtle generosity. The defining influence on him are not the great writers that he has read and reread and learned from, but his parents. The father Herman, the hardworking Jew in a gentile insurance colossus, and his mother's husbandry. She put two dollars a week into a jug so the family could go to Jersey shore for the annual hol. His book *Patrimony*, about his father's illness, is a painful book, of course, but it is leavened with an amazing tenderness, and in the end the son, the brilliant son for all the hubris becomes the little child with the child's conscience and the father the Moses figure, forever sitting in judgment on what that child does, and what that child writes.[120]

Likewise, Roth saw heritage as the crucible of O'Brien's work, as he told journalist Roslyn Sulcas in 2015: "It is our good luck that she has never gotten over her ancestry." At Roth's birthday, O'Brien continued, "It has been assumed that we were lovers. I have to confess to you we were not," before directing the audience to some resemblances between her and Caesara O'Shea, an Irish actress that bewitches Roth's Zuckerman.[121] O'Brien toys with the audience's lewd (and human) curiosity, and in doing so maintains the ambiguous relationship between life and art that is the animating force of her corpus—and of Roth's. What emerges from their letters, interviews, and paratexts is a puckish and mutually supporting friendship that grew stronger as the years went by.[122]

While there are potent similarities between these writers' lives—marginal backgrounds, perceived exogamy, ambivalent early reception, and remarkable creative longevity—there are also trenchant differences. Whereas Roth had a sometimes strained relationship with his father, Herman was never physically abusive like O'Brien's father. Roth's mother—unlike his fictionalized mother characters—was not shocked and ashamed by his writing; O'Brien's mother, Lena, strongly disliked her daughter's writing (though her letters to O'Brien hint at an unconscious literary flare of her own) and famously went through *The Country Girls* with a black pen, censoring out any vulgarity. Roth spent his career walking the tightrope of his Jewish American identity, further complicated by his relationship with Israel. O'Brien, on the other hand, unearths the secrets of her Irish and Catholic inheritance, a process made both easier and more difficult by her habitation for sixty years in London. This divided loyalty has generated some of her richest insights, as she writes in *Country Girl*: "It was as if the two countries warred and jostled and made friends, inside me, like the two halves of my warring self."[123] In 2015 O'Brien's first novel in ten years, *The Little Red Chairs*, appeared to widespread acclaim.[124] On the cover, Roth declares the book "her masterpiece." When, in 2018, I informed O'Brien that *Fine Meshwork: Philip Roth, Edna O'Brien, and Jewish-Irish Literature* had been accepted for publication, she mused, "I think our main resemblance is a certain innate defiance of the rules." It is the credo of the true artist, as Roth says of his best-loved authors: "Stand alone. Like Swift and Dostoevsky and Joyce and Flaubert. Obstinate independence. Unshakable defiance. Perilous freedom. No, in thunder."[125]

While in one sense Roth and O'Brien stand alone, in another they stand together. In one of her notebooks now held in the James Joyce Library at University College Dublin, O'Brien inscribed an epigram: "What seems to be lacking is a firm sense of a common cause, a coherent community, a genuine purpose in life—Saul Bellow."[126] In this group of Jewish American authors, Heller, Malamud, Bellow, Salinger, Singer, Brodsky, Mailer, Roth, and Jong, O'Brien found a writerly community that provided support and friendship to a fellow outsider.[127] Across their twentieth- and twenty-first-century straddling careers, Roth and O'Brien have investigated "the self" in relation to community, nation, history, and the world at large. But they have also been fascinated by other selves, other communities, other nations, and other histories. Roth has always been interested in other Jewish lives, be it in Europe or the Middle East, while O'Brien has been drawn to Irish lives in Britain and the United States (along with women's lives throughout the world). At the same time, he has shown his inquisitiveness toward Irish writers, themes, and characters, just as she has been enamored by Jewish texts and cultures. For both, then, their writing is not only a delving into the self, but a diving out into the Other. For Roth, this pursuit is always doomed to failure. As his most enduring creation, Zuckerman, puts it: "The fact remains that getting people right is not what living is all about anyway. It's getting them wrong that is living, getting them wrong and wrong and wrong and then, on careful reconsideration, getting them wrong again. That's how we know we're alive: we're wrong." If we know little about ourselves, we can only know infinitely less about another. O'Brien shares this sentiment. In her archives at Emory University, there is a notebook that contains several quotations from Virginia Woolf's *The Years* (1937), to which O'Brien has appended her own summation: "the general impossibility of any two people understanding each other." She puts it eloquently in her novel *Night*: "To have met and not met, like cyclists, in a spinner at night, greeting, without a snatch of conversation, without a holler; recognisable to each other only by the strength or the weakness of their flashlights, or their tail-light . . . Not known."[128] This book illuminates those moments Roth and O'Brien, and Jewish American and Irish literature more generally, cross paths and catch in one another a glimpse of their reflected selves.

2

"A Nice Catholic Irish Girl Ruined by a Dirty Foreigner"

Censorship and Minority Voices in The Country Girls *Trilogy*

Like the country it depicts, Edna O'Brien's *Country Girls* trilogy (1960–64) contains a multitude of voices. Many of these voices, discordant to the dominant Catholic male chorus of Irish life in the 1940s–1960s, were suppressed and otherwise expunged from the national narrative. The trilogy is peopled by marginalized characters (Protestants, Jews, and migrants), the presence of whom challenges the fallacy of a monocultural Ireland. Alongside these maligned social voices, the trilogy is filled with intertextual voices, some much-discussed Irish ones—W. B. Yeats, James Joyce, and Maria Edgeworth, for example—and some ignored Jewish American ones, such as J. D. Salinger, Bernard Malamud, and Philip Roth. This chapter sets out to give a more open hearing to these muffled societal and allusive expressions in O'Brien's early fiction.

It is difficult today to separate the trilogy (*The Country Girls* [1960], *The Lonely Girl* [1962], and *Girls in Their Married Bliss* [1964]) from the controversy that surrounded its publication, as Eimear McBride notes in her preface to the 2017 edition: "The book's journey—from pen to pyre and thereafter to the status of much-cherished classic, which it enjoys today—automatically frontloads any approach to what O'Brien actually wrote with political meaning." O'Brien says something similar of the reception of J. M. Synge's *Playboy of the Western World* (1907): "The fate of the play reads like a play itself." As with Synge's play, O'Brien's critics focused their public ire on the portrayal of sex. However, as Patricia Coughlan argues, "in fact the number of specifically sexual scenes . . . is not large, and the content . . . is not really calculated to inflame the passions, being the very reverse of romantic."[1] This chapter argues that it is not the depiction of sex but O'Brien's rebuke of the formal and informal systems of censorship at work in Ireland that saw her books banned there. Through rereading O'Brien's "foreign" characters and unearthing flirtatious interactions between her work and contemporaneous global texts, this chapter exposes how censorship allowed for the silencing of contrarian sentiment. Her fiction will be shown to contest the cultural autarky of midcentury Ireland by ridiculing the state's attempts to keep the Irish spiritually and racially "pure" through the Irish Censorship Board and other institutions.[2]

In 1962 the archbishop of Dublin, John Charles McQuaid, wrote to the then justice minister, Charles Haughey, to express his displeasure over the publication of *The Country Girls* books, deeming *The Lonely Girl* in particular to be—in words that echo Arthur Griffith's censure of Synge's drama—"a smear on Irish womanhood."[3] McQuaid said of Haughey's reaction: "Like so many decent Catholic men with growing families, he was just beaten by the outlook and descriptions."[4] In subsequent decades, it was revealed that Haughey (who became taoiseach in 1979) accepted copious bribes and conducted an extramarital affair during his time in office. These hidden instances of impropriety capture something of the hypocrisy of the Irish state, which, in conjunction with the church, purported to uphold the morals of Irish society. McQuaid was also duplicitous in relation to sexual conduct. The 2009 Murphy Commission found that in 1960—contemporaneous with the banning of *The Country Girls* for "sexual immorality"—McQuaid covered up clerical child abuse at a Dublin hospital in order to "avoid scandal in both Ireland and Rome."[5] *The Country Girls* trilogy targets such insidious forms of concealment, and it is for this reason, more so than these books' muted descriptions of sex, that they were so abhorrent to the Irish establishment. As McBride puts it, *The Country Girls* shines "an unwelcome light on the hidden human costs of the rigorously enforced cultural, social, and intellectual stagnation" of 1940s, 1950s, and 1960s Ireland.[6]

The Country Girls trilogy follows two teenagers, the romantic Caithleen Brady and her pragmatic friend Baba Brennan, as they grow up in rural 1940s Catholic Ireland and make their way into both adulthood and exile.[7] In these girls O'Brien renders the opposing extremes of traditional Irish female literary representation, as she tells interviewer Mike Murphy: "I invented two divergent characters—[Caithleen] who is docile, devout and subordinate, and Baba, the outspoken rebel. I was able to give a voice inside myself, and therefore on the page to the conflicts and ambiguities I felt. I wanted to be a good girl, particularly to my mother, and not offend her. On the other side of the coin, what they call the dark side, I wanted to kill her, indeed I did kill her—she dies in the first fifty pages of *The Country Girls*." In concordance with this reading, Declan Kiberd says of the girls: "Together, the duo might have the makings of a whole person."[8] The pair escape their rural village and convent school for the relative freedom of 1950s Dublin, where *The Lonely Girl* begins. The focal point of this book is Caithleen's love affair with Eugene Gaillard, an exotic filmmaker of elusive foreign heritage. In the final book in the trilogy, *Girls in Their Married Bliss*, the "girls" have moved to London, where they are both unhappily wed: Baba to a brutal Irish builder, Caithleen to the controlling Eugene. Owing to equivalence between the plots of these books and O'Brien's life, commentators have frequently read her fiction as lightly disguised autobiography. Terence de Vere White's review of *The Lonely Girl* is representative: "What I fear is that Miss O'Brien (*vide* her failure to bring her heroes to life) is drawing for material like a spider from her own inside. Her writing is egocentric."[9] The seemingly biographical nature of O'Brien's fiction teases the reader with the sensation of reality. Yet the apparent inward-looking nature of her work belies an engagement with a diverse range of Irish, European, and American texts, just as Ireland, despite the prevailing narrative of national self-sufficiency and exceptionalism, was inescapably linked, culturally and economically, to the wider world.[10] The dust-covered maps of "Ireland and Europe and America" that line the walls of Caithleen and Baba's classroom quietly signal these external influences.[11]

"You Little S——": *The Country Girls*

In the public imagination, *The Country Girls* was primarily remembered for being banned because of its sexual content. It was less frequently acknowledged that within its pages, the novel itself subverted the conspiracy of silence that buttressed censorship policy. This point is best observed in one of the opening scenes, in which Caithleen's violent, alcoholic father, James, returns home (having spent the mortgage money on a drinking spree) and attacks his daughter, exclaiming as he strikes her, "Always avoiding your father. You little s——." However, his demeanor immediately changes when he realizes that Baba is also present: "He took his hands off me at once. He didn't like people to think he was brutal."[12] If the house can be taken as a metonym for the Irish state (a common trope in Irish fiction), then James's attempt to camouflage violence at a family level acts as a metaphor for censorship at a national level.[13] It also portends the critical reception of *The Country Girls*, with O'Brien indicted for divulging national confidences to strangers, thereby confirming British and American stereotypes of the vicious, vinous Irish. O'Brien tells Julia Carlson, "There's the official censorship and the everyday censorship," suggesting that one informs the other. As such, *The Country Girls* is not simply a passive target of a draconian censorship law; rather, within its own pages, it vigorously contests the premises upon which Irish literary and social suppression rested. Moreover, the novel replaces the image of the heroic Irishman fighting for freedom against the British with a man who saves his violence for his wife and children. In *The Country Girls*, the independence generation has failed to build a successful national structure, and instead presides over a crumbling edifice: "The Tans burned the big house and my father, unlike his forebears, had no pride in land, and gradually the place went to ruin."[14]

The novel is filled with incidents that midcentury Irish society would have considered unmentionable. Caithleen speaks of sharing secrets with Baba: "Once we took off our knickers . . . and tickled one another. The greatest secret of them all." In Catholic Ireland, where there was little tolerance for the expression of heterosexual desire, there was complete silence about "deviant" behavior. This repressive attitude means that the girls have a skewed view of sexuality, a fact that Baba takes advantage of: "Baba used to say she would tell, and every time she said that, I gave her a silk hankie or a new tartan ribbon or something." Sexuality is thus simultaneously shrouded in secrecy and connected with ideas of reward. Caithleen learns this lesson both from Baba and from her mother, who allows the local shopkeeper and village scholar Jack Holland (to whom the impecunious Bradys owe money) to put his hand on her knee; for Kiberd, the transaction is representative: "The mother, like many docile women of the time, accepts this without a word of rebuke, despite the bad example it gives to her daughter."[15] Women's subordinate position in a patriarchal culture meant that such actions were necessary survival mechanisms. Jack Holland too is trapped by malformed social norms. The nature of Irish rural life for much of the twentieth century meant that men often had to wait for their elderly mothers to die before they married, as Patrick Kavanagh depicts in *The Great Hunger* (1942):

> He stayed with his mother till she died
> At the age of ninety-one.
> She stayed too long,
> Wife and mother in one.[16]

Jack's mother has been "dying" for years. When Caithleen visits his shop, she finds Jack's mother with her shoes in the fire. "Jack, I'm dying," she says, but many months later she "was still dying," according to Caithleen.[17] O'Brien here breaks another taboo, with Jack's lingering mother exposing Ireland's sacred social unit, the family, as warped and broken decades after the country's emergence from British rule.

A society in which men either marry late or emigrate normalizes relationships between older men with some wealth and young women, as Jack's open attraction for the fourteen-year-old Caithleen makes apparent. As her family are indebted to him, Jack feels free to ask Caithleen for a kiss, or "a little favour": "'I'm too young, Jack,' [Caithleen] said helplessly." Jack is not alone in his attempts to seduce Caithleen. More successful is Mr. Gentleman, a graying married French solicitor, who tells Caithleen on a trip to Limerick: "Men prefer to kiss young girls without lipstick, you know." O'Brien unveils the open secret of these malign relationships, a predominant feature in rural Ireland at this time. As Kiberd says, novels like *The Country Girls* and John McGahern's *The Dark* (1965) were unheeded "early warning systems" for the abuse rife in Irish society that would become evident in the 1990s. For Kiberd, Caithleen is a "sort of Irish Lolita, destined to be at once infantilized and sexualized."[18] In one of O'Brien's early unpublished short stories, "Cottage in the Mountains," a young woman awaits the arrival of her English guests: "These were the people I wanted . . . angels straight from the culture beds of London, with anecdotes, duffle coats and forbidden books of the *Lolita* category in their duffle pockets." Perhaps books like Vladimir Nabokov's tale of pedophilic obsession were banned in Ireland because they—like *The Country Girls*—held the mirror too close to Irish reality.

The Country Girls also uncovers other unspoken aspects of Ireland at this time, such as a man who "poisoned himself" with Lysol and a nun who "run[s] away with the gardener." Domestic violence also goes unmentioned, whether it is against a family member—James again strikes Caithleen a "terrific blow"—or toward servants, as is seen with Baba's mother, who "often beat [the family maid] Molly, and locked her in a bedroom whenever [she] asked to go to a dance in the town hall." The novel is a sustained disavowal of Eamon de Valera's pastoral vision of Ireland: "a land with cosy homesteads . . . the romping of sturdy children . . . and the laughter of happy maidens." Indeed, it specifically critiques de Valera by linking him to Jack Holland. When Caithleen's mother leaves home in an attempt to borrow money to pay the mortgage that her husband has squandered (a mission she does not return from, being washed away while crossing a flooded river), she puts Jack in charge of the house—he later takes full control of the estate as a result of James's indebtedness. Caithleen despairs at the choice, worried no doubt about Jack's unwanted affections while also remembering that it was "Jack [who] was in charge of the lorry that De Valera nearly fell through during an election speech."[19] Jack's association with de Valera intimates a bond between micro and macro patriarchal authority. This reading is strengthened by a biographical parallel: de Valera visited O'Brien's hometown of Scariff to sell his 1937 constitution to the local populace, an instance that may have inspired the truck anecdote. The constitution formally cemented women's ancillary place in Irish society, a position *The Country Girls* portrays and seeks to overturn.[20]

Jack eulogizes the Brady women with frequent references to the work of Yeats, while his courting of both mother and daughter parodies Yeats's own unsettling proposals of marriage to Maud and Iseult Gonne. Jack quotes from Caithleen's namesake, Yeats and Lady Gregory's *Caithleen Ni Houlihan* (1902), when he describes her mother as having "the ways and walks of a queen." The play symbolically conflates women and the nation by personifying Ireland as an old woman who becomes young and beautiful again through throwing off British rule: "I saw a young girl, and she had the walk of a queen." Against the intentions of its Anglo-Irish writers, it also provided fuel for ethnocentric visions of Irish identity, with the old woman warning that there are "too many strangers in the house." For Julieann Veronica Ulin, "The trope of the stranger in the house has functioned as shorthand for the colonial presence in Ireland, regularly surfacing in literary and political discourse to invoke hostility toward and to demand the expulsion of an outsider inside."[21] The play effectively paints an Ireland of idealized women under threat from demonized invaders. This fear fed into nationalist rhetoric of the need to "protect" Irish women from foreign influence, an ideological foundation of the nationalist movement. Caithleen's attraction toward Mr. Gentleman and other exotic outsiders threatens this tenet.

At their convent school, Caithleen develops a (doubly forbidden) crush on an older half-Swedish schoolmate, who takes the younger student under her wing. Meanwhile, Baba spends her time plotting expulsion from the claustrophobic and draconian convent. In this maneuvering she reflects J. D. Salinger's Holden Caulfield, another 1950s hero of youth rebellion, who is also at odds with the purported values of his society and hypersensitive to the hypocrisies of the adult world—her repeated use of Holden's favored epithet, "phony," strengthens the affinity between these two characters. Kiberd draws the same comparison: "As a coming-of-age story of confused teenagers, [*The Country Girls*] might be read alongside *The Catcher in the Rye* [1952]."[22] The girls eventually achieve Baba's goal, by writing an obscene note and leaving it for the nuns to find: "Father Tom stuck his long thing . . ." Ostracized by church and community—in a manner that foreshadows O'Brien's own treatment after the publication of the book—Baba and Caithleen make their way to the capital. There they find shelter in a boardinghouse run by an Austrian woman named Joanna and full of lodgers from around Europe, which provides a contrast to the homogeneity of their West of Ireland village. Julia Obert proposes the boardinghouse as an antiparochial environment and Joanna as a "potential surrogate mother" who "signifies O'Brien's look beyond Mother Ireland."[23] The novel ends with Caithleen—free from Mr. Gentleman, who has broken off their romance because of scandal at home—living in this multicultural milieu, a space that presages the concerns of *The Lonely Girls.*

"I Would Never Marry One of My Own Kind": *The Lonely Girl*

In *Race in Modern Irish Literature and Culture* (2009), John Brannigan observes: "The history of the Irish state, as indeed the history of every state, is a history of self-constitution determined not just through acts of assertion and definition but also exclusion and rejection. There is no state, no 'home,' without the foreigner." "Foreigners," whether actual or perceived, are at once essential to a nation for the purposes of self-conception, yet paradoxically they are at the same time marginalized or censored out of that nation's story of itself. Minorities exist at the outskirts of *The Country Girls.* For example, the local Connor sisters are described as "Protestant but well thought of." O'Brien further explores the lives of these characters in her short story "The Connor Girls," where one sister becomes engaged to a lapsed Catholic bank clerk to the consternation of the villagers, who puncture the tires of his motorbike and leave him a hilarious and horrifying note: "Go to Mass or we'll kill you." Of the betrothal, the narrator's mother asserts her belief that "Catholics and Protestants just could not mix." This prediction proves to be true, as objections from the village and the big house—her father refuses to "see his daughter marry a Papist"—serve to doom the romance. This rupture acts as an unheralded harbinger for the narrator, who, many years later, would marry "a man who was not of our religion" and suffer the repudiation from family and relatives that followed.[24] In *The Lonely Girl* relationships between insiders and outsiders (and the implications they have for a community) take center stage.

O'Brien's intertextual flirtations with other international writers link this book with texts that explore how societies deal with newcomers by enforcing racial, ethnic, and religious boundaries. In doing so, these books suggest how such attitudes can be challenged, inverted, and overturned.

The novel also continues O'Brien's rebuke of the Irish Censorship Board, as is evident in Jack Holland's possession of "Bryan Merriman's *Midnight Court.*" In 1946 the Irish Censorship Board banned Frank O'Connor's English translation of Merriman's ribald eighteenth-century poem, *Cúirt An Mheán Oíche*, in which a fairy court is convened to hear the grievances of the women of Ireland. Kiberd says of this interdiction: "[It] seemed to confirm J. M. Synge's contention that an artist would be permitted many freedoms in Irish which might not be deemed appropriate in genteel, post-Victorian English." Asked by an interviewer if she had read *The Midnight Court* in school, O'Brien responds, "Oh yes—expurgated, naturally, and in Irish," before praising it as evidence of the "Rabelaisian streak in the Irish." Her friend David Marcus, a Jewish Irish writer and editor, protested what he describes as the "culturally criminal nonsense of leaving the Irish original unbanned but banning the English" by writing his own translation, which placed even greater emphasis on the poem's subversive sexuality. In November 1952, O'Brien heard Marcus read his version by Lake Graney, next to her home place of Tuamgraney, where Merriman himself had lived in the late eighteenth century and where he "dipped his fingers and soaked his vision."[25] Jack's ownership of the book not only ridicules his desire to marry Caithleen—such unions are relentlessly mocked in the poem—but also derides the judgment and effectiveness of Irish literary censorship.

In *The Lonely Girls*, O'Brien paints a 1950s Dublin distrustful of foreigners, as Baba warns Caithleen at a Sunday-night dance: "Don't take cigarettes from those Indian fellows with turbans; they might be doped." Caithleen's response—"Doped cigarettes! We didn't even get asked up for one dance; there wasn't enough men"—implies that 1950s Ireland's problem is not so much immigration as emigration. However, as this novel shows, societal attention focused on the former usefully diverted it from the latter. According to Clair Wills, "Half a million people (from a population of less than three million) left the country between 1945 and 1960."

This statement is another unpalatable truth that O'Brien's novels make plain: the failure of independent Ireland to stem that tremendous outward migration that as a colony it had blamed on Britain. It is a theme that runs through O'Brien's writing from the beginning. In one of her earliest published pieces, a 1952 account of a trip to the Aran Islands in the *Irish Press*, O'Brien reflected on the depopulation of the Irish countryside: "A girl was being hugged and smothered with Failtes. I asked the reason. 'Home from England after five years,' the policeman told me. 'To stay?' I asked. 'Hardly,' he shook his head, and in that negative I saw a hundred young women and an army of strong men go out of Aran and my mind did not show them coming home again."[26] More engrossed than alarmed by the unfamiliar, Caithleen disregards Baba's warning and once again falls in love with someone from outside the pale of traditional Irish identity.

Kiberd notes that *The Country Girls* "rejigs, at certain moments, *Castle Rackrent*," as when Caithleen's father retires from the big house to the gatehouse and a supposed social inferior wins control of the estate. In *The Lonely Girl* O'Brien adapts another trope from Edgeworth's 1800 novel: an Irish/Jewish marriage. O'Brien provides a summary of the book in her memoir *Mother Ireland* (1976), drawing implicit parallels between it and her own life and work: "*Castle Rackrent* . . . [is] about an eighteenth-century castle in Longford and its profligate owners. . . . Sir Kitt . . . was compelled to marry a crippled Jewess in order to pay his gambling debts. But she was canny, and refused to hand over her dowry which was contained in the thousands of diamonds which she wore about her person. As punishment he had her locked in one of the large damp rooms where she had to while the time away looking at her diamonds and eating the pork that for spite he had sent her to eat." In *The Lonely Girl*, O'Brien reverses the relationship, with the Irish Caithleen drawn to an exotic outsider, Eugene Gaillard, a socialist, and possibly Jewish, documentarian. It is widely accepted that Eugene emanates from O'Brien's husband, novelist Ernest Gébler, whom Michelle Woods describes "as a kind of malevolent muse for her fiction."[27]

Though this chapter intends to complicate this assumption, the resemblance deserves some explication. In his memoir, *Father and I* (2001), Carlo Gébler (son of Edna and Ernest) relates his father's tangled lineage: "The

Géblers were originally Armenian. Towards the end of the nineteenth century, they were thrown out of Turkey by the Ottomans. . . . They may or may not have been Jews." Interestingly, the Jewish element drops from the equation in Carlo Gébler's more recent biography of his father, *The Projectionist* (2015): "His ancestors were Armenians who settled in German speaking Bohemia, which later became Sudetenland before reverting to Czechoslovakia."[28]

In a 1950s letter to her mother, O'Brien says of her then husband: "He has inherited traits that he himself is a stranger to, being of Armenian, Jewish, Czech and German and Irish stock." As such, there is a great deal of vagueness surrounding the extraction of Gébler père, while Eugene's heritage is similarly indeterminate. What is certain, as Woods explains, is that Eugene, like Gébler, is *perceived* as "a foreigner, whom the Irish suppose, in negative and racist terms, to be a Jew." While Eugene does not overtly self-identify as Jewish, he is drawn to the work of Jewish artists, borne out in his love of Gustav Mahler—a composer who considered himself "thrice homeless—as a native of Bohemia in Austria, as an Austrian among Germans, and as a Jew throughout the world . . . an intruder, never welcomed."[29]

Fixed as cultural outsiders in the Irish imagination, Jews were regarded as a sexual threat to pure Irish womanhood. Women were at once symbolically central to the Irish state, yet because of their reproductive capacity they were also the weak link in guaranteeing racial integrity. Laura Doyle analyzes this fear: "The mother herself remains a borderline figure. Her doubleness, even as it secures cultural boundaries, also vexes them."[30] Exogamy or any sexual contact between different cultural groups therefore destabilizes Manichaean perceptions of national and religious identity. These fears meant that Jews became ensnared in Irish censorship laws in strange and revealing ways. In 1929 Rev. Richard Devane submitted in evidence to the "Committee of Evil Literature"—which led to the setting up of the Irish Censorship Board—the following anecdote: "There arrived in the town a Jew with a lorry . . . and he started selling contraceptives made up as pencil holders. . . . Someone told the parish priest about the traffic. . . . He notified the police who could do nothing. [The priest] then set up a court of his own and tried him and fined him £10. The Jew paid £10 and cleared out."[31] The story best highlights how the presence of contraceptives—and the sexual immorality they represented for the Catholic authorities of the embryonic Irish state—could be blamed on Jews, sexual fifth columns bent on undermining the virtue that set Ireland apart from the rest of the world. In the same year Devane made his report, Irish film censor James Montgomery prohibited the American Jewish/Irish love story film *Abie's Irish Rose* (1928) as "subversive to public morality" and "likely to offend religious and *racial* susceptibilities."[32] Historian Kevin Rockett argues, "Any film that infringed [the] Christian [family] was banned. . . . Films that sympathetically depicted divorce, extra-marital affairs, illegitimacy, birth control, abortion, or homosexuality were systematically banned."[33] To this list can be added relationships between Irish women and "foreign" men.

Making Eugene appear Jewish allows O'Brien to draw attention to one particularly striking consequence of Irish wartime censorship. Joanna, the girls' Austrian landlady, questions Caithleen about Eugene's background: "'Is he a Jew, eh?' Her eyes narrowed. 'I do not like Jews, they are a little mean.'"[34] Though she is herself a migrant, Joanna is clearly no touchstone of toleration. Her sentiment may have been shaped by her upbringing in early 1900s Austria. However, such views would not have been regarded as unusual in 1950s Ireland, as historian Eugenio Biagini attests: "Anti-Semitism was deeply embedded in both state practice and popular attitudes." Even while overt anti-Semitism began to disappear from Western society following the Second World War, Dermot Keogh explains that stringent Irish censorship—with even the war's name effaced and replaced with the euphemistic "Emergency"—left "many members of the public in a state of near ignorance about what was going on in continental Europe." Donal Ó Drisceoil concurs: "All war news had to be 'neutralized'—its intrinsic propagandist content, or intent, removed. . . . Reports that revealed cruel or inhuman behaviour were banned as 'atrocity stories,' including coverage of the Holocaust." Wartime censorship in Ireland contributed to a sense of disbelief and denial regarding the Holocaust, as David Marcus shows in his memoir, where he recounts a 1946 encounter with a woman on a Cork-bound train: "They steal and scheme until they get their way. Monsters. Horrible, ugly creatures, with black, oily hair and hooky noses. . . . Oh I'd know a Jew anywhere!"[35] The *cordon sanitaire* of "Emergency" censorship stoked the hyperdistrust of "outlanders," contributing to the inhumane response to Jewish war refugees, based on the inverted logic that Jews cause anti-Semitism: "It has always been the policy of the Minister for Justice to restrict the admission of Jewish aliens, for the reason that any substantial increase in our Jewish population might give rise to an anti-Semitic problem."[36] In the reactions to Eugene, O'Brien thus explores Ireland's inhospitable response to those persons deemed outside the bounds of Irish Catholic nationalist identity.

Caithleen's family finds out about her relationship with Eugene through an anonymous letter, which warns that she is about to become "a nice Catholic Irish girl ruined by a dirty foreigner." Her enraged father retrieves her from Dublin and brings her home by train against her will. En route, James meets some old hurling buddies, who commiserate with him over his almost compromised daughter before drunkenly singing the rebel song "Kevin Barry," while lambasting the "bloody English." None appears to recognize the irony inherent in singing of freedom while Caithleen is effectively held captive. Caithleen manages to escape back to the city and from there to Eugene's home in the countryside outside of Dublin. This escape spurs Caithleen's father's second attempt to "rescue" his daughter from Eugene's hold. James and a collection of inebriated cronies arrive, demanding the return of Caithleen, and subject Eugene to barely coded anti-Semitic attacks: "Look at the nose of him—you know what he is? They'll be running this bloody country soon." If there are any doubts as to what this question insinuates, they are dispelled by looking at O'Brien's contemporaneous short story "Irish Revel," in which an Irish village girl snidely remarks upon the foreign love interest of another: "'He was a Jew,' Doris said. 'You could tell by his nose.'" Denounced as "a foreigner," Eugene asserts his Irishness, retorting, "Not at all as foreign as *your* tiny, blue, Germanic eyes, my friend." Eugene is asked if he is a Catholic ("No"), before the inquisition—having, it seems, little experience of non-Catholics—comically demands to know whether he attends Mass and eats meat on Fridays.[37] Unhappy with his acerbic responses, they knock Eugene to the floor and savagely beat him—before he is saved by his shotgun-wielding housekeeper. At its simplest, the scene can be read as a fictionalization of the reaction of O'Brien's family to her elopement with Gébler.[38] Yet these obvious parallels between Eugene and Gébler can effectively blind readers to subtler intertextual correspondences between Eugene and a variety of fictional personages.

Though born in Ireland, Eugene's atypical parentage (Irish mother, Central European father) means his fellow countrymen do not regard him as Irish. While he shares this stigma with Gébler, he also has much in common with Leopold Bloom of Joyce's *Ulysses*.[39] Bloom is, in Catherine Hezser's words, "constantly stereotyped as Jewish by his Irish Catholic contemporaries and therefore forced to defend himself as if he were Jewish, although he sees himself as an Irishman." Indeed, the assault on Eugene bears an uncanny resemblance to an incident in *Ulysses*, specifically in the Cyclops episode, where the rabid and bibulous Citizen questions Bloom's nationality: "We want no more strangers in our house." His words uncomfortably recall both *Caithleen Ni Houlihan* and the anti-Semitic sentiment of Arthur Griffith. In the Citizen's dualistic mind, all intrinsic and extrinsic "threats" to the Irish nation merge. Thus, Jews and English are conflated, and women function as the window through which these exterior forces gain access to the Irish hearth and home: "Swindling the peasants . . . and the poor of Ireland. . . . The adulteress and her paramour brought the Saxon robbers here."[40] Past invasions are blamed on women, who must be guarded against future onslaught. "Protecting" them from foreign sexual threat gives nationalism, at its most rudimentary, its raison d'être.

In *The Lonely Girl*, James and his cohort share the Citizen's worldview, with Eugene seen as at once Jewish and at the same time implicitly tied to British colonial domination. "We won our freedom. It's our country now," he is told by one of Caithleen's relations. The implication is that the Irish have gained their liberty and, with it, the right to defend women from "alien" influence, even if it means institutionalizing women who stray outside the fold: "We can have her put away. She's not all there." Like that of the Citizen, the men's purported nationalism is thus revealed to be little more than rancorous xenophobia crossed with a desire for power and control. Moreover, their religious devotion is likewise twisted, with accusations of blasphemy somewhat undercut by their unchristian acts of violence. This point is particularly evident when the exasperated Eugene exclaims, "God help Ireland," and is shouted down, with cries of "None of that blasphemy," echoing Bloom's baited outburst in *Ulysses*—"Christ was a jew like me"—and the Citizen's unintentionally ironic response: "By Jesus . . . I'll brain that bloody jewman for using the holy name in vain."[41] Consequently, O'Brien rewrites the horrifying comedy of the Cyclops episode in the confrontation between Eugene and the Irish mob, and in doing so she continues Joyce's exposure of the hypocrisies and absurdities of Irish nationalist discourse.

The upholders of Irish racial integrity seek to silence Eugene for his sexual transgressions, yet it merely has the effect of driving Caithleen more firmly into identifying with him, as the Irish establishment equally suppressed the sexual (and inherently political) expression of its female population. One of her father's friends unwittingly reveals this tenet of Irish nationalism when he assures Caithleen, "Don't worry . . . you'll meet a nice boy yet, one of your own kind." She (silently) spurns this prediction: "I did not tell him this but I now knew that I would never marry one of my own kind." She thus marks her own difference from Irish ideals of archetypal womanhood by aligning herself with Eugene, who embodies political, religious, and racialized Otherness. However, O'Brien complicates any oversimple symmetry between Irish society's attempted silencing of Eugene and that of Caithleen, as Eugene, despite his supposed egalitarian principles, is also complicit in her muzzling. In the fight scene, Eugene speaks for Caithleen, articulating her wish to be free of her family's strictures, as she lies hidden from her father's wrath: "Your daughter is escaping from you. . . . She is running away from you and your way of living." Eugene becomes, for this brief moment, Caithleen's surrogate.[42] Yet it quickly becomes apparent that he reenacts his own persecution on Caithleen. He speaks for her and finds he likes it all too well.

On one final attempt to convince his daughter to return to the family fold, James calls at Eugene's home with some ecclesiastical muscle, a Bishop Jordon, but is turned away by Eugene, who has threatened legal action over their previous attack. Perhaps this affront to the power of the bishopric in Ireland contributed to Archbishop McQuaid's strong reaction to the book. Alternatively, it might have been the relationship between the

Irish Caithleen and the "Jewish" Eugene that stoked his hostility. Worse than depicting a sexual relationship between a young woman and a married man, the book depicts a sexual relationship between an Irish woman and what looks to be a Jewish foreigner. Such a story line fed into Irish stereotypes of the lecherous Jew. It thus seems feasible to argue that it was the deduced ethnic implications of Eugene's relationship with Caithleen as much as the sexual ones that saw the book proscribed. More than jeopardizing Irish morality, according to Heather Ingman, it "threatens the boundaries on which the Irish nation is constructed." In a 1932 sermon, (then) Fr. McQuaid ranted against an anti-Catholic conspiracy led by Jews, in league with Freemasons, Protestants, and communists: "From the first persecutions till the present moment, you will find Jews engaged in practically every movement against Our Divine Lord and his Church." He goes on to attack what he regarded as Jewish control of Hollywood and the implications for Western culture: "I hold here copies of the telegrams by which . . . [a] powerful Masonic and Jewish group . . . compelled the Jewish film producers even to alter the sacred history of the Gospel [in films such as *Ben-Hur* and *The Ten Commandments*]."[43] Though McQuaid had outwardly muted his anti-Semitism by the time he became archbishop in 1940, he continued to connect Jews with troubling foreign influence, especially in cinema. In a 1950s memo, he notes his command over Irish cinemas, but not over the extraneous forces he saw as providing the films: "Five of seven large cinema *managers* are K. of C. [Knights of St. Columbanus, a Catholic lay fraternity]. Cinema renters are very different: English, Jewish."[44] It seems possible then that it was the racial as much as sexual elements of the relationship that spurred McQuaid's reaction to O'Brien's book.

In addition to his "race" and his vocation, Eugene's left-wing sympathies are an affront to Catholic Ireland. Though it is not made explicit, it seems possible that, considering his politics and the novel's setting in the early 1950s, Eugene has left his work as a filmmaker in Hollywood owing to the McCarthyite witch hunts then sweeping the United States. It would certainly add bite to a joke told to Eugene by one of his American friends about the unseemly ambition of the ardently anticommunist (and stalwart supporter of Senator McCarthy) Cardinal Spellman of New York: "The last time the Virgin Mary appeared at Knock she revealed that the next Pope would be tortured. Upon hearing this Cardinal Spellman fainted."[45] Autobiographical convergences back this reading, with Ernest Gébler supposedly taking great delight in the fact that his novel *The Plymouth Adventure* (1948)—a historical novel based on one of America's foundational myths that he infused with a covert protosocialist ethos—was made into a Hollywood film in 1952. He would later use his experience in Hollywood during the making of this film to address the McCarthy witch hunts in his novel *A Week in the Country* (1958). Just as with Gébler, Eugene is viewed in Irish society as politically suspect and denounced for having "no religion."[46] As a filmmaker, a socialist, and a "Jew," Eugene is triply suspect.

The Lonely Girl is filled with plangent references to Joyce: the girls have a drink in "Davy Byrne's," and Baba warns Caithleen to stop using *Dubliners* as a topic of conversion: "Leave James Joyce blow his own trumpet."[47] Yet these resonances can potentially drown out other, less heralded, intertextual voices. Just as Eugene is not wholly drawn from O'Brien's autobiography, neither is he merely plucked from the Irish literary tradition. In a 1962 letter to Bernard Malamud, another potential inspiration becomes apparent. O'Brien applauds Malamud's novel *A New Life* (1961) as the "most moving I [have] read since *Portrait of the Artist*."[48] The comparison is not random. *A New Life* is a *kunstlerroman* in the tradition of *Portrait of the Artist*, and it makes clear its debt to Joyce by quoting *Ulysses* in the epigraph: "Lo, levin leaping lightens in eyeblink Ireland's westward welkin."[49] Malamud's book follows a Jewish protagonist, Seymour Levin, as he escapes New York for a new life in the American Northwest during the 1950s. Teaching in an agricultural college in a small white, conservative town, Levin finds himself isolated for his liberal politics, his romance with Pauline Gilley (his boss's wife), and, it is implied, his Jewishness. While not as blatant as the attacks on Eugene, the lexicon of abuse against Levin is not entirely cryptic: "The next thing you'll be advising the [college president] to step aside so you can take over"; "You are . . . an outsider looking in"; "I'll bet you led them by the nose"; "Why don't you go back where you came from . . . ?"[50] As O'Brien read this novel during the period she was composing *The Lonely Girl*, it seems credible that she drew upon Malamud's characterization of this communal interloper denounced as amalgamated Jew, communist, and sexual threat in her fashioning of Eugene and how he is received by Irish society.

Levin's college is a microcosm of McCarthyite America, where "fear manifested itself . . . in what was missing: ideas, serious criticism, a liberal position." Levin challenges this notion by protesting when college authorities decide to remove an anthology containing Ernest Hemingway's short story "Ten Indians," because a student's parent complains about "the sex parts." He is told through some tortuous and disingenuous logic that retaining the story might see "the Un-American Committee here investigating us and making all sorts of nasty charges," leaving him to fume that "censorship is dangerous business." Significantly, while "Jews" form empty cyphers for the Irish community in O'Brien's novel, an Irishman fulfills a similar role for Levin in Malamud's. Levin finds himself following in the footsteps of an offstage character named Leo Duffy, who has previously worked in Levin's job, which he lost for supposed political (and sexual) indiscretions. The rumors surrounding Duffy's departure inspire Levin to take up his (in the end futile and self-defeating) stand against censorship: "The little you do may encourage the next man to do more." Just as Levin looks to Duffy for moral aid in combating censorship, O'Brien looked to Malamud (himself looking to Joyce) for artistic tools to accomplish the same task. Still, O'Brien did not incorporate elements of Malamud's work into her novel uncritically—Eugene's inability to see Caithleen's perspective mirrors Levin's disregard for Pauline's. Malamud, it seems, noted some implicit criticisms of Levin's point of view in O'Brien's novel, apparent in his critique: "I've read *The Lonely Girl* in a gulp and was moved and charmed by Cait, her good looks, wit, naturalness, innocence and potentialities. Eugene I thought less interesting—possibly your point of view keeps him from being fully realized."[51] It is a charge, mutatis mutandis, O'Brien might have leveled against Malamud's novel.

The Lonely Girl explores Caithleen's own ambivalent position in Irish society as a woman through Eugene's "foreign" status. Yet while they are drawn together by their unwillingness to follow the Irish national narrative—Caithleen in not marrying one of her "own kind," Eugene merely in existing—any empathetic connection is made impossible by Eugene's reproduction of the authoritarian masculine control she has fled. Eugene is at once a victim and a perpetrator of hierarchical power. *The Lonely Girl* ends like its predecessor, with Caithleen rejected by her lover. She rejoins Baba, and they take the boat together for England, the promise and freedom of which begin to loosen Caithleen's bound tongue: "The gulls flew slowly with us, their screaming unwinding the scream inside of me."[52]

"The Courage to Say the Word Fuck": *Girls in Their Married Bliss*

In the ironically titled *Girls in Their Married Bliss*, Baba and Caithleen move to Britain, representative of a journey made by hundreds of thousands of Irishmen and -women in the 1950s. This exodus was yet another of the unutterable truths of Irish society at this time. Four decades after the end of British rule, the great exodus that began during the Famine had not been staunched by independence. While *The Lonely Girl* investigates Ireland from a minority perspective, *Girls in Their Married Bliss* depicts how the Irish were themselves the minority in Britain. As Wills says of that generation, "They left familiar environments and, as they disembarked at Tilbury, Southampton, Liverpool or London Airport, instantly became strangers." O'Brien's book tracks these immigrants as they moved from low to high—from society's bricklayers to its cornerstones. In this, *Girls in Their Married Bliss* flirts with the work of Fitzgerald, whose *Great Gatsby* (1925) epitomizes the experience of assimilation and its ills in the United States. Irish poet Brendan Kennelly recognized a darker note of "disillusionment" in O'Brien's work at this time, suggesting that *Girls in Their Married Bliss* "owes something to Scott Fitzgerald." It also owes something to Roth, whose first book, *Goodbye, Columbus*, draws on Fitzgerald to express disenchantment with Jewish entry into complacent, bourgeois America. Writing in 1967, one anonymous Irish commentator lists the reasons that the three books in *The Country Girl* trilogy were banned in Ireland: *The Country Girls* for "unconsummated sexual experimentation," *The Lonely Girl* for "illicit sex," and *Girls in Their Married Bliss* for "infidelity, abortion, sterilisation, fetishism, voyeurism, exhibitionism, venereal disease, and general sexual frustration and failure."[53] This extended charge sheet points to O'Brien's darkening vision and her continued subversion of censorship.

O'Brien makes no secret of her love for Fitzgerald, with Caithleen fervently reading *Tender Is the Night* (1934) to see if "the man would leave the woman or not" and Baba quoting the novelist back to Caithleen when she falls into a deep depression: "You know what old Scott Fitzgerald said about the three-o'-clock-in-the-morning state."[54] Baba increasingly takes over the narration, as Caithleen experiences progressive mental dissolution in *Girls in Their Married Bliss*, through her inability to adapt to the expectations of English society and married life. Throughout, *Girls in Their Married Bliss* pays particular homage to *The Great Gatsby*. Literary critic Joe Cleary suggests that Fitzgerald's most famous book is inspired by the author's family's Irish immigrant roots and the anxiety of entering American society: "*The Great Gatsby* is essentially . . . [a] passing narrative in which an ethnic parvenu finds his way into the gorgeous upper echelons of American WASP society, there to discover the great vacuity concealed at the heart of the American dream." *Girls in Their Married Bliss* mimics this rise. While Caithleen is reunited with the corrosive Eugene (with whom she has a baby boy, Cash), Baba marries the nouveau riche Frank, an Irish builder who has made it big in London: "You won't believe it but I felt sort of sorry for him, the way he worried about not being educated . . . or being taken for an Irish hick by waiters. Never mind that they're Italian hicks." Like Gatsby, Frank affects an English accent, getting voice lessons from an Englishwoman; according to Baba, "You'd pay not to talk like her." Like Gatsby, Frank ostentatiously displays his wealth, with a house full of rooms "done like the Vatican" and a retinue: "He never stirred with less than ten or twelve people." At one of his parties (sad copies of Gatsby's banquets), Baba finds one of the Jewish guests attractive and "sort of wronged" looking. His presence recalls Gatsby's Meyer Wolfsheim, who, for Cleary, connects "Gatsby with another recent immigrant ethnicity despised by WASP America." Baba lampoons Frank's attempts to become "civilized," such as his courting of the English gentry, which is hilariously frustrated one night when a washerwoman nicknamed "the Duchess" is accidentally invited over for drinks—her family crest, as she later admits to an infuriated Frank, is the "mop and pail."[55] Throughout, O'Brien's book gestures toward Fitzgerald's seminal account of acculturation.

If Frank is like the arriviste Gatsby, he is at the same time analogous to the brutal, racist Tom Buchanan, who, despite his upper-class breeding, has no compunction about beating his wife or his mistress: "With a short deft movement, Tom Buchanan broke her nose with his open hand." Though now in Britain, not much has changed in this regard for Baba and Caithleen. Both are still under male control and the threat of male violence. Helen Jones says of 1950s England: "Domestic violence was probably the greatest threat to women's safety, it remained within the 'private' domestic sphere, neighbours most typically turned a blind eye." By depicting this reality, O'Brien challenges the code of silence surrounding violence toward women not only in Ireland but in Britain as well. Just as in *The Country Girls* Caithleen's father tries to hide his violence toward his family from the wider community—who collude by ignoring it—so too do Eugene and Frank attempt to conceal their own domestic misconduct. Of Frank, Baba says: "[He] was very careful; you know, slaughter your wife so long as you do it indoors." She risks his rage to have a brief fling with a foreign drummer, which ends with her pregnancy and failed attempts to induce a miscarriage. When Eugene finds out that Caithleen—trapped by their loveless marriage—is also conducting an apprehensive affair, he strikes her, a change from his usual methods of dominance: "He believed in the gentle art of persuasion, in change through knowledge, in the twentieth-century game of brain washing." When confronted, Caithleen, wavering between defeat and defiance, tells Eugene she did not sleep with the other man: "She wished she had the courage to say the word fuck and offend him more."[56] While the unuttered word does not offend Eugene within the book, it did defy established publishing norms and unofficial British censorship outside of it.

Girls in Their Married Bliss shifts O'Brien's attack on censorship from the Irish state to the self-censorship of the British publishing industry. This chapter has hitherto demonstrated that James Brady's hushed attack on his daughter in *The Country Girls* is an instance of the everyday censorship that formed the popular backbone of state censorship. While that scene acts as a metaphor for Irish governmental censorship, the expurgation of the word "slut" in her father's rebuke—"you little s——"—signals another mode of silencing. As Marjorie Howes notes: "Nearly all western nations had some form of censorship at this time."[57] Published less than a year after two 1959 obscenity trials—one in New York, the other in London—lifted the ban of D. H. Lawrence's *Lady Chatterley's Lover* (1928), O'Brien's early novels were born into a publishing world still very uneasy with offending readers, even after official sanctions had been lifted.[58] And so these books encountered many forms of potential censorship beyond the most obvious. A culture of self-censorship developed in the wake of these British legal censorship watersheds, shifting from a hard model of government oversight to a more specialized form of capital hegemony based on markets and sales. This model imposed restrictions on artistic expression, founded as it was on deductions made by publishers about their audiences' moral tolerance level. The absent word "slut" is a rare instance when these publishing negotiations surface and become apparent to the reader.

In the 1960s, O'Brien was frequently criticized as a writer who produced popular Irish melodrama for American and British audiences. Irish novelist John Broderick described her readership as the sort that "likes to know, before it opens a book, just exactly what it is about to read" and scolded the "silly . . . reviewers and critics in England and America" who took her seriously. This supposition is contradicted by correspondence between O'Brien and her editorial manager Isobel Ross at Jonathan Cape regarding the publication of *Girls in Their Married Bliss*. Ross asks O'Brien to remove a certain passage, "which is extremely blasphemous and will undoubtedly give offense. Please will you either delete it or change it. Also, I expect you already know that Boots have an absolute veto on books that contain four-letter words." The passage in question concerns Baba summing up a woman's place in an excoriating address to God: "Oh God, who does not exist, you hate women, otherwise you'd have made them different. And Jesus, who insulted your mother, you hate them more. . . . I thought of all the women who . . . saying their rosary with their rosary beads held over the side of the bed, and others saying, 'Stop, stop, you dirty old dog, you're hurting me,' and others yelling desperately to be jacked right up their middles, and it all leading to nothing." Had O'Brien wished her novel to be included in the Boots lending library and gain the large popular fiction audience that that market would all but guarantee, it seems likely she would have removed or altered this scene. O'Brien remained adamant, and

Jonathan Cape editor Tom Maschler eventually decided to go ahead with publication, but with a caveat he lays out for O'Brien's agent, Mark Hamilton: "It is not easy for us to judge the exact degree of risk involved but we would be prepared to go ahead provided that Edna understands the implications and guarantees that she will be responsible for any costs or damages which might be incurred as a result of a case being brought against us."[59] Such a responsibility was not a light one for a woman who was paid a fifty-pound flat fee for her first, wildly successful, novel and whose estranged husband held the film rights to its sequel.[60] This correspondence obviously says something about O'Brien's artistic integrity, but it also points to her awareness of and fight against censorship beyond the formal Irish variety. Furthermore, the offending scene communicates intertextually with other texts struggling against censorship of one form or another.

Just as *The Lonely Girl* flirts with Malamud's *A New Life*, *Girls in Their Married Bliss* converses with Roth's early fiction. According to O'Brien, *Goodbye, Columbus* (1959) was the "first book of [Roth's] that I read." Roth's debut novella is a satirical snapshot of the Jewish community in America as it made its rapid postwar transition from a loathed immigrant group to the essence of the "American Dream." Critics have long drawn connections between Roth's first book and *The Great Gatsby*, with Alfred Kazin's review arguing, "One catches lampoonings of our swollen and unreal American prosperity that are as observant and charming at Fitzgerald's," and Norman MacLeod suggesting that both stories start when a "major protagonist is introduced to an alien social milieu." The novella follows a summer love affair between working-class Jew Neil Klugman—described in a *New York Times* review as sharing the "smug self-righteousness of Joyce's Stephen Dedalus"—and Brenda Patimkin, a member of the newly wealthy and suburban Jewish middle class.[61] At heart, it is a novel of assimilation, as Neil reflects on the changing landscape of his hometown of Newark, New Jersey:

> On the streets, instead of Yiddish, one heard the shouts of Negro children playing. . . . The neighborhood had changed: the old Jews like my grandparents had struggled and died, and their offspring had struggled

> and prospered, and moved further and further west, towards the edge of Newark, then out of it, and up the slope of the Orange Mountains, until they had reached the crest and started down the other side, pouring into Gentile territory as the Scotch-Irish had poured through the Cumberland Gap. Now, in fact, the Negroes were making the same migration, following the steps of the Jews.[62]

It is also a novel about the dangers of prosperity, one that critiques the gaudy excesses of the recently enriched Jewish community and, more broadly, 1950s American materialist culture.

Like O'Brien's trilogy, *Goodbye Columbus* was attacked for pandering stereotypes to the wider world, with one rabbi revealingly admitting in a letter, "Your story—in Hebrew—in an Israeli magazine or newspaper—would have been judged exclusively from a literary point of view," with the implication that Roth's unadorned portrayal of the Jewish community merely confirmed the opinions of a hostile Gentile audience.[63] Along with *The Lonely Girl*, Roth's book was banned in Ireland in 1962 for its depiction of premarital sex, contraception, and blasphemy.[64] In New York's Saint Patrick's Cathedral, Neil contemplates his relationship with Brenda and his ambivalence toward the wealth and materiality of her family, which both attract and repel him. It is noteworthy that this moment occurs in an Irish Catholic space, perhaps an acknowledgment that the Jewish leap into American affluence mimicked prior Irish assimilative success. He addresses his introspection to "God":

> I wondered if I looked like a Catholic, and in my wonderment I began to make a little speech to myself. Can I call the self-conscious words I spoke prayer? At any rate, I called my audience God. God, I said, I am twenty-three years old. I want to make the best of things. . . . What is it I love, Lord? . . . Which prize is You? . . .
>
> Which prize do you think, *shmuck*? Gold dinnerware, sporting-goods trees, nectarines, garbage disposals . . .
>
> And God only laughed, that clown.[65]

Like Roth, O'Brien uses the device of a mocking prayer to indict the false pieties, moral stagnation, and cultural complacency of 1960s society.

With her trilogy, O'Brien confronts censorship both within Ireland and without. Her focus on characters marginalized in the Irish national discourse evolves as the Irish themselves become marginal figures in Britain. O'Brien makes common cause with American writers who were themselves confronting the accepted mores of their day. Her willingness to defy publishing standards as a young author at the expense of sales and financial gain serves as a rebuttal to Roy Foster's contention that she produces "Irish melodrama for non-Irish audiences."[66] While midcentury Irish authorities strove to present Ireland as a place of religious and racial purity, O'Brien dispels this myth by portraying a country of moral hypocrisy and hidden diversity. Bursting with minority voices, her books symbolize this heterogeneity. Full too of discreet intertextual flirtation, *The Country Girls* trilogy acts as a metaphor for a country that was, for all its outwardly distrust, deeply connected to the wider world. Yet she received little thanks for her work at the time. As she said of Synge: "He gave Ireland what Ireland needed and he was crucified for it."[67]

3

"A Contrast of Explosive Nature"

History and Buried Politics in Night *and* Portnoy's Complaint

The censure and censorship that greeted the debut novels of Philip Roth and Edna O'Brien, discussed in the last chapter, proved to be formative experiences. Their books were attacked for breaking sexual taboos, but beneath this overt censure lay a more profound charge: betraying tribal secrets. Roth's and O'Brien's subsequent fiction was fueled by the anger they felt as a result of these hypocritical accusations, and it ultimately led to the volatile experimentation of Roth's *Portnoy's Complaint* (1969) and O'Brien's *Night* (1972). These novels appeared at a time of great historical change, with Ireland emerging fitfully from the long conservative rule of Eamon de Valera and America undergoing a cultural revolution that repudiated the deference of the Eisenhower era. In their home countries, Roth and O'Brien became symbols of this era of sexual and social upheaval. Neither *Night* nor *Portnoy's Complaint* was well received, with commentary focusing on the explicit sex of the novels, rather than their implicit politics. The *Times* of London, for instance, dismissed *Night* as "self-indulgent whimsy . . . a mixture of narcissism and Irishry . . . one long act of public literary masturbation." A *New York Times* editorial inveighed against *Portnoy's Complaint* for "wallowing in revolting sex excesses" and regretted that the courts could no longer ban such "descents into degeneracy." It was an Irish newspaper, ironically, that glimpsed something beyond the salacious, with Bruce Williamson of the *Irish Times* reflecting on Roth's protagonist: "One wonders, from time to time, whether he uses sex to cover up a simple and selfish instinct for power: people seldom talk so freely unless they are putting up a smokescreen."[1] This chapter concurs, arguing that *Portnoy's Complaint* is primarily concerned with how power functions—particularly in 1960s Israel and America. Equally, *Night* is not, as Irish novelist Eilís Dillon deplored, "the recollections of a soured, middle-aged woman of shaky standards"; rather, it is an exploration of Irish identity at a time of civil strife in 1970s Northern Ireland.[2] Here I argue that Roth and O'Brien use these novels to question not the intoxicating allure of sex but the dangerous appeal of nationalism.

"Here *We're* the WASPs!": *Portnoy's Complaint*

In the wake of the controversy surrounding *Goodbye, Columbus* and its attendant short stories of Jewish adultery, duplicity, and blasphemy, and having declared "I'll never write about Jews again," Roth wrote two deeply serious novels, *Letting Go* (1962) and *When She Was Good* (1967), in which Jews and Jewishness are marginal or absent entirely.[3] Yet the indignation with his critics appears to have built up throughout the decade, only to erupt with *Portnoy's Complaint*, which returns with a vengeance to the setting and subject matter of his first book. Irish writer Kevin Stevens observes that "like Swift and Twain, Roth is aesthetically propelled by anger; it supplies the energy needed for the massive, self-imposed task of dissecting . . . the suffocating paradoxes of twentieth-century America."[4] *Portnoy's Complaint* tells the story of Alexander Portnoy, a former "good Jewish boy" who, through his frenzied sex life (real and imagined), attempts to break free of the moral inhibitions of his Jewish childhood in 1930s and 1940s Newark, New Jersey.

The epigraph, purporting to be an entry in a psychoanalytic encyclopedia, institutes the principal theme of the novel: "Portnoy's Complaint: n[oun]. Strongly-felt ethical and altruistic impulses are perpetually warring with extreme sexual longings, often of a perverse nature." In a frenetic monologue directed at his taciturn psychiatrist, Dr. Spielvogel (addressed as Herr Doctor), the thirty-three-year-old Portnoy narrates his life as a series of vivid episodes, each one loaded, in his own mind, with Freudian significance. He begins with his mother, Sophie, who dominates his early life: "She was so deeply imbedded in my consciousness that for the first year of school I seem to have believed that each of my teachers was my mother in disguise." From this point on, it is clear that the supporting characters of Portnoy's life are not objectively sketched, being rather an exaggerated product of his churning brain, as Debra Shostak avers, "Roth makes us aware that the speaker is examining the inhabitants and memories of his conscious mind."[5]

His insurance salesman father is rendered with the same satirical eye, his constant constipation a symbol of his "social impotence" as a Jew in an overwhelmingly Christian insurance company and society, according to Alan Cooper. As he contemplates his parents, Portnoy's thoughts flow back past his earliest memories to his birth: "I might be remembering his sperm nosing into her ovum . . . so sweeping and unqualified is my love." Portnoy's imaginative return to his origin appears to flirt with Lawrence Sterne's *Tristram Shandy* (1759–67), in which the eponymous hero also narrates his own birth: "I wish either my father or my mother, or indeed both of them, as they were in duty both equally bound to it, had minded what they were about when they begot me." Like Sterne's novel, *Portnoy's Complaint* is filled with digressions and double entendres, as well as crusades against oppressive seriousness and propriety. Portnoy's motivating factor is his attempt to reject what he sees as the bequest of his parents and of the Jewish community: "Shame and shame and shame and shame—every place I turn something else to be ashamed of."[6]

Portnoy's father sells insurance in the poorest sections of Newark, to "the callow Poles, and violent Irishmen, and illiterate Negroes." Portnoy's childhood education, as he subsequently recalls it, bears out this Manichaean sense of difference: "The very first distinction I learned . . . was not night and day or hot and cold, but *goyishe* and Jew . . . Jew Jew Jew Jew Jew Jew!" For Portnoy's parents' generation, this wariness is well earned; in the 1930s, the family has to leave their first home in Jersey City after "a swastika was painted on the front of [their] building." Yet America was rapidly changing at this point, not least in its attitude toward Jews—spurred on by Jewish economic advancement and military enrollment, alongside the postwar revelations of the Holocaust. Portnoy's boyhood then is shaped not by the debilitating anti-Semitism of his parents' and grandparents' generations, but by another myth: Jews as paragons. Gentile perfidy and

Jewish perfection become the two poles of his experience. *Portnoy's Complaint* continues *Goodbye, Columbus*'s aim of showing the Jews of America to be just as capable of dishonesty, lechery, and prejudice as their Christian American counterparts: "Imperfection . . . is, after all, maybe only human!" As a teenager, Portnoy rebels against the weight of Jewish tradition, exemplified by his father, and comes into conflict too with his sister, who, through her collection for the Jewish National Fund, represents Jewish American loyalty to Israel. Yet what frequently comes across is the utter reasonableness of Portnoy's opponents' points of view and the fevered nature of his own arguments. As Roth later said of his writerly process: "Of course you give the other guy the best lines. Otherwise it's a mug's game."[7]

Roth wrings great comedy out of Jewish attempts to set themselves apart from Gentile America, as the strictures of Portnoy's young life make plain: "The goyim . . . will eat *anything*. . . . And the terrifying corollary, *they will do anything as well*. . . . Yes, it's all written down in history, what they have done, our illustrious neighbors who own the world and know absolutely nothing of human boundaries and limits."[8] Portnoy's father reinforces the logic behind this belief, by painting Christians as irrational and hypocritical in their attitudes toward Jews: "They worship a Jew, do you know that, Alex? Their whole big-deal religion is based on worshiping someone who was an established Jew at that time. . . . [He] was a Jew, like you and me." These words echo Leopold Bloom's response to the Citizen in *Ulysses*, "Your God was a jew. Christ was a jew like me." *Portnoy's Complaint* flirts further with Joyce, its structure mimicking the episodic nature of *A Portrait of the Artist as a Young Man*—a book Portnoy's sister reads at camp—as Roth explains in an interview with George Plimpton: "[it] proceeds by means of what I began to think of as 'blocks of consciousness,' chunks of material of varying shapes and sizes piled atop one another and held together by association rather than chronology." Beyond stylistic links, Roth elaborates on thematic ones: "Obscenity as a usable and valuable vocabulary, and sexuality as a subject, have been available to us since Joyce, Henry Miller, and Lawrence." Whereas the young Stephen Dedalus travels to Dublin's red-light district—which he confuses with the "quarter of the Jews"—Portnoy's desires are directed elsewhere.[9] One predictable result of his ethnic conditioning against Gentiles is that the growing Portnoy is fascinated by all things non-Jewish.

His desire to escape his community develops into longing for the forbidden fruits of American culture, and subsequently for Gentile women. Foiled, however, his adolescent predilections find other, more solitary, outlets. He begins to masturbate constantly, at home, at school, even on community outings: "Oh shove it in me, Big Boy, cried the cored apple that I banged silly on that picnic." In an emphatic rebuke of Jewish dietary rules and all they signify, Portnoy goes as far as befouling his family dinner: "Come, screamed the maddened piece of liver that, in my own insanity, I . . . violated behind a billboard on the way to a bar mitzvah lesson." Roth may have also come upon this particular obscenity in *Ulysses*, in the hallucinatory Circe episode filled with Bloom's lurid fantasies: "if desire act awfully bestial butcher's boy pollutes in warm veal liver."[10] As Portnoy later reflects: "What else, I ask you, were all those prohibitive dietary rules and regulations all about to begin with, what else but to give us little Jewish children practice in being repressed?"[11]

Enamored by Christians, Portnoy is particularly beguiled by Irish Catholics, as evinced in two childhood incidents he calls to mind (and embellishes) from the analyst's couch. In one he recounts a cautionary tale that his mother is fond of retelling, pertaining to how she was "bamboozled (which is to say, flattered and shamed simultaneously) into eating lobster Newburg by a mischievous, lush named (could it be better?) Doyle." As with the enigmatic Doyle in Bernard Malamud's novel *A New Life*, the Irishman here is figured as both potentially menacing and sexually enticing. Portnoy further summons up the image of an Irish American work colleague of his father, Anne McCaffrey, who is brought to the Portnoy home for "a real Jewish meal." Reinterpreting this scene in analysis, Portnoy sees it as a sign that his father was having an affair: "A question has just occurred to me, twenty-five years later (not that I have a single shred of evidence . . .), a question has arisen in the audience: why did you bring . . . [her] into our home? . . . because . . . of your forbidden lust! . . . I recognize the syndrome perfectly."[12] Portnoy's words mock the tendency of traditional Freudian analysis to reductively see (or falsely instill) sexual transgression as the core of all psychological problems. These "memories" likely tell us more about Portnoy than his parents. Yet they also tell us about ethnic formation and exclusion: Portnoy reimagines his parents betraying their family, community, and religion through liaisons with Irish Catholics, and in so doing shows that latent desire often lurks behind one cultural group's distrust for another.

For Portnoy, sexual encounters with Gentiles not only are a means of rejecting the unyielding religious directives of his childhood, but also serve to annul the cultural homogeneity imposed by his inward-looking Jewish milieu, in which outsiders were treated with suspicion and exogamy was sternly discouraged. If the embroilment between Caithleen's family and the "Jewish" Eugene furnishes the pivotal point of *The Lonely Girl* by unmasking Irish Catholic hatred of outsiders, then a reversed example can be found in *Portnoy's Complaint*. Portnoy recounts the story of his highly assimilated, athletic older cousin, whom he idolizes: "To me, Heshie was everything." Before Heshie is drafted into the army in 1943, he becomes engaged to the Polish Catholic Alice Dembosky. Horrified by this prospect, Heshie's father convinces Alice that his son has a rare blood disease and pays her a hundred dollars to never speak to him again; he then wrestles his distraught son to the ground to ensure his compliance. Frantically and hilariously uproariously narrated up to this point, the story suddenly turns somber: "When Heshie was killed in the war, the only thing people could think to say to my Aunt Clara and my Uncle Hymie, to somehow mitigate the horror, to somehow console them in their grief, was, 'At least he didn't leave you with a *shikse* wife. At least he didn't leave you with *goyische* children.'"[13] With this abrupt tonal shift, Roth presents that the reader with an ugly manifestation of Jewish xenophobia.

As an adult, Portnoy escapes to New York from the confines of Jewish Newark: "The hysteria and the superstition! The watch-its and the be-carefuls! You mustn't do this, you can't do that—hold it! Don't! you're breaking an important law! What law? Whose law?"[14] Portnoy goes on to relate his continued pursuit of American women as an adult to Dr. Spielvogel. These characters are crudely drawn by Portnoy, being, like his parents, hyperbolic oral reconstructions rather than rounded human portraits. It becomes increasingly clear, however, that it is not the Jewish mother or the Gentile love object that sits at the novel's satiric center, but

Portnoy himself. Portnoy—who has now become the assistant commissioner for human opportunity in New York—works himself into a frenzy and disparages his parents as racist, his lovers as ignorant, and the Jews as "narrow-minded" and "self-righteous," yet all the while it is he who best displays all of these basest instincts.

In 1972 literary critic Irving Howe, who once robustly defended *Goodbye, Columbus* from rabbinic disapproval, reassessed Roth's fiction. It was the perceived failure of *Portnoy's Complaint* to live up to a Swiftian standard of satire that, according to Howe, induced this backlash:

> To compose a satire is not at all to free oneself from the obligation to social accuracy; it is only to order that accuracy in a particular way. If it can be shown that the targets of the satirist are imprecisely located or that he is shooting wild, the consequences may be more damaging than if the same were shown for a conventional realist. And if it can be shown that the satire is self-serving . . . then it becomes—well, imagine how absurd *Gulliver's Travels* would seem if we became persuaded that the satiric barrage against mankind allows for one little exception, a young hero troubled by the burdens of being English and resembling Jonathan Swift.[15]

For Howe, the narcissism of the protagonist becomes inseparable from that of the author. Yet such a reading ignores the multilayered irony of Roth's work. Swift's own satirical work was similarly misread during his lifetime, as with his late poem "Verses on the Death of Dr. Swift," in which he imagines his own demise:

> This maxim more than all the rest
> Is thought too base for human breast:
> In all distresses of our friends,
> We first consult our private ends;
>
> While Nature, kindly bent to ease us,
> Points out some circumstance to please us.
>
> . . . .
>
> Vain human kind! fantastic race!
> Thy various follies who can trace?

> Self-love, ambition, envy, pride,
> Their empire in our hearts divide.[16]

Swift's friend Alexander Pope famously dismissed it as "too Vain in some respects, & in one or two particulars, not true." Alive to the mischievous manner at work of the dean, Swift scholar Barry Slepian argues that Swift's inclusion of himself within the poem does not negate his "thesis that all mankind is egotistical, selfish, and proud," but rather resoundingly affirms it.[17] There is something provocative in playing with the divide between fact and fiction that causes even astute critics like Howe or Pope to miss the point: biography clouds satire. The same is true for Roth's deceptively autobiographical creation. Far from being excluded from Roth's social satire, the outrageous Portnoy is the epitome of it.

Portnoy is torn by contradictory impulses. On the one hand, he wishes to be known as the defender of the downtrodden—"Who do you think got the banks to begin to recruit Negroes and Puerto Ricans for jobs in this city, to send personnel people to interview applicants in Harlem?"—yet on the other, he wants to rewrite the old prescription of the Jews as powerless, like his father: "How could he oppress?—he was the oppressed. How could he wield power?—he was the powerless. How could he enjoy triumph, when he so despised the triumphant—and probably the very idea." Portnoy's boasts of virility—"through fucking I will conquer America"—are an attempt to replace the stereotype of the weak and helpless Jew with an image of the ultramasculine Jew. Like the Irish, Jews were categorized as feminine in nineteenth- and early-twentieth-century racial discourse. And like the Irish, hypermasculine nationalism became an attractive means of rewriting this position. As Aidan Beatty argues, "Both Jewish and Irish cultures were greatly affected by their weakness vis-à-vis the stronger majority, and Jewish and Irish men faced some conceptually similar stereotypes about their supposed deficiencies. Zionism, like Irish nationalism, was also a concerted effort to refute popular racial stereotypes and create a more prideful image of Jewish strength and power." Drawing on large-scale Jewish service in the US armed forces (exemplified by Heshie), and the violent foundation of Israel, the novels of Jewish American writers such as Herman Wouk and Leon Uris launched this figure into the popular cultural imagination. In Uris's *Exodus* (1958), American nurse Kitty Fremont differentiates old Jew from new when describing the Israeli Ari Ben Canaan: "This Ben Canaan, doesn't act like any Jew I've ever met. . . . You don't particularly think of them in a capacity like this . . . of fighters." Portnoy parodies these creations. In fleeing one stereotype (the feeble Jew), Portnoy tumbles into another: the lecherous, perverted Jew. Worse, the angst caused by his sexual desires means that he becomes, in Shostak's terms, "not only emasculated but linked to the hysteria associated with the feminine."[18] Portnoy's masculinity thus ends up undermining itself, becoming the thing it is attempting to escape. Roth's novel challenges corrosive masculinity in the United States, but its aim is broader, as becomes evident when Portnoy, fleeing America and his Gentile lovers, makes his way to Israel.

Provocatively titled "In Exile," the final chapter of Roth's novel is set in Israel, ostensible home of the Jews. Yet while the plane is circling over the country, Portnoy cannot help fondly reminiscing about his home in the "Diaspora": "I look down . . . upon the land of Israel, where the Jewish people first came into being, and am impaled upon a memory of Sunday morning softball games in Newark." Once on the tarmac, however, Portnoy is immersed in the ultramasculine world of Israel, where the recently ended Third Arab-Israel War (1967) has fundamentally altered the position of the Jewish nation in the region. In the words of Israeli revisionist historian Ari Shavit, "Within a few weeks the mighty Arabs were transformed into victims, while the endangered Israelis became conquerors." Forgetting his airborne epiphany, Portnoy is enthralled by this land of strong, triumphant, and unapologetic Jews: "One simple but wholly (to me) implausible fact: I am in a Jewish country. In this country, everybody is Jewish." This ignores the non-Jewish citizens (Christian and Muslim) in Israel at this time, along with those under military occupation in the West Bank and Gaza Strip after 1967. Yet they are there, subconsciously at least, as Portnoy notes the "tombs, synagogues, fortresses, mosques, shrines, harbors, ruins, the new ones, the old." The "mosques" signal a Muslim presence, while the "new ruins" connote the recent wars. Overjoyed at being surrounded by Jews, Portnoy cries, "Here *we're* the WASPs!"[19] His exclamation contradicts his assertion that everyone in the country is Jewish; for there to be WASPs (or an elite), there must also be a despised Other, a role the Jews (and the Irish, inter alios) previously played in American society and one Arabs play in Israel. Portnoy, so revolted by the toxic insularity of his Jewish American family—as evinced in the Heshie story—does not realize that in Israel, he is guilty of the same crime.

Portnoy's wonder is more consciously undermined as he wanders through Tel Aviv after dark: "They are going to assault me! But how can that be? If they are Jewish and I am Jewish, what motive can there be for them to do me any harm?" It is unclear whether the Jewish youths actually want to attack Portnoy, simply make fun of him, or whether he misinterprets this situation entirely. What is clear is that the Jewish American Portnoy finds himself not bolstered by Israeli masculinity but rather threatened by it. According to historian Ian Black, the "New Jew" was "tough, dedicated, muscular and Hebrew-speaking [and] rejected the values of the Diaspora." Portnoy, as the embodiment of Diasporic Jewry, becomes in his own mind at least a target rather than a beneficiary of Jewish nationalism. Despite this incident, Portnoy is spellbound by Israeli women and contemplates marriage to Naomi, a kibbutz member he meets on his travels: "Why don't I marry her and stay?" According to Joshua Lambert, Portnoy's infatuation "parod[ies] the intense attraction of post-1967 Zionism to American Jews, seeming, as it did, to offer a dramatic solution to the instabilities of Jewish identity." She rejects his advances, but when he persists she knocks him to the ground and lectures him on how "[the Diaspora] had produced just such disagreeable men as myself—frightened, defensive, self-deprecating, unmanned and corrupted by life in the gentile world . . . who had gone by the millions to the gas chambers without ever raising a hand against their persecutor."[20]

Portnoy, with the upper arm muscles he has built up using weights inherited from Heshie, once again grapples with Naomi, attempting to force himself upon her, but finds himself impotent. As Shostak notes, Portnoy experiences "sexual failure with an Israeli woman, in the one place where he might have expected to feel confident in his power as a Jewish man." Bernard Avishai asserts that Portnoy's attempted rape "suggested, prophetically, that if Jews had power . . . this only meant they'd be struggling with the world's historical sinfulness they had customarily projected onto Gentiles." Israel is not the promised land, but one that forces Jews to become rulers, with all the negative consequences it entails. Disabused by Naomi of his fatal nationalist attraction, Portnoy celebrates not the certainties of Israel but the complexities and contradictions of the Diaspora: "This is what it's like in the Diaspora . . . Temptation and disgrace! Corruption and self-mockery! Self-deprecation—and self-defecation too! Whining, hysteria, compromise, confusion, disease! . . . I am soiled, oh, I am impure—and also pretty fucking tired . . . of never being quite good enough for the Chosen People!" Portnoy attacks the moral convictions of the Jewish nationalism that he has only moments ago himself professed. As Alan Cooper argues, "Roth probes myths of Jewish history by suggesting that not Israel but America may be the true Zion."[21]

In *Portnoy's Complaint*, Roth questions the pieties of postwar Jewish American identity by undermining idealistic portrayals of the community in America and mocking the unquestioning support of Israel. Yet at the same time, he is aware of the strong pull of nationalism and does not completely negate it. As Portnoy tells Naomi, "I am a patriot too . . . only in another place! (Where I *also* don't feel at home!)." The novel closes with Portnoy, whipped into a delirium on his analyst's couch, imagining himself on trial for his lifetime of sexual misdeeds and ethnic treachery: "This is the police speaking. You're surrounded, Portnoy. You better come on out and pay your debt to society."[22] The scene recalls Leopold Bloom's own trial scene in the Circe episode, in which both his allegiance to Ireland and his masculinity are challenged by a phantasmagoric mob. Like Joyce, Roth subverts the accepted tenets of nationalism by deconstructing the masculinity on which it is built.

"The Original Hooligans": *Night*

In 1972 Isaac Bashevis Singer wrote to Edna O'Brien: "I think we both have in common the fact that we are rooted in the soil and culture of our people. Most of modern writers are rootless and they consider it being 'cosmopolitan.'" Yet O'Brien's work had up to that point oscillated between soil and city, Ireland and England, and solemnity and satire. Following *The Country Girls* trilogy, O'Brien's next two, deeply serious, novels, *August Is a Wicked Month* (1965) and *Casualties of Peace* (1966), were set on the Continent and in Britain and were less overtly concerned with themes of Irishness. *A Pagan Place* returned to Ireland, but not to the searing comedy of the trilogy. In a 1971 *Palatinate* interview she separates her work into two distinct groups: "My writing about Ireland is always . . . my deepest writing. I tend to write two kinds of things, one is urbane, like say *August is a Wicked Month* . . . urbane works, fairly shrill, fairly raucous, but Ireland is more in my gut. My last book is about Ireland, *Pagan Place*, the most Irish book I have written."[23] Her remarks suggest O'Brien was searching for a way to amalgamate such seemingly contradictory impulses in a single work—just as she had earlier wed the ribald and the demure traditions of Irish female literary representation in *The Country Girls*. Here I will suggest that O'Brien uses her 1971 *Vogue* essay, "The Artist and His Country," as a testing ground in which to experiment with how such a merger might be accomplished. In this flirtatious paratextual space O'Brien sets forth the relationship between a writer and her nation.

O'Brien begins "The Artist and His Country" by reflecting on the relative lack of oppression she encounters as an artist in British society: "In another part of Europe a writer may expect a knock on the door in the middle of the night and be carted off for interrogation or death. . . . Maybe England is too benign. Artists require a struggle."[24] She instead sees congruence between her position and that of contemporary America writers, the literature of which she divides into two camps: "At the moment there are two very different kinds of writing going on in America. There are the works set in *urban places*, *shrill*, *raucous*, the themes are fornication, divorce, [and] marriage-swopping."[25] The use here of the terms "urban[e]," "shrill," and "raucous" (previously seen in her *Palatinate* interview) suggests that O'Brien correlates her own "cosmopolitan" novels with this strand of American fiction. Her professed aversion for such American writing may then be based on an internalization of the criticisms her "urban" fiction faced, frequently dispraised as inauthentic, in contrast with her "genuine" rural stories.

O'Brien makes a distinction between this emerging irreverent urban tradition and what she sees as the disappearing politically driven rural tradition of writers like John Steinbeck: "The themes that engaged the writer of the American thirties are now the province of television and journalism. It is journalists who describe the journey of the Mexican grapepickers who cross the frontier and work in appalling conditions. . . . It is on television that we see what is happening, or some of what is happening, in Vietnam. No writer could dare compare with the goriness of the events." Here her views coincide with Roth's, who, in his 1961 essay, "Writing American Fiction," argued, "The American writer . . . has his hands full in trying to understand, and then describe, and then make credible much of the American reality. It stupefies, it sickens, it infuriates, and finally it is even a kind of embarrassment to one's own meager imagination."[26] However, in "The Artist and His Country," Roth is denounced as the zenith of the "shrill," "raucous" contingent, with O'Brien reproaching *Portnoy's Complaint* for its popular "titillation" and thus its lack of gravitas relative to more partisan, socially conscious (American) predecessors like Steinbeck.[27] In critiquing Roth, O'Brien therefore projects onto her American counterpart the negative appraisals her own work faced, specifically her supposed failure to address "serious" themes.[28]

O'Brien's repudiation of *Portnoy's Complaint* for its sexual sensationalism suggests an anxiety over similarly erroneous dismissals of her own fiction. However, as this chapter has shown, Roth's book engages with one of the preeminent geopolitical events of its time, the Third Arab-Israeli War, just as O'Brien's own work is concerned with Irish identity at the moment Northern Ireland erupted into patent violence. Many of the accusations O'Brien levels against Roth are thus issues with which she herself struggled at this time. Regarding a writer's relationship with nation, history, and violence, O'Brien is not so much questioning Roth's methods and motivations as investigating her own.

In 1984 Shusha Guppy put it to Edna O'Brien: "You are not a political writer because, as you say, politics are concerned with the social and the external, while your preoccupations are with the inner, psychological life. Nonetheless, considering your emotional involvement with Ireland, how have you kept away from the situation in Northern Ireland—terrorism, the IRA, et cetera?"[29] This chapter contests Guppy's binary political-psychological writer and her subsequent premise that O'Brien "kept away" from the North. Rather, *Night* is intimately engaged with the "Irish question," looking as it does at the Irish in England, the English in Ireland, power relations, violence, xenophobia, and nationalism. Though it does not address Northern Ireland directly, as a novel published in the bloodiest year of the Troubles it contains multitudinous, understated intimations of the crisis in Irish identity brought about by events in the "six counties." *Night* discreetly probes the anguished position of the Southern Irish writer and citizen, balancing dismay over IRA murders with a deeply rooted indigenous affiliation with downtrodden Northern Catholics.

O'Brien's response to Guppy captures some of this ambivalence:

> My feelings about it are so manifold. I think it is mad, a so-called religious war, in this day and age. At the same time, I can't bear the rhetoric of the Unionists; I mean Ireland is *one small* island, and those six counties do not belong to Britain. Equally I abhor terrorism, whoever does it, the IRA, the Arabs, the Israelis. But . . . Catholics are second-class citizens. . . . I have not set a novel in Northern Ireland simply because I do not know enough about it . . . so far I have refrained from bringing the topic into a book merely as a voyeur.[30]

Though O'Brien does not set *Night* in the North, the novel nonetheless has much to say about Irish nationalism and where women fit into this traditionally masculine narrative. The novel is set in England, interspersed with never fully trustworthy anecdotes from and reflections on Ireland. Its meditations on Irish history and the republican movement are not confined either to the South or to the past, but have implications for the then unfolding upheaval in the North as well. That this is the case should perhaps be obvious, but restricted and lingering conceptions of the thematic range of a woman author in the early 1970s, added to O'Brien's own adroitness in sublimating her politics into her text, have thus far occluded such a reading.

Night's protagonist, Mary Hooligan, is a forty-year-old Irishwoman living in early 1970s Britain. Caretaker of an empty country house, she has ensconced herself in the master bedroom—"I am in a bed, a fourposter no less"—from which she looks back on her life and her lovers. While Roth draws on Leopold Bloom to confect Portnoy, Mary's interior monologue echoes Molly Bloom's, as Helen Thompson suggests: "By mimicking the style and character of the Penelope episode, O'Brien effectively rewrites

Joyce's stream-of-consciousness narrative."[31] Like Molly, Mary considers her current existence, while ruminating on past events and paramours: "I have had unions, tête-à-têtes, ripping times." Yet these encounters are rarely without trouble, leaving her to fantasize about the separation of man from member: "bloodless, jovial, obedient; twittering, hanging, maybe even fluttering, like sparrows perhaps, or socks." Here she reiterates Molly's view: "Id cut them off so I would."[32] Thus, in their stream-of-consciousness depictions of desire, both Roth and O'Brien flirt with Joyce.

As a narrator, Mary is far from reliable, recalling what she "saw" and "mis-saw." She does, however, have vivid memories of her father, "the Boss," who was always, in her mind, "on the edge of a cataclysmic ire." The Boss's subordinate position in the village—along with his alcoholism—spurs this fury. Her mother, Lil, is such a ubiquitous force in her life that she haunts Mary after her death: "She actually got into the bed, the single bed. . . . She arched and tilted and bowed her body so that she fitted exactly into mine, my tumescence and my curves, her tumescence and her curves, and it felt as if we were being welded together, or at least moulded together, like one of her legendary carragheen soufflés in its wetted mould." Mary seeks to escape these restrictive parental bonds: "Not to be a member of the communion of saints or angels or gods or Demi-gods or fathers or mothers or grandfathers or grandmothers or brother or sisters or brethren of any kind, germane to me through consanguinity, affinity, or any other kind of linear or genitive or collateral bond." She is driven by the same centrifugal force as Portnoy, yet also shares his backward-facing vision, as evinced when her mind drifts back beyond these childhood moments to her conception: "The seed of my father I reach out to you, as you once did to me, pitifully, passionately, idiotically, to small avail. What caused us to embark on such a maraud? Her buttocks, flaunched and ordinary, the slit, the slit of absurdity into which we chose to pass." Like Portnoy too, even before birth she is filled with the shame: "Already I, with some cursed inkling, some predilection towards shame and calamity and stupor, already liturgicalised before entering that dark, damp, deep seasous place."[33] This dream of genesis then playfully draws on both Roth and Sterne.

Mary recounts her adolescence in the West of Ireland village of Coose, a time when "purity prevailed, yet lapsed." She remembers a fancy dress in the local village hall where she dances with a falconer, as she sings "Sweet Rosie O'Grady." This ballad also appears in Joyce's *A Portrait of the Artist as a Young Man*, where it evokes in Stephen Dedalus an idealistic vision of Irish Catholic womanhood: "The figure of woman as she appears in the liturgy of the church passed silently through the darkness." Far from vestal, the figure's "falling girdle" subverts notions of exemplary femininity, and in *Night* O'Brien similarly destabilizes this ideal. The winner of the fancy dress competition is an unsettling entry, a child wrapped up in packaging like a Russian doll: "The winner turned out to be none other than a brown paper parcel. A parcel, within it another, and another and another, until at the very center a very underfed creature came peering through, screeching." Though the mother of the child wins a prize for the costume, she will later be taken "to the Castle, the choice name for the loony bin." The scene suggests that if Ireland is to be symbolized as female, then an institutionalized woman and her concealed child provide a more accurate emblem than Caithleen Ni Houlihan. Significantly, the woman in fancy dress and her packaged child win out over local men dressed as "bauld Fenian men," a rebuke of the focus on Ireland's imagined glorious past to the exclusion of its draconian present. It is not Dublin Castle—the former headquarters of British rule in Ireland—that Irishwomen need to fear, but its new namesake, a constitutive element of the Irish state's own regulatory apparatus. As Lisa Colletta and Maureen O'Connor put it: "The Irish Free State . . . reproduced all of its previous master's oppressive structures, its technologies of control and prohibition. The exercise of power in independent Ireland has continued to be patriarchal and exclusionary."[34] Throughout *Night*, O'Brien tips over the sacred cows of twentieth-century Ireland, saving particular ire for the men who milk the country's subjugated history while reenacting that very subjugation on Irish women.

Following the fancy dress ball, Mary flees Coose fearing pregnancy after a farcical assignation with the falconer, who ejaculates on her Snow White costume: "Not very au fait with the facts of life and bred on melodrama, I began to get a touch of morning sickness even though it was after midnight." Less funny is how this incident makes apparent the complete lack of sexual information given to Irishwomen at this time. Moreover, the only education women such as Mary did receive—a nationalist one—was spectacularly unsuited to an economic and social climate that made emigration almost inevitable. As one participant in Sharon Lambert's study on Irish female out-migration ruefully exclaimed, "They taught us to hate England and then they sent us here!" Mary arrives in Liverpool with the usual anti-English prejudices—"Among the foe. The Brits, the painted people"—yet is also best placed to comprehend and expose the deplorable nature of the nationalist state in its failure to provide its citizens with the pecuniary means (or social liberties) that would allow them to remain in their own country. This reality did not stop the Irish polity from exporting sentimental nationalism alongside its citizens, a ploy Mary becomes acquainted with when she travels to New York as part of a tourism campaign: "Very laughable. My task was to lure the unfortunate exiles back to the Old Bog Road." She is thus alert to the potentially cynical claims of national belonging. In escaping Ireland, Mary (like Portnoy) throws off the restraining chorus of her youth: "Do this, Do that, Don't do this, Do do it, I'll cut the tongue out of you, How bloody dare you, D'you hear?"[35]

In England Mary meets Dr. Flaggler: "Very aristocratic he seemed compared with . . . the Coose Romeos and I was carried away with his airs and the interest he showed in me." They are quickly wed and have a son, Tutsie. However, Mary finds that she has escaped one form of constraint for another, and so (after Flaggler locks her up for suspected infidelity) she flees once more. She is a consummate storyteller, and as Tutsie grows up she regales him with tales from her youth. One in particular features all the customary ingredients of an Irish nationalist paean—the hearth, an intruder, and the invocation of past heroes—but is conveyed with a telling slant. The Boss hears a trespasser in the kitchen late at night. Fearing it is the ghost of British invasions past, the Boss declaims, "Who goes there, and Sarsfield is the word, and Sarsfield is the man," summoning up the spirit of Patrick Sarsfield, hero of the Battle of the Boyne and the Siege of Limerick during the Jacobite (or Williamite) War of 1688—a war that provided foundational tropes for competing Catholic and Protestant ethnohistories in Ireland. However, the apparition turns out not to be a marauding ghoul, but rather a confidence man who arrives in the middle of the night with the "express intention of covering the hayshed with his miracle spray to protect it from the rude elements." Finding his services angrily rejected, he retreats, shouting, "Up the Republic." Both men thus employ empty nationalist slogans in a manner that resembles James Brady's unintentionally ironic singing of Irish freedom (while at the same time trying to imprison his daughter Caithleen) in *The Lonely Girl.* When the trespasser leaves, Mary's mother, Lil, unleashes a divergent narrative, not an account of British colonial despotism, but a distressing litany of catastrophes that followed Irish independence: "and there she was, rambling on about dead beasts, the economic war, a sacked land, dead beasts gaping at us, the workhouse."[36] Lil's outburst suggests continuity between British rule (the workhouses) and Ireland's postindependence policies (the economic war), linked by the hardship they inflicted on the Irish populace. This scene shows popular nationalist sentiment to be farcical and nationalism as a ruling ideology to be calamitous. In telling this story to Tutsie, Mary plays her part in demythologizing Irish history for the next generation.

While *Night* denigrates the ruling Irish nationalism in the Republic, it also scorns British and Unionist rule in Northern Ireland. This disdain is evident in the epigraph, which, according to Bertrand Cardin, "[offers] a gloss on the text to follow." As with *Portnoy's Complaint*, *Night* takes as its epigraph a scholarly definition that illuminates the central character. The explanation of the word "Hooligan" is attributed to the British philologist Ernest Weekley—whose wife absconded with D. H. Lawrence—taken from his linguistic study *The Romance of Words* (1912): "The original Hooligans were a spirited Irish family whose proceedings enlivened the drab monotony of life in Southwark towards the end of the nineteenth century." The epigraph clearly sets up the novel's love affair with language, the most commented-upon aspect in reviews of the 2014 edition: "Here is a work saturated in its own language, the balladeer's native yawp and an Elizabethan gift of phrase, all passion, all mind."[37] Yet for readers of the first edition, the coupling of "Irish" and "hooliganism" would likely have had a more specific connotation. Northern Irish civil rights marchers were habitually dismissed as "hooligans" by British authorities. Nowhere is this point more prevalent than in the Widgery Report, the investigation into the events of January 30, 1972, otherwise known as Bloody Sunday, when British paratroopers shot dead thirteen unarmed Catholic protest marchers.[38] "Hooligan" appears nineteen times in the report, calling into question the innocence of the victims, a fact bitterly mocked in poet Thomas Kinsella's response to the tribunal, "Butcher's Dozen," published in its immediate aftermath:

> Once there lived a hooligan.
> A pig came up, and away he ran.
> Here lies one in blood and bones,
> Who lost his life for throwing stones.[39]

In her memoir *Country Girl* (2012), O'Brien relates how at this time her mother "saw the pity of war; whereas, for many in the south, increasingly the IRA were 'the mindless hooligans' who brought shame on their fellow Catholics and a stain on the altar of the nation. The 'mindless hooligans' on the other side were not nearly so vehemently rebuked."[40]

For O'Brien, much of the discourse on the war was marked by a sort of moral purity that eschewed nuance. The condemnation of "terrorist" violence sometimes excluded an awareness of its state-backed equivalent. O'Brien's seemingly innocuous epigraph thus takes on a darker political shade when considered in its immediate historical context. However, she adroitly avoids overt politicization by burying her commentary in a densely allusive subtext, the intricacies of which reflect the complexities of the nationalist question. She succeeds so well that she does not use the words "Ireland" or "Irish" outside of the epigraph, yet there is no doubt that the novel is about Ireland. It is the whole island that concerns O'Brien, however, not just the South. Lying in her four-poster bed, Mary begins her dream reverie: "I take a tablet, break it down its central line and swallow one half, with some of the waters of the Malvern hills." This refreshment is not incidental; the Malvern Downs were the fond rural home of W. H. Auden during the "low dishonest decade" of 1930s. Speaking of "the Troubles," O'Brien discloses: "I admired those who had written about war, especially Hemingway, Orwell and Auden. But this was a different war, the 'dirty war,' . . . fought openly and in the shadows, deaths and devastation by the IRA, the four Protestant paramilitary organisations, the security forces and the British army."[41] Even though they dealt with what were, in some ways, dissimilar wars, O'Brien had much to gain from Auden's work, especially his maxim: "Those to whom evil is done / Do evil in return."[42] The inconspicuous reference to Malvern thus sets the scene for a dialectical exploration of artistic loyalty in times of war.

In a 1972 *Times* article, O'Brien speaks out on escalating violence and state coercion in the North: "Such a situation will go on as long as it remains a war between the British and the Irish, the longest-lasting war that Britain has to her credit. . . . Ireland is the world's problem as much as Czechoslovakia was in 1969, and still is, as much as poverty, and pollution and theft and brainwashing and the fouling of men's minds, is the world's problem." Whereas in "The Artist and His Country" O'Brien deliberates upon the absence of obvious oppression in British society, here she is cognizant that such a state of affairs now exists in at least one British jurisdiction. The nightmarish concept of being pulled from one's house and held in legal limbo is no longer, in O'Brien's view, singular to the communist bloc: "The police knock in the middle of the night [is] a feature through Eastern Europe. The same knock [is] now true in Ulster."[43]

O'Brien's take on nationalism in the North is tempered by her awareness of how it functions in the South, specifically in how it is used to regulate the lives of women. However, this understanding does not mean she is hostile to Northern nationalists and their legitimate anger over the subservient position of Catholics in the Protestant state. These concerns are apparent throughout *Night*. Mary has taken over the country house where she is supposed to be the hired help—"I have managed to pick the lock of the wardrobe and am on the lookout for a crowbar to invade the cellars"—a situation that has obvious analogies with the growing Catholic demand for civil equality in Northern Ireland in the 1960s and early 1970s and the ferocious response it engendered in the Unionist community, or the sense that the Irish in England were, during the Troubles, seen as a potential enemy within.[44] Indeed, housing was one of the foundational issues of the civil rights movement, and early leaders such as Austin Currie (Protestant himself) squatted in and were evicted from Protestant allocated housing to attract national and international attention to the unjust access to accommodation.

In an evocative and comic scene, O'Brien shows Protestant and Catholic identities to be performative and unfixed rather than stable and intrinsic through acts of semantic subterfuge. Mary thinks of how Tutsie used to dress up his pet: "Sometimes he had the dog on the table with a headscarf or a bowler hat on her. Laughing they used to be. The dog was called Rosie, a mongrel."[45] Here O'Brien parodies the feminine personification of Ireland as Róisín Dubh, instead transforming the country into the canine Rosie. The two apparently inconsequential items of clothing thus take on an enigmatic significance. The bowler hat might be taken to represent the Orange Order, an important piece of their marching-season attire, while the head scarf nods to the stereotypical image of the Mass-bound Catholic mother. That both can be switched with ease suggests the nonessentialist nature of the "Irish" and "Scotch" labels in the North. As these items are placed on the mongrel Rosie, they are also stripped of their requisite seriousness. Further, Tutsie is himself a "mongrel"—Irish on his mother's side, English on his father's—his hybridity chiming with Kinsella's description of the people of Ireland: "We are what we are, and that / Is mongrel pure."[46] He thus belies concepts of ethnic or cultural purity, those indeterminate ideals both sides in the conflict held up to discourage, often violently, intermarriage or other amatory intercommunity relationships. As ever, it is not simply the policing of physical borders that interests nationalists and unionists, but also the guarding of women's bodies. Mary ultimately opts for a position outside both traditions: "The truth is I do not wish to lie with my own kith and kin. Another blow for King James and for the green. I do not want to lie with anyone else's kith and kin either. One for King Billy."[47]

As she tosses in her bed, Mary reflects upon a feather that she has wrenched loose from the pillow: "It has been irking me for some time, but I have managed to wrench it from the ticking. . . . The feather of whom, of what."[48] "Of whom" suggests the feather, at least in Mary's mind's eye, comes not from a bird, but a human, rousing images of the tarring and feathering of Northern Catholic women thought to have flirted with "the enemy."[49] O'Brien's prose tickles the reader with this potential interpretation, while remaining evasive. These attacks occurred with great frequency around the time O'Brien was composing *Night*: "In the third incident of its kind during the week [November 11–18, 1971], a seventeen-year-old Derry girl has hair shorn and ink poured over her for 'fraternising' with British soldiers."[50] O'Brien is conscious that the heroic narrative propagated by republicans often contains within it the continued patriarchal jurisdiction over women's lives. She is aware of this contradiction through her own experience of sexist governance inherent within Irish nationalism in its manifestation south of the border. In the North, too, O'Brien balances admiration for the IRA in its original capacity as protector of the civil rights marchers with a clear-eyed knowledge of the misuses to which violent, fanatical ideologies can be put—most commonly against women.

O'Brien does not, however, unequivocally reject the nationalist tradition. Mary lampoons her father's nationalism yet at the same time professes herself enamored by "guerrillas, men on the move, . . . like . . . a volunteer called McKann. I only know McKann by hearsay but I often think he's the one, the destiny for me. I saw photos of him, very still and mild, like a crock of milk, and yet he burns with a fierce indignation like a burning bush."[51] In this description, Mary mirrors Portnoy, at once contemptuous of nationalism and at the same time romantically drawn to it. O'Brien complicates this attachment through an intertextual flirtation, which implies that the most robust, self-aware nationalism can arise from the Irish satiric tradition. The reference to McKann's "fierce indignation" calls to mind the excoriating satires of Swift.[52] As an Anglican dean who was just as derisive of the superstitious Catholic Irish as he was of the self-serving Protestant Irish ascendancy and of distant British rule, Swift provides a suitably ambivalent role model for the sort of patriotism O'Brien strives for in *Night*. For Swift, satire always starts with the self, evinced in "Verses on the Death of Dr. Swift," and as affirmed by A. J. McConnell: "Swift's real offence against good taste and decorum is that he makes us see the Yahoo that is in us all."[53] As such, O'Brien never fully rejects her own clannish bias. She recognizes that impartial perspective is unattainable, and instead confronts the prejudiced, fallible self, in all its egotism, narrow-mindedness, and insularity.

It is not only the conflicting nationalisms of the British Isles that *Night* explores. Mary's grown son, Tutsie, visits Israel and writes of sleeping in fields "under a mosque wall." He says of Jerusalem, "The rituals at the Wailing Wall are too much, you should witness these. What a contrast of explosive nature between what occurs on the surface of this land

and what the archaeologists find right under it."[54] Tutsie's letter places Irish-English strife in conversation with the Israeli-Arab conflict.[55] Mary provides her own sly answer as to how barriers between hostile communities might be sapped: a wailing wall of sex. "There ought to be crèches where poor people can go when their glands ignite," Mary reasons, "just as there are wailing walls, and temples to chant in." Throughout her life she has followed this formula, rebelling against Irish chauvinism through desire for and trysts with a range of foreign partners: "A motley crew, all shades, dimensions, breeds, ilks, national characteristics." Mary implicitly draws connections between the Jewish and Irish tragic pasts, as she remembers looking at the newborn Tutsie and thinking that "the crown of his head spoke to me of former massacres, his little bones used to suggest holocausts."[56] She is also aware of how past wrongs done to a group can be used to shift the debate from current wrongs done by the same group—apparent in her father's jingoistic anti-British slogans drowning out her mother's mumbled chastisement of the Irish Free State. *Night* rejects exclusionary historical narratives; rather, it embraces a multiplicity of histories, making connections between the troubled pasts of different groups in order to break cycles of violence.

Portnoy's Complaint and *Night* agree that the remedy for nationalism is exile. O'Brien makes this apparent in an early draft of "The Artist and His Country": "While you are still tied to it you do not know, cannot know how deeply the country abides in you . . . its language, its history, its geography, its prejudices. It is only at the moment of losing it . . . that one fully realizes the strength of the heritage. So it is that exiles make good artists." Though O'Brien is scathing of *Portnoy's Complaint*, *Night* seems in many ways very much like it: scholarly epigraphs; horizontal narrators delivering associative monologues; flirtations with Swift, Sterne, and Joyce; the destabilization of accepted gender roles; and sex as a means of escaping an inward-looking ethnic group. O'Brien does praise one specific element of Roth's book. She suggests that it derives its power from the "vengeance" it takes "on those erstwhile [Jewish] victims/heroes."[57] Roth rejects idealization and muddies the Manichaean divide between oppressor and oppressed—the dualism upon which Zionism is built—proving that one does not necessarily preclude the other.[58] O'Brien likewise dismantles facile and hazardous binaries of the Irish nationalist tradition.[59] Both novels warn of the dangers of the confluence of masculinism and nationalism. The diasporic subject—akin to a traitor in ultranationalist discourse—is best placed to spot the hypocrisies demanded by unquestioned national allegiance. Both Roth and O'Brien learn from Swift that diaspora is the real home of the artist, and, ironically, the best vantage point for the patriot.

Before the 1990s, Roth and O'Brien were habitually disparaged as "autobiographical" novelists—too busy endlessly retelling the stories of their lives to engage with the vast upheavals of the 1960–90 period. In effect, they were damned either way: to write about war left them open to accusations of tendentiousness; to ignore it condemned them as narcissists. Though their 1990s trilogies (the subject of chapter 5) did something to dispel such views in later years, this chapter has shown that both writers have long engaged with the world around them. In these earlier novels, Roth's and O'Brien's focus on sex and the self is not egotistical, but rather the most appropriate way to evade the pitfalls of nationalism and sectarianism's snares. A relentless scrutiny of the psyche leads to the realization that where emotional subjects of kinship and identity are in contention, detachment is impossible. It is with this awareness that Roth and O'Brien turn to Israel and Ireland and, through the biases, faults, and hatreds of their protagonists, simultaneously brandish and banish quixotic nationalisms. In delving inward they find the tools to outwardly address society; in the "perpetual warring" of the human mind, they discover a fitting metaphor for factional strife. This chapter has primarily argued that the psychical and sexual focuses in *Portnoy's Complaint* and O'Brien's *Night* have an important political valence. Yet, just as important, this chapter has suggested that O'Brien both challenged and channeled Roth. By contrast, the next will consider the ways in which Roth turned to O'Brien to sharpen his exploration of nation and race.

4

"A Harp in the Hallway"

Mother Ireland *and Jewish/Irish Whiteness in* Zuckerman Unbound

In 1984 Philip Roth asked Edna O'Brien: "Why do you write so many love stories? Is it because of the importance of the subject or because, once you grew up and left Ireland and chose the solitary life of a writer, sexual love inevitably became the strongest sphere of experience to which you continued to have access?"[1] Roth's inquiry is not, however, entirely serious, nor is it directed exclusively at O'Brien. As Darren Hughes suggests, the angle of Roth's line of questioning gives the impression he is "conducting another of his self-interviews." This point corroborates David Gooblar's contention that the presence of other writers such as "Franz Kafka and Anne Frank in Roth's fiction [often] tells us more about Roth himself than about those ostensible subjects." Roth's speaking of and to other writers can thus be read as a displaced commentary on himself. An important corollary to this insight can be extrapolated from it: when Roth writes of another cultural group, he is also writing about American Jews. As O'Brien does with Roth in "The Artist and His Country" (as discussed in the previous chapter), so Roth does with O'Brien in his *New York Times* interview of her. This reasoning can also be extended to his foreword to her anthology *A Fanatic Heart*, in which he says of her short fiction: "Many are love stories, among them eerily intimate stories relating to sexual love, and these are what people chiefly associate with Edna O'Brien. But her range is wider than that and there is an acute, sometimes searing, social awareness."[2] Perhaps this description is how Roth wishes his own work to be read, with the understanding that it addresses a far greater array of themes than an often sex-fixated media credits him with. These suppositions frame this chapter and its consideration of the presence of O'Brien in Roth's fiction.

Roth's 1981 novel, *Zuckerman Unbound*, is most often considered as an autobiographical disquisition on fame, a view substantiated in critics' minds by the biographical crossovers between Roth and the protagonist, Nathan Zuckerman, a literary novelist "afflicted" by the high sales and mass popularity of his 1969 novel *Carnovsky*—a stand-in for Roth's *Portnoy's Complaint*. However, traces of O'Brien in this work provide an alternative interpretation. Though by no means as immediately tangible as that of Frank and Kafka, O'Brien's presence was revealed at Roth's eightieth birthday, when she teasingly proposed herself as a likely model for the Irish actress Caesara O'Shea, with whom Zuckerman becomes enraptured. Just as Zuckerman shares significant biographical data with Roth, Caesara does so with O'Brien. As Roth summarizes, O'Brien was "born in the isolated reaches of Ireland, raised on a lonely farm in the shadow of a violent father and educated by nuns behind the latched gate of a provincial convent." Caesara grows up in an identical milieu, the rural confines of Connemara, under a father who "drank whiskey" and beat her mother. More significantly, both Caesara and O'Brien share with one another (and with Zuckerman and Roth as well) the experience of being ostracized from their communities as a result of their provocative vocations. Caesara thus in many ways offers an Irish female "counterlife" for Zuckerman, as O'Brien might be said to do for Roth. Just as Roth employs Kafka and Frank to delve into parallels between Jewish experience in Europe and America, he engages O'Brien to examine the equivalences between Jewish and Irish cultural identity. In doing so, Roth uses the example of the Irish as a warning to Jewish Americans against unquestioningly supporting a mythologizing nationalism abroad and falling into an unaware ethnic whiteness at home. Brett Ashley Kaplan has already explored how "race figures in *Zuckerman Unbound* in ways that echo the tension between identification and anxiety," looking specifically at black-Jewish interrelations in America. Meanwhile, Scott W. Klein unearths traces of James Joyce in the 1980s Zuckerman books, which highlight Roth's use of the Irish modernist writer to investigate "national difference." Building on these foundations, this chapter adds another layer of interpretation to *Zuckerman Unbound*'s complex analysis of race by focusing on its representation of Irishness—and specifically on Caesara, "the very heart of Ireland."[3]

Caesara is introduced to the reader through a letter she has left for Zuckerman: "I was so sad to leave without saying goodbye. But when Fate changes horse the rider is carried along. . . . Vague memories, nothing but memories." While the note is deceptively simple, Zuckerman is attuned to its allusive content: "'Vague memories, nothing but memories' was Yeats. 'Fate changes horse' was Byron." Zuckerman's close reading intimates that the reader should exercise similar caution in approaching the deceptively simple character of Caesara. To begin with, Zuckerman is fascinated by her exotic name. He listens as she explains its ancient Irish origins: "'[named] for a Hebrew woman, the niece of Noah. She sought refuge in Ireland from the universal flood. My people,' she said, her white hand to her white throat, 'were the first to be interred there. The first of the Irish ghosts.'" Though Zuckerman dismisses her explanation as "gentle, harmless, hypnotic blarney," this is in fact a classic act of Rothian misdirection, as Klein makes evident: "Caesara understates the significance of her name. . . . More usually spelled . . . 'Cessair' in Celtic mythology, Caesara's namesake appears in the Irish *Book of Invasions* as one of the earliest settlers in Ireland. As the niece . . . of Noah . . . Cessair is a marker in Irish myth for the continuity of Irish and biblical prehistories. She is the link between Jewish and Irish identity, the imagined proof that Ireland was founded by biblical Jews."[4] Klein rightly cites the *Book of Invasions* (in Irish, *Lebor Gabála Érenn*) as the mythological basis of Caesara's story. However, I would submit that Roth appropriated the name and its history from a more modern version of the myth—one found in O'Brien's memoir *Mother Ireland*.[5] The relevant section of the *Book of Invasions* reads, "Cessair daughter of Bith [son of] Noe, she it is who took Ireland at first, forty days before the Flood. . . . Her [follower] Ladra the pilot . . . is the first dead man who went under the soil of Ireland." Roth's rendition thus appears to be closer to O'Brien's, not least of all considering the unique spelling of "Cessair": "a Hebrew woman, a lady, Caesara, niece of Noah, hearing her uncle's prophecy about a universal flood, decided to seek refuge [in Ireland]. . . . Her people were the first to be interred there, the first in a long line of hardy Irish ghosts."[6] To better understand the implications behind this intertextual connection between Roth and O'Brien, it is first necessary to linger for a moment on the *Book of Invasions*.

Klein's argument that "Cessair is a marker . . . for the continuity of Irish and biblical prehistories" requires expansion. The twelfth-century *Book of Invasions* (from which all versions of the Caesara myth ultimately derive) is, as Francis J. Byrne suggests, a pseudohistory: "a fantastic compound of genuine racial memories, exotic Latin learning and world history . . . euhemerised Celtic mythology, dynastic propaganda, folklore, and pure fiction." John Carey elaborates on these myths' external origins: "The Bible . . . exercised a pervasive influence on the evolution of Ireland's legendary history, providing not merely information about distant times and places but also narrative models which could serve as templates for elaborating an artificial past." The term may sound anachronistic, but the *Book of Invasions* is a transnational text, one composed to "put Ireland on the same footing as Israel and Rome" by adopting and adapting the historical and literary accounts of those entities for Irish purposes.[7] It is not then a purely "Irish" text, but rather one inflected by outside influences. Likewise, the book's theme of invasion (tracing the imaginary migrations into Ireland of the peoples of Cessair, Partholón, and Nemed, and of the Fir Bolg, the Tuatha Dé Danann, and the Milesians) argues against Ireland as a purely "Irish" place. *Zuckerman Unbound* thus invokes a book that structurally and thematically rejects the concepts of textual and racial purity.

Irish mythology has been more often used to demonstrate the racial and cultural exclusivity of the Irish than the opposite. For early-twentieth-century Irish nationalists, modified versions of the legends of Cú Chulainn, Fionn Mac Cumhaill, and the Fianna provided a heroic past from which to draw sustenance in their fight against British imperialism. Pádraig Pearse, the executed leader of the failed 1916 Rising, proclaimed his mission "to recreate and perpetuate in Eire [*sic*] the knightly tradition . . . the high tradition of Cuchulainn . . . the noble tradition of the Fianna . . . the Christlike tradition of Colm Cille." Here Pearse comfortably amalgamates fictional and factual Irish figures, from pagan and Christian traditions, to limn the Ireland he wished to create—a homogeneous Catholic, nationalist, and masculine state. Through the auspices of Eamon de Valera, this ethos would guide official policy in the Irish Free State. O'Brien's entire canon undermines these false ideals, and her work frequently rewrites Irish mythology in an attempt to decontaminate it from these patriotic appropriations. As Maureen O'Connor argues, "Certainly the Irish Free State exploited Irish myths to its own masculinist ends, but I would like to suggest that O'Brien also attempts to 're-mythologize' Irish experience in her fiction, reaching back to earlier Irish traditions found in archaic narratives which represented . . . a social order in which women and the natural world were given political and spiritual significance." Nowhere is it more apparent than in *Mother Ireland*, where O'Brien explains the Irish nationalist interpretive slant on the myths of the *Book of Invasions*: "These infiltrations have been told and fabricated by men and by mediums who observed the violation of [Ireland's] body and soul." These interpretations were fed into the Irish psyche through the nationalist education system: a repetition of "the same grinding themes . . . victimisation, misapprehension, aborted revolutions, informers, chaos and bungle."[8] By opening her book with the myth of Caesara, O'Brien takes an alternative route. She emphasizes not invasion but rather Ireland's heterogeneous social landscape, that is, Ireland as an island that has seen inward migrations stretching far into a mystical past—along with the more historically certain arrival of Vikings, Normans, English, Scottish, French Huguenots, and Lithuanian Jews.[9]

It is Jews in particular to whom O'Brien turns throughout her work, both to upset the de Valerian image of Gaelic cultural uniformity and to probe twentieth-century Ireland's deep xenophobia. O'Brien's friend David Marcus published a short-story collection titled *Who Ever Heard of an Irish Jew?* (1988). By his very existence the Jewish Marcus answers the question posed by his title, yet at the same time it points to the seeming incongruity of an Irish Jewish identity. It was Joyce who first explored the ostensibly strange juxtaposition of Irish and Jewish identity in *Ulysses*, with Mr. Deasy informing Stephen Dedalus that Ireland never persecuted the Jews, "Because she never let them in."[10] The headmaster's poor joke perfectly captures two Irish chauvinist canards: first, that Ireland is a monolithic racial entity and, second, that as a result of this uniformity (coupled with their long history of oppression) the Irish cannot be racist. Joyce employs the Jewish Irish Leopold Bloom to disprove these fallacies, and O'Brien performs a similar maneuver in *Mother Ireland.*

O'Brien relates the fear and suspicion with which the Irish treated the nation's small Jewish population, and in doing so challenges Irish society's complacent self-conception as a place of Christian virtue. Though the Caesara legend conveys a sense of Jewish-Irish assimilation, other, more typical, myths are divisive, as with the tale of King Conchubar, uncle of Cú Chulainn, who dies of violent rage when informed by a druid of the death of Jesus at the hands of the Jews, which O'Brien recounts in *Mother Ireland*: "[Conchubar] observing the unusual darkness . . . asked what it omened, [and was told the] Son of God was being crucified by the Jews, upon which the king . . . got into an unholy dither, rushed to the grove and began hewing . . . to demonstrate how he would deal with those wicked Jews." This hatred was not, unfortunately, relegated to fable, but was alive and well in the Ireland of O'Brien's youth. Channeling the contemporary and casual anti-Semitism of her childhood, O'Brien ventriloquizes its discourse: "The Jew man was shunned as were the gypsies and the hawkers, all bringing upon themselves unvoiced odium, which was mysteriously connected with sex and connected with the fact they had sallow skin and quivering nostrils. Furriers were Jews, jewellers were Jews, and they were not above taking the precious jewels out of your watch or the best strips of fur and replacing it with counterfeit. There had been a pogrom in Limerick half a century before and a redemptionist priest told the faithful to stone the moneylenders which they did." In this light, the opening of the next paragraph, "Limerick was an exemplary city," can only be read as sardonic.[11] In this nation of hypocritical rectitude, the Jews are the all-encompassing Other—suspect not only in business matters but in sexual affairs as well. O'Brien uses the Irish treatment of the Jews to undermine idealized visions of the state and its people, disproving myths of moral innocence that she as a woman in Catholic Ireland knows lack any basis in reality.

Like the transient Zuckerman and his ever-increasing tower of books that he lugs from one home to another, Caesara comes laden with textual baggage. By reading beyond Caesara's "hypnotic blarney," the reader can unpack encrypted criticisms of Irish society and a warning of the dangerous and manipulative malleability of myth. While Irish nationalists took mythological invasions as a confirmation of Ireland's perpetual oppression, and O'Brien reinterprets them as a symbol of Irish diversity. Madison Grant, author of the eugenicist screed *The Passing of the Great Race* (1916), used them for his own purposes:

> Ferocious gorilla-like living specimens of Paleolithic man are found not infrequently on the west coast of Ireland and are easily recognized by the . . . wild and savage aspect. . . . The other traits of this Irish type are common to many primitive races. This is the Irishman of caricature and the type was frequent in America when the first Irish immigrants came in 1846 and the following years. It seems, however, to have almost disappeared in [America]. If, as it is claimed, the Neanderthals have left no trace of their blood in living populations, these Firbolgs are derived from some very ancient and primitive race as yet undescribed.[12]

Citing the Fir Bolg, Grant draws on the pseudohistory the *Book of Invasions* to promote his pseudoscience, proposing the Irish of the West of Ireland as the missing link between modern man and some prior incarnation.[13] Yet what is fascinating is Grant's distinction between the barbarous Irish of Ireland and Irish Americans, who by the 1910s had ascended the American social scale enough to be accepted (grudgingly) as white by the ruling WASP majority.[14] Tellingly, his ambivalence does not extend to Jews and blacks: "The cross between a white man and a negro is a negro"; "The cross between any of the three European races and a Jew is a Jew."[15] The Irish guarded their newfound position in America by absorbing the tenets of this racial hierarchy. As Matthew Frye Jacobson argues, "Having emigrated to North America, many [Irish] took on a new racial identity, now participating in a politics of white supremacy."[16] A preponderance of nineteenth-century Irish immigrants took to American racism with ease and violently set themselves apart from the waves of overseas labor that preceded them, black slaves and their descendants, and those persons who came after them, especially the Jews.

One might contend that Roth, diligent as he is, likely did not know of the connection to, nor did he intend to invoke, early-twentieth-century racial science when he plucked Caesara and her lineage from O'Brien's memoir. Yet a seemingly flippant comment in the opening pages of *Zuckerman Unbound* adds weight to this reading. In an attempt to remain unchanged by his newfound wealth, Zuckerman comically rides the bus to his meeting with an investment banker. Unfortunately, a fellow passenger unmasks him as a millionaire. This realization draws the attention of two young girls, whom Zuckerman imagines from their uniforms to be Catholic convent students. Though reminding them politely that it is rude to stare, Zuckerman is faced with their continued scrutiny: "Must be phrenology they were studying at St Mary's." Zuckerman's passing quip can be read simply for its comic value or (more intentional obfuscation on Roth's part) as a muted indicator of the novel's fundamental concern with race. By reminding the reader at the novel's outset that racial categories are not stable, objective entities, but rather the consequences of bad science in the thrall of power, Roth preempts whiteness theorists such as Jacobson, who avers, "Race resides not in nature but in politics and culture."[17] Further, that the two girls Zuckerman jokingly imagines to be studying phrenology are viewed as Catholic and (from the name of the school) Irish, might be taken as a sign of how quickly the Irish in America took on the racial prejudices they themselves suffered under in colonial Ireland.[18] It also evokes the historical animosity that existed between Jewish and Irish immigrants and their descendants in urban America, an animosity notably absent throughout the bulk of *Zuckerman Unbound*.

Just as the Irish entered American whiteness in the nineteenth century, the Jews did so in the twentieth. Anthropologist Karen Brodkin traces this transition, noting how succeeding generations of twentieth-century American Jews had "different ethnoracial identities," with Jews "granted many institutional privileges of white racial assignment after World War II." This shift explains *Zuckerman Unbound*'s uncertainty in locating Jews on the American racial spectrum. When a former Jewish Newark resident tells Zuckerman the name of his high school, Zuckerman remembers it as "almost half black even in Zuckerman's day, when Newark was still mostly white." In this retrospective view, the Jews seem to be a part of white Newark. Yet toward the novel's close, on Zuckerman's return to Newark, he considers the city's contemporary demographics: "Except for the elderly trapped in nearby housing projects, the Jews had all vanished. So had almost everyone white." Here Zuckerman appears hesitant in uniting the elderly Jews and the white-flight masses. This confusion denotes the shift in Jewish racial designation over Zuckerman's lifetime, drawing attention to the inconsistent and constructed nature of race in twentieth-century America. In light of this midcentury Jewish entrance into whiteness, it is worth probing the novel's perhaps surprising lack of focus on past Irish-Jewish urban hostility. Absent here are some of the anti-Semitic bugbears of Roth's Jewish American generation that he attacks elsewhere in his work, most prominently Father Charles Coughlin, Henry Ford, and Joseph McCarthy. Rather, as Klein deduces, there are many instances of affirmative Jewish-Irish "ethnic confluence."[19]

Chief among them is Zuckerman and Caesara's brief affair, which begins with an unusual topic of flirtation: "They had both read Ellmann's biography of Joyce and, from the sound of it, had never dared to confess the depths of their admiration for the book to anyone before."[20] The scene is remarkable in its dissimilarity to previously discussed moments of cross-cultural romance, as in *The Lonely Girl* and *Portnoy's Complaint*. Here, there are no community and family impediments to a relationship between two people perceived to be from two distinct ethnic groups; rather, the opposite is true. Klein sees Zuckerman and Caesara's intimacy as a sign that "cultural confluence and assimilation are both possible and desirable while reminding readers of the fissures within the idea of 'Americanness' as a marker of identity."[21] The first clause points toward a positive reading of this Irish-Jewish integration, while the second connotes a more negative exegesis. Focusing on art, Klein lays more emphasis on the positive, likely because *Zuckerman Unbound* seems to stress this side of the relationship. However, this positivity can be conceived of as more Rothian dissimulation, a stratagem to conceal the less appealing parallels between the Jews and Irish.

Taking the positive interpretation first, *Zuckerman Unbound* is replete with references to Irish literature, underlining the importance of writers like Joyce and Yeats to the Jewish American literary tradition, as Klein expertly traces. The novel also champions the Irish influence in the sphere of American education, with Zuckerman's father's liberalism derived in part from his Irish American eighth grade teacher. This liberalism is evinced in his antiwar letters to President Lyndon B. Johnson, in which he "elucidate[s] his argument against the war with wisdom, not always assigned with the utmost scrupulosity, from either the Talmud or a long-deceased spinster named Helen MacMurphy."[22] Further, Zuckerman himself seems to become symbolically interchangeable with two antiwar Catholic priests, one who partly inspires *Carnovsky*—"Recycled and fused with Nathan's own recollections, some of Douglas's best stories made their way into the life of Carnovsky, a budding soul no less bedeviled by onanism in Jewish New Jersey than Douglas growing up in Catholic Wisconsin"—while the other, in Zuckerman's imagination at least, replaces him in his former wife's affections: "A priest had taken his place."[23] Yet there is a darker side to these conflations of Jewish and Irish Catholic identity, insinuated in the last pages of the novel when Zuckerman remembers that all he knew of priests as a child was that "they hated Jews"—more than an adolescent fantasy considering Father Coughlin and the Limerick redemptionist priest cited in *Mother Ireland*.[24] In this light, while these Irish-Jewish fusions outwardly celebrate cultural intermixing, they simultaneously warn that this coalescing can occur only because Jews have joined the Irish in whiteness.

Richard Dyer explains the power of whiteness: "Because whiteness carries such rewards and privileges, the sense of a border that might be crossed and a hierarchy that might be climbed has produced a dynamic that has enthralled people who have had any chance of participating in it." According to Dyer, "Two examples of people who have counted as white under particular historical circumstances are the Irish and the Jews." Part of the attraction between Jews and Irish beyond the simple allure of the Other is that the latter offered the former a model of assimilation into white American society. Zuckerman's infatuation with Caesara can be viewed as an instance of this dynamic. In *Zuckerman Unbound*, Caesara is repeatedly referred to as white: "her white hand to her white throat."[25] Her tryst with Zuckerman can thus be taken to signify the passing over of Jews into whiteness, thereby joining the Irish. This interpretation is underpinned by Zuckerman's frantic activities the morning after his night with Caesara, in which he (the supposed intellectual and ethnic outsider) has six suits made by the tailor of New York's WASP elite, the emblematically named Mr. White. Zuckerman in effect "dresses white," in a scene that comically recalls the early gangster films of James Cagney, such as *The Public Enemy* (1931), where the newly rich Irish mobster poses in a gaudy suit, signaling the Irish arrival into American wealth and privilege. Zuckerman (here a stand-in for the Jewish American community as a whole) makes the leap from "not-quite-white" to ivory, and is spurred to do so by his enchantment with the Irish Caesara.

What is the significance behind the setting of *Zuckerman Unbound*, balancing as it does on the hinge between the 1960s and the 1970s? A biographical answer might simply say that 1969 was the year Roth published *Portnoy's Complaint*, the model for *Carnovsky*, or even that it was the year Roth met O'Brien, the model for Caesara. Yet Roth is at pains to set the novel in its historical (as opposed to personal) context: "In the spring of 1969. . . . Vietnam was a slaughterhouse. . . . Martin Luther King and Robert Kennedy had been gunned down. . . . At the Democratic convention the summer before, hundreds had been beaten with clubs and trampled by horses." Roth's novel looks back on this tumultuous decade from the high ground of the early 1980s, and he surreptitiously imbues it with a commentary on the social conservatism and political retrenchment of the 1970s. This consideration is especially relevant in any discussion of race in the novel. Historian Dominic Sandbrook describes the rise of the "cult of ethnicity" in the 1970s, a backlash against the civil rights movement and welfare programs that "supposedly favored lazy, greedy blacks over their hardworking white neighbors"—a sentiment given intellectual heft by books such as Michael Novak's *The Rise of the Unmeltable Ethnics* (1971). For Sandbrook, Roth's rise in popularity owes something to this unsavory development: "Half-forgotten immigrant sagas found new audiences, while Chaim Potok and Philip Roth attracted critical praise with novels steeped in the second or third-generation experience." However, any Jewish reader turning to Roth for unproblematic ethnic nostalgia would surely be disappointed. As Timothy Parrish says, "Roth is not a conventional ethnic writer," but rather one for whom "no identity, ethnic or otherwise, is stable." *Zuckerman Unbound* actively challenges this troubling white ethnic pride that developed in part as a response to the 1960s government expansion of the rights of African Americans. In an echo of Jacobson, Kaplan notes the fear in Roth's work, "that the Jewish victims of anti-Semitism have become, across the passage to America, white racists."[26]

On his perambulations to escape the writer's block caused by his newfound status as a famous writer, Zuckerman runs into a fan named Alvin Pepler. A fellow Jewish Newarker, Alvin Pepler is a deeply embittered man whose own claim to fame lies in a brief stint on (and scandal-filled dumping from) a popular 1950s quiz show. Limned by Zuckerman as "Zeitgeist overspill," Pepler is the embodiment of the white ethnic revival. At the outset, he attempts to present himself as a fair-minded social commentator, describing what he sees as the difference between Zuckerman's artistic portrayals of Newark and the writings of the African American poet Amiri Baraka (LeRoi Jones): "I say this without racial prejudice . . . but what he writes is not literature. In my estimation it's black propaganda." As Kaplan explains, "If someone says, 'I say this without racial prejudice,' he or she actually harbors much racial prejudice." This point becomes apparent in Pepler's closing speech, when the mask of civility is ripped away and the ugly actuality of racial hatred is revealed: "Newark is a nigger with a knife! Newark is a whore with the syph!" These two sides of Pepler's character—"reasonable" surface and raging underbelly—represent the two sides of the white ethnic revival: its seemingly objective political front (where bigotry is couched in euphemism) and its murderous street-level manifestations, as revealed in (for example) the Irish American response to desegregation in Boston. Zuckerman (and, by extension, Roth) exempts neither the Jews nor himself from this racism, recognizing the possibility that Pepler is "my Pop self."[27]

White ethnic pride is undergirded by a sense of victimization, based on ordeals that have been overcome by previous resilient and admired immigrant generations. As a failed TV quiz show contestant, Pepler is a farcical instance of Jewish victimhood: "What it came down to was that they could not afford to let a Jew be a big winner too long on 'Smart

Money.'" His criteria for persecution are intentionally absurd: "From nineteen fifty-five to fifty-eight, you won't find a single Jew who won over a hundred thousand. That was the limit for a Jew to win, and this is on programs where the producers, nearly every single one, were Jews themselves." In Pepler's story, Roth parodies not the undoubted prewar structural discrimination experienced by his parents' generation, but rather the misuse of this history to suggest that Jews were still an oppressed minority in the postwar era. Speaking of white ethnic groups in general, Jacobson calls out this anachronistic sleight of hand: "Seizing upon their forebears' status as racial Others, writers like Michael Novak . . . now disavow any participation in twentieth-century white privilege on the spurious basis of their parents' and grandparents' racial oppression." Tresa Grauer outlines how this worked in a Jewish context: "Many American Jews who had once embraced the dominant cultural narrative of assimilation began to seek alternative plots that could be read as particularly 'Jewish.'"[28] The 1970s fetishization of ethnic identity allowed groups such as the Irish and the Jews a selective whiteness: a share in its benefits and a pass on its costs.

Zuckerman touches on the dangerous emphasis on and pride in rapid social advancement among Irish Americans, when he sums up the idealized lineage of Mary Schevitz, wife of Zuckerman's agent: "You couldn't put anything over on Mary; not even on upper Park Avenue was she out of touch with the lower depths. Her mother had been an Irish washerwoman in the Bronx—the Irish washerwoman in the Bronx, to hear her tell it." This bootstrap fantasy can often act as an oblique commentary on African Americans, who through lack of social progress are marked as mentally and morally unsuited to work and success. Thus, the propagation of the American Dream myth can be a way of avoiding discussion of the systemic barriers to economic development for African Americans. Roth uses an Irish American example here, but Brodkin notes that this tendency is also apparent in the Jewish community: "A Jewish version of Horatio Alger has become a point of entry for some mainstream Jewish organizations to adopt a racist attitude against African Americans especially and to oppose affirmative action for people of color."[29] Roth's displaced commentary on the dangers of ethnic pride does not equate Jewish-black relations with Irish-black relations—many Jews played a prominent part in the civil rights movement, while the Irish, largely, were wary if not downright hostile toward it—but it does warn against a rise in Jewish narrow-mindedness in the wake of the 1967 Newark Riots and the more general disillusionment of the 1970s.

The novel's closing scene can be reread in light of the shifting scale of racial Otherness, not just as black-Jewish-white, but as black-Jewish-Irish-white. Following his father's funeral—signifying his separation from family and community—Zuckerman returns to Newark. As he is driven through his childhood streets, Zuckerman remembers the now long-closed Catholic orphanage that was his "first momentous encounter with caste" and the subject of his first short story. It is here that Zuckerman is reminded of his youthful impression of priests: "They hated the Jews." Yet Zuckerman is no longer a member of a despised minority, as becomes obvious when he is confronted by a "young black man" who looks at Zuckerman and sees only a "white man in the back seat" of a "chauffeur-driven limousine." Any sense of identification between Jews and African Americans, as in Roth's earlier work, has evaporated. Zuckerman has become symbolically as well as socially white, and he has become so through sitting inside the ultimate mark of power and wealth in America, the limousine. Moreover, it is a limousine, as Roth pointedly emphasizes, previously used by Caesara: "It was from the same outfit that drove Caesara around in New York"; "It was Caesara's young driver."[30] It is the final fitting image of how the Jews followed the Irish highway into whiteness.

Zuckerman Unbound also clarifies how the Jews came across these models of Irish American assimilation and looks at how this process had unintended transnational consequences. The novel criticizes the myth-making of American popular culture and its potential by-products of chauvinistic nationalism and white ethnic pride. It does so most overtly through Caesara's career as a movie star but also, as we will see, through Pepler's fantasies. In both cases, chaotic Irish and Jewish history is made all too clear-cut and consumable.

Where did Irish America get its sense of history? In *Mother Ireland* O'Brien relates the source of her version of the Caesara myth: "Around 1860, a nun of a contemplative order in County Kerry spent her time compiling her country's history as an incitement to Irishmen and Irishwomen in America to remind them of their noble and glorious annals." By the twentieth century it was Hollywood that fulfilled the role of purveyor of emotive Irish "history." Cinema formed the new mythological medium, imparting tales of Irish suffering, resilience, and bravery, in both the Old World and the New. Where, for example, does Mary Schevitz's image of her mother come from, personal experience or Hollywood stereotypes of the drudging immigrant mother, such as the "Bridget" figure, as seen in *Amarilly of Clothes-Line Alley* (1918)? It was through such films that the Irish understood their rise in American society: the old, hardworking, unassimilated Irish immigrants producing and then giving way to a new American generation. As Sandbrook insists, "It was in Hollywood that the ethnic revival made the greatest cultural inroads." It was not only the Irish to which these films were aimed, however, as Lee Lourdeaux confirms: "Hollywood elected the Irish to serve as role models of assimilation for other immigrants." For example, Irish American novelist Peter Quinn remembers watching *The Bells of St. Mary's* (1945) as a child: "This was how we wanted the world to see us, America's best-behaved ethnic group: a big-screen refutation of the lies once spread by nativists."[31] Indeed, this particularly popular cinematic example of ethnic perfection might be on Zuckerman's mind when he refers to his two young phrenological inquisitors on the bus as students of St Mary's. While such narratives could act as a guiding light for succeeding immigrant groups, they could also create a dangerous sense of ethnic superiority over those who did not fit into this formula, primarily African Americans. *Zuckerman Unbound* questions the role of hegemonic popular culture in informing ethnic discourse by interrogating the formulaic historical plotting on which Hollywood and Broadway thrived.

The novel's most overt critique of these systems lies in Caesara's studio-constructed identity. Her first film role as a nun in *Divine Mission*, remembered fondly by Zuckerman and Pepler, evokes *The Bells of St. Mary's*, in which Ingrid Bergman plays the mother superior of an educational order trying to save an inner-city Irish Catholic school. In this manner, Caesara's cinematic persona epitomizes Irish assimilation in America and the attraction this process held for other, later, immigrant groups. Her appeal to American audiences appears to be as much ethnic as it is erotic. She is marketed as "the tragic empress of sex," with "all the sorrow of her race." Hollywood's cynical blurring of history and sex appeal is evident in these epithets. In the popular American imagination, Caesara embodies both stories of social uplift in America and tales of tragedy in Europe. As Mary tells Zuckerman, "Do you really not know what you're getting in Caesara O'Shea? Aside from the most beautiful thing in creation? Dignity, Nathan. Bravery. Strength. Poetry. My God, it's the very heart of Ireland you're getting!"[32] In actuality, however, her childhood experiences of domestic abuse, coupled with O'Brien's encoded reproofs of nationalism, suggest a much more complex vision of Ireland and the Irish, not held down by perfidious Albion, but rather perfectly capable of enacting oppression upon themselves, particularly women and Jews.

Caesara's on-screen image symbolizes how popular cultural products can manipulate history and cultivate myth. In this regard, Caesara represents an Irish reiteration of Roth's attack on the kitschification of Jewish history in *The Ghost Writer* (1979), where the musical of *The Diary of Anne Frank* exemplifies this cultural nadir.[33] To remedy this bowdlerization, Roth reincarnates Anne Frank in the mind of Zuckerman, in a knowingly subjective (and thus doomed-to-fail) attempt to salvage her from myth. Arguably, Roth attempts an analogous stratagem in *Zuckerman Unbound*, using Caesara's roles to challenge the manipulation of Irish history to sell movie theater seats. Strengthening this crossover, Caesara starts her stage career "Playing Anne Frank at the Gate Theatre" in Dublin.[34] Caesara is not just full of Irish ghosts, it seems, but Jewish ones as well.

Zuckerman Unbound continues *The Ghost Writer*'s attack on emotionally manipulative and historically distorting instances of "Jewish kitsch," singling out in particular the musical *Fiddler on the Roof* and the Israeli folk song "Tzena, Tzena." It is Pepler who most fully personifies this dilution and misrepresentation of the past, a state Zuckerman describes as "mythomania." Pepler does so through his magnificent creations, Mr. Perlmutter and Marty Paté, two Broadway producers he dreams up and fleshes out before Zuckerman's eyes. In this act, Zuckerman sees Pepler as pseudoartist, a debased copy of himself: "Perlmutter? Mythical gentlemanly father or the mythical producer Paté? . . . This novel is some novel."[35] Pepler tells Zuckerman that Paté wants to make a musical of his life story as a cheated quiz show contestant, disseminating to a wider audience his ludicrous story of Jewish victimization in America. This show is not Paté's only project, however; he is also in talks with Moshe Dayan for a musical of the Six-Day War, as Pepler relays: "Yul Brynner is already as good as signed to star as Dayan. With Brynner it could be something for the Jews." Zuckerman sardonically adds, "And for Paté, too," to which Pepler concurs, "Christ, how can he miss? He'll rake it in."[36] The invented Paté is thus engaged in two related, cynical, moneymaking enterprises: cultivating a sense of past Jewish oppression (and thus present grievance) in America in Pepler's story and stoking Israeli nationalist fervor among American Jews in his war musical.

When combined with his fictitious creations, Perlmutter and Paté, Pepler actually appears to parody a very real producer of sentimentalized popular Jewish history: Leon Uris. Uris's best-selling fictional account of the founding of Israel, *Exodus* (1958), played a huge role in shaping how Americans (Jews and non-Jews) viewed, and continue to view, Israel. In 2001 Edward Said argued that the novel still provides "the main narrative model that dominates American thinking" on Israel and the Middle East. Louis Gordon describes Uris as "mythographer of history," while for Ira Nadel, "Uris employed the Hollywood tradition of personalising history and reducing politics to family romance." Uris's novels reject historical and social complexity in favor of dualistic renderings of good and evil. Grauer asserts, "The pioneering and patriotic Israeli served as one model for a new kind of Jew—particularly after the Six-Day War of 1967, when the image of the Jewish fighter elicited such pride among American Jews that it affected their self-definition as well as the depth of their affiliation with Israel." Drawing on the Old Testament as some Irish nationalists drew on Irish myth, Uris played a major role in promoting this new image of the hypermasculine warrior Jew. It is a construction that Roth found deeply disturbing and one he rebuked in his 1961 article "Some New Jewish Stereotypes": "Mr. Uris's discovery that the Jews are fighters fills him with pride; it fills any number of his Jewish readers with pride as well." Roth counters that it should be no cause of celebration that "the Jew is no longer looking out from the wings on the violence of our age, nor is he its favorite victim; now he is a participant."[37] As an antidote to Uris's one-dimensional adventure yarn, Roth upholds Elie Wiesel's novel *Dawn* (1961), in which a Holocaust survivor who has made his way to Palestine and joined a Jewish paramilitary group there must execute a captured British soldier.[38] Roth closes his argument: "I should like to tell Uris that Wiesel's Jew is not so proud to discover himself in the role of a fighter. . . . No matter how just he tells himself are the rights for which he murders, nothing in his or his people's past is able to make firing a bullet into another man anything less ghastly than it is."[39]

Several instances in *Zuckerman Unbound* suggest that Roth is once more upbraiding Uris and his unsophisticated outlook on history. First, Paté's visit with Moshe Dayan mirrors Uris's own extensive interviews with the Israeli general, on whom he partly bases his protagonist, Ari Ben Canaan. Second, Zuckerman, trying to come to terms with his new fame, thinks to himself, "You are not Paul Newman, but you're no longer who you used to be either," reminding the reader of Newman's role as Ari Ben Canaan in the 1960 film version of *Exodus*. Finally, there is Alvin's television sobriquet, the "Jewish marine," which chimes with Uris's own past and the image of the pugnacious Jew he wished to promote. Uris sums up his philosophy thus: "I have drawn inspiration from the Marine Corps, the Jewish struggle in Palestine and Israel, and the Irish."[40] It is this last clause that provides a potential answer as to why Roth would renew his assault on Uris in *Zuckerman Unbound*, two decades after "Some New Jewish Stereotypes."

Like Uris, Pepler is obsessed not only with the Jews, but with the Irish as well. He tells Zuckerman that he and Perlmutter—who, despite his name, is imagined by Pepler to be "from Ireland"—have recently stayed up late to watch Caesara in *Divine Mission*: "I watched it with Paté's father." As he describes Paté's sumptuous apartment, Pepler adds an apparently innocuous detail: "There's a harp in the hallway, just sitting there." Yet like phrenology and Paul Newman, this element has wider implications, implying that Ireland lurks at the edges of Pepler's consciousness. This point becomes all the more apparent when Alvin seeks to impress Zuckerman with his photographic memory, listing out all the great events that happened in years ending with "98." On reaching 1798 he catalogs the following, "Casanova dies, Battle of Pyramids makes Napoleon master of

Egypt. I could go on all day." Had he gone on, he might have mentioned one of the most significant events of that year, the 1798 Irish Rebellion. Yet Pepler cannot use his vast store of data in a beneficial manner; he has, as Zuckerman describes it, a "maniacal memory, without maniacal desire for comprehension."[41] He can only put his gift to use in an ever-growing tragicomic litany of wrongs done to him (and by egomaniacal connotation to the Jews as a whole), in a manner that recalls the xenophobic ranting of the Citizen in *Ulysses*.

Like Pepler, Uris had a strong interest in Ireland. In 1976 he published *Trinity*, an epic saga of Ireland, which Ann McGlinn, mimicking the heightened prose of the novel, describes as "a detailed picture of that beautiful green isle and its tribes who have never stopped fighting." It displays all the simplification of *Exodus*'s Israel mapped onto Ulster in the final decades of the nineteenth century and the beginning decades of the twentieth. His wildly popular book (more than a million sold in the first two years) did much to shape American (and Irish American) views of the conflict in Northern Ireland. In his wide-ranging survey of Irish American views on Ireland, Reginald Byron noted, "Leon Uris's novel *Trinity* . . . was reported to have been read, remarkably, by fully half of our informants, who said that the book had helped them to put Irish history in perspective. The book appeared in 1976, at a time when the concern of Irish Americans with the Troubles of the 1970s was at its height." Such popularity carries responsibilities; at this time many Irish Americans' only experience of Ireland was through films, songs, and novels. Kevin Kenny relates how the pro-IRA organization "NORAID and its hard-line position had emerged by the early 1970s as the dominant and most popular form of Irish American nationalism." Popular works like Uris's offered an enticing Manichaean vision of the conflict in Northern Ireland, one that spurns historical complexity. Uris himself stated he started the book with the (narrowing and historically inaccurate) premise that "Irish Catholics have been screwed for a thousand years." This one-sided perspective encouraged some notable blind spots for Irish Americans; as Kenny points out, they "oppos[ed] civil rights for African Americans even as they endorsed the cause of civil rights for Ulster Catholics."[42] As an author who always strives for subtlety and precision, Roth abhors texts that recklessly and inaccurately stir up ethnic nostalgia and foreign nationalism for their own profit. If in "Some New Jewish Stereotypes" Roth validates Wiesel's portrayal of Israel as curative to Uris's *Exodus*, in *Zuckerman Unbound* he appears to lionize O'Brien's depictions of Ireland as the answer to Uris's *Trinity*.

Caesara's "hypnotic blarney" warns that Irish identity, like all ethnic and national identities, is performative. This idea is especially important to remember in 1970s America, when the white ethnic revival publicized the idea of certain essential immigrant-heritage qualities, such as hard work and social advancement. O'Brien burlesques the constructed Irish identity in America in *Night*, the first novel of hers that Roth read, as "doling out shamrocks and doing a bit of step dancing, inveigling, boggling them with Kiltartan wisps."[43] Irish actuality is somewhat darker, however: "The children inherit a trinity of guilts (a shamrock): the guilt for Christ's Passion and Crucifixion, the guilt for the plundered land, and the furtive guilt for the mother frequently defiled by the insatiable father." Yet even the highly self-aware Zuckerman, who has earlier congratulated himself on seeing through Caesara's blarney, is tricked by her performance. Inquiring about her acting career, he asks, "How did you get into all this?" to which she replies, "'All this,' meaning what?" she said sharply. "Showbiz? Masochism? Whoredom? How did I get into all this? You sound like a man in bed with a prostitute."[44] For a second, the charming mask of the Irish colleen is dropped, and a much more complex identity is glimpsed lying beneath. So too with Ireland, the moral of Roth's story seems to suggest, a place that actively frustrates the simple fables American popular culture seeks to foist upon it.

Just as Roth's interpretation of other authors inversely functions as self-interpretation, so his exploration of other nationalities and ethnicities acts as a displaced examination of Jewish and American society. In drawing such parallels, Roth scripts a cautionary tale that forewarns against mythologizing nationalism and racist ethnic arrogance. He makes clear the constructed nature of these communitarian identities by seeking out the narratives that form their linchpin and exposing them as myth. Myths can be played in diverse ways, as evinced in the Caesara myth, which variously denotes negative invasions, positive migrations, diasporic patriotism, and, in *Zuckerman Unbound*, fantasies of whiteness. Roth invokes O'Brien for her relentless struggle against Irish myths of racial and moral purity, and he does so through intertextuality—the recognition that no text is pure but is rather inescapably bound up with a vast network of other texts. As such, intertextuality can function as a metaphor for a multicultural society. Just as Jews looked to Irish Americans for a template of assimilation, Jewish writers turned to Irish writers for the means to analyze this immense social process. The Jewish-Irish confluences in the novel first show the instability of ethnoracial identity, but they also remind of the uncomfortable trade-offs made in becoming white. Roth's book is an admonishment to American Jews not to let this whiteness dazzle them, as Zuckerman is dazzled by Caesara. It is a timely warning, as his book was published in the wake of another "Irish" movie star taking office as president of the United States.[45] Ronald Reagan did so with the support of large numbers of Irish Catholic voters, who had drifted away from the Democratic Party in the wake of its support for civil rights. He also received the highest-ever percentage of Jewish votes for a Republican candidate, at 39 percent.[46] Reagan's rhetoric shared much with the language of the white ethnic revival, most particularly his repellent invention, "the welfare queen," which played up to white (and newly white) fears that granting African Americans' civil rights would lessen their own social positions. Roth rejects this language of division and hatred and the simplified (even falsified) historical narratives that inform it. By flirting with both O'Brien's work and her performative image, *Zuckerman Unbound* illustrates the fluctuating shades of national identity, proving race to be the most powerful and deleterious myth of all.

5

"Dark Knowledge"

House of Splendid Isolation, American Pastoral, *and the Transnational Origins of the "National" Trilogies*

In chapter 4, intertextuality acted as a metaphor for multicultural society, with the many voices of the text reflecting the many (often stifled) voices of the modern state. Here intertextuality provides a similar model, calling into question the dominant, undeviating account of the nation: the multivalent text bespeaks a polyphonic history. Commentators have misread the 1990s trilogies of Roth and O'Brien, seeing in them a turn toward nationalism, with Roth unproblematically extolling the virtues of America, in effect becoming a Republican neoconservative, and O'Brien supporting IRA violence in the North, in effect becoming an Irish republican. These commentators focus not on the combined effect of the cacophony of opposing voices in these trilogies, but rather settle on which particular one proves their point, to the exclusion of dissenting testimony. This chapter argues that Roth and O'Brien insert within their trilogies—in the forms of intratextual argument and intertextual flirtations—diverse views and internal contradictions.

When in 2012 I asked O'Brien if she and Roth shared any influences, she replied, "I know he greatly admires Faulkner, as do I." At Roth's eightieth birthday, O'Brien praised her friend's powers of literary exegesis: "Philip is for me, the most sedulous reader I've ever come across. He gets to the pith. . . . Ask him, 'what for him is so great about Faulkner?' and he thinks, and this is what he says: 'Dark knowledge.'"[1] O'Brien does not elaborate on what Roth may mean by "Dark knowledge," but his description appears to allude to William Faulkner's fascination with the intertwined subjects of race and history, the words suggesting at once racial identity and hidden histories. This chapter argues that these two subjects are central to the later work of Roth and O'Brien and, further, that their flirtations with Faulkner's fiction provide original critical means of addressing their apparent "turn" toward history.

In 1994 O'Brien published *House of Splendid Isolation*, the first in "a trilogy of three themes important to Ireland and to me: politics, sex, and land." Roth published *American Pastoral* in 1997, beginning "a thematic trilogy, dealing with the historical moments in postwar American life that have had the greatest impact on my generation."[2] Until the 1990s, Roth and O'Brien had principally focused on the painstaking painting and repainting of the self, as the comparison with the art of Georgia O'Keeffe in this book's introduction suggested. Now they turned to larger canvasses, as Roth explains: "I'll give you a painting analogy. [In] Jackson Pollock's big paintings . . . everything is covered, they're covered with energy, they're covered with pictorial substance . . . it's dramatized in every square inch, that's the amazing thing."[3] In their seventh decade, Roth and O'Brien shifted their attention from selfhood to statehood, from self-portraiture to megalography.

At least this transition is how reviewers understood their new work. Those who had previously written off the pair as incurable narcissists were forced to make reassessments. In 1993 Eileen Battersby had summed up Roth's career: "*Operation Shylock* is silly, pretentious, soaked in ego and manically unfunny. . . . [Evidence of] a creatively exhausted writer doomed to reproduce ponderous, self-obsessive, witless stories devoid of physical description, landscape or even the weather—books chronicling his life, his neuroses, and little else." Yet four years later, she hailed *American Pastoral* as "a haunting, haunted masterpiece. . . . [T]he energy and rich invention of his prose are here brilliantly matched by a thoughtful eloquence and awareness of change." In a similar vein, Helen Meany asserts that *House of Splendid Isolation* "marks an expansion from the traditional O'Brien terrain of doomed love affairs and melancholy, disappointed women, into politics and history."[4] These perspectives implicitly set up a false dichotomy between Roth's and O'Brien's supposedly ahistorical and self-centered earlier fiction and their expansive late-career historical bent. *Fine Meshwork* has endeavored to provide a counternarrative, arguing that from the outset of his career as a writer Roth has contended with issues of race, class, nationalism, ethnicity, masculinity, war, power, and oppression.[5] Similarly, O'Brien's pre-1990s range comprises, inter alia, the contemplation of state censorship, war and the demands it makes on citizens and writers, and the heterogeneity and xenophobia of the Irish nation. Nevertheless, *House of Splendid Isolation* and *American Pastoral* did mark a change in emphasis for O'Brien and Roth. Both authors achieve this enlarged purview through their reading of Faulkner, as this chapter will show by unraveling their paratextual and intertextual entanglements with the pivotal southern modernist writer. Both adopt Faulkner's formulation, "The past is never dead. It's not even past," to scrutinize the ways in which the past is continuously manipulated for the present needs of the powerful. "Memory and language are the two best things a writer has," O'Brien tells us, while for Roth, "To be alive is to be made of memory."[6] Their own career-long study of fallible personal memory swells here in these books into a more spacious examination of collective memory. In the process, history is shown to be not linear and determined, but multiple and unforeseeable. In their 1990s trilogies, Roth and O'Brien challenge the grand (and grandstanding) historical narratives of their nations.

The chapter is divided into two sections. The first looks at how *House of Splendid Isolation*'s textual relations with Faulkner's fiction inflect the novel's commentary on Irish racial identity and on traditional interpretations of Irish history. The second performs a similar operation on *American Pastoral*, looking at how Roth flirts with Faulkner to shape his novel's confrontation with whiteness and the American Dream.

"The Passion and Ignorance in the Deep South of America and the West of Ireland Are the Same": *House of Splendid Isolation*

O'Brien made no secret of her deepening fascination with Faulkner in the latter stages of her métier: "All his books are in the glass-fronted cabinet among those books that I love most."[7] Critics have observed his presence in her work, such as Sandra Manoogian Pearce, who describes her as the "Irish Faulkner," and Roth, who, on finishing *Wild Decembers* (1999), remarked, "You're not like Colette after all. . . . You're more like Faulkner." However, there has as yet been no extended scholarly scrutiny of this important transnational relationship. How does Faulkner's Yoknapatawpha inform O'Brien's fiction, and how does that fiction in turn unsettle our understanding of Faulkner's imaginative universe? The beginnings of an answer may lie in O'Brien's epitextual flirtations with Faulkner. Just as chapter 2 takes O'Brien's reading of Roth in "The Artist and His Country" as a dislocated investigation of her own conflicted attitude toward the North in the 1970s, this chapter uses O'Brien's essay "Compelled by the Dark Sensibility of William Faulkner" as a prism through which to view her relationship with Irish nationalism in the 1990s. O'Brien sets up an implicit parallel between the harsh handling Faulkner received in the South and her own treatment in Ireland: "Naturally, like all writers who seek the truth, Faulkner was accused of not loving his native South, so much so that he has a character say again and again: 'I don't hate it, I don't hate it, I don't hate it.'"[8] For O'Brien, love for one's country is expressed not through obsequiousness toward its institutions but through relentlessly exposing their faults and thereby forcing them to measure up to the nation's purported principles. Roth endorses this method in *The Counterlife*: "Disillusionment is a way of caring for your country too."[9]

For O'Brien, Faulkner's greatest strength is a paradox, his intrepid refusal of the partisan position, coupled with his knowledge that no one escapes his or her prejudices: "Never is there the obvious and unbudging political stance. . . . He does not simply marshal the black man and the white man with loaded muskets confronting one another; he depicts them in ongoing . . . enmity, but opts for the higher and harsher judgement that all are compelled by greed and vindictiveness."[10] These particular elements of Faulkner's writing guide this chapter's reading of *House of Splendid Isolation*, a novel virulently attacked not for O'Brien's more usual "crime" of not loving her country enough, but for apparently loving it all too well. "To write about the North was to enter troubled waters," O'Brien testifies in her recent memoir, "wrath and accusations from some, fractured friendships, along with the sneering insinuation that I was 'sleeping with the provos.'"[11]

In 1984 O'Brien declared, "Any small, claustrophobic, ingrown community resembles another. The passion and ignorance of the Deep South of America and the West of Ireland are the same." She is not the first Irish author to imaginatively perceive such primitive commonalities between these two distant regions. Her words echo the writings of Sean O'Faolain, who was struck by the resemblances between post–Civil War Ireland and the post–Civil War American South: "There is the same passionate provincialism; the same local patriotism; the same southern nationalism . . . the same vanity of the old race; the same gnawing sense of defeat; the same capacity for intense hatred." For O'Faolain, all of these elements are interlinked. Both he and O'Brien see insularity and intolerance as the qualities that unite these disparate lands and lie at the core of their social dilemmas, explaining the sense of shared purpose that may often be discerned between Irish and southern writers. Cleanth Brooks considers these literary symmetries, looking at Yeats and the Yeats-smitten Faulkner, both fascinated by their territory's vanishing aristocratic caste and by "the big-house tradition." Of Faulkner, O'Brien says, "When accepting the Nobel Prize, he said that the only thing worth writing about is the problem of the human heart in conflict with itself," a sentiment that echoes Yeats's great insight, "We make out of the quarrel with others, rhetoric, but of the quarrel with ourselves, poetry." Or as O'Brien deftly puts it: "A lot of people crowd inside one poor head."[12]

Scholarly interest in the interconnections between these two regions continues to grow. Kieran Quinlan expands on their mutual liminality: "Ireland is to England, the argument sometimes goes, as the American South is to the United States: both places have long been the 'problem,' if also frequently romanticized regions, of otherwise 'progressive' nations. They exist if often unwillingly, as the untamed peripheries of their respective civilized centers."[13] Kathryn Stelmach Artuso relates the literary consequences of these outlying locations: "In their quest for new literary forms that would undermine local-color fiction and oppose the oppressive outside influences of the North or of England, both southern and Irish writers made massive contributions to literary modernism." She goes on to argue that both places apotheosized womanhood and "conflated woman with the land," much to the disadvantage of the actual women who inhabited these spaces. Male modernist authors on both sides of the Atlantic at times defied these images and at times deferred to them. The experiences of other minorities who live in these areas have also been compared, with historian Brian Dooley taking stock of the sundry interconnections between the southern black and Northern Irish civil rights movements: "Civil rights activists in Northern Ireland borrowed slogans from black American protesters, called themselves 'white negroes' and identified in a positive way with the struggle across the Atlantic led by Martin Luther King."[14] Through its flirtation with Faulkner's oeuvre, *House of Splendid Isolation* touches on all of these diverse correlations.

House of Splendid Isolation is narrated by Josie O'Meara, an Irishwoman, born around the turn of the last century, who emigrates to America during the Irish War of Independence, only to return in its aftermath and marry into the rising Catholic large-farmer class then supplanting the Anglo-Irish gentry. Her marriage to the alcoholic, violent, and emotionally stunted James is an unhappy one. She becomes pregnant, but fearing to bring a child into the relationship or to further tie herself to James, she procures an horrific illegal abortion from a local medicine woman.[15] She seeks an unlikely form of escape from her bleak life through an unconsummated later-life affair with a visiting priest, Fr. John.[16] After discovering this infidelity, James beats Josie so badly she goes mad for a time, a madness compounded by the end of her quasi-relationship with John and the rumors circulating in the locality: "She'd stand in front of the long mirror of the wardrobe and decide that the sockets of her eyes were filling up with blood. She was tasting blood. She saw her priest being boiled in oil and skinned, skinless." As James is rendered increasingly helpless through alcoholism and pecuniary mismanagement, a truce (built on their inescapable proximity) settles between them: "They sat side by side of an evening, in the conservatory, numb with cold."[17] This truce is broken once more, however, when Josie opposes James's 1970s abetment of the IRA and he again viciously attacks her. Visiting an arms dump on his land, James is killed by Gardai. Josie once more suffers a mental collapse, but again recovers. In the 1980s, as the Provisional IRA campaign in the North enters its second decade, McGreevy, a republican assassin on the run from the authorities, hides out in Josie's house. O'Brien uses the confines of the house to set Northern and Southern Irish conceptions of nationalism in conversation with one another. A similar device is used by Bernard Malamud in *The Tenants* (1971), a book that examines American interracial dissension by portraying a black writer and Jewish writer as the last occupants of a decrepit New York tenement house about to be torn down.[18]

There were several reasons O'Brien's novel was seen as too positive in its portrayal of the IRA. First, she wrote a balanced profile of Gerry Adams for the *New York Times* at a time when it was more common to paint him simply as a terrorist; second, she interviewed Dominic McGlinchey, a republican prisoner who had murdered dozens of people, and used some of his biographical details in her creation of McGreevy. As in chapter 2, I will argue that O'Brien's fiction is considerably more nuanced than her public statements on the North have been framed in the print media. More than anything, it is the representation of McGreevy that impelled the media backlash against *House of Splendid Isolation*. John Dunne fumed, "Personally I detested McGreevy as much as I detested what I felt were Ms O'Brien's attempts to make me like him. I'm sure that Attila the Hun loved his mother too." While praising the sections that focus on Josie's life story and document her survival as a woman in androcentric Catholic Ireland, Rüdiger Imhof is less impressed with the portions of the book that focus on McGreevy: "It is when it comes to assessing the book as a novel about Ireland's blood-soaked present, which obviously *House of Splendid Isolation* aspires to be, that one begins to have Reservations." McGreevy is shown as an intelligent and principled man, despite having killed in the region of twenty people in support of his cause. This ostensible contradiction infuriated journalists, who often found it easier to render violent republicans as psychopaths than as rational beings. Ed Moloney reflects on the reductive thinking of some Irish journalists regarding the IRA prior to the peace process: "If you wanted to write about . . . the IRA . . . [y]ou had to be a fellow traveler because how else could you write about such people unless you talked to them like they were human beings and not . . . mindless monsters. . . . And if you did that, then you must secretly sympathize with them. It was media McCarthyism Irish-style."[19] Forced into this Manichaean framework, McGreevy becomes a straightforward expression of O'Brien's sympathy toward Irish republicanism in the North.

However, for such accusations to hold value, one must ignore not only O'Brien's career-long quarrel with Irish nationalism—most pertinently its confinement of women to the hearth or the institution—but also the evidence of *House of Splendid Isolation* itself. Just because O'Brien is contemptuous of British imperialism and its divide-and-rule legacy between Protestants and Catholics in Ireland, does not mean her book cannot be equally scathing of masculinist theories of Irishness. As Eve Stoddard points out in her discussion of the novel, "This nationalism versus revisionism debate is often presented as a binary opposition between 'truth' and 'myth,' which can apply in either direction."[20] Rather, like Faulkner, O'Brien abjures the static stance. Far from celebrating the violence of the IRA in Northern Ireland, O'Brien's book is a continuation of her chastisement of the faux patriotism of the Irish state, exposing its multifarious contradictions: a place that force-feeds its inhabitants heroic Irish mythology yet fails to see the cognitive dissonance it creates, a place that condemns current violence in the North while commemorating past violence in its schools and public forums, and a place where women are upheld as emblems of a nation and held down as citizens of that nation. O'Brien's sensitivity to the plight of Catholics in the North should not be confused with an endorsement of the IRA. Rather, her book is at pains to argue that the triumph of unreconstructed nationalism there would likely see a protraction and deepening of patriarchal oppression, as happened in the postindependence southern state.

Chapter 2's reading of *Night* can counteract the reactionary accusations of IRA apologia leveled at *House of Splendid Isolation*. Indeed, O'Brien appears specifically to invoke her previous novel (thereby reshaping her past creations for present purposes) in the section titled "Captivity." It opens with the words "Night again" and sees the first encounter between McGreevy and Josie: "He lowers his gun when he sees that all which confronts him is an elderly woman in a four-poster bed." This beginning recalls Mary Hooligan—"I am in a bed, a fourposter no less"—and suggests that O'Brien is flirting not only with Faulkner but with her own canon as well.[21] Written at the outset of the Troubles, *Night* berates both the divisive inheritance of British imperialism in the North and the abuses of Irish republicanism. Composed as the North stumbled toward peace, *House of Splendid Isolation* continues O'Brien's policy of avoiding the "obvious or unbudging political stance." The major difference is that while in *Night* the deliberation on imperialism and nationalism takes place in the shadows, in *House of Splendid Isolation* it is brought into the light of day. Faulkner's self-revisions seem to have been on O'Brien's mind at this time and perhaps offered a model for her own. This idea is discernible when looking beyond O'Brien's public epitextual flirtations with the southern writer (in interviews and essays) toward her private ones, as evinced in her archives. In one of her *House of Splendid Isolation* notebooks O'Brien has inscribed a series of entries relating to Faulkner's work, including "Quentin Compson," "*The Sound and the Fury*," "*Absolom, Absalom!*"[22]

Quentin has a complicated relationship with the South. He is the one who declaims, not fully convinced, "I dont! I dont hate it! I dont hate it!"[23] He has internalized the region's poisonous ideology, which rests on the concept of the eternal preservation of pure, white, womanhood. In *The Sound and the Fury* (1929), this is revealed in his incestuous obsession with his sister Caddy's loss of virginity, a mania that eventually leads to his suicide. In *Absalom, Absalom!* (1936), Faulkner returns to Quentin to stress the elemental cause of his (and the South's) fanatical defense of southern women: the threat of miscegenation. Through the story of the Sutpen family, which Quentin reconstructs with the help of other narrators and much poetic license, the impossibly tangled nature of race in the South becomes evident (in the end reminding us that race is a fiction, though a fiction that continues to wield great power). O'Brien turns to Faulkner's South to dispute the fallacy of a racially homogenous "Irish" Ireland, a fallacy often at the heart of Irish jingoistic sentiment. In their fear and hatred of the Other, and their interrelated control of women's bodies, Ireland and the American South were indeed "the same."

O'Brien's rebuke of Irish nationalism is most apparent in James, Josie's republican husband. Though seen as an upstanding member of the community, James is a brutal man who habitually rapes his wife. While doing so, he "calls her muddy, short for mother and mud." This incestuous confusion of land and lineage echoes Quentin's association of his sister's "muddy . . . drawers" (seen at their grandmother Damuddy's funeral), with sin, adulteration, and the forfeiture of his southern honor. Diane Roberts says that "as a southerner, Faulkner inherited the images, icons, and demons of his culture . . . sometimes accepting [them], sometimes rejecting." Though he discards the romanticized iconography of the southern woman, his characters (and he himself) display a disquieting obsession with women's "unclean" bodies and menstruation, what Quentin's father terms "periodic filth."[24] O'Brien thus seems to be at once aligning her work with Faulkner's in the refutation of the impossibly pure woman of the South while simultaneously deriding the always impure woman that he alternatively proposes.

Though O'Brien sharpens her criticism of the propensity of chauvinist ideology to splice woman and nation through reference to Faulkner and the South, she is just as sensitive to this tendency in the Irish literary tradition. While he does not give the appearance of realizing it, James's archetypal Irishwoman is not a perpetual feature of the Irish landscape, but is rather plucked from nineteenth-century popular culture. On his wedding day, drunken James and his leering brother describe to Josie the mating ritual of the mayfly: "It's the female that makes the play and does the tricks." Vaguely aware of Josie's dismay through his alcoholic haze, James changes tack, with innuendo becoming homily: "But they give life." In this oscillation between lewd sexuality and venerated motherhood, O'Brien encapsulates the virgin/whore syndrome that governed the view of women in twentieth-century Ireland. Reflecting on the failure of the mayfly story to arouse or inspire Josie, James "wondered if perhaps his wife would not have preferred a more romantic story attached to the Shannon lake, the one about the Colleen Bawn, the jilted woman who was drowned and whose death was exposed later by the appearance of a corset on the water."[25] In her essay "Why Irish Heroines Don't Have to Be Good Anymore," O'Brien traces the bawdy representations of Irishwomen in eighteenth-century poetry, arguing that the "gentle, tremulous, gullible, devout, masochistic" Irishwoman (emblematic of a weak and threatened land) is a nineteenth-century trope rather than a historical constant.[26] O'Brien saves particular ire for Gerald Griffin's

1829 novel *The Collegians* (later adapted by Dion Boucicault into the 1860 play *The Colleen Bawn*):

> It charts the fate of a young girl called Eily O'Connor, a rope maker's daughter, of "a timid hesitancy, downcast gentleness of manner which shed an interest over all her motions and a tongue that seemed to move on silver wires." She is of course extremely devotional, an adoring daughter and a wonderful cook. Naturally this perfect vessel is ready for contamination and the redemption that eventually comes with it. . . . [S]he leaves home, meets a cad called Hardress, falls hopelessly in love with him, gets married in secret, is banished . . . and eventually has to be bumped off because his mother wishes him to marry a rich heiress. However, her body is washed up on the shores and true to the mores of sentiment Eily is found lying in the mud, her blue mantle over her frame, her small feet in Spanish leather shoes and in her death her virtue inviolate.[27]

Lying in the mud, Eily is united with the Irish land that she has, in her tragic fate, come to betoken. James's elicitation of this paragon of Irish feminine virtue, the Colleen Bawn, hence contains traces of this reductive nationalist symbolism.

House of Splendid Isolation parodies the melodramatic conventions of the Colleen Bawn story. The "corset on the water" that James speaks of (in Griffin's book it is a straw bonnet) is reworked, with Josie's relationship with Fr. John discovered when the farmhand Paud finds her corset—flung off in anticipation of the priest's arrival at their rendezvous—on a ditch and gives it to James, thereby revealing the affair. To reassert his mastery over his wayward wife, James ferociously assaults Josie before parading her around in front of a group of inebriated men he has invited home from the local village: "a rough line of jaws, side by side, like men on a chapel bench, except that they are drunk, too drunk and too skittish to even look at her in her bedraggled state and too settled to go home." Danine Farquharson and Bernice Schrank read this appalling scene as follows: "[James]'s physical and verbal brutalities, although plainly seen, are ignored. This schmoozy male camaraderie countenances [James]'s transgressions." Not only do they countenance them, but they also celebrate the reestablishment of indigenous patriarchal order. The townspeople presume that Josie's "assignation" has been with a "foreigner." Here the scene appears to redraft not only Griffith but O'Brien's own earlier fiction. The intoxicated gaggle of men come to witness the triumphant subjugation of the rebellious Irishwoman, thought to have betrayed her family and race through fornication with a foreigner, is an episode already seen in *The Lonely Girl*, as discussed in chapter 2. Here, however, no shotgun-wielding housekeeper is present to save the protagonist from her fate. In *House of Splendid Isolation*, O'Brien has stripped away the dark comedy of the attack on Eugene Gaillard's house—except perhaps for the great irony that the Lothario is not an alien but a priest, the very embodiment of Catholic Ireland—leaving intact only the fierce, raw tribalism of the earlier work. Rereading Josie's affair in light of Griffith, Faulkner, and *The Lonely Girl* brings to the surface latent Irish fears of racial invasion. It also gives new meaning to Josie's wish to "flee her own house and flee the prison of her white body and go somewhere, anywhere, escape."[28]

In some important ways, James mirrors Thomas Sutpen, creator (and destroyer) of the house of Sutpen. Both crave and are denied heirs. Both occupy houses that act as metonyms for their homelands, Ireland and the American South. According to Stoddard, in O'Brien's book, "The big house allegorizes the Irish republic as a post-colonial state that has failed to nurture the nation by virtue of occupying the big house rather than inventing another form for the nation. It replaced the 1916 ideals of equal rights for all in the nation with a Catholic and patriarchal regime."[29] In a similar manner, the plantation house in America continued to represent white rule for African Americans following the Civil War, in spite of the freedom promised in the Emancipation Proclamation and the subsequent Reconstruction amendments.[30] These houses were still occupied by powerful whites, while blacks continued to till the land, though now under the crushingly inequitable sharecropping system. As such, they provided concrete symbols of the largely unchanged structures of white power, with the Jim Crow laws and extralegal lynchings regulating black lives just as comprehensively as enslavement. O'Brien is not drawing direct analogies between American slavery and women's position in Irish society, but she is at pains to demonstrate that all revolutions have the potential to fail in their promise by merely reestablishing under different names the old forms of control they have set out to overthrow.

In Faulkner's and O'Brien's books the personifications of these systems of control are in due course revealed to be pitiable figures. As Farquharson and Schrank note, "Jamie's bankruptcy is more than a commentary on his financial situation. It is a judgment on the quality of the patriarchal arrangements in which he is participant and creator." Likewise, Sutpen's insolvency following the Civil War can be taken as a judgment on the moral bankruptcy of the plantation class. Indeed, it appears that O'Brien had Sutpen specifically in her thoughts while constructing *House of Splendid Isolation*. Her notebooks reveal several quotations from *Absalom, Absalom!* concerning him: "the ancient varicose and despairing Faustus"; "Creditor's hand already on his shoulder." In these descriptions we see Sutpen not as a commanding hero of Confederate mythology, "who at one time could have galloped for ten miles in any direction without crossing his own boundary," but as a pathetic character, full of patriotism and whiskey: "reaching after the third or second drink that old man's state of impotent and furious undefeat in which he would rise, swaying and plunging and shouting for his horse and pistols to ride single-handed into Washington and shoot Lincoln (a year or so too late here)." James's drunken jingoistic passion is similarly misdirected, aimed verbally at the ancient enemy across the Irish Sea, but landing physically on Josie's body, when she warns him not to aid the IRA in stashing weapons on their land: "he resurrecting every bit of Fenian feeling that he ever had and she saying that it was out of the question and his slapping her. . . . His old rage reared up in him as he took swipes at her, his hiccups going like mad."[31] James's actions suggest that nationalism is often merely a cover for self-interest and a justification for the control of women, along with anyone else falling outside the ethnocentric narrative of the nation.

Despite James's and Sutpen's ruthless treatment of their families and social "inferiors," both are well respected within their communities. When Josie and James marry, he is seen as a man of power and position; as one of his acolytes reminds her, "you've married into the best family in the country." Throughout their five-decade marriage, Josie discovers just how false this gentlemanly veneer actually is. However, so ingrained is this all-encompassing belief that Josie cannot help but perpetuate the myths of James's manly endeavor following his death, telling McGreevy of the "big fish, the biggest fish ever caught on the lake, caught by her husband and having to be sent to Dublin to a taxidermist and then put in a glass case in a hotel." Slowly, through these recurring conversations between the southern woman and northern man, Josie is able to reveal the actual circumstances of her life, though even then they are expressed in typical Irish circumlocution, with James eventually described, as "the wrong kind of drinking man." Her talks with McGreevy allow Josie to dredge up long-repressed memories of her life, challenging not only the public character of her husband, but also the public face of the Irish nation. McGreevy and Josie's dialogues do not produce political synthesis; rather, the very act of conversation shows signs of providing a possible way forward for Ireland, North and South. These conversations between Josie and McGreevy symbolize several different things. First, they advocate a political sphere in which dialogue, not dogmatism, triumphs. Second, they stand in for a polyphonic view of history, one that emphasizes the multiple perspectives often stifled by the dominant narrative of a nation. Here, *House of Splendid Isolation* again corresponds with *Absalom, Absalom!* in which Quentin and his conarrators question southern history through their creative investigation of the life of Sutpen and in doing so unveil both his own immoral nature and that of the slave-owning society he represents. That O'Brien was cognizant of Faulkner's narrative strategies seems clear in her notebooks, in which she has jotted down the names of the narrators of *Absalom, Absalom!*—"Quentin C, His Father, His Roommate Shreve, Miss Coldfield"—along with the appended commentary: "Sutpen's story[,] talking either actually or imaginatively[,] voices entered through the minds of a single speaker."[32]

House of Splendid Isolation does not advocate Irish republican ideals. However, it is fascinated with its pervasive appeal, particularly among those individuals—such as women—oppressed by it. Despite the negative example set by her republican husband, Josie has internalized some of the same beliefs. Though she realizes something is wrong with this ideology, she cannot fully express her misgivings. Thus her inchoate pleas to McGreevy, "If women ran your organisation there would be no shooting . . . No bombs." McGreevy counters that his organization has "plenty of women"—failing to note that while women participated in the struggle, they are rarely permitted into positions of power. Josie is trying to communicate the idea that any community philosophy built around masculinity and race will almost inevitably lead to hatred of those persons thought to fall outside these categories. Further, the control of women is central to such a community, lest through intermarriage women undermine racial purity. That Josie finds it so hard to verbalize her acute experiences of the abject failure of Irish nationalism as the guiding ethos in the Irish Free State is not surprising. The Irish were intensively indoctrinated in anti-British rhetoric, indicated in the novel by Paud's understanding of Irish history: "At once he burst into a recitation of what Miss McCloud his teacher had dinned into him and others day after day, how their country, their beloved country had been sacked, plundered and raped by the sister country." It is this view of history that instills a prevalent sense of defeat in Irish discourse while also disabling any fair-minded criticism of the southern Irish state and its economic and social shortcomings. The Republic's tribulations could be blamed on the repercussions of British rule, and any talk of the oppression of internal others could be drowned out by loud orations of Ireland's own history of oppression. A kindred dissimilation was perpetrated in the American South, one that, as Artuso argues, Faulkner's literary generation set out to counter: "It looked round and saw for the first time since about 1830 that the Yankees were not to blame for everything."[33] O'Brien interweaves her work with Faulkner's to accentuate how heroic myths often shield horrific deeds.

Liam Harte claims that *House of Splendid Isolation* is "politically partisan" and laments O'Brien's "decision to eschew moral or ironic scrutiny of McGreevy's political outlook and activism in the course of her sustained humanization of him."[34] Tempering this view is, first, the fact that McGreevy is not the only republican present in the book—the sexually abusive James and the callous IRA operatives that McGreevy meets on the run could not be described as affirmative recruitment posters for the movement. Second, as a mass murderer McGreevy himself is not necessarily a positive image of republicanism. Third, it is imperative to remember that McGreevy is not O'Brien's unproblematic mouthpiece; neither, for that matter, is Josie. It is their dialogue, and the subtly shifting space between their two positions, that exemplifies the book's standpoint on conflict and the North. This dialogue explores the incongruities between Irish republican discourse and practice. Through their conversations, there is an (ultimately unsuccessful) effort on Josie's part to establish a vision of community that moves beyond the "vanity of the old race" and "a capacity for intense hatred" that are central to the ethnocentric Irish republican movement.[35]

Outwardly, McGreevy is certain of the goals of his struggle. When Josie asks him, he answers candidly, "To get the British out of Ireland. . . . Justice for all. Personal identity. Racial identity." Though superficially unambiguous, these goals in fact highlight a contradiction at the center of the Irish republican viewpoint: the tension between the warring concepts of "Justice for all" and "Racial identity."[36] The former gestures toward the IRA's modern socialist agenda, the latter, darkly, toward its primitive sectarianism. McGreevy's focus on race as a marker of identity does not appear of great consequence until read in conjunction with James, specifically his thrashing of Josie for (what is seen in the community's eyes as) the sexual betrayal of the Irish race.

For her part, Josie tries to push past the idea of race as the foundational characteristic of a nation. In attempting to decipher what draws her and McGreevy together, beyond the "anvil of circumstances," Josie ruminates: "The saddest bit is that we're the same stock, the same faith, we speak the same tongue and yet we don't. Language to each of us is a braille that the other cannot know. Words like justice or love or bread turned inside out or outside in."[37] Josie lists the conventionally accepted traits of their connection to each other as fellow Irish people, race, religion, and language, yet finds them inadequate and even false. Neither of them, for example, places much value in Catholic rituals, with McGreevy saying that "others pray for him but he does not pray," while for Josie, "her religion had never been a comfort."[38]

Though both speak English (in itself a failure of early Free State Gaelic objectives), language, too, fails to unite them, the gulf between their experiences in two thoroughly different milieus seemingly too great to bridge. O'Brien makes this chasm apparent by having Josie's words flirt with those of Stephen Dedalus.[39] Stephen, in conversation with a college dean, "a countryman of Ben Jonson," despairingly reflects: "The language in which we are speaking is his before it is mine. How different are the words *home, Christ, ale, master*, on his lips and on mine! I cannot speak or write these words without unrest of spirit. His language, so familiar and so foreign, will always be for me an acquired speech. I have not made or accepted its words. My voice holds them at bay. My soul frets in the shadow of his language."[40] Whereas Joyce suggests a social and conceptual divide between the English and Irish "races," O'Brien bravely does so between Northern and Southern Irish. If religion and language fail to unite her with McGreevy, race is thus similarly undermined. This seemingly eternal, unchanging phenomenon is revealed to be a shifting label, one just as open to interpretation as words like "Justice." By rejecting the transcendental signifiers, stock, faith, and language, Josie argues for a view of Irishness that transcends these exclusionary structures.

O'Brien has spoken of her admiration for the war poetry of W. H. Auden, as mentioned in chapter 3. His poem "September 1, 1939," written on the eve of the Second World War, warns that a failure to heed history begets endless violence:

> I and the public know
> What all schoolchildren learn,
> Those to whom evil is done
> Do evil in return.

McGreevy is trapped in this deadly cycle. He writes down the basis of his ideology to Josie: "Don't worry, I am not going to give you a 1916 litany. Not to grow up in hate, not to have been Papist leper scum, not to have been interned at fourteen and fifteen and sixteen. . . . What I would love is for you to have met some of the boys that I was in the blocks with . . . it only takes being with people like that and one's faith is invincible." McGreevy's one-sided view of history is understandable, but contributes to the ongoing enmity. O'Brien interrogates this myopia in reference to Bobby Sands, of whose motives she says, "I read his writings, which were full of pity for his own and loathing of the enemy." It is this inability to see the stories of the other side, the belief that your side's aims are unsullied and justified, while their goals are tainted and wrong, that helps drive sectarian conflict. O'Brien's book points out the folly behind this purity of victimization, with McGreevy imagining the Irish Republic as a place of "love and strawberries," where people "forgot their brothers and sisters across the border, let them rot."[41] Josie's life story challenges this simplistic view.

Empathizing with the struggles of others can have positive outcomes, while too exclusive a focus on persecution of one's own community can lead to problems in identity formation, as seen when the Irish blame their faults on Britain and the people of the American South on the Union. In *House of Splendid Isolation*, Ireland is stuck in a repetitious cycle of violence exactly because of the inability of its various groups, unionist and nationalist, to reflect on the injury done to those groups not their own—that is, to apply the lessons of history in a nonvindictive manner. Those groups who overcome subjugation inevitably turn and reenact that subjugation on others. Therefore, Ireland repeats its colonial oppression on its internal others, embodied in James's treatment of Josie. There seems to be every danger that in coming to power McGreevy may do the same, seeking revenge for lost loved ones and former indignities. A worrying sign of his capacity to do so can be seen when he hijacks a van, because the driver "was a woman." Yet even Josie is not immune from the thrill of power over others. Though in Brooklyn she is a maid, "a mere skivvy to a plump woman from beyond the Ukraine who could be soft while her husband was around but then fuming the moment he left," back home in Ireland she learns nothing from this maltreatment: "Those years were a bad dream now to a woman standing in her room. . . . Yes mistress of a house and a serving girl whom she could call to wait on her, to iron her clothes, to amuse her if necessary." If Paud's mother is to be believed, Josie once locked her servant in a room "for two days . . . for a theft that she had not done. It was the Missus herself who had stolen the scarf."[42] The refusals of McGreevy, Josie, and James to learn from their personal stories reflect the larger inability of the Irish nation to learn from its history.

In Ireland history is reified, given a tangible immediacy, best evinced by a guard hunting McGreevy, who says of a passing pub, "There's two bullet holes in there, where the 'Tans shot through a toilet door. . . . Shot a man dead." Faulkner's South has a similar problem, where the weight of history is everywhere, obfuscating past and contemporary wrongs of the South. Shreve, Quentin's Canadian college roommate, parses the difference between their upbringings: "We don't live among defeated grandfathers and freed slaves . . . and bullets in the dining room table and such, to be always reminding us to never forget. What is it? Something you live in and breathe in like air? A kind of vacuum filled with wraithlike and indomitable anger and pride and glory at and in happenings that occurred and ceased fifty years ago."[43] In Quentin's mind, it is impossible for an outsider to understand this history, as he tells Shreve: "You cant understand it. You would have to be born there." Thinking that no one else can comprehend your tragic experience is the basis of an exceptionalist, insular worldview. It is significant then that McGreevy's words flirt with Quentin's; he tells Josie the same thing: "Look, you would have to be born there to know it." That O'Brien was thinking of Quentin here is confirmed through her notebook, where the quotation "You would have to be born there" can be found alongside other Faulkner excerpts.[44]

O'Brien does not make the obvious connection between McGreevy and disenfranchised blacks in the American South, but rather makes it between him and a privileged white voice. She gives McGreevy Quentin's words. True, they are the words of a white southerner who is more willing than most to contest the shibboleths of his region's history, but they are the words of a white southerner nonetheless.[45] In doing so, O'Brien destabilizes McGreevy's claim to victimhood, while at the same time reminding us of the role the Irish played in enforcing racial prejudice in America, as discussed in chapter 4. This acknowledgment complicates simple associations between the more recognizably related Irish civil rights movement and its African American equivalent. Further, O'Brien does not give McGreevy Quentin's uncertainty and willingness to question everything, even his own beliefs. When Shreve asks Quentin does he, Quentin, understand the South, even having been born there, he receives the ambivalent response: "'I dont know,' Quentin said. 'Yes, of course I understand it.' They breathed in the darkness. After a moment Quentin said: 'I dont know.'" If Quentin *has* come any closer to understanding his region, however, it is through dialogue with Shreve. The same is true for McGreevy and Josie. Through his investigation and artistic invention, Quentin comes closer to fathoming the detrimental state of his country's relationship with history. O'Brien, in her direct references to Faulkner, covertly suggests that dialogue between different ethnic groups is the antidote to nations built on racial exclusivity. As such, intertextuality acts as a metaphor for a multicultural society. The text of many voices represents the many-voiced nation. *House of Splendid Isolation* argues for just such a welcoming nation, one that will embrace both internal and external others. At the end of her life Josie dreams, "She will give the house over to young people, a youth hostel for those who travel, a place to be lived in."[46]

In conclusion, *House of Splendid Isolation* rejects the fantasy of racial purity hinted at in its title, dismissing the idea that Ireland is a place kept apart for the "Irish" Irish (whoever they might be), when in fact it has always been a land of in-migration. O'Brien's interviews and archives provide the maps that guide this reading, yet the book does not herald an end point, instead endorsing a process. That process is political and social interchange between antagonistic communities, symbolized intratextually by the discussions between McGreevy and Josie and intertextually by the dialogue O'Brien instigates with Faulkner's South. If the book has a moral, it is to radically distrust morals and the ideologies that paint them as essentialist phenomena, rather than as ever-shifting concepts motivated by power.

"Undercurrents of Awfulness": *American Pastoral*

O'Brien was not the only one to suffer schematic misinterpretation in the 1990s. Roth's fiction was also misread, with conservative commentators seeing *American Pastoral* (1997) as evidence of a Pauline conversion to the "cultural right."[47] In both cases, these myopic elucidations emerge from the autobiographical fallacy that has haunted the reception of the novels of Roth and O'Brien since the 1960s. Inculcated in this sort of reasoning, reviewers took the most obvious central characters of *House of Splendid*

Isolation and *American Pastoral* and ascribed their views to the authors. Neoconservative Norman Podhoretz looked at Roth's protagonist, the all-American hero Swede Levov, and gushed, "I myself, and many other people too, detected in this book a born-again Philip Roth whose entire outlook on the world had been inverted." To come to such a conclusion, one must ignore the presence of a multitude of conflicting perspectives within the novel.[48] Roth's intertextual flirtations with Faulkner, with O'Brien, and with his own earlier canon provide a means of uncovering these counterperspectives, and thus of modifying perceptions of how race and gender function in the novel.[49]

American Pastoral begins in the 1990s with Nathan Zuckerman, now in his sixties, meeting Seymour "Swede" Levov, a former schoolmate revered in 1940s Jewish Newark for his sporting aptitude and for the aura of assimilative American masculinity he exuded: "[He was] the boy we were all going to follow into America, our point man into the next immersion, at home here the way the Wasps were at home here." The Swede is the son of Lou Levov (himself the uneducated son of a Jewish immigrant) who built up a large glove manufacturing business, which the Swede has inherited. Seymour's wealth allowed him leave behind not only dwindling 1950s Newark but also the well-to-do Jewish suburbs that surround it. He instead moves to the overwhelming white and genteel Old Rimrock with his Irish Catholic wife, Dawn Dwyer, where they have a daughter, Merry. Meeting the Swede in later life piques Zuckerman's nostalgia, but, as a seemingly all-too-perfect man, not his novelistic interest. This opinion changes when, soon afterward, Zuckerman finds out that Seymour, seemingly so confident and healthy when they met, has died. His brother, Jerry, informs Zuckerman that the Swede's life had been destroyed in 1968 when his then sixteen-year-old daughter blew up the nearby post office to protest the Vietnam War, killing the local doctor. Amazed by this dark history lurking behind the facade of the Swede's seamless American life, Zuckerman decides to "imagine a realistic chronicle," by mixing scant biographical details of the Swede (the Gentile wife, the glove factory, the grand country house) together with formidable poetic license to fictionally render his inner life.[50] From this point on, Zuckerman disappears below the surface of the narrative, reemerging only indirectly.

Zuckerman invents a kiss between Seymour and his then eleven-year-old daughter, a scene to which Zuckerman's Seymour returns repeatedly, wondering whether it is the cause of his daughter's radicalization. The entire novel becomes a mediation on the possible causes of Merry's actions: her stutter, the incestuous kiss, her reaction to the televised self-immolation of Buddhist monks, Lyndon Johnson, Vietnam, the influence of nefarious liberalism (in Podhoretz's reading), her parents' intermarriage, her secret baptism, or simply a sign of history's inexplicability, a rejection of clear-cut cause and effect. That there is no point to the suffering of the Levovs might well be the point, borne out in the William Carlos Williams epigram "the rare occurrence of the expected," with its connotations of history's arbitrariness and unpredictability. Roth offers no definitive answer. Still, one appears to loom larger than the others, and it is the Swede's inability to question anything, but particularly his success in America, a success that in various ways is predicated upon the subordination of women and African Americans. The Swede is the embodiment of 1950s American masculinity—"Aryan" sporting hero, titan of industry, wed to a former Miss New Jersey—and his downfall comes, arguably, through his "considerable powers of suppression," his ability to ignore the signs of deep unrest within himself, his family, and his nation.[51] In unthinkingly joining the white American elite, he in effect acquiesces to its historical role in the exploitation of women and people of color. In the Swede's family Zuckerman finds an apposite emblem of consensus America and of the racial and sexual tensions that tore that fiction asunder.

American Pastoral intentionally reminds readers of Roth's older books, as Ross Posnock says, "[Here the author] revisits the historical moment of *Goodbye, Columbus*. . . . [To explore] the road not taken, the path of assimilation as sacrifice that entails identifying America as a WASP nation founded on a myth of pastoral innocence."[52] *American Pastoral* also summons to mind *Zuckerman Unbound*. As explained in chapter 4, *Zuckerman Unbound* covertly explores how Jews became white in America by using the Irish as a model. The novel is concerned that this process potentially entails the rejection of previous bonds of affiliation between blacks and Jews (forged and frayed in the civil rights movement and its aftermath): that becoming white necessitates fearing, distrusting, even despising blacks. It thus seems significant that many instances in *American Pastoral* radiate a sense of uncanny familiarity. For example, in researching Seymour's life, Zuckerman visits his old house in Newark, a recursion of the closing scene in *Zuckerman Unbound*, in which Zuckerman returns to his own home place in Caesara's limousine and is confronted by a young African American man: "a street where it didn't seem like a good idea to get out of the car. . . . Three black kids were sitting on the front steps eyeing me. . . . I explained to them, 'A friend of mine used to live here.' When I got no answer, I added, 'Back in the forties.' And then I drove away."[53] While the disconnection between the city's former Jewish and current African American residents is palpable in both novels, it gains greater effect in its repetition.

At his forty-fifth high school reunion, where he finds out about the Swede's death, Zuckerman ponders the ostentatious nostalgia for a lost Newark, dismissing it as "mythomania"; significantly, he used this same word to describe Alvin Pepler's fantasies in *Zuckerman Unbound*.[54] More worryingly, Lou Levov, the very epitome of postwar Jewish Democratic liberalism, echoes Pepler in deploring the "fall" of Newark following the 1967 riots: "A whole business is going down the drain because of that son of a bitch LeRoi Jones. . . . I built this with my hands! With my blood! They think somebody gave it to me? Who? Who gave it to me? Who gave me anything, ever? Nobody! What I have I built! With work—w-o-r-k!" The implication here is that those individuals who did the rioting (predominantly disenfranchised African Americans) did not work, evoking stereotypes of the indolent, violent black of popular American imagination—despite the fact that it is predominantly African Americans that staff the Levov glove factory. Also reappearing in *American Pastoral* are draft-resisting Catholic priests, opposed to the Vietnam War, who become symbolically linked to Zuckerman in *Zuckerman Unbound*. Dawn articulates the conservative backlash these priests often faced within the Irish American populace: "Priests are *not* great forward thinking liberals. Otherwise they don't become priests. It's just that that's not what priests are supposed to *do*." The link to the racial discourse of the earlier novel is further strengthened by the fact Dawn's brother has attended "St. Mary's," the same school as Zuckerman's bus-bound phrenological inquisitors.[55]

This seemingly innocuous moment reminds us of the once intense dislike of Jews by the Irish in America (and of the Catholic Irish by Protestant Americans).

American Pastoral's concern with race is evident through its engagement not only with Roth's own *Zuckerman Unbound*, but also with Faulkner's *Absalom, Absalom!* This chapter builds on Jessica G. Rabin's adept comparative analysis of *American Pastoral* and *Absalom, Absalom!*—though it disputes some of her conclusions. Rabin lays out the arresting parallels between Swede and Thomas Sutpen, who "utilize similar strategies in their ill-fated pursuits of social mobility and the American dream, and both men's quests are guided by careful plans to which the protagonists adhere with single minded focus," and "use symbol-laden houses and strategic marriages as pathways to mainstream respectability." Moreover, both Sutpen and Swede are related to us through "outside narrators who try to imagine and even place themselves inside the story and its main subject. . . . Events are repeated, revised, and told out of order." However, Rabin too readily links the miscegenation of Faulkner's novel to the Jewish-Irish intermarriage of Roth's and in doing so elides the latter's more pressing, though less immediately obvious, concern with twentieth-century Jewish-black relations. For Rabin, "If marrying Dawn was a mistake . . . the Swede doesn't seem to have learned from it," as his second wife also appears to be a non-Jew.[56] However, it is not intermarriage that is the problem with Swede's life, just as it is not miscegenation that is the problem with Sutpen's; rather, in both cases, it is their unwillingness to query the structures of white male privilege by which their lives are lived.

Far from being Swede's *hamartia*, Jewish-Catholic intermarriage affords an occasion for much-needed comic relief in the lead-up to the novel's deeply unsettling denouement. Lou is staunchly against his son's marriage to the Irish Catholic Dawn (he has already broken up a similar previous engagement). Yet Roth seems to play the scene for comedy, albeit of the darker sort, rather than treating it with the seriousness it receives in, for example, *Letting Go* (1962) (see chapter 1). In 1973, five years after Merry's bomb, Swede remembers how his father interviewed his future daughter-in-law back in 1950. Ever the businessman, Lou bargains with her over Jewish and Catholic ritual: "I'LL GIVE YOU CHRISTMAS EVE AND

I'LL GIVE YOU CHRISTMAS DAY AND I'LL GIVE YOU EASTER. BUT I'M NOT GIVING YOU THE STUFF WHERE THEY EAT HIM."[57] While intermarriage may have been an issue in the 1950s, it was less contentious by the 1970s and a nonissue in the 1990s, when Roth wrote the novel.[58] This subject does not seem to be the thematic core of the novel, but on the contrary an instance of Rothian misdirection. It is not Jewish-Irish animus that the novel troubles over but rather black-white rancor, with Jews now firmly entrenched in the latter camp.

When Lou questions Dawn about her father, she shrewdly notes, "You and my father aren't that different, when you come down to it." Lou retorts, "HE IS A DEVOUT CATHOLIC AND I AM A JEW. THAT'S NO SMALL DIFFERENCE." Dawn, however, recognizes that the differences are small and the similarities manifold. The major point of correspondence is the patriarchal basis of both communities. Dawn expands on her father's faith, describing him as "someone who is very caught up in the issues of right and wrong and the prohibitions against sex." Lou concurs: "I WOULDN'T DISAGREE WITH THAT." Following the feared marriage, as Dawn expected, her father, Jim Dwyer, and Lou get on exceptionally well: "Two great memories meet, and it is futile to try to contain them. They are on to something even more serious than Judaism and Catholicism—they are on to Newark and Elizabeth—and all day long nobody can contain them." Jim always begins his stories, "All immigrants down at the port." In this vision, history is whitewashed, with immigrants becoming a single, supportive, constituency, rather than a collection of warring tribes. The novel warns against this tendency of "mythomania" to reorder the past, elsewhere reminding the reader of the animosity between various new arrivals at the turn of the century, when the Swede's grandfather, "com[ing] to Newark from the old country in the 1890s . . . found work fleshing sheepskins fresh from the lime vat, the lone Jew alongside the roughest of Newark's Slav, Irish, and Italian immigrants in the Nuttman Street tannery."[59] In Jim's retrospective, Jewish-Irish enmity is drowned out by sentimentality, but, as chapter 4 argued, this revision can occur only because the Jews have joined the Irish in whiteness and are no longer competing for scarce resources at the bottom of American society. As much as intermarriage, it is this shared social assent, along with a comfortable ability to mythologize history and to control women's bodies, that dissolves the barriers between these two communities.

Swede believes he can move beyond race and ethnicity simply by leaving Newark for the countryside. In this belief, he is representative of the placidity of the 1950s, its ability to ignore the racial and gender concerns bubbling below its surface. As David Halberstam contends of that generation in general, "The middle-class living standard had been delivered in an obvious trade-off for blind acceptance of the status quo." On moving to Old Rimrock, Low tells Seymour, "This is rock-ribbed Republican New Jersey. . . . this place was Republican when Roosevelt was living. Republican during the New Deal. Think about that. . . . they didn't like Roosevelt because they didn't like the Jews and the Italians and the Irish—that's why they moved out here to begin with." Swede's unwillingness to question the president and his agenda is sharply divergent from Roth's own views during the fifties: "Eisenhower, who as president, [I] despised." Eisenhower, famed for sending federal troops into Arkansas to guard the desegregation process instigated by *Brown v. Board of Education*, is less well remembered for telling Chief Justice Earl Warren, "[Segregationists] are not bad people. . . . All they are concerned about is to see that their sweet little girls are not required to sit in schools alongside some big black bucks." The quotation reminds us that the "protection" of white women from miscegenation remained embedded both in the popular American imagination and at the highest government levels. This led to one of the most glaring defects of the civil rights legislation, according to Hannah Arendt, "for it left untouched the most outrageous law of Southern states—the law which makes mixed marriage a criminal offense."[60]

The Swede, nominally liberal, not only assents to the governing Republican ideology of the 1950s, but is also obsessed with unreconstructed American history, particularly in the American South. His fascination with the lineage of his genteel neighbor William Orcutt III is telling in this regard. Rabin sees Orcutt's family links to Thomas Jefferson—father of both the nation and numerous slave children—as a reminder of what Kurt Anderson terms America's "original sin." Jefferson symbolizes the unsettling fact that slavery was not simply a dark footnote in American history but rather a seminal chapter; to paraphrase Faulkner, "Slavery is never dead. It is not even past." However, Rabin overlooks an Orcutt connection that drags slavery and its legacy out of the past and into the twentieth century: "His grandfather was a classmate of Woodrow Wilson's. At Princeton." The historical footprint of Wilson's presidency is a contested one. On the one hand, he was a champion of the Jews, as Herman Roth elucidates in Roth's 2004 novel *The Plot against America*—"Man of dignity, President Wilson. . . . Who had the courage to appoint Louis D. Brandeis to the Supreme Court. First Jewish member ever of the Supreme Court." However, as a southerner, he was no friend to the African American community, refusing to reprimand the Ku Klux Klan; bringing segregation to Washington, DC; and allegedly describing W. T. Griffith's rabidly racist *The Birth of a Nation* (1915) as "like writing history with lightning."[61]

The Swede's passion for southern culture mirrors that of America at the time, in an era when the film adaptation of *Gone with the Wind* (1938, successfully rereleased in 1947, 1954, and 1961) was viewed by one in two Americans. For him, Old Rimrock is an outpost of the southern way of life. In his army service, Seymour has been to the South, and while he has seen "how the Negro lives," it does not dampen his enthusiasm for the place: "In South Carolina . . . it used to thrill him to think, 'This is the Old South. I am below the Mason-Dixon line. I am Down South!' Well, he couldn't commute from Down South [but he could . . .] get as far out west in New Jersey as he could while still being able to make it every day to Central Avenue in an hour."[62] This fixation runs counter to liberal sentiment in the late 1950s, when "the anger and hatred that had been smoldering . . . in the South since the enactment of *Brown v. Board of Education* had finally exploded, and . . . because of television, the whole nation . . . could watch America at war with itself."[63] From this perspective, the Swede's passion for what Jerry describes as "quaint Americana" takes on a distinctly problematic tone. For example, the Swede's glove manufacturing memorabilia includes "a copy of a ship's manifest from 1790, in which skins were landed in Boston . . . from . . . Africa." While the manifest refers to animal skins used in the leather industry, considering the location, date, and the cargo, this apparently incidental moment calls to mind the slave trade. Moreover, the Swede's house was constructed around this time, "built in 1786, its exterior walls constructed of stones collected from the fireplaces of the

Revolutionary army's former campsites in the local hills," making it possible that it—like the United States Capitol—was erected by slave labor.[64] If the house functions as a metonym for America (as the one in O'Brien's novel does for Ireland), its foundations are rotten and threaten the structural integrity of the entire edifice.

While *Goodbye, Columbus* rages against the bland and choking Eisenhower era, there is at least a tentative sense that the flood of prosperity that swept WASPs, then Irish, and then Jews out of the inner cities might also raise African American boats: "The neighborhood had changed: the old Jews like my grandparents had struggled and died and their offspring had struggled and prospered and moved further and further west towards the edge of Newark then out of it. . . . Now in fact the Negroes were making the same migration following the steps of the Jews, and those who remained in the Third Ward lived the most squalid of lives and dreamed in their fetid mattress of the piny smell of Georgia nights."[65] Certainly, there is ambivalence toward black economic advancement here: some escape poverty, but more recent arrivals from the South, part of the Great Migration of six million blacks from southern states to northern cities between 1916 and 1970, face a less certain future. However, any cautious optimism that African Americans will make this transition en masse is considerably lessened in *Zuckerman Unbound* and is stripped completely from *American Pastoral*, a depressing indictment of the failure of progressive history.

Just as Zuckerman intimates that Pepler may represent his own repressed racism in *Zuckerman Unbound*, in *American Pastoral* the novelist uses his version of the Swede to examine the prejudice that can skulk behind a liberal facade. Jerry ridicules his brother's lack of introspection and his failure to question the slogans of equality he professes: "Refusing to give offense. Blaming yourself. Tolerant respect for every position. Sure, it's 'liberal'—I know, a liberal father. But what does that mean? What is at the center of it? Always holding things together. And look where the fuck it's got you!" In this light, the Swede's remembrances of the Newark Riots deserve careful scrutiny. Zuckerman imbues the Swede with liberal America's never fully articulated exasperation with African Americans, as if civil rights advances were somehow expected to obliterate the legacy of two and a half centuries of slavery and another hundred years of Jim Crow.

The Swede's tolerant mask begins to slip as he drives into Newark to find his terrorist daughter, who, five years after the bomb, is thought to be hiding out there. Waiting in his expensive car on an economically deprived street, the Swede is greeted by an African American woman who asks him if he knows where the Salvation Army center is: "Anything beginning with sir or ending with sir usually means 'I want money,' and so he reached into his pocket, passed her some bills."[66]

This incident sends him into a reverie of the riots in which his dormant bigotry appears to erupt:

> Looting crowds crazed in the street, kids carrying off radios and lamps and television sets, men toting armfuls of clothing, women pushing baby carriages heavily loaded with cartons of liquor and cases of beer, people pushing pieces of new furniture right down the center of the street, stealing sofas, cribs, kitchen tables, stealing washers and dryers and ovens—stealing not in the shadows but out in the open. . . . The not paying for things is intoxicating. . . . The fire this time—and next? After the fire? Nothing. Nothing in Newark ever again.[67]

The Swede's thoughts channel the liberal backlash against blacks; the riots are portrayed as evidence of the inherently flawed black character, prone to violence and thievery, rather than an expression of comprehensible anger against unremitting systematic oppression. Yet here Zuckerman surfaces and plants a counterpoint amid Seymour's inner antiblack fulminations.[68] In a book with a notable lack of obvious allusions to illustrious authors (unlike practically every other Roth hero, the Swede is no bibliophile), here, amid the protagonist's stream of consciousness, is a reference to James Baldwin's *The Fire Next Time* (1963).[69]

In the first essay in his book, "Letter to my Nephew on the One Hundredth Anniversary of Emancipation," Baldwin writes, "This innocent country set you down in a ghetto in which, in fact, it intended that you should perish." Swede is representative of this pseudoinnocence, loath to interrogate the social and economic structures upon which his wealth and status are based. Baldwin continues his excoriation of white America: "The country is celebrating one hundred years of freedom one hundred years too early."[70] Recent protests by African Americans in St. Louis,

Baltimore, and other American cities bear out Baldwin's prophecy, while also demonstrating the depressing circularity of racial history in America (Baltimore's disaffected black community rioted in 1968, while St. Louis suffered America's worst racial massacre in 1917).[71] The assumption in Baldwin's time that blacks should have reached economic parity a century after abolition ignored the effects of legally enshrined segregation in the South. Similarly, anyone today making the same argument must overlook the continued, if informal, segregation of modern America, after fifty years of redlining, predatory lending practices, and employment prejudice.

American Pastoral comes to a close at a garden party thrown by the Levovs in 1973. It is an eventful day. After a tip-off, the Swede finds Merry and discovers that she has killed three more people as part of her revolutionary activities. He does not tell Dawn or his father, stoically repressing this additional horror. But the multiplying fault lines in his once faultless life now threaten to shatter it. Reeling from his encounter with Merry, Seymour overhears Dawn telling Bill Orcutt (with whom, it is further revealed, she is having an affair) that she has always hated their home: "That she was there only because her husband had 'dragged' her there when she was too young to have any idea what it would be like trying to run a huge, antiquated, dark barn of a place in which something was always leaking or rotting or in need of repair."[72] Dawn's outlook is the antithesis of Swede's; she is no longer willing to be simply an element of her husband's master plan. Her conflicting narrative is demonstrative of the hidden minority histories silenced by the drone of triumphant postwar American history, her hatred of the house symbolizing the growing consciousness of women in the 1960s and 1970s to the gendered societal structures previously so pervasive as to be near invisible. Roth's women have been criticized for their lack of depth, mere sketches rather than the layered portraiture his men receive.[73] In *American Pastoral* he attempts to turn this fault into an advantage. The little the reader sees of Dawn is through the Swede's myopic gaze. Her interiority remains unreachable, but what is certain is that it in no way equates to what the Swede presumes it to be. The recognition of this blind spot continues in the final novel in Roth's trilogy, *The Human Stain*, in which the character Faunia Farley is thought by Zuckerman (again the narrator) to be illiterate. Yet that novel comes to a close with the revelation that she had kept a diary, one Zuckerman, assiduously writing about Faunia, is frustratingly unable to access. The inaccessible diary symbolizes the unheard stories of the women that populate both the trilogy and the periods of American history it dramatizes.[74] While Roth uses metatextual tricks to note his awareness of the absent female perspective in his novel, this tactic (which bears out his general thesis of the ultimate unknowability of another person) is in danger of reproducing ideas of feminine mystery. Countering this assumption, O'Brien describes Faunia favorably: "As regards women, Philip has been mistakenly accused of not liking or understanding them. That's tosh! Take Faunia, his most recent heroine: she is generous, funny, astute, and, like many a woman, castigated for her sexual robustness."[75]

Equivalences between the Swede and Sutpen undermine the former's apparent goodness, the basis of reading Roth as a conservative reactionary, retroactively denouncing the social upheaval of the 1960s. Correspondences between the Swede and one of the characters in O'Brien's trilogy reinforce this conclusion. In a letter to Roth, O'Brien describes *American Pastoral* as "a grave book filled with the undercurrents of awfulness."[76] Arguably, some of these undercurrents originate in O'Brien's own *Down by the River.*[77] The story revolves around a thirteen-year-old girl who, having been raped and impregnated by her father, seeks an abortion in England. The novel is a fictionalization of a controversial Supreme Court case (popularly known as the "X case") and forms a devastating appraisal of Ireland's archaic abortion laws specifically and its treatment of women more generally. In the closing pages of *American Pastoral*, Seymour recalls his walks with young Merry down by the "strong trout stream where she'd fished with her father," admiring a "countryside that had been tamed over the centuries by ten American generations." However, the remembered pastoral idyll is marred by the sexual undertones of the descriptive language of the surrounding countryside: "wild pinks . . . sturdily spilling . . . simple lavender blossom . . . distended little sac . . . that she loved to pop loudly in the palm of her hand, the erect mullein whose tonguelike velvety leaves she plucked . . . pussy willows . . . walnut trees nearing fruition, only weeks from dropping the nuts whose husks when she pulled them apart would darkly stain her fingers and pleasantly stink them up with an acid pungency."[78] Such wordplay remolds this loving father-daughter nostalgia into something altogether darker, an indirect expression of Seymour's repressed malevolent sexuality and of his misused power. Moreover, it is a literary device Roth appears to borrow from O'Brien, just as in *Zuckerman Unbound* he turned to O'Brien to challenge myths of identity.

Down by the River opens with a similarly idyllic scene. James McNamara and his adolescent daughter, Mary, march through the father's land, as he measures out "his empire." He is in a jovial mood as he fishes in various bog holes, but the daughter perceptively notes that such "a spiral of gaiety . . . was sometimes short-lived and often followed by some argument." His playacting quickly transforms into "feel[ing] the stuff of her dress [and] pinching the bodice underneath it." Heather Ingman notes the symbolism: "Mary's father measures out his property before proceeding to rape his daughter, showing that he has both land and female bodies under his control." In O'Brien's novel, too, it is the fauna and encompassing landscape that symbolize the aberrant sexual impulses that underlie the scene: "It was too early, berries on the stalks showed rawly pink, little excrescences purposing to come forth in a pained fruition." Images such as an ancient bog corpse's "shrivelled little bags, which in the paper were given the Latin name of Testa" and the father "extend[ing] the metal ruler down the moist seams of the black-brown soil . . . [and spinning] the metal tape in a wide and apostolic arc, a wand, pronouncing his claim over the deserted . . . landscape riches which had lain so long, prone and concealed, waiting for the thrust of a slane" combined with his sinister fishing pantomime—"something to get his bait into . . . juicy worms which had been suffocating in his trouser pocket"—prefigure the rape. In an interview O'Brien emphasized the intentionality of her word choice: "The prologue to *Down by the River* . . . was deliberate. I wanted nature to be bursting forth, to be giving birth in order to foreshadow what would happen to that young child."[79] Roth's use of language must be seen as similarly calculated. Manuscripts of the novel show that, at some point between November 1995 and July 1996, Roth added the quoted *American Pastoral* scene, infused with sexual suggestiveness.[80] Considering that *Down by the River* was published in 1996 and that O'Brien sends Roth a copy of each of her novels, it seems possible that the Swede was shaped, at least in this important closing instance, by Roth's reading of Mary's father.

In McGreevy, James O'Meara, and James McNamara, O'Brien fashions men whose monstrous deeds are all the more appalling for being committed by humans: "It is as if up to then he had succeeded in walling up what had happened and now is seeing it, made to see it, like a man awakening from a dream and finding the monster he has dreamed, agape, beside him on the pillow."[81] The theme of incest in both *American Pastoral* and *Down by the River* is representative of more sweeping national pathologies. In O'Brien it signals the malign consequences of unchecked Irish male power, ironically the greatest threat to the family and nation it presides over. In Roth incest similarly indicates the destructive import of white male dominance. These men look outward for blame, refusing to see the dark impulses within their own minds and homes.

According to Brauner, "Most critics have argued that Roth's vision of history in *American Pastoral* is essentially deterministic." He offers a divergent take, seeing in the 1997 novel a "vision of history as dynamic, fluid, and startling." Inspired by the emotions of his forty-fifth high school reunion, Zuckerman ruminates on the seeming inevitability of the past, while hinting at the unpredictability of the future: "What is astonishing is that we, who had no idea how anything was going to turn out, now know exactly what happened. That the results are in for the class of January 1950—the unanswerable questions answered, the future revealed—is that not astonishing?" O'Brien has been similarly misconstrued. For Harte, *House of Splendid Isolation* is deterministic; history moves along a predestined path: "There is no sense that a liberating future might be fashioned from a selective use of the past."[82] I have suggested otherwise. The many voices of *American Pastoral* and *House of Splendid Isolation* signify not only the multiple histories of their nations, but also those nations' multifarious conceivable futures.

6

"We're All in Our Own Coffins"

Displacement and Intolerance in the Late Novels

In 2003 Edna O'Brien wrote to Philip Roth to tell him that she had hit the "doldrums" on her new book and was looking forward to returning to America, both for inspiration and to see him: "I often think of you but don't ring. We're all in our own coffins."[1] That book would become *The Light of Evening* (2006), in which O'Brien explores the twentieth-century migratory lives of succeeding Irish generations, a theme she returns to and expands upon in her 2015 novel, *The Little Red Chairs*. In both she not only gives voice to the Irish diaspora, but also sets it in conversation with other mass displacements. At the same time, Roth wrote (among other things) *The Plot against America* (2004) and *Nemesis* (2010), which use the ambiguous condition of the Jews in early-twentieth-century America to speak to the position of other oppressed minorities within a hostile society. Roth and O'Brien thus recast their traumatic ethnic and national histories in solidarity with ethnic and national groups that at first glance appear very different from their own.

In recent years, critics have commented on the similarity between the late writing of Roth and O'Brien. For example, Janan Ganesh praised their remarkable continued productivity: "Philip Roth wrote a sequence of immediate classics (*Sabbath's Theater*, *American Pastoral*, *The Human Stain*) that culminated in *The Plot against America* when he was seventy-one. . . . Edna O'Brien was a Bellovian eighty-five when she published *The Little Red Chairs* to general rapture two years ago."[2] For Claire Lowdon it was their ever more apparent deployment of historical circumstance that unites them: "Late Roth and late O'Brien have something in common. . . . [Both are] increasingly interested in exploring real-life events." It is James Wood, however, who best catalogs the correspondences between these writers' mature achievements: "In late work by Muriel Spark, Philip Roth, Saul Bellow, William Golding, and now Edna O'Brien, you can detect a certain impatience with formal or generic proprieties; a wild, dark humor; a fearlessness in assertion and argument; a tonic haste in storytelling, so that the usual ground-clearing and pacing and evidentiary process gets accelerated or discarded altogether, as if it were (as it so often can be) mere narrative palaver that is stopping us from talking about what really matters." What really matters for Roth and O'Brien is what Wood terms "the present age and . . . the lives of those displaced by its turbulence." In his essay "Thoughts on Late Style," Edward Said writes, "The accepted notion is that age confers a spirit of reconciliation and serenity on late works. . . . But what of artistic lateness not as harmony and resolution, but as intransigence, difficulty and contradiction?"[3] This chapter outlines how the fiction written by Roth and O'Brien over the past two decades reaches back into their own histories and into each other's literary traditions to create complex, unresolved parables of hospitality and hostility, concord and discord, and welcome and warfare in the modern world.

"The Unfolding of the Unforeseen": *The Plot against America*

Irish author John Banville describes Roth's *The Plot against America* as a "muted, post-Orwellian [dystopia]." The novel is an alternative history set in a reimagined 1940s America, where a young Philip Roth and his lower-middle-class Jewish family grapple with a society in which fascist forces have come to power (for clarity, this chapter will use the name "Roth" to refer to the author of the novel, and "Philip" for the protagonist). It opens historically in 1940, at the end of Franklin D. Roosevelt's second term, with the Roths taking a trip from Newark to see Union City, where Philip's insurance-agent father, Herman, has been offered a promotion. However, the city has a large German enclave, and as the family reconnoiters their new prospective home they happen upon a beer-garden gathering of the German American Bund (an organization set up to promote favorable views of Nazi Germany in the United States), which punctures the optimism of even the usually sanguine Herman: "Fascist bastards!" he exclaims.[4] For Philip's mother, Bess, a move away from the Jewish section of Newark to Union City would reenact her own childhood in a neighboring Irish-dominated city:

> Elizabeth, New Jersey, when my mother was being raised there in a flat over her father's grocery, was an industrial port a quarter the size of Newark, dominated by the Irish working class and their politicians and the tightly knit parish life that revolved around the town's many churches . . . Should we have the good fortune to buy and move into a house on any of the Union streets . . . not only would her status slip back to what it had been when she was growing up the daughter of a Jewish immigrant grocer in Irish Catholic Elizabeth, but worse than that, [her children] would be obliged to relive her own circumscribed youth as a neighborhood outsider.[5]

Herman turns down the promotion (and with it the chance to fulfill the American dream of home ownership), placing himself in a precarious position in the Gentile insurance company Metropolitan Life.

This economic uncertainty at a family level is mirrored by political uncertainties at a national level, as isolationist and anti-Semitic voices gain traction in the public sphere. Roth did not have to invent this xenophobic chorus to satisfy his alternative history; rather, he simply amplifies the latent suspicion of outlanders already prevalent in American society, particularly among Irish Americans. The eight-year-old Philip hears the radio tirades of "Father Coughlin, the Detroit-area priest who edited a right-wing weekly called *Social Justice* and whose anti-Semitic virulence aroused the passions of a sizable audience during the country's hard times."[6] Historian Jay P. Dolan says of Coughlin:

> By the late 1930s his anti-Semitic attacks found a receptive audience among many young unemployed Irish living on the margins of society. Tapping into their discontent, he supported them as they formed neighbourhood clubs to act as self-defense units to defend America against the threat of communism and other anti-Christian forces. Known as the Christian Front, these clubs were popular among the Irish in Boston

> and New York. Gangs of Irish youths attacked Jews in the Bronx and northern Manhattan as well as in South Boston and Roxbury. They vandalized synagogues and boycotted Jewish merchants, breaking store windows and painting anti-Semitic graffiti.[7]

Historian David Nirenberg corroborates the widespread presence of anti-Semitic views in America at this time: "American citizens, asked to name the greatest threat to the United States in a series of polls taken by the Opinion Research Corporation between 1939 and 1949, consistently chose 'the Jews' over the Japanese or the Germans, with fear peaking in June of 1944, just as the Jewish population of Europe was close to fully exterminated."[8] *The Plot against America* does not fabricate the prejudice already extant in the United States in the 1930s and 1940s, but instead provides a catalyst that transforms it into open xenophobia.

It is in his depiction of tragic aviation hero Charles Lindbergh—the first man to fly solo across the Atlantic, whose infant son was later kidnapped and killed in one of the most publicized crimes of the interwar years—that Roth significantly alters the historical record. The author does not change Lindbergh's pro-Nazi, anti-Jewish worldview, but does transmute his position in American society. In *The Plot against America* this isolationist, political-neophyte, Aryan-supremacist celebrity defeats Roosevelt to become the president of the United States. Lindbergh has made his views explicit on the campaign trail, giving a "famous radio speech before a hall full of cheering supporters in Des Moines that named among the 'most important groups who have been pressing this country towards war . . . [as] the Jewish race'"—words spoken by the real-life Lindbergh. Though told through the eyes of Philip as a child, the novel is narrated by his much older self, who reflects back on Jewish American identity before the election, when he is bewildered by a man collecting money for a Jewish national homeland in Palestine, despite the fact that "we'd already had a homeland for three generations." However, following Lindbergh's nomination, "everything changed." He decries the "dilution by foreign races" and "infiltration of inferior blood" into the American bloodstream, while warning of "the greatest danger to this country . . . [Jewish] large ownership and influence in our motion pictures, our press, our radio, and our government." The older narrator captures both the horror and the irony of these widely accepted views: "The Republican Party . . . chose as its candidate the bigot who had denounced Jews over the airwaves to a national audience as 'other peoples' employing their enormous 'influence . . . to lead our country to destruction,' rather than truthfully acknowledging us to be a small minority of citizens vastly outnumbered by our Christian countrymen . . . and surely no less loyal to the principles of American democracy than an admirer of Adolf Hitler."[9]

The Roth family hopes against hope that Lindbergh will renounce his anti-Semitism once in office and accept that "though Ireland still mattered to the Irish and Poland to the Poles and Italy to the Italians, we retained no allegiance, sentimental or otherwise, to those Old World countries that we had never been welcome in and that we had no intention of ever returning to." When he becomes president, the reticent Lindbergh does in fact mute his rhetoric, but his actions speak loudly enough. He sets in motion various programs to "Americanize" immigrant populations, with particular emphasis falling on the Jews. These initiatives divide the Roth family and the wider Jewish community. The shock of the election is described as "activat[ing] an atavistic sense of being undefended that had more to do with Kishinev and the pogroms of 1903 than with New Jersey thirty-seven years later" and causes American Jews to respond in different ways.[10] The majority go on, cautiously, with their everyday life, while some flee to Canada and others ingratiate themselves with the incoming administration.

To further his agenda, Lindbergh sets up the benignly named Office of American Absorption, which instigates the "Homestead 42" and "Just Folks" programs: "to encourage America's religious and national minorities to become further incorporated into the larger society." The office falls under the control of the secretary of the interior, the Irish American automotive baron Henry Ford. As with Coughlin, Roth does not fictionalize Ford's anti-Semitism. In 1922 Ford bought a local Michigan newspaper, the *Dearborn Independent*, and transformed it into an anti-Semitic platform, and subsequently printed the four-volume work *The International Jew: The World's Foremost Problem* (1920–22). He also organized the publication in the United States of *The Protocols of the Elders of Zion*, a virulent anti-Jewish forgery that first appeared in Russia in 1903. "Just Folks" sends urban Jewish children to rural Christian farms to instill in them the pioneering American spirit that they lack, as the program implicitly suggests. Philip's older brother, Sandy, is chosen for this social experiment. Unlike his parents, however, Sandy is not worried about the separation; rather, he relishes it and returns after two months full of praise for his host father and a deepening dislike of his own, as Philip explains: "It went without saying that Mr. Mawhinney was a Christian, a long-standing member of that great over-powering majority that fought the revolution and founded the nation and conquered the wilderness and subjugated the Indian and enslaved the Negro and emancipated the Negro and segregated the Negro . . . while my father, of course, was only a Jew."[11] While the work of the Office of American Absorption echoes on a minor scale the legislation enacted against Jews in Nazi Germany, and reviewers such as J. M. Coetzee saw parallels between its "sinister programs with reassuring titles" and George W. Bush's Patriot and Homeland Security Acts, Roth also had an inspiration much closer to the temporal setting of this novel, the Jim Crow laws.

The invented plight of the American Jews in *The Plot against America* brings a fresh perspective to the real predicament for African Americans living under southern segregation and northern bias. The novel acts as an allegory for the actual racial history of pre–civil rights era America. Literary critic Jennifer Glaser confirms this reading: "Roth uses the ambiguous whiteness of Jews in [1940s] America as a site from which to critique race and ethnicity in the United States." In the book, Sandy wins an art competition, with a poster based on one of the stamps Philip collects. He adds a black child to the work to "protect him[self] from the charge of 'copying.'" Significantly, this boy is a black facsimile of Philip: "He [the black child] stands back and to the side of the sapling and holds ready a watering can—as I [Philip] held one when I modelled for Sandy."[12] To view this doubling on a wider scale, and in the context of the alternate history Roth has created, Jews are used as a substitute for blacks, and Roth's alternate Jewish history in fact replicates African American reality.

This idea is further borne out in the immediate aftermath of the Roth family's first experience of overt bigotry, when, on a trip to Washington, DC, Herman is called a "loudmouth Jew," just as the tour guide points out "an angel of truth freeing a slave" at the Lincoln Memorial.[13] This juxtaposition of prejudice and emancipation jars and through displacement makes the reader consider anew the continuing legacy of slavery and the wider politics of exclusion in America.[14] There are also hints throughout of America's treatment of Native Americans, as when Philip's teacher tells the class of the Lenni Lenape tribe that once roamed the land where Newark now sits before the Indian Removal policies of the nineteenth century.

As restrictions on Jews increase, Philip begins to dream of escaping Jewish life. The Catholic orphanage that appears throughout Roth's fiction as a site of difference takes on an ominous centrality in *The Plot against America*: "The orphanage stood within the fenced-off grounds of St. Peter's, the parish church that oddly monopolized some three square blocks at the very heart of our unredeemable [Jewish] neighborhood." Though more threatening than in previous novels, Catholics still remain symbols of exotic sexual desire, as the young Philip experiences while waiting at the bus stop beside two nuns: "[My mind was filled with] all the questions concerning their female bodies and its lowliest functions, and all tending toward depravity. . . . I couldn't manage to be anywhere near a nun, let alone a pair of them, without a mind awash in my none-too-pure Jewish thoughts." He sits near them on the bus, "simultaneously hoping and dreading that I'd overhear them say something in Catholic." It is during this period that Philip and a school friend, Earl, begin to follow Christians home and in doing so perform escaping from the Jewish community: "We never followed anybody we thought was Jewish. They didn't interest us. Our curiosity was directed at men, the adult Christian men who worked all day in downtown Newark."[15] As part of their game, Philip's friend teaches him how to spot a Jew, and Philip begins to internalize the racial profiling inherent in American culture.

According to W. E. B. DuBois, the subservient status of African Americans created a "double consciousness" or a "sense of always looking at oneself through the eyes of others." This painful process develops in Philip, as he comes to see himself and his family not simply as Americans, or people, but as Jews: "It was then that I realized—employing all the criteria imparted to me by Earl—that my mother looked Jewish . . . unmistakably Jewish. But then so must I, who so strongly resembled her. I hadn't known." This painful realization of otherness is similar to moments found throughout African American fiction, best seen in James Weldon Johnson's *The Autobiography of an Ex-Colored Man* (1912), in which the narrator, upon being made aware of his color, also "re-views" his mother through "white" eyes: "I had thought of her in a childish way as only the most beautiful woman in the world; now I looked at her searching for defects." Roth's scene also conjures up the experience of Jews in Nazi Europe, as Roth is told by his friend Israeli author and Holocaust survivor Aharon Appelfeld: "It took years to understand how much my parents had internalized all the evil they attributed to the Jew, and, through them, I did also. A hard kernel of revulsion was planted within each of us."[16] Thus, whereas in *Portnoy's Complaint* Roth jestingly has Portnoy "pass" for Christian to impress non-Jewish girls, in *The Plot against America* the young Philip increasingly passes as an unconscious method of survival.[17]

The family divisions continue to grow, as Sandy increasingly pulls against what he terms the "ghetto" attitudes of his parents and becomes "intimidating to have around the house"—not unlike children in Nazi Germany who were deployed as spies against their parents. Sandy becomes closer to his aunt Evelyn and her new husband, Rabbi Bengelsdorf, who has endorsed the new regime and become head of the Office of American Absorption. Philip's mother, Bess, on the other hand, pushes for the family to escape to Canada, while his cousin Alvin joins the British army fighting Germany in Europe, where he is wounded and loses his leg. Philip watches on helplessly as his family is torn asunder by the strain caused by Lindbergh's regime. *The Plot against America* reverses Roth's previous work, in that the worst fears of the older generations (derided in books like *Portnoy's Complaint*) here come true. Irish writer Joseph O'Neill takes note of this reversal: "Over the course [of Roth's career], mother and father figures, troublesomely overbearing at first, appear in a progressively heroic and frankly loving light."[18] In *The Plot*, Herman and Bess, inspiration for the domineering parental figures throughout Roth's oeuvre, are given roles commensurate with their tenacity: protecting their family not from the normal travails of 1930s and 1940s American life—no easy task in itself—but rather from the terrors unleashed in a country sliding toward fascism. In doing so, the novel rewrites Roth's earliest satires of American

Jewish life, which work on the premise that Jewish experience in the New World was radically different from the Old.

As Lindbergh's presidency continues, his approval ratings soar, as he resolutely keeps America out of war in Europe and the Pacific. Yet resistance against him also gathers momentum. Walter Winchell, the infamous Jewish syndicated gossip columnist, decides to run for president, campaigning on a platform to reveal the anti-Semitism of Lindbergh's supporters, whom he nicknames the "ratzis": "Winchell, in short, was the candidate of the Jews, and himself a Jew of the coarsest type, in no way resembling the inner circle of well-bred, dignified Jewish Democrats like . . . the recently retired Supreme Court justice Louis Brandeis. [He was] a Jew of no background who embodied just about every vulgar trait that made Jews less than welcome in the better strata of American social and business society."[19] His presence in many pro-Lindbergh parts of the country sparks protests that quickly morph into anti-Jewish riots:

> From Quincy he went on to Boston, where he planned to spend three days moving through Irish Dorchester and South Boston. . . . However, on his first afternoon at South Boston's busy Perkins Square the few jeering hecklers who'd been baiting him as a Jew ever since his departing his native New York burgeoned into a mob . . . [In Detroit] in the city's biggest Jewish neighborhoods, shops were looted and windows broken, Jews trapped outdoors were set upon and beaten. . . . American history had recorded its first large-scale pogrom.[20]

Yet Winchell achieves his aim: "He had at last brought the Lindbergh grotesquery to the surface, the underside of Lindbergh's affable blandness, raw and undisguised."[21]

Liberal and even Jewish opinion is split on Winchell's campaign, with some hailing him as a champion and others denouncing him as a troublemaker. Roth's representation of Winchell flirts with James Joyce's Leopold Bloom, who himself fends off anti-Semitic attack in his mock-heroic battle with the biscuit-tin-wielding Citizen, when the *New York Times* editorial headline on Winchell's campaign reads, "At It Again": "There is nothing Walter Winchell has more talent for than himself." "At it again" are the words Bloom emits as he masturbates in his pocket overlooking

Sandymount Strand. Roth tells his biographer Claudia Roth Pierpont, it is one of the "greatest lines in literature": "'At it again'! That combination of resignation, delight, and tolerance! That's what I want it to say on my tombstone . . . 'At it again.'"[22] Here then *The Plot against America* winks at *Ulysses*; just as Bloom unveils Irish chauvinism, so Winchell uncovers American racism.

The violence peaks when Winchell is assassinated in Louisville. Fiorello La Guardia, Democratic mayor of New York, speaks at Winchell's funeral: "Our president is an admirer of Adolf Hitler and more than likely a Nazi himself—and Walter Winchell was Hitler's first American enemy and his worst American enemy. There's where our imperfect Walter was incorruptible—where it mattered. Walter is too loud, Walter talks too fast, Walter says too much, and yet, by comparison, Walter's vulgarity is something great, and Lindbergh's decorum is hideous." The choice of Louisville as the location for this murder is not random. The town was also a turning point for multitudes of slaves in antebellum America. Louisville could alternatively mean salvation or destitution for the slaves who passed through it, depending on their direction. It was a central slave-market town where troublesome slaves were sold "downriver" to the Deep South. Conversely, the town also formed the final leg of one of the Underground Railroad routes. The Ohio River, which runs through the town, separated slaveholding Kentucky from the free state of Ohio and was known by slaves as the river "Jordan," as in *Uncle Tom's Cabin* (1850): "Her first glance was at the river, which lay, like Jordan, between her and the Canaan of liberty on the other side." Roth draws attention to this era by having Winchell shot from one of the "large, austere, beautifully proportioned front windows" of the Jefferson County Courthouse, named for Thomas Jefferson, whose "commanding statue" stands outside.[23] Jefferson, signatory of the Declaration of Independence, slaveholder, and possessor of a shadow slave family, exemplifies white America's intimate and paradoxical relationship with its black counterpart.

Roth does not contrive the racism found in *The Plot against America*, or the anti-Semitic hatred, but rather portrays real, influential figures such as Ford and Coughlin, whose large followings underscore the reach and scope of their beliefs. The novel also references the profascist, anti-Semitic, isolationist group that attempted to stop American involvement in the Second World War, the America First Committee, the exclusionary mantra of which continues to reverberate through the contemporary American political sphere. Roth's novel ends with the deus ex machina disappearance of Lindbergh as he returns to Washington, DC, after flying to Louisville to reassure its (white) citizens following the Winchell assassination. In the panic that ensues, Vice President Burton K. Wheeler takes over and instigates the arrest of leading opposition figures for what he says is a global Jewish conspiracy to kidnap the president and force America into the war. The country is saved from plummeting into dictatorship by the first lady, who surprisingly denounces Wheeler's power grab and calls for fresh elections, which are subsequently won by Roosevelt. This abrupt return to the historical record attests to Wood's idea of the "tonic haste" of late storytelling, leaving the reader deeply uneasy in the face of this deceptively simple resolution. As Michael Gorra notes in his review, this "narrative machinery is the very opposite of reassuring."[24]

Such a whiplash denouement suggests that what really matters to Roth is the idea that the characteristics that can lead to fascism—suspicion of outsiders, love of strong leaders, excessive nationalism—are not uniquely European traits but rather human ones. Polish American historian Timothy Snyder writes, "We are no wiser than the Europeans who saw democracy yield to fascism, Nazism, or communism in the twentieth century." Former secretary of state Madeleine Albright concurs: "Fascism is not an exception to humanity, but part of it."[25] Roth shows us that while his particular alternate history did not take place in the United States, the component parts existed then and continue to exist today. For Michel Foucault, fascism exists not only in society but in the individual: "[Fascism is] in our heads and in our everyday behavior, the fascism that causes us to love power, to desire the very thing that dominates and exploits us."[26]

Roth uses the tool of historical displacement to make his readers consider once again the experience of American minorities, be it in the 1940s when the book is set, the 2000s when it was written, or in today's America, where many commentators have reread *The Plot* as a prescient parable of the current administration. In a 2004 *New York Times* article, "The Story behind *The Plot against America*," Roth dismissed suggestions that his book was a roman à clef for the Bush administration, while at the same time admonishing the president: "George W. Bush . . . merely reaffirmed for me the maxim that informed the writing of all these books and that makes our lives as Americans as precarious as anyone else's: all the assurances are provisional, even here in a 200-year-old democracy. We are ambushed, even as free Americans in a powerful republic armed to the teeth, by the unpredictability that is history." In denying the parallels between Bush and Lindbergh, Roth actually emphasizes them, a rhetorical figure known as paralipsis, which he describes in his retirement speech as "saying you are not going to talk about something and then, for a doubtful ironic effect, talking about it."[27]

In the aftermath of the 2016 election, Richard Brody wrote, "*The Plot against America* dramatizes the American character as vast, manifold, and inchoate; it can use its prodigious and uninhibited energy for good or for evil, and it shifts under the sudden force of unforeseeable events."[28] In an interview with Judith Thurman, Roth denies any obvious parallels between his alternative history and America's current leadership:

> It is easier to comprehend the election of an imaginary President like Charles Lindbergh than an actual President like Donald Trump. Lindbergh, despite his Nazi sympathies and racist proclivities, was a great aviation hero who had displayed tremendous physical courage and aeronautical genius in crossing the Atlantic in 1927. He had character and he had substance and, along with Henry Ford, was, worldwide, the most famous American of his day. Trump is just a con artist. The relevant book about Trump's American forebear is Herman Melville's *The Confidence-Man*, the darkly pessimistic, daringly inventive novel—Melville's last—that could just as well have been called *The Art of the Scam*.[29]

In fact, the character that Trump more closely resembles is not the taciturn President Lindbergh at all, but the loud-mouthed media personality Winchell, an outrageous New York fringe candidate who belittles his opponents with school-yard epithets. This paradox merely proves Roth's point about the impossibility of predicting what he terms the "American berserk." In *The Plot against America*, he addresses the contingency of history: "Turned wrong way round, the relentless unforeseen was what we schoolchildren studied as 'History,' harmless history, where everything unexpected in its own time is chronicled on the page as inevitable. The terror of the unforeseen is what the science of history hides, turning a disaster into an epic."[30] In the end, Roth's book is not tied to any historical place or period but rather tells a universal story of human experience, trapped as it is in the nightmare of history.

"Memories of Their Homelands": *The Light of Evening*

Fittingly, considering the novel's transoceanic settings, *The Light of Evening* flirts with texts from both sides of the Atlantic, evinced in the title—derived from W. B. Yeats—and the epigraph, taken from William Faulkner. In a letter to O'Brien, her friend Harold Bloom applied his Oedipal paradigm to the novel: "Joyce I think is your mother, in this book, and the Joyce influenced Faulkner, your father."[31] This description, however, elides the text's less conspicuous intertextual voices. *The Light of Evening* uses multiple stream-of-consciousness narratives to tell the story of the life and family of Dilly, an Irishwoman born at the turn of the last century who leaves Ireland for America during the Irish War of Independence. O'Brien's book was partially inspired by the life of her mother, Lena, who worked in Brooklyn as a maid for a "wealthy Jewish family" in the 1910s.[32] The novel opens with the now aged Dilly admitted to the hospital in Dublin, where, under the power of a pill that sets her mind racing, she half remembers and half dreams of her life in Ireland and America: "She clutched at the rungs of the bed, only to feel . . . the bed itself beginning to sink as before her eyes there galloped a riderless horse and the consultant who had examined her is wringing the neck of a dead Rhode Island cockerel." Here *The Light of Evening* echoes its near namesake, Faulkner's *Light in August* (1932), in which the Reverend Gail Hightower fixates on his grandfather, a Civil War cavalry officer, "shot from the galloping horse" for his inglorious theft of a chicken.[33] It is a sign that O'Brien takes history not as objective fact but as contested memory, borne out in the epigraph from Faulkner's *Requiem for a Nun*: "The past is never dead. It's not even past."

Dilly remembers her life as a child in County Clare and the pull of the Atlantic: "There was always so much talk about America, every young person with the itch to go." Discovering her desire to emigrate, Dilly's mother beats and berates her: "Why should America claim Ireland's sons and daughters, Ireland needing them. . . . Had I no nature to want to leave, to bolt?" Despite her mother's opposition, Dilly leaves for America on a third-class passage from Queenstown: "For nearly two weeks a world of water, pounding and sloshing. . . . A hole. People bickering and fighting and broken hearted." In Ellis Island, Dilly is overwhelmed by the mass of humanity: "I had never known, never thought, that God had created so many different races—different attires, different hairstyles and headgears, men with ringlets and small skullcaps, women the size of tubs because of the clothes, the bundles they had wrapped around themselves, and their children roped to them in case they got lost."[34] By the early 1900s, the mass Irish immigration of the nineteenth century was being superseded by the arrival of Italians and Jews. Historian John Powell delineates this change, along with the similarities between these two waves:

> The main tension in this period was between the old-line . . . culture and the newly arrived, slum-dwelling Irish. Fleeing from the terrors of the Great Irish Famine (1845–51), the Irish usually arrived poor, hating the English, and committed to their Catholic faith. By the late nineteenth century, however, Irish New Yorkers were beginning to gain access to important positions of political and financial power. . . . After the 1880s the immigrant source countries shifted from northern and western Europe to eastern and southern Europe, significantly altering the character of the city. The peoples of [this new immigration], drawn from dozens of ethnic groups from Italy and the Austro-Hungarian, Ottoman, and Russian Empires, were generally poor and by American standards of the day dressed oddly and practised strange customs.[35]

At immigration, Dilly and the other immigrants are "subject to every kind of humiliation . . . our eyelids lifted with a buttonhook . . . our bodies hosed down." To test literacy, they are given biblical passages taken from the book of Joshua, which follows the Israelites out of Egypt and into Canaan, reflecting the newly exilic condition of the migrants: "This our bread we took hot for our provisions out of our houses on the day we came forth unto you." Throughout the novel O'Brien draws subtle analogies between the Irish and other minority groups in America. Dilly observes an ill Jewish husband separated from his wife by customs officials who prepare to deport him: "[She] spat onto her fingers, wiped them on his eyelids, and then ran her damp fingers across her own, to contract the eye disease that she guessed he had. The guards were on her like dogs." This poignant scene of marital devotion is undercut by the husband's response—"her husband looking at her with such coldness, as if he did not love her"—which foreshadows Dilly's own disastrous future marriage.[36] Mocked by the border agents who find household tips inscribed on her passport and smarting at the label "domestic servant" that they stamp there, Dilly is accepted into America, joining the roughly "four million Irish who emigrated to the United States in the post-Famine era," alongside the same number of Italians and three million Jews.[37]

Dilly's cousin picks her up from the docks and brings her to her boardinghouse, telling Dilly with no trace of irony that "all the other lodgers were foreign except us." The cousin's distrust suggests that despite their own expatriate status, the Irish in America did not necessarily empathize with other migrants. Norman Mailer, in whose company O'Brien researched the New York sections of *The Light of Evening*, reproduces the extremes of this tension in the backstory of his Irish American character Roy Gallagher in *The Naked and the Dead* (1948). Gallagher, a member of an anti-Semitic gang called Christians United, fulminates against the "International Jews [who] is trying to get us to war, an' we gotta get them first, ya see the way they take away all the jobs, we let it go an' we won't have a fuggin chance." Mailer further personifies the violence that marks Jewish and Irish relations in interwar urban America: "There is a deadening regularity and a sullen vicious temper that rides underneath the surface. . . . [I]t rides the brow when the kids are beaten up in the alleyways, and the synagogues and cemeteries are fouled with language and symbol, 'The fuggin kikes' and the cross."[38]

Dilly strikes out to escape this insular notion of community, just as she has left Ireland. Leaving her cousin's house, she is accosted by a blind man who raves to her about Walt Whitman's "masts of Manhattan and tall hills of Brooklyn," a reference to his poem "Crossing Brooklyn Ferry":

> Ah, what can ever be more stately and admirable to me than mast-
> hemm'd Manhattan?
>
> . . . .
>
> What is more subtle than this which ties me to the woman or man
> that looks in my face?
> Which fuses me into you now, and pours my meaning into you?[39]

This welcoming sense of America continues as Dilly makes her way to Mass, where she listens to a visiting priest:

> The congregation, he said, was indeed lucky to be living in such a leafy borough with its clapboard houses, its stone mansions . . . but that such comforts had been obtained at a price. The past could not be blotted out. The very site on which we knelt had been stole from others. He cited the first settlers . . . [who] cheat[ed] the tribes of Lenape Indians . . . gradually acquiring the deeds of those lands so that the native tribes were driven out. . . . And what, he asked, did the newspapers and politicians do? They colluded in their corruption, in their greed . . . ensuring the cunning few reaped the fat of the land.[40]

The sermon is not, however, well received, and the zealous cleric is shunned by the comfortably established and parochial Irish community. The Irish do not want parallels drawn between their own experiences in Ireland and those of other suffering groups.[41] Moreover, the Irish are not even particularly welcoming of their own kind, as Dilly finds out when she takes up a position as a maid in the home of the McCormacks, wealthy second-generation Irish Americans, where she is mocked and belittled by the woman of the house for her "brogue" and greenhorn mannerisms.[42]

Christmas dinner at the McCormacks glimmers with flashes of Joyce's great table scenes in "The Dead" and *A Portrait of the Artist as a Young Man*. Prosperous Irish Americans attend the party, "vying with each other over memories" of the old country, while admonishing popular anti-Irish vaudeville shows (in terms similar to the ones used against J. M. Synge and O'Brien herself): "Paddy the drunken Irishman and Mrs. Paddy his half-drunken wife, fighting it out . . . Scandalous altogether. *A bloody slur on the race* . . . depicted with ape lips and grass hair." The drunken guests do not entirely reverse this stereotype, with two of them, Felim and Mr. Keating, arguing "both at opposite political poles. A flood of accusation and counter-accusation . . . Mr. Keating going too far by claiming that the men of 1916 were nothing but boy scouts." Affronted, Felim declares, "No Irishman had ever done a dishonourable deed in his life." Their farcical quarrel represents competing revisionist and nationalist perspectives of Irish history. Keating sardonically asks Felim what he ever did for Ireland, in response to which Felim bares his chest to the gathered company to show them "the knife wounds he had incurred from a bastard who simply could not stomach the fact that Christopher Columbus was not the first man to discover America, that an Irishman, Patrick McGuire, was the first to step on American soil."[43] As in *The Lonely Girl* and *Night*, O'Brien skewers such self-serving nationalist bluster. Drawing on Joyce, she makes use of a Christmas dinner party to bring together and explore the contending orthodoxies of Irish identity.

Dilly eventually leaves the McCormacks', finding work instead in the then largely Jewish garment industry. At a dance, she falls in love with an Irish American logger named Gabriel (his name again recalling "The Dead"), who sympathizes with her when she finds out her brother has been killed by British soldiers back home in Ireland in the closing days of the War of Independence.[44] They become engaged, but a rival convinces her that Gabriel has left her. Desolate, she returns to an Ireland free of British rule, but a home life more claustrophobic than when she left. Her father is ill and her mother in deep mourning for her son. Here she meets Cornelius, a well-to-do Catholic landowner and member of the new postindependence elite. He courts her by showing her around the rubble of his country house: "He told how it had had to be burned at the height of the Troubles to prevent the English from using it as a headquarters. . . . He had done it himself along with three other lads." A new house is to be built beside it, "a replica of the old"—a symbol of the continuity between the Protestant Ascendency and the new Irish Catholic elites. Dilly is unsure about Cornelius, but her mother (fearing she will return to America) prevails: "Seeing that I was in two minds, [my mother] made speech after speech of famine times and times when our forebears were evicted." Dilly's fifty-year marriage, illuminated for the reader in remembered glimpses, is tragic—a long litany of trials and humiliations brought upon her by Cornelius's fecklessness, alcoholism, and violence. Her romance with Gabriel hints tantalizingly at a road not taken: "Gabriel, the man she might have tied the knot with except that it was not meant to be. Putting memories to sleep, like putting an animal down."[45]

The narrative shifts back to the hospital, where the elderly Dilly relates to one of the ward sisters her relationship with her daughter, Eleanora. The novel then turns to Eleanora's story, her marriage to "an infidel and madman" and their move to England in the 1950s. Though she has longed to escape Ireland, there is a subconscious sense of loss bound up in her exile, evinced in her dream of another diasporic people: "In her dream life a white swan attached itself to her so that she was ferried to where she imagined to be London, standing on a bridge with its chain of lampposts, when a stranger, a robed man, held up card after card of ancient Hebrew lettering, telling her that she must discover the hidden meaning of the word." Inspired by this sundering, in England Eleanora becomes a novelist, who (not unlike O'Brien herself) is ostracized in Ireland for "books that have scandalized the country." As Ellen McWilliams suggests, *The Light of Evening* "self-consciously writes back to O'Brien's early work, in particular *The Country Girls* and the controversies that surrounded its publication." Eleanora finds it hard to separate her life from fiction: "Literature was either a route out of life or into life and she could never be certain which." Her reading of books like Charlotte Brontë's *Jane Eyre* and Gustav Flaubert's *Madame Bovary* encourages her to rethink her relationship: "What it wanted was for them to be more equal, not to be master and slave because already she was ceasing to be that slave, finding in the books she read not only riches but also rebellion."[46]

After her marriage collapses, she takes a lover named Quentin. Here *The Light of Evening* again toys with Faulkner, whose presence is particularly felt at Dilly's funeral. In the cortege, Eleanora's thoughts linger on the overflowing rivers "swishing the shores" and the swooping crows, both of which recall the Bundrens' funeral march in Faulkner's *As I Lay Dying*, with the flooded river that almost carries off Addie's coffin and the ever-present circling vultures. In a 2006 interview O'Brien said that "if there was one book she would have loved to have written herself, it would be *As*

I Lay Dying."[47] The novel thus flirts with Faulkner's epic tale of matriarchal demise and family disintegration, while at same time using autobiographical parallels between the life of Eleanora and that of O'Brien to tease the reader. As Faulkner himself maintained, it is this interaction between life and art that lies at the heart of fiction: "I'm telling the same story over and over which is myself and the world. That's all a writer ever does, he tells his biography in a thousand different terms."[48]

The Light of Evening frequently draws attention to its own textual status, underlining its reality as a mosaic of contradictory texts, a "combination of journals with diary entries, unsent letters and paper notes."[49] This structure mirrors the novel's development, which had a long and varied gestation. In 1986 O'Brien sent Roth a five-page draft of a short story titled "Friday Appointment" with the qualification, "I wrote this in the last week or so—a precursor of things to come. Not best-selling material! Ah, the brain, the brain."[50] Dreamlike, the story revolves around a series of visits to a psychiatrist. Drawing comparisons with Virginia Woolf, Roth responds, "I think with 'Friday's Appointment' you're off at a gallop in a very Dallowayish way. Wait to see where you wind up. I like the way you get in and out of you, it, her."[51]

The story was a precursor of things to come, but not for another two decades, as it was not until she was writing *The Light of Evening* that O'Brien returned to this short-story draft. In Eleanora's diary, an entry of a past visit to a psychiatrist begins with the heading "Friday's Appointment." She remembers the experience as "a sort of seizure, everything flooding in, truths, half-truths, limbs, litter." This rewrites the opening of the "Friday's Appointment" draft, where the protagonist questions the motives of her visit: "For what. Peace of mind. *Truth. Half-truth.* Confrontation maybe. . . . Jesus, I might not be able to get up. I might have lost the use of the *limbs*. What then? Panic stations. You'd have to eject me. Men or even women would have to come in here and carry me out as on a *litter*." Both scenes end in the same manner: "My legs are like stalks. However, I get up. I do stagger through the doorway. . . . The street has not changed, the sky is cold and pewter"; "I don't know how I get out of there, possibly I stagger. The street is bedlam, but a quiet in all the treetops." O'Brien's rewriting also nods to *Portnoy's Complaint*, as in Eleanora's mock description of her psychiatrist as "Herr Inquisitor," recalling Portnoy's "Herr Doctor." O'Brien was certainly reading Roth at this time, as she tells Mike Murphy, when he asks her to name her favorite authors: "A lot of people at different times, depending on my own emotional stew. Philip Roth is a good friend and I admire the way he makes language potent, the bravura in his work. I am more of a re-reader than a reader. I read Joyce all the time, I read Faulkner."[52] All four writers are concerned with the furthest reaches of the mind, the conflicted nature of memory, and the interaction between the frail self and the flawed world.

The closing pages of *The Light of Evening* resonate with "The Dead"—"the soul's magnanimity, falling timorously through the universe and timorously falling upon us"—but also chime with a more recent writer. Eleanora remembers an encounter with Dilly, free from the strain of their lifelong strife, in which she massages the twisted muscles of her mother's neck: "She began to bask in it, her expression melting, a happiness at being touched as she had never been touched in all her life, and it was as though she was the child and I had become the mother."[53] Here O'Brien's image of the reversed parent-child relationship recalls not Joyce but Roth, and in particular *Patrimony*, his haunting memoir of Herman Roth's final year, where he writes of his decrepit, helpless father: "He was kicking his legs forcefully up and down now, rather like a baby playing in the water, but there was nothing of a baby's delight in his grimly set half-face. He seemed in deadly earnest about this bath, as though, like nearly everything of late, it, too, must be undertaken with the utmost determination."[54] O'Brien cites this book as an inspiration for her own memoir, *Country Girl*, and explains its power at Roth's eightieth birthday: "His book *Patrimony*, though raw and searing, is infused with tenderness, in which ultimately, he the son, with a child's conscience, is at the mercy of the father, the Moses-like figure, sitting in judgment on what the son does and what he writes."[55] In these deeply self-reflective novels, Roth and O'Brien transfigure the autocratic, oppressive parents of their early fiction into stoic sentinels that somehow survived the upheavals of the twentieth century, the wars and depressions, the "daily trails, the inescapable crises, the stunning losses and the unavoidable conflicts engendered simply by going about one's business for" eighty years or more.[56] In doing so, they embody the vicissitudinous histories of the Irish and Jewish peoples over the last one hundred years. Yet these ambivalent parental relationships should not be read as metaphors for Roth's and O'Brien's struggle with overbearing literary influences. Rather, Roth's and O'Brien's playful encounters with a range of international writers and each other challenge outward hostilities and inward-looking national visions.

"Fleeing Catastrophes": *The Little Red Chairs*

Throughout her late fiction, O'Brien increasingly mixes blunt realism with mythic storytelling (as in *Down by the River, Wild Decembers*, and *Into the Forest*). Nowhere is this more evident than in her 2015 novel, *The Little Red Chairs*, as numerous reviewers noted: "[a] fairy tale, O'Brien's novel is both harrowing and absurdly funny"; "[a] malevolent Irish fairy tale"; [it] "marries myth and fact in a new form"; "[a] mythic resonance . . . tempered by sidelights into . . . ordinary lives." For Maureen O'Connor, "O'Brien's gritty, unsentimental portrayals of rural Irish life place the ordinary into unexpected relationship with the legendary past, sometimes ironical, but often in poignant and spiritual ways, and frequently all at once."[57] In a 1993 *New York Times* article, O'Brien discusses two Jewish authors whose work roams the porous frontier between reality and mythology:

> Each of us looks for something different in a work of fiction. Some like the ordinary so as to feel reaffirmed and "at home," and some seek the extraordinary, those daring distortions of realism that, by stunning verbal feats, hurtle the reader to fantastic latitudes. There is, however, just that element of strain when the conscious and not the unconscious is seen to be pulling the strings. Magic, as I see it, is simple eeriness, as in . . . the enchanted stories of Isaac Bashevis Singer, in which New York is often fleetingly transformed into an exile's dreamland; or in Kafka's work, in which the ordinary glides inexorably into the gilded labyrinths of nightmare.[58]

O'Brien's here deliberates at a remove upon her own fiction, which becomes ever more concerned with the "exile's dreamland" and "labyrinths of nightmare."[59] In *The Little Red Chairs*—chapter drafts of which she sent to Roth as she wrote it—O'Brien sets her writing in dialogue with

Jewish writers, while at the same time placing traumatic Irish history in conversation with that of oppressed communities in modern Europe.[60]

As *The Light of Evening* shows, throughout her almost six-decade literary career, O'Brien's fiction has always focused on migratory characters (and their descendants) and how they are treated by the society they have entered. Her stories revolve around marginalized characters who do not fit comfortably into a nation's homogenous narrative. In *The Lonely Girl* (1962), Caithleen Brady falls in love with the exotic Eugene Gaillard who—though born in Ireland—is labeled as Jewish and foreign by her xenophobic family. In *Girls in Their Married Bliss* (1964), Caithleen and Baba are themselves made "foreign" when they emigrate to London. O'Brien continues to trace the lives of the Irish in England, as evinced in her 2011 story "Shovel Kings" that follows the broken Irishmen that rebuilt postwar Britain. Minor characters found throughout her 1990s and 2000s novels attest to her interest in the "new Irish," whose experiences of expatriation so often mirror those of the Irish diaspora. In *The Little Red Chairs* O'Brien continues to expand this range. As her compatriot Banville says of her work, "The most striking aspect of [her] . . . stories, aside from the consistent mastery with which they are executed, is their diversity. This writer knows many worlds, and delineates them for us with . . . accuracy, wry fondness, and, always, compassion."[61]

The Little Red Chairs tells the story of Dr. Vladimir Dragan, a healer of uncertain origins, who arrives in a sleepy West of Ireland village.[62] His alien character fascinates the locals, particularly the women. One of them, the protagonist, Fidelma, visits Dragan, searching for a cure for her childlessness, but instead ends up beginning an affair with him. His past is not what it seems, however, as it is revealed that he is hiding in Sligo from the consequences of his role in Yugoslav war crimes in the early 1990s. Fidelma suffers grievously at the hands of Dragan's lieutenants who have come to Ireland to capture their erstwhile leader for the promise of a substantial reward. In the aftermath of this attack, Fidelma leaves the village, rejected by the townspeople for the affair she has conducted and, implicitly, for the rape and maiming she has endured. She makes her way to Britain, where she finds work and affiliation with the traumatized migrants who have escaped war and poverty in the rest of the world to take up their invisible positions in London's underclass. The final section takes place many years later, with Fidelma at The Hague to hear the rabid nationalist testimony of the captured Dragan before the International Court of Justice.

The fairy-tale nature of the story serves to heighten the often shocking realism. As Ganesh points out: "There is always humour competing with pain for space on the page. Reading the book, it takes a while to realize it will not be a rural comedy."[63] The shifts from one register to another—be it fable to material world or comedy to horror—are intentionally jarring for the reader. O'Brien's greatest juxtaposition here, however, is that of a peaceful post–Good Friday Agreement Ireland with a war-torn and devastated Balkans. The rape and mutilation of Fidelma transplant terror from Europe's eastern edge to its western shore. In doing so, the book jolts the reader from his or her comfort zone, forcing a reconsideration of a conflict—and the migration crisis it engendered—largely ignored in Ireland and the West.

The novel opens with submerged warnings of the dangers of unrestrained nationalism and the violence it can generate. Dragan enters the West of Ireland village of Cloonoila by a parkland river walk: "The current, swift and dangerous, surges with a manic glee, chunks of wood and logs of ice borne along in its trail. In the small sidings where water is trapped, stones, blue, black and purple, shine up out of the river bed, perfectly smoothed and rounded and it is as though seeing a clutch of good-sized eggs." These trapped stones contain ripples of Yeats's own examination of violent fanaticism: "Enchanted to a stone / To trouble the living stream."[64]

Dragan arrives in the village pub and engages the bartender in conversation, drawing parallels between their two homelands, through religious devotion, warrior spirit, and a supposed shared Celtic origin: "the links between Ireland and the Balkans were indisputable." The bartender draws more contemporary links, speaking of the 1923 Ballyseedy Massacre in which Irish Free State troops killed eight Irregular prisoners by tying them to a land mine and then detonating it. This atrocity echoes the horrors committed in Yugoslavia's own civil war. Dragan is a consummate storyteller, regaling the villagers with supposed tales of his life: "Soon he had them in the palm of his hand, as he pieced events together, adding a few flourishes." Such small reflexive moments remind the reader of the subjective and selective characteristics of all narratives, be they novels or history tracts. Significantly, the villagers cannot decide on a single interpretation of Dragan and his stories. When he leaves, some regard him as a welcome addition to the locale, while others denounce him as a Rasputin figure, a "newcomer one of those sharks, speculating for gas or oil." The scene's realism then seems to dissipate as it closes: "Spirals of smoke drifted through the room, the faces curious, jovial, dreamy, wreathed in smoke, like beings captured in some strange nocturnal bacchanalia."[65] In this the novel calls to mind not only Singer's short fiction but also Yeats's *Stories of Red Hanrahan*, a book the villagers later present to Dragan.

In addition to Yeats, the book makes allusion to a range of other seminal Irish writers. A mention of Synge's *The Playboy of the Western World* refigures Dragan as a reverse Christy Mahon, a stranger who has committed far greater violence than he lets on at the outset. Joyce is present too, in the description of Dragan and his new friend, the local priest, who are referred to as the "two gallants," suggesting both represent predatory ideologies. The priest is not the only religious convinced by Dragan. A resident nun undergoes his therapy and feels "a wildness such as she had not known since her youth, out in the fields when she pissed against trees, the way men did, pissed unashamedly." Living adjacent to these remnants of Ireland's past are members of its future, whom O'Brien sketches in a conversation between the workers in the town hotel: "They are a mixed group, Irish, Burmese, Italian, Spanish, Czech, Slovakian, Polish. In their small bedrooms . . . are the emblems of their own land, maybe a flag, or a map . . . [or] family photographs." These Irish, old and new, stand at the back porch of the hotel at the end of the night, telling tales about of their pasts. The broken English of the migrants—reflecting the severed worlds they have left behind—fits harmoniously with the Hiberno-English of the natives. For Claire Messud, such group scenes "serve as a Greek chorus. In each assembly, individuals recount their stories of loss and lamentation, a recurring reminder of the suffering behind so much contemporary 'globalisation.'"[66]

The story of Dragan's former life as a Serbian nationalist leader during the Yugoslav Wars is revealed to the reader in a dream in which he envisions a bomb exploding in the besieged city of Sarajevo: "surreal, limbs, arms, heads, torsos, all mixed in with potatoes, cabbages, onions and kohlrabi." An old army comrade known as K.—echoes of Kafka's *The Trial* (1925) and *The Castle* (1926)—appears to him and derisively dismantles Dragan's life's work: "Ethnic purification must happen, even if in the end you ruled over a land of ghosts." The villagers have not yet, however, found out about Dragan's past or about his affair with Fidelma. She becomes pregnant and tries to hide it from her husband: "She was inventing stories to tell him, all of them lacking credence, like a child making sandcastles that the incoming tide will sweep away." When the affair becomes known, Dragan is outed as a war criminal, for which he is arrested and imprisoned in The Hague. The once enthralled villagers immediately revise their views of the stranger (just as in *The Playboy of the Western World*). His landlady remembers their gardening together and his saying "what good clay it was and little did she guess that in his own country were all those thousands of remains, with worms eating them." His capture becomes national and international news, with footage of Sarajevo played repeatedly on television: "They saw the shells of burned houses, a gutted landscape, marching frightening families, a boy on a pile of rags calling a name and behind the bars of a concentration camp, skeletal young men staring out in gaunt and hopeless despair."[67] The violence is not containable to the Balkans, however, and spills over into Ireland in different ways.

Elements of the Yugoslav Wars find their way to Ireland, first in the memories of Mujo, one of the migrants working at the local hotel, who has suffered horrifically in Bosnia under Dragan's military rule. As a Muslim, Mujo was compelled by the Serbian forces to cannibalize his countrymen, torture that actually took place during the 1990s, according to journalist Ed Vulliamy, who documents this case along with those of "thousands of non-Serbs [who were] . . . killed, tortured, raped."[68] That war arrives more directly on Irish shores in the ferocious rape of Fidelma by Dragan's former henchmen, now out to betray their leader for financial reward. Fidelma is left to die in a barbarous scene, with rats who have "come to sup and she can hear their tongues lapping up the pools of warm blood." O'Brien's fiction has always excelled at describing the collapse into madness induced by trauma and the subsequent silencing of victims in Irish society. When asked to tell the Gardai what happened to her, Fidelma can only stutter, "I don't have the . . . vocabulary," before adding, "They butchered me" and giving an "insane little laugh." The village uses Fidelma's affair as a convenient excuse to blame her for what has happened, as Irish novelist Éilís Ní Dhuibhne points out: "As often in O'Brien's novels, an Irish country community punishes and expels a woman who has broken the tribal rules of sexual behavior"—a process of control seen also in *The Lonely Girls* and *House of Splendid Isolation*.[69] Fidelma flees Ireland and makes her way to London. Her past, however, follows her there: "In all my dreams there is blood. It gushes from the pump in Cloonoila, where several women stand to fill their buckets. They are blaming me for the terrible curse that I have brought on their village. It oozes from mattresses and spills onto the floor, out into the hall and the pathway that leads from . . . [the] apartment to the entrance gate."[70]

The savagery of the rape scene might have left O'Brien open to charges of sensationalism, had not such horror actually taken place, though not in Ireland. The testimony that has emerged from Bosnia in the 1990s makes for nightmarish reading. O'Brien displaces these atrocities and in doing so focuses a Western audience to consider the Yugoslav Wars in something more than simply abstract terms. In doing so, she unmasks Western complacency toward distant brutality. O'Brien's book argues that in a global world, the seemingly pastoral first world cannot close its eyes to the discord of the third; she does so by reminding us that one does not have to look back very far in the history of Ireland or Europe to find similar eras of destruction. O'Brien thus employs artistic displacement to explore human displacement.

Fidelma finds work as a cleaner in a City of London bank, along with others fleeing impoverishment, stasis, and violence in Africa and the Middle East. One of Fidelma's coworkers shares her belief that someday a bank executive will fall in love with her and rescue her from her predicament: "It was not a dream as she said, it was a fairy tale and in their predicament, fairy tales were crucial." O'Brien shows how people and societies under great stress often turn to fantasy as a coping mechanism. Fairy tales provide a space to escape domineering reality, but also a place to potentially overturn social structures and imagine nonoppressive societal models. O'Brien gives insight into the lives of the lowest-paid and least-respected workers in Western society and the extreme strain that they bear to survive: "In the mornings, after they had clocked out, they ran, recklessly, they ran as if they were fleeing catastrophes. The fear that governed their whole lives was now compressed into this urgency to catch a bus or a train to allow a husband or a mother or a cousin to go to work." O'Brien questions which is the fairy tale, the myths and legends of these supposedly backward exiles or the comforting lies of global capitalism. Returning home from work, the exhausted Fidelma sees "figures drenched and half-blind, bumping into one another. Cars, buses and cyclists all on a collision course, fighting for their footing and the tour buses, coming in twos and threes, send lashing of water in all directions, so that pedestrians are even more wrathful, their patience spent, in their urgency to get to where they belong or half belong."[71] This image presents urban poverty as a Hobbesian experience of all against all.

Fidelma finds solace in attending a center for migrant support, where one worker, a survivor of the Yugoslav Wars, ruefully tells her, "There was a time when Sarajevo was thought to be the biggest issue in the world." In this remark lies the world's ability to quickly forget about atrocities not taking place in the immediate present and a hint at the many tragedies that have occurred and been consigned to oblivion. Fidelma listens to the stories of other survivors, such as a Bosnian refugee: "From the bus we are put on boxcars on a train . . . and we are brought to camp. . . . Many bodies packed in there on top of each other, one toilet for hundreds and all the time shouting, guards shouting and people beaten, begging until they had no breath." Oghowen has fled Nigeria because as a twin she is anathema to Igbo culture. She has undergone genital mutilation, during which she recalls being asked if she wanted to be blindfolded: "But I say no, I want to see. Even then I know God's plan for me is to live my life with my eyes open." A girl from Senegal speaks of the more routine migrant misery of not being able to return to see her dying mother, in response to which another woman becomes indignant: "She goes ballistic, asking why they have to listen to this crap when they are there to talk politics and not somebody's mother. [The discussion leader] interrupts and very gently points out that everything in this world is political." Here is one of O'Brien's great themes, the dismantling of boundaries between the political and the personal. A conduit for these stories, Fidelma is, as O'Connor describes, "an Everywoman travelling alone through the fallen world, looking for salvation, she is the occasion for other stories told by representatives of the world's migrant, dispossessed population."[72] All of these characters bear witness and speak testimony to the inequalities and degradations of contemporary society.

This theme of story sharing and empathy building clashes with another idea, voiced by one of O'Brien's characters: "We don't know others. They are an enigma. We can't know them especially those we are most intimate with, because habit blurs us and blinds us to the truth." O'Brien's writing allows us catch a brief vision of other realities made at once strange and familiar. In the novel's final section, Fidelma achieves stability in her London life, before traveling to The Hague to find closure at Dragan's war criminal trial. In his defense, Dragan tells the court, "I am not a nationalist . . . but I think races should not mix," and "If I am crazy then patriotism itself is crazy." The book suggests that hybrid identities, ideas, and cultures can ameliorate the brutalities of patriotism. *The Little Red Chairs* closes with a haunting migrant rendition of *A Midsummer Night's Dream*, chaotic and cacophonous until "one woman stepped forward and took command, her voice rich and supple, a wine-dark sea filled with the drowned memories of love and belonging. Soon other followed, until at last thirty-five tongues, as one, joined in a soaring, transcendent Magnificat. *Home. Home. Home.* It rose and swelled, it reached to the rafters and through the walls, out onto the lit street, to countryside with its mash and meadow, by graveyard and sheep fold, through dumbstruck forests, to the lonely savannahs and reeking slums, over seas and beyond, to endless, longed-for destinations."[73] This conclusion suggests that new communities can be, painstakingly, forged out of the fragments of war and exile. Moreover, it encourages us to reflect on our own shell-shocked past as a way to understand the scarred present of those now arriving in Europe.

Reviewing *The Little Red Chairs*, Joyce Carol Oates draws attention to the continuities and breakages with O'Brien's earlier work: "[The book] is both an exploration of those themes of Irish provincial life from the perspective of girls and women for which she has become acclaimed and a radical departure, a work of alternate history in which the devastation of a war-torn Central European country intrudes upon . . . rural Ireland." Clair Wills concurs: "O'Brien's audacious counter-history of Karadžiæ dissolves any comfortable boundary between the nice people of Sligo and the nasty history of Serbia. . . . Contemporary Ireland is implicated in the fratricidal violence of Eastern Europe." Alternate historical fiction—much like Shakespeare's drama—draws from a range of epochs. Beyond the Balkan Wars and Irish history, the book makes most obvious allusion to the Second World War and the Holocaust. The Serbian Dragan's genocide of Bosnian Muslims echoes the Nazi destruction of European Jews, as references to concentration camps and atrocities bear out. O'Brien appears to have had such correspondences in mind when she created Dragan, as she tells journalist Philip Maughan, "Think of the Nazis in South America, mowing their lawns and washing their cars. I find it unbelievable that a man (and they usually are men) could live with the thousands of deaths and not go mad. That I cannot understand. Can you?"[74] Though the conclusion of *The Little Red Chairs* makes allusion to "The Dead," Oates aptly describes the book as "a new unsettling fabulist vision that suggests Kafka more than Joyce."

"A Malicious Absurdity of Nature": *Nemesis*

Kafka hovers too over Philip Roth's *Nemesis*, in which humanity is prey to the whims of unseen and unstoppable malignant forces. Critic Morris Dickstein describes Roth's voice in the book as "pitched like Kafka's between humor and anguish."[75] Kafka's presence is felt throughout Roth's work, most particularly in his 1973 short story "I Always Wanted You to Admire My Fasting; or, Looking for Kafka," this seminal modernist writer does not die in 1924, but instead emigrates to America in time to become the unassuming Yiddish teacher of an unenthusiastic nine-year-old student named Philip, who uses his literary skills to nickname his tutor "Kishka," or intestines. *Nemesis* is similarly a work of alternate history on a minor scale. It presents an imagined 1940s New Jersey polio epidemic, the response to which simultaneously evokes the ghettoes of the Third Reich and the fearmongering of America's twenty-first-century political discourse.

Nemesis is set in Newark in the closing years of the Second World War and follows the protagonist, Bucky Cantor, a young summer sports coach whose shortsightedness frustratingly prevents him from joining his friends fighting in Europe. Bucky faces a more invidious scourge, however, when polio afflicts his city, including the parks he supervises. Arnie Mesnikoff, one of Bucky's students who falls victim to the disease, narrates the story from a thirty-year vantage point. For reviewer Leah Hager Cohen, "The narration is evocative of a Greek chorus, at once communal and all-knowing. More than a hundred pages go by before we discover who is telling the story." Bucky battles helplessly against the disease, as more and more of his students become infected. His peace of mind and dreams of the future are crushed by the seemingly ceaseless flow of events. As in *The Little Red Chairs*, realism and mythical narration sit side by side. Christopher Tayler describes it as "part sinewy historical fiction, part inscrutable moral fable," while Victoria Aarons says the Newark of the novel "[exists] in a kind of mythic time and place as well, out of real time. . . . Indeed, Newark would seem here to be isolated, cut off, and dispossessed." Stripped of extraneous elements (or in Wood's terms discarding "ground clearing" and the "evidentiary process"), the book speaks not only of a polio epidemic but of something more primal. As Bucky reminds himself, "What's important is not to infect the children with the germ of fear." In this way, *Nemesis* can be read as a companion piece to *The Plot against America*. Whereas the latter transfers characteristics of the Holocaust to America on a sweeping magnitude—a fascistic president, resettlement programs for Jews—the former takes a subtler approach. Nicholas Lezard says of it, "Here we have something similar to the counter-factual approach in his magnificently terrifying *The Plot against America*. Only the threat is more ambiguous, more existential."[76] *Nemesis* sees the ominously faceless Board of Health quarantine the Jewish quarter of Newark to contain the epidemic. The book then explores the fear caused among the entrapped inhabitants and the hatred it stirs up among the ethnic Irish and Italians who share the city.

Allusions to the Holocaust reverberate throughout *Nemesis*, with telling metaphorical language conspicuous in the burning summer heat: "The sun was so hot that you would think that rather than darkening your bare skin it would bleach you of all color before cremating you on the spot." Bucky cannot help picturing his fighter pilot brother: "Invariably he wound up instead imagining Alan roasting like a piece of meat in his box."

Eric Sundquist posits the novel as a rewriting of Roth's friend Aharon Appelfeld's 1978 novel, *Badenheim 1939*: "Echoes . . . reappear in *Nemesis*, where the multiplying deaths, rampaging fear and guilt, xenophobia, and anger at God . . . take on the coloring of the far greater plague ravaging the Jews of Europe."[77] Appelfeld's novel is set in a spa town in Austria, where a nefarious and seemingly disembodied Sanitation Department instigates ever-greater limitations and degradations on the wealthy visiting Jewish population, who do everything they can to ignore the increasingly evident nature of their fate as the town slides dreamily from a place of mirth to a transit depot for the death camps. For the inhabitants, "It still seemed that some other time from some other place, had invaded the town and was silently establishing itself."[78] This aptly captures the temporal and spatial dislocation at the heart of Roth's novel and its creation of alternate history.

The simmering ethnic tensions of midcentury urban America spill over in the novel, as a group of Italian toughs arrive on Bucky's playground to intimidate the young Jews: "We're spreading polio. We don't want to leave you people out." Bucky faces them down, but the fear spread by the disease enflames relations not only between Jews and Catholics but within the Jewish community as well: "Fear unmans us. Fear degrades us." And the Jews themselves are not immune to the bigotry they suffer from other ethnic groups: "There was talk . . . of keeping the colored cleaning women from coming to the neighbourhood for fear they carried the polio germs up from the slums." There are undertones too not just of the massacre of Jews in Europe, but the atrocities committed in America itself, as when Bucky remarks on the trees at the summer camp he absconds to when he can no longer take the relentless march of the polio in Newark: "[They] bore black slashes encircling their bark as though they'd been scarred by a whip."[79] As in *The Plot against America*, Roth suggests that racial slaughter did take place in America, just not to Jews. Slavery is subtly alluded to here, and the fact that Bucky's discovery takes place in "Indian Hill, a camp for Jewish boys and girls," may hint at the genocidal clearing of Native Americans as well. This alternate history intimates many possible analogies: the Jews in Europe, African Americans and Native Americans in the United States in the nineteenth and twentieth centuries, and immigrants in the United in the twenty-first.

Bucky faces down the derision of his Newark boss, Mr. O'Gara, to quit his summertime playground position for a less harrowing job at the Indian Hill summer camp. He does not escape polio, though, and in fact seems to regard his abandoning of the city children for the supposed safety of the countryside as deserving of a sort of cosmic punishment, duly delivered when he finds out he is a carrier for the disease and has perhaps infected many of his charges, before being struck down himself. When protagonist Arnie meets Bucky many years later, he finds an embittered and devastated man: "[The polio] seemed to him not a malicious absurdity of nature but a great crime of his own." Arnie tells us, "I was constantly torn by the thought it could so easily have been the other way," reminding the reader of the unpredictable nature of life that is at the core not only of alterative historical fiction but of history itself.[80]

Nemesis and *The Little Red Chairs* are both timeless and timely. They force the reconsideration of abstract and unfamiliar wars and atrocities by embedding traces of them in familiar landscapes. Though very different in many ways, these late novels share the invention of understated alternate histories to warn against the rise of exclusionary nationalism and racial scapegoating in Europe and America. In their most recent fiction, Roth and O'Brien use lessons from Irish and Jewish history to map out the crossroads where humanity and fate collide. At Roth's eightieth birthday, O'Brien spoke of the change in her friend's late work: "There was still the ebullience that he likes, the precision that he insists on, the occasional blasphemy, and something else deeper, a gravity, a Greek gravity—the artist's dissection of fate and hope in a world, our world, gone berserk."[81] This living eulogy might just as readily be applied to O'Brien. Both authors have bequeathed to us deeply empathic parables that impel readers to see the world through the eyes of others and to face the world with eyes open. By refusing to ignore the dark corners of our cultures and of our minds, these writers warn us against the dangerous self and national mythologizing that feed the flames of racism, isolationism, and fascism.

Conclusion

"A Beautiful, Baffling Synthesis"

At the beginning of 2018, Edna O'Brien was awarded the PEN/Nabokov Award for Achievement in International Literature in New York for breaking down "social and sexual barriers for women in Ireland and beyond." Chief among the special guests was Philip Roth, who himself received the award in 2006. In her speech O'Brien emphasized "the importance of literature, the necessity for literature in our unhinged times. . . . It is essential to us as breathing. It brings other worlds, other pain, other grief, other humanity, other paradoxes to us through language. . . . Language lives longer than people and therefore its permanence is vital. It moves us from one generation to the next; it's immortal."[1] What emerges from this study are two authors obsessed less with sex and themselves—as trivializing commentary has long had it—than with power and nations. Yet to fully gauge Philip Roth's and Edna O'Brien's textual engagement with their respective nations, it is necessary to look beyond those entities. This aim is best achieved through a flirtatious, transnational intertextuality: querying the defined bounds of the text allows us question the demarcated boundaries of the nation-state. Further, intertextuality acts as a metaphor for a country's inevitable, if often denied, heterogeneity; it fulfills a similar role in symbolizing history's multiperspectival nature. Through its hybridity, playfulness, and amorphous constitution, the fiction of Roth and O'Brien seeps into and helps erode the false conceptual monoliths of linear history and racial uniformity that remain dangerously central to each of their nations' sense of itself.

The first chapter surveyed the lives and literary careers of Roth and O'Brien over the past fifty years and mapped out each author's uncanny relationship with the culture and literature of the other. Chapter 2 looked at how in Ireland "the Jew" was shorthand for the foreign, the strange, the perverse, and the suspect, while the Irish Catholic performed a similar role in the Jewish American imagination. O'Brien has confronted community and national orthodoxies through relationships that cross perceived ethnic frontiers, but also through textual dialogues with Bernard Malamud, F. Scott Fitzgerald, and Roth. Roth did likewise by flirting with the works of Joyce and Mary McCarthy. The third chapter reread O'Brien's 1970s fiction in light of the Troubles and found that, like unexploded ordnance, her politics lies hidden beneath the surface. Critical reconsiderations of Roth's supposedly frivolous fiction—discovering a deep ambivalence toward post-1967 Israeli triumphalism, though one long obscured by sex—aided this revision of O'Brien's work. For both, their refusal to take sides is at once bolstered and undermined by the knowledge that such objectivity is ultimately illusory.

Chapter 4 reassessed Roth's 1980s work in the context of race, charting the shifting conceptions of American Otherness on a scale that ranged from black to Jewish to Irish to white. His reading of O'Brien's memoir *Mother Ireland* provided Roth with the means of questioning mythologizing nationalism *and* its benighted offspring, white ethnic pride, by pointing to the peculiarity of Irish xenophobia being blindly emulated by American Jews who not so long before suffered from it. The fifth chapter was interested in this very process, in which formerly tyrannized groups reprise that tyranny on others. This knowledge tempers Roth's and O'Brien's 1990s trilogies, which are both concerned with history and with breaking cycles of violence through destabilizing the moral purity of victims and heroes. Once again, we saw Roth turning to O'Brien, here for the literary means to address a nation facing a new millennium with many of its greatest social predicaments sitting stubbornly on its shoulders rather than at its back. Both authors flirted with Faulkner, ironically gaining enlightenment from his "dark knowledge."

According to Hannah Arendt, the Jewish political theorist (and close friend of Mary McCarthy), "there can be no patriotism without permanent opposition"—a point Roth recapitulates when he suggests that "disillusionment is a way of caring for your country too."[2] Roth and O'Brien are each, in their different ways, patriots, sharing a deep love of their respective nations. Yet this love is expressed not through paean but through the perpetual exposure of national faults. To dismiss Roth and O'Brien as mere vendors of reheated autobiography, to argue that their books had no impact on their nations, is to ignore the response they incurred from figures such as Charles Haughey, Archbishop McQuaid, and Richard Nixon. Throughout their long careers, Roth and O'Brien have challenged the transcendental signifiers of their states and societies, and their books provide us with the tools to do the same. As such, these texts are not mere barometers of changing times but are themselves catalysts of change.

Paraphrasing Joyce, Malamud once wrote, "I am the foolish writer of a wise book." Art transcends the inevitably limited vision of its creator, because it sets internal contradictions in motion. Roth agrees with this sentiment, arguing, "The intelligence of even the most intelligent novelist is often debased, or at the least distorted, when it's isolated from the novel that embodies it. Detached from the fiction, a novelist's wisdom can even be just so much talk." Alvin Pepler, that fantastical Roth creation, describes his own fictional characters, Gayle Gibraltar and Marty Paté, as having the "secret of perpetual motion."[3] The novels of Roth and O'Brien exemplify this secret. Their texts are built like the intricate timepieces so lovingly described by the young protagonist of Roth's *Everyman* as he works in his father's jewelry store: they continue to tick in our minds, their arguments and counterarguments reverberating, long after we have closed the cover. Like artificial intelligence, these novels are designed—through the intratextual interchange between characters and the intertextual flirtations between texts—to outthink their creators, powered endlessly by new readers and new responses.

For Roth and O'Brien, recognizing inner conflict is key to understanding our conflict-ridden world. O'Brien is now honored by the state she for so long attacked—made Saoi, or wise one, of the Aosdána. Meanwhile, Roth received, among other distinctions, the National Humanities Medal from Barack Obama (the title of this conclusion comes from O'Brien's "A Poem for Barack," inspired by Obama's 2008 election). These honors have not blunted their ability to produce the "permanent opposition" essential in a democratic state. Rather, their most recent fictions have taken on even weightier targets, as chapter 6 showed. O'Brien's *The Little Red Chairs* presciently tells the story of the world's displaced people, with subtle analogies drawn between these refugees and the Irish diaspora and between the Holocaust and genocide in the former Yugoslavia. Concordantly, Roth's *Nemesis* tells a timeless fable of a dreamed-up 1940s Newark polio epidemic, while simultaneously evoking the ghettoes of the Third Reich and the xenophobic fearmongering of America's current political discourse.

Fine Meshwork has uncovered flirtatious interactions between the fictions of Roth and O'Brien, yet they are merely a glimpse of the broader links now becoming apparent between Jewish and Irish writing. These crosscurrents show no sign of abating almost a century after Joyce's *Ulysses*. The generations that have followed Roth and O'Brien are just as entranced by literatures that fall outside their own immediate experience and just as eager to home in on correspondences and contradistinctions between Jewish and Irish life. Joseph O'Neill has written about Roth at length, analyzing the interaction between "the self and the other," the "self and community," and "the quarrel that subsumes every other: *Self v. Self. v. Self v. Self.*" John Banville is alternately dismayed and amazed by Roth's late work, scolding *Everyman* for its "slackness," yet professing himself moved by the "almost Shakespearian" graveyard scenes.[4] Kevin Barry has ruefully admitted, "For a long time I was trying to be the next great Jewish-American writer. You know, the next Saul Bellow or Philip Roth. This was in Cork city, Ireland. As a pale ginger twenty-something."[5] Despite this, flirtatious traces of Jewish literature remain in Barry's fiction, as in his dystopian alternative history, *City of Bohane* (2011), which appears to draw sustenance from Roth's *The Plot against America* (2004). Roddy Doyle, too, has professed his love of this particular Roth novel, along with the more obvious impact of E. L. Doctorow on his work.[6]

On the Jewish side, writers far beyond the old triumvirate of Roth, Bellow, and Malamud continue to be engrossed by O'Brien's fiction. Erica Jong saw her as a model for upsetting "the male literary establishment," which lacked the "consciousness to take" in the work of female writers.[7] The Jewish African American writer Walter Mosley became alive to the "riches" of his hybrid identity through O'Brien's mentorship at City College of New York.[8] Lev Raphael, one of the first writers to openly address the intersection between Jewish and gay (male) identity in *Dancing on Tisha B'av* (1990), admires *Wild Decembers* (1999), while second-generation Holocaust survivor and novelist Melvin Jules Bukiet writes appreciatively of *Down by the River*, praising it as an "angry, grief-stricken book."[9]

Irish and Jewish writers continue then to turn to one another to find new modes of expression. Joshua Cohen's review of Eimear McBride's *A Girl Is a Half-Formed Thing* (2014) is exemplary of this persistent mutual need for both groups to push against the bounds of the language. Cohen, whose work has been hailed as a mixture of Roth and Flann O'Brien, praises McBride (herself acclaimed as the next O'Brien and compared favorably with Faulkner), particularly her ability to "subject the outer language the world expects of us to the inner syntaxes that are natural to our minds. . . . [I]n doing so [she] refuses to equate universal experience with universal expression."[10] Emerging Irish author Ruth Gilligan's novel *Nine Folds Makes a Paper Swan* (2016) tells the story of Jewish-Irish love and migration across three generations, while drawing on the self-reflexive fiction of Nicole Krauss—herself captivated by Roth, Bellow, and Joyce. Thus, as a new generation of Jewish authors faces a post-Roth era, Ireland remains in their peripheral vision. Equally, today's Irish authors not only look back to their own literary tradition, but also continue to gaze beyond their shores. Together, these writers reject ideologies of purity. Together their writing weaves a piece of fine meshwork.

Notes

. . .

Bibliography

. . .

Index

Notes

Introduction

1. Edna O'Brien, "A Conversation with Edna O'Brien," 42; Debra B. Shostak, *Philip Roth: Countertexts, Counterlives*, 60.

2. Maureen O'Connor, "Edna O'Brien, Irish Dandy," 44. Lisa Colletta and O'Connor elaborate on this point in their introduction to *Wild Colonial Girl: Essays on Edna O'Brien*: "O'Brien's deliberate, stylized, highly theatrical stagings of the self . . . make porous the boundaries between author and text . . . [and] also reveal the constructed nature of national and sexual identities, as well as the unacknowledged interdependence of those structures" (5).

3. Philip Roth, "The Ghosts of Roth," 130. Wilde made a strong impression on Roth's work. His play-like novel *Deception* (1991)—a title O'Brien loved—held the prepublication title of "The Importance of Being Clever." For more on Roth and Wilde, see Steven Sampson's *Corpus Rothi: Tome 2, le Philip Roth tardif, de pastorale américaine à némésis*.

4. Timothy Parrish, "Introduction: Roth at Mid-Career," 2; Oscar Wilde, "The Decay of Lying," 87.

5. Oscar Wilde, "The Truth of Masks," 126; Philip Roth, "On *The Breast*," 65; O'Brien, "A Conversation with Edna O'Brien," 46. She puts it more forcefully in a draft of her 1972 article "The Artist and His Country": "The poet's business is to rage, rage and storm. He has two criteria, truth and excellence. He should not be in the pay of the politician or the bureaucrats or the middle man. Art is not for appeasing people, it is for expanding them." O'Brien, "The Artist and His Country," galleys, Edna O'Brien Papers, Emory University, Atlanta (hereafter cited as O'Brien Papers, Emory). Reprinted by permission of Peters Fraser & Dunlop (www.petersfraserdunlop.com) on behalf of Edna O'Brien.

6. James Joyce, *Ulysses*, 2.264.

7. Marjorie Howes, introduction to *The Cambridge Companion to W. B. Yeats*, 1; Parrish, "Introduction: Roth at Mid-Career," 2; Amanda Greenwood, *Edna O'Brien*, 103.

8. Philip Roth, *The Counterlife*, 310; Sigmund Freud, *Civilization and Its Discontents*, 88; Werner Sollors, *The Invention of Ethnicity*, xi.

9. Philip Roth, foreword to *A Fanatic Heart: Selected Stories*, by Edna O'Brien, ix; Kathryn Laing, Sinéad Mooney, and Maureen O'Connor, eds., introduction to *Edna O'Brien: New Critical Perspectives*, 4.

10. Philip Roth, *The Professor of Desire*, 200.

11. Philip Roth, "Lovely, lovely, lovely . . . ," undated letter to Edna O'Brien, box 10, folder 45, O'Brien Papers, Emory. Copyright © by Philip Roth, used by permission of The Wylie Agency LLC.

12. Edna O'Brien, "Manhattan Medley," 136. They also recall O'Keeffe's husband, the Jewish American modernist photographer Alfred Stieglitz, and the hundreds of photographs he took of his wife between 1917 and 1937.

13. Roth quoted in O'Brien, "A Conversation with Edna O'Brien," 43; James Joyce, "Ireland, Island of Saints and Sages," 165–66.

14. Harold Bloom, *A Map of Misreading*, 19. Bloom befriended Roth and O'Brien, and he included Roth's novels *Portnoy's Complaint, My Life as a Man, Zuckerman Bound, The Counterlife, Patrimony,* and *Operation Shylock* as well as O'Brien's short-story anthology *A Fanatic Heart* in his *Western Canon.* He is also one of many Jewish American literary academics very much taken with Irish literature: "Isn't it interesting that all of the drama post-Shakespeare that really matters in English . . . is written by the Irish. . . . Congreve is Irish, Sheridan is Irish, and of course Oscar and Shaw and O'Casey and Synge." Harold Bloom, "Harold Bloom Interview."

15. Asha Varadharajan, "The Unsettling Legacy of Harold Bloom's *Anxiety of Influence*," 462; Patricia Coughlan, "Irish Literature: Feminist Perspectives," 13.

16. Moynagh Sullivan draws attention to an example of this oversight in Declan Kiberd's *Inventing Ireland* (1995) in which Mary Lavin and Kate O'Brien appear in a chapter promisingly titled "Mothers and Daughters," yet which fails to suggest any "intergenerational model of influence" based on this relationship. For Michael Cronin, Edna O'Brien fares worse; he points out she is "relegated" to one of the book's interchapters. Moynagh Sullivan, "Raising the Veil: Mystery, Myth, and Melancholia in Irish Studies," 257; Michael Cronin, *Impure Thoughts: Sexuality, Catholicism and Literature in Twentieth Century Ireland*, 180.

17. Michel Foucault, introduction to *Anti-Oedipus: Capitalism and Schizophrenia*, by Gilles Deleuze and Félix Guattari, xii–xiii; Gilles Deleuze and Félix Guattari, *A Thousand Plateaus: Capitalism and Schizophrenia*, 51.

18. Adam Phillips, *On Flirtation*, xvii, xix.

19. Julia Kristeva, "Word, Dialogue, and Novel," 37. As if to prove her point while making it, Kristeva's words echo Wilde's aphorism (itself a reworking of Ralph Waldo Emerson): "Most people are other people. Their thoughts are someone else's opinions, their lives a mimicry, their passions a quotation." Oscar Wilde, "De Profundis," 612.

20. Roland Barthes, *The Pleasure of the Text*, 5–6 (emphasis in the original), 17.

21. Roth and O'Brien first met in 1969 in New York, and the pair became friends when he moved to London in the mid-1970s. They remained so until his death, as O'Brien

eloquently outlines in her recent memoir, *Country Girl*. Roth described O'Brien as "the most gifted woman now writing fiction in English," a high compliment from a man who did not bestow praise lightly—he told his dying mentor Malamud not to publish his final unfinished novel, believing it substandard. O'Brien has reciprocated this tribute in her 2013 short-story anthology, *The Love Object*, which she dedicated to Roth. See chapter 1 for more details on their lives and friendship.

22. Edna O'Brien to Philip Roth, June 14, 1987, and Aug. 20, 1993, MS, box 26, folder 10, Philip Roth Papers, Library of Congress, Washington, DC (hereafter cited as Roth Papers, LC). Reprinted by permission of Peters Fraser & Dunlop (www.petersfraserdunlop.com) on behalf of Edna O'Brien.

23. O'Brien to Roth, Jan. 14, 1993, MS, box 26, folder 10, Roth Papers, LC. Reprinted by permission of Peters Fraser & Dunlop (www.petersfraserdunlop.com) on behalf of Edna O'Brien.

24. Edna O'Brien, "Roth@80: The Life and Work of Philip Roth." Incidentally, I was this "zealous student." Having posited that O'Brien had inspired Caesara in an email interview in October 2012, I received no answer to this particular question. It was pleasant then to receive this indirect answer at Roth's birthday lecture in 2013, which I was lucky enough to attend.

25. Philip Roth, "On *The Great American Novel*," 75.

26. Philip Roth, "A Conversation with Philip Roth," 98.

27. Roth's characters, for example, frequently appeal to the spirit of Yeats. Yet these moments of high-mindedness are often comically undercut: Mickey Sabbath of *Sabbath's Theater* (1994) finds a copy of "Meru" while furtively rummaging in the underwear drawer of his friend's daughter; the girlfriend of Alexander Portnoy—of *Portnoy's Complaint*—mocks his pompous attempts to seduce her with a rendition of "Leda and the Swan"; and David Kepesh of *The Dying Animal* recites "Sailing to Byzantium" as he masturbates to the memories of his lost love.

28. Philip Roth, "Art of Fiction, No. 84."

29. Philip Roth, *The Ghost Writer*, 110.

30. Roth, "Art of Fiction."

31. In his short story "'I Always Wanted You to Admire My Fasting'; or, Looking at Kafka," Roth performs another literary resurrection, this time of Franz Kafka, whom he fictionalizes as coming to America—rather than dying in Europe—only to become the uninspiring Hebrew teacher of a young boy named Philip.

32. Derek Parker Royal, "Roth, Literary Influence, and Postmodernism," 23. O'Brien wrote to Roth to commend *The Professor of Desire* as "very dark and very funny." O'Brien to Roth, n.d. [1978], box 26, folder 10, Roth Papers, LC. Reprinted by permission of Peters Fraser & Dunlop (www.petersfraserdunlop.com) on behalf of Edna O'Brien.

33. *Academic Dictionaries and Encyclopaedias*, s.v. "flirt," def. 2.2; Philip Roth, *Zuckerman Unbound*, 275.

34. Edna O'Brien, *Country Girl: A Memoir*, 223; Michael Patrick Gillespie, "Edna O'Brien and the Lives of James Joyce," 82–83.

35. In *The Facts: A Novelist's Autobiography* (1988), Roth notes how the genre of memoir must—through its selectivity, emphasis, and elisions—always necessarily be a type of fiction: "It isn't that you subordinate your ideas to the force of the facts in autobiography but that you construct a sequence of stories to bind up the facts with a persuasive *hypothesis* that unravels your history's meaning" (8 [emphasis in the original]).

36. Gerard Genette, "Introduction to the Paratext," 261.

37. O'Brien asserts this very point in an essay called "Clothes": "Clothes are at once a disguise, a symbol of power and of course a means of seduction." N.d., box 57, folder 6, O'Brien Papers, Emory. Reprinted by permission of Peters Fraser & Dunlop (www.petersfraserdunlop.com) on behalf of Edna O'Brien.

38. Genette uses the term "coquetry" in his exposition of the paratext, echoing Barthes's use of the term "flirtatious" in reference to the relationship between text and reader ("Introduction to the Paratext," 269). Jacket enticements or blurbs form a more peripheral (and more playful) portion of the peritext. The blurb can provide a patent and positive link between authors: one author reads another and is so moved that she or he provides a recommendation. In this regard, Roth has provided blurbs for *The Country Girls Trilogy* (1987), *Country Girl: A Memoir*, and *The Little Red Chairs* (2015). However, blurbs can also hint at the power dynamics of the publishing industry, which in many ways remains a gender-biased world. In 1907 B. W. Huebsch (the first American publisher of Joyce and D. H. Lawrence) described the recently coined term "blurb" as "the picture of a damsel—languishing, heroic, or coquettish—anyhow, a damsel on the jacket of every novel." As an author who has suffered much critical flak over the covers of her books, which—against O'Brien's wishes—have repeatedly featured damsels of one sort or another, Huebsch's comment reminds us how books are marketed. Until recently, O'Brien's work was blurbed mostly by male writers, such as John Updike and Harold Pinter, hinting that publishers (and presumed audiences) thought her work required male validation. Allan A. Metcalf, *Predicting New Words: The Secrets of Their Success*, 38.

39. Philip Roth, afterword to *The Book of Laughter and Forgetting*, by Milan Kundera, 230.

40. Jiøí Weil was one such author, suffering under both Hitler and Stalin, and Roth's preface to the 1989 edition of his novel *Life with a Star* (1964) conjures up an alternative reality for Roth, had his grandparents not left Europe for America, a theme he would build on to great effect in alternative historical novel, *The Plot against America* (2004).

41. Roth's interest in Synge would find full expression in *The Humbling* (2009), in which he reimagined the relationship between Pegeen Mike and Christy Mahon in the twenty-first century. Aware of his affection for Synge, O'Brien sent Roth a copy of the Irishman's collected works as a thank-you for his preface to *A Fanatic Heart*.

42. Edna O'Brien, preface to *The Playboy of the Western World*, by J. M. Synge, x; Arthur Griffith, editorial, *United Irishman*, Oct. 17, 1903; Arthur Griffith, editorial, *United Irishman*, Apr. 23, 1904.

43. It is not the first time that O'Brien has lingered on this relationship. Her anthology *Some Irish Loving* (1979) gathers together a selection of Irish prose, poetry, and letters through the shared theme of love. It is dedicated "to Synge for his letters to Maire O'Neill because these to me are the last word in truth, in beauty and in love."

44. Greenwood, *Edna O'Brien*, 96.

45. Shostak, *Philip Roth: Countertexts, Counterlives*, 3.

46. My paper was briefly mentioned in Charles McGrath's coverage of Roth@80 for the *New York Times*, giving global coverage to Roth's Irish models: "There were papers on . . . Roth and Joyce, Roth and Yeats, Roth and Synge." Charles McGrath, "Goodbye, Newark, the Place Roth Never Left," *New York Times*, Mar. 20, 2013.

47. O'Brien, "Roth@80."

48. Declan Kiberd, *Inventing Ireland: The Literature of a Modern Nation*, 1; Elizabeth Butler Cullingford, *Ireland's Others: Gender and Ethnicity in Irish Literature and Popular Culture*, 7; Scarlett Baron, *"Strandentwining Cable": Joyce, Flaubert, and Intertextuality*, 3.

49. As one example of many, in the third volume John Wilson Foster patronizingly contrasts Joyce's implicitly "pure" exile with "later departures of Edna O'Brien," which seem to him "less like aesthetic compulsion than the simple search for a bigger pond to swim in . . . the attraction of a livelier publishing market and a potentially larger readership." He gives little consideration to the fact O'Brien first moved to London with her intensely controlling husband or to the fact (borne out by Richard Ellmann's study of Joyce) that Joyce's own exile was as calculating as Wilson Foster imagines O'Brien's to have been. John Wilson Foster, "Irish Fiction, 1965–1990," 941.

50. Shostak, *Philip Roth: Countertexts, Counterlives*, 7.

51. Paul Gilroy, *The Black Atlantic: Modernity and Double Consciousness*, 19.

52. Scholarship in Jewish/Irish literary and cultural connections in Ireland and America continues to grow, with Abby Bender's *Israelites in Erin: Exodus, Revolution, and the Irish Revival* (2015) and M. Alison Kibler's *Censoring Racial Ridicule: Irish, Jewish, and African American Struggles over Race and Representation, 1890–1930* (2015).

53. Stephen Watt, *"Something Dreadful and Grand": American Literature and the Irish-Jewish Unconscious*, ix; George Bornstein, *The Colors of Zion: Blacks, Jews, and Irish from 1845 to 1945*, 2.

54. Watt, *"Something Dreadful and Grand,"* ix.

55. In the Irish context, the poem's title has connotations of the 1916 Easter Rising and the Irish Proclamation of Independence; in the Jewish context, it alludes to the length of David Ben-Gurion's famously hurried declaration of Israel's independence in 1948.

56. Quoted in Kiberd, *Inventing Ireland*, 35.

57. Standing as counternarrative to these correspondences, however, is Abby Bender's timely reminder that such historical parallels are not fixed, stable, phenomena, but are "often paradoxical": "in their mutual insistence on exceptionalism (two chosen peoples, alike in their uniqueness) and . . . in the contradictoriness of the comparisons: the Irish, like the Jews, were a territorial nation; the Irish, like the Jews, were a diasporic nation; . . . the Irish, like the Israelites, resisted the temptations of cultural assimilating . . . the Irish, like the Israelites, could not resist." The most striking sign that analogies between groups (like groups themselves) are conceptual constructs is the shift over the twentieth century from comparisons between Irish and Jewish nationalisms to comparisons between Irish nationalism (particularly its post-1969 manifestation) and Palestinian nationalism. Bender, *Israelites in Erin*, 1–2.

58. Bernard Malamud to O'Brien, Oct. 15, 1962, box 7, folder 49, O'Brien Papers, Emory, copyright © 1962 by Bernard Malamud, permission granted by Russell & Volkening as agents for the author's estate; Bellow to O'Brien, Dec. 31, 1965, in *Saul Bellow: Letters*, 254; Joseph Heller to O'Brien, May 15, 1962, box 5, folder 34, O'Brien Papers, Emory; O'Brien, *Country Girl: A Memoir*, 255–56; Isaac B. Singer to O'Brien, Oct. 30, 1971, box 11, folder 46, O'Brien Papers, Emory; Erica Jong to O'Brien, Aug. 5, 1977, box 6, folder 19, O'Brien Papers, Emory, copyright © Erica Jong, 2018, all rights reserved.

59. Edna O'Brien, email interview with the author, Oct. 2, 2012, reprinted by permission of Peters Fraser & Dunlop (www.petersfraserdunlop.com) on behalf of Edna O'Brien; O'Brien to Roth, Aug. 20, 1999, Roth Papers, LC. Reprinted by permission of Peters Fraser & Dunlop (www.petersfraserdunlop.com) on behalf of Edna O'Brien.

1. "The Body Contains the Life Story Just as Much as the Brain"

1. Philip Roth, "A Confusion of Realms," 192; Julia Carlson, *Banned in Ireland: Censorship and the Irish Writer*, 73.

2. Irish author Joseph O'Neill warns the danger of this task: "Nowadays, to attempt a critical investigation of the work of Philip Roth is to put oneself in the humiliating position of the flatfoot arriving at the scene of the crime only to discover that, yet again, he's been beaten to it by the private eye, the eye who has not just cracked the case but got the girl and held the press conference. The eye is, of course, Roth himself. Any idea that might occur to us about the author has already occurred to him, only more intelligently." Joseph O'Neill, "Roth v. Roth v. Roth."

3. Henry Roth, *Call It Sleep*, 85.

4. As David is drawn to the rosary beads, so was Henry Roth to Irish literature, as Alfred Kazin delineates in his introduction to *Call It Sleep*: "Anyone who recognizes Joyce's immense achievement in *Ulysses* will recognize his influence of Roth" (xiv). Philip Roth pays homage to his namesake in his novel *Exit Ghost* (2007).

5. Saul Bellow, *The Adventures of Augie March*, 38; James T. Farrell, *Studs Lonigan*, 78, 54. As Stephen Watt says of this latter scene: "What the fourteen-year-old Studs

sees in the mirror, whether he likes it or not, is an Irish Jew, a highly ironic motif that runs throughout the trilogy given Studs's and his father's recourse to ethnic slurs." Watt, *"Something Dreadful and Grand,"* 37.

6. E. L. Doctorow, *Ragtime*, 14. Doctorow taught creative writing alongside Edna O'Brien at New York University in the 1990s.

7. Bornstein, *Colors of Zion*, 18. "There were no less than twenty-two movies over the period from 1921–1930 that featured Irish-Jewish relationships from romances and marriages, to shared vacations, to business partnerships, to the strangest of all, interfaith, interethnic adoptions—almost always a Jewish parent or parents adopting an Irish infant or child," according to Meagher. Timothy Meagher, "Abie's Irish Enemy: Irish and Jews, Social and Political Realities and Media Representations," 47.

8. Roth, *The Facts*, 20. Roth originally named this book "A Counterbook: Portrait of the Artist as a Young American."

9. Claudia Roth Pierpont, *Roth Unbound*, 19; Meagher, "Abie's Irish Enemy," 47.

10. Pierpont, *Roth Unbound*, 19.

11. Philip Roth, *Patrimony: A True Story*, 203, 132.

12. Pierpont, *Roth Unbound*, 19. Roth's mother, Bess, had grown up in the neighboring city of Elizabeth, "the only Jewish child in an Irish Catholic milieu." Driving through it many years later, Roth's father, Herman, deliberated upon its changing demographics: "Used to be only Jews around this part of Elizabeth when Mother and I moved from Newark. Not when she was growing up here, of course. It was Irishmen, then. All Catholics. No more. Spanish, Koran, Chinese, black. The face of American is changing every day." Pierpont, *Roth Unbound*, 17; Roth, *Patrimony: A True Story*, 85.

13. Pierpont, *Roth Unbound*, 327. Watt argues that it was as much through theater, film, and radio as through youthful street battles and intermarriage that the Irish and Jews encountered one another in the New World: "Positioning Jewish characters in familiar narratives, particularly ones in which Irish characters had previously occupied central roles . . . encouraged audiences to reconceive or transcode the foreign as the familiar, the exotic as the domestic: in short, the Jewish as the Irish and, later, vice versa." Watt, *"Something Dreadful and Grand,"* 73.

14. Philip Roth, "The Conversion of the Jews," 141.

15. Roth, *The Facts*, 37; Philip Roth, *Indignation*, 15.

16. William Karel and Livia Manera, *Philip Roth: Unmasked*.

17. Roth later said of Bucknell: "I've always been intrigued by the Other. Why did I go to a nice Christian college? Not because I wanted to be like then, but because I wanted to find out what they were like." Quoted in David Plante, "Conversations with Philip: Diary of a Friendship," 159.

18. Pierpont, *Roth Unbound*, 25. Roth was far from the only Jewish American intellectual interested in Irish literature. Some of the great voices in the field are Jewish American, such as Joyce scholars Richard Ellmann, Maud Ellmann, and Harry Levin. George

Bornstein reflects on this attraction in his own academic career: "I gravitated towards a thesis on Ireland's greatest poet W. B. Yeats, partly because of the beauty of his poetry but also because as an Irishman he was the closest thing to a fellow-outsider available to me as a choice." George Bornstein, "Hybrid Identities," 136. In the field of history too, Jewish American academics were drawn to Irish subjects. The half Jewish Arthur Schlesinger Sr. made his academic mark studying the nineteenth-century flood of Irish immigration to America, before applying its lessons to subsequent Jewish waves. His son, Arthur M. Schlesinger Jr., friends with both Roth and O'Brien, was the court historian for the first Irish American president, John F. Kennedy.

19. Pierpont, *Roth Unbound*, 27.

20. Philip Roth, "Writers Have a Third Eye"; Bellow to Roth, Dec. 26, 1957, in *Saul Bellow: Letters*, ed. Taylor, 162.

21. Philip Roth, "Writing about Jews," 206.

22. Quoted in Pierpont, *Roth Unbound*, 14. At the same time, Roth published the essay "Writing about Jews," in which he spoke of the shared concerns of writers, but also of the need for cultural specificity: "Someone else might have written a story embodying the same themes, and similar events perhaps, and had at its center Negroes or Irishmen; for me there was no choice." Roth, "Writing about Jews," 213.

23. Roth and Ellmann would became good friends, and the academic would help the author secure permission to quote Yeats's poem "Leda and the Swan" in *Portnoy's Complaint* (1969) from the Yeats estate. Ellmann also befriended O'Brien and after a visit to Oxford wrote to tell her that she caused a sensation at the college.

24. Saul Bellow, "The Swamp of Prosperity"; James T. Farrell to Roth, Aug. 12, 1963, box 9, folder 7, Philip Roth Papers, Library of Congress, Washington, DC (hereafter cited as Roth Papers, LC).

25. Roth, *Patrimony: A True Story*, 90.

26. William Styron, "Dear Dirty Dublin: My Joycean Trek with Philip Roth," *New York Times*, June 9, 1991. Less amused at the time, Styron described the city in a letter to a friend: "Dublin is a crashing horror of a city, with the shade of Joyce inundated by a spinechilling amalgam of S. S. Kresge, hamburgers, Pat Boone, atrocious food, ugly girls, malnourished men, and the Son of Tarzan at the corner flickers." Styron, *Selected Letters of William Styron*, 301.

27. Philip Roth, *Letting Go*, 77, 104, 186.

28. Roth, *Letting Go*, 185.

29. Roth, *Letting Go*, 374.

30. Philip Roth, "In Response to Those Who Have Asked Me: 'How Did You Come to Write That Book Anyway?,'" 29.

31. Though not well received in America, *Letting Go* was praised by Bruce Williamson in the *Irish Times*: "Well-plotted, full of character and characters, and with dialogue that's a treat, this is a professional novel of a high order, with overtones of Dreiser and

Erskine Caldwell." Williamson, "Don't Judge a Judge by His Cover," *Irish Times*, Nov. 11, 1967, 10.

32. Philip Roth, "Imagining Jews," 274.

33. Roth, "On *The Great American Novel*," 89. As O'Brien says of *Portnoy's Complaint*: "It was a repellent book, a burst of rage and romp, filled with fetid indiscretions and blasphemies. . . . The author protested . . . his only crime was to have observed the human granules all around him and hone it into fiction." Edna O'Brien, "The Great Comic Literary Conquistador," Faber and Faber website, Oct. 22, 2018.

34. Edna O'Brien, email interview with the author, Oct. 2, 2012. Reprinted by permission of Peters Fraser & Dunlop (www.petersfraserdunlop.com) on behalf of Edna O'Brien.

35. Philip Roth, "On Satirizing Presidents," 47. Roth drew further parallels to Irish writing, suggesting that literature at its best should enrage and goad a response: "Reading *Crime and Punishment* is a disgusting, if not repellent, experience, among other things; so is watching *Othello*. Even Synge's *Playboy of the Western World*, which just toys with the theme of parricide, has been known to cause audiences in Ireland to riot" (54).

36. Quoted in Pierpont, *Roth Unbound*, 73–74.

37. Philip Roth, *My Life as a Man*, 263.

38. Quoted in Frances Kiernan, *Seeing Mary Plain: A Life of Mary McCarthy*, 724. McCarthy speaks about her own childhood ambivalence toward Jews in *Memories of a Catholic Girlhood* (1957): "I myself had a curious attitude, I now realize, in which the crudest anti-Semitism . . . mingled with infatuation and with genuine tolerance and detachment." McCarthy's own life captures the intertwined nature of the Irish and Jewish American communities. She had a Jewish grandmother, whose religion brought on "dark innuendoes dropped by my father's people"; she would later have an affair with Jewish intellectual Philip Rahv. Kiernan, *Seeing Mary Plain*, 179, 178.

39. Velichka Ivanova, introduction to *Philip Roth and World Literature: Transatlantic Perspectives and Uneasy Passages*, 2; Roth, *The Professor of Desire*, 190.

40. Kepesh notes that one of the prostitutes he observes must have been born "before the publication of *Ulysses*." Roth, *The Professor of Desire*, 28.

41. In 1978 Bloom, O'Brien, and Roth all signed a demand to release the Kenyan novelist Ngugi wa Thiong'o: "We find it difficult to believe that Professor Ngugi, whose works are read and admired internationally, constitutes a threat to Kenya's security. We urge the Kenyan government to release him as soon as possible." James Baldwin et al., "Release Ngugi," *New York Review of Books*, June 15, 1978.

42. O'Brien, "Roth@80."

43. O'Brien, "Roth@80."

44. Unlike Roth, Pinter loved to visit Ireland, having begun his acting career touring the country in the early 1950s. In one of his early 1980s letters to O'Brien, he sends her his poem "The Islands of Aran Seen from the Moher Cliffs": "The three whales of Aran /

Humped in the sun's teeth, / Make a tough bargain with the cuff / And statement of the sea." Harold Pinter, *Collected Poems and Prose*, 13.

45. Lonoff is frequently thought to be a combination of Roth's elder peers Bernard Malamud and Saul Bellow, though Irish author John Banville sees him as "based on Henry Roth." Banville, "Z/R," review of *Exit Ghost*, by Philip Roth, *London Review of Books*, Oct. 4, 2007.

46. Roth, *The Ghost Writer*, 71.

47. Philip Roth, *The Anatomy Lesson*, 310. The irony here is that Zuckerman still struggles to escape the crushing weight of family, heritage, and propriety.

48. Alan Cooper, *Philip Roth and the Jews*, 3; Philip Roth, "An Exchange with Mary McCarthy," 113.

49. Philip Roth, "Conversation with Philip Roth," 263. This point is repeated in his novel *Deception* (1990): "I never hear about Northern Ireland when I'm out on the town here. I hear only about Nazi Israel and Fascist America" (82).

50. Ross Posnock, *Philip Roth's Rude Truth: The Art of Immaturity*, 125.

51. Roth, *The Facts*, 5. Mark Shechner says of the letter from Zuckerman to Roth that closes the novel that the fictional character acts as the author's "devil's advocate and . . . psychotherapist digging out of the book's bland narrative the grievances and terrors and culpabilities—the sly motives, the slick defenses, the punishing self-delusions—that the main text leaves unspoken." Shechner, *Up Society's Ass, Copper: Rereading Philip Roth*, 20.

52. Roth, *The Facts*, 7, 172.

53. His body failing, Herman Roth becomes incontinent: "The shit was everywhere." As he cleans his father, Roth promises not to tell anyone, yet even as the son apologizes, the writer betrays, as we the readers see Herman's distress in clinical detail. Roth acknowledges this point in the closing lines of the book: "In keeping with the unseemliness of my profession, I had been writing [this book] all the while he was ill and dying." Roth, *Patrimony: A True Story*, 172, 190.

54. O'Brien wrote to Roth to say, "Thank you again for *Operation Shylock* and for the 'fireworks' within it. . . . I enjoyed it a lot, full of leaps and bounds and your unique humour and full of daring too." O'Brien to Roth, June 9, 1993, box 26, folder 10, Roth Papers, LC. Reprinted by permission of Peters Fraser & Dunlop (www.petersfraserdunlop.com) on behalf of Edna O'Brien.

55. Elaine B. Safer, "The Double, Comic Irony, and Postmodernism in Philip Roth's *Operation Shylock*," 113.

56. Quoted in David Remnick, "Into the Clear: Philip Roth," 107; Pierpont, *Roth Unbound*, 178.

57. Bloom writes about their relationship and its breakdown in her memoir, *Leaving a Doll's House* (1996).

58. O'Brien, "Roth@80" (ellipses in the original).

59. Philip Roth, *Sabbath's Theater*, 164. In a folder marked "Sabbath's Theater: Notes and Background Material," Roth has written "*Ginger Man*" and "*Ulysses*," suggesting J. P. Dunleavey and Joyce might have been on his mind while constructing Sabbath.

60. The novel also contains one of Roth's great Irish American characters, communist steelworker Johnny O'Day, who mentors the young, idealistic Ira.

61. Coleman passes first by joining a Jewish boxing club and fighting against "Italians from Barringer, Poles from East Side, Irish from Central," again invoking those early Newark ethnic rivalries that Herman Roth tells his son about in *Patrimony*. Philip Roth, *The Human Stain*, 103.

62. Roth, *The Human Stain*, 242.

63. O'Brien wrote to Roth before publication: "Thinking of you a lot today as Houghton Mifflin sent me a proof of 'Shoptalk.' I read the Primo Levi and thought it a gem." O'Brien to Roth, n.d. (1999), box 26, folder 10, Roth Papers, LC. Reprinted by permission of Peters Fraser & Dunlop (www.petersfraserdunlop.com) on behalf of Edna O'Brien.

64. John Banville, "Grave Thoughts from a Master," review of *Everyman*, by Philip Roth, *Guardian*, Apr. 29, 2006; Philip Roth, *Everyman*, 10; Roth, *Exit Ghost*, 6.

65. John Banville, review of *Indignation*, by Philip Roth, *Financial Times*, Sept. 20, 2008. This accolade joins almost every major American and international commendation, such as the PEN/Faulkner Awards, Pulitzer Prize, Franz Kafka Prize, PEN/Nabokov Award, PEN/Saul Bellow Award, and the Man Booker International Prize.

66. Carmen Callil, "Why I Quit the Man Booker," *Guardian*, May 21, 2011; Elaine Showalter, "Many Feminists Find Philip Roth's Work Off-Putting"; Zadie Smith, "Zadie Smith Remembers Philip Roth," *New Yorker*, May 23, 2018.

67. David Simon, creator of *The Wire*, is currently adapting *The Plot against America* as a miniseries.

68. Philip Roth, "No Longer Writing, Philip Roth Still Has Plenty to Say," interview by Charles McGrath, *New York Times*, Jan. 16, 2018.

69. Nicole Krauss, "The Presence of Philip Roth," *New Yorker*, May 24, 2018; Kevin Powers, "Philip Roth," *RTÉ Radio One*, May 24, 2018; quoted in Suzanne Lynch, "Philip Roth: 'The Greatest American Novelist of Our Postwar world,'" *Irish Times*, May 24, 2018.

70. Norman Manea, "Nearby and Together: Norman Manea on His Friend Philip Roth," *Los Angeles Review of Books*, June 23, 2018.

71. O'Brien, "Great Comic Literary Conquistador." O'Brien elaborates: "[Roth's] favourite [Kafka] story is 'The Burrow.' A creature is building a vaulted chamber, a safe hole to hide in. His one tool is his forehead, just as a writer's one tool is the mind. The creature is joyous when blood flows. It means he has worked unrelentingly, and the walls are beginning to harden. Philip chose the story as a testament of how art is made."

72. Bender, *Israelites in Erin*, 1.

73. In the book, an Anglo-Irish lord marries an Anglo-Jewish heiress—before subsequently imprisoning her for refusing to hand over a dowry of diamonds to service his

gambling debts. A Jewish American woman, Rachel Mordecai Lazarus, wrote to Edgeworth to complain about her depictions of Jews in her novels. As a corrective, Edgeworth wrote her novel *Harrington* (1817), the story of a recovering anti-Semite who learns the error of his ways and marries a Jewess—though the final revelation that the Jewess is in fact Christian somewhat undermines the book's intention.

74. Eugenio Biagini, "Minorities," 443.

75. James Joyce, *A Portrait of the Artist as a Young Man*, 76. In his book *Joyce and the Jews: Cultures and Texts* (1989), Ira Nadel sees Joyce's attraction to Jews as both textual, "the roots of [Joyce's fascination with] Judaism [lies] in the analysis and creation of texts," and sexual: "For most of his life, Joyce was strongly attracted to Jewish women . . . who embodied the dark, mysterious qualities of the Orient" (4, 11). See also Marilyn Reizbaum's *Joyce's Judaic Other* (1999).

76. Stanley Price, *James Joyce and Italo Svevo: The Story of a Friendship*, 63; Bryan Cheyette, *Constructions of "the Jew" in English Literature and Society: Racial Representations, 1875–1945*, 206. Cheyette recently said of Irish authors, "There is a link between lapsed Catholics and philo-semitism. As well as Joyce, as an example, you can think of writers like Maeve Binchy or Edna O'Brien." Quoted in Patsy McGarry, "Lapsed Irish Catholics 'Most Sympathetic' to Jews," *Irish Times*, June 20, 2017.

77. O'Brien, "A Conversation with Edna O'Brien," 43; Edna O'Brien, *Mother Ireland*, 96; O'Brien, *Country Girl: A Memoir*, 285; O'Brien, *Mother Ireland*, 51; Edna O'Brien, *Some Irish Loving*, 102.

78. O'Brien, *Country Girl: A Memoir*, 24. Lena returned home from Brooklyn and met Michael O'Brien in 1921. They then married and went to America in 1922 (passing through Ellis Island) as the Civil War raged in Ireland and lived there for another year before returning home.

79. O'Brien, "A Conversation with Edna O'Brien," 43.

80. O'Brien's father was involved on the outskirts of the nationalist movement during the revolutionary era, as is noted in a local Tuamgraney man's submission to the Bureau of Military History: "A Company of Irish Volunteers was first formed in Tuamgraney early in 1914. There were about thirty members. . . . We met for drill about twice a week in the ball alley in Tuamgraney and in one of O'Brien's fields in Drewsboro." Joseph H. Noonan, Witness Statement 1,287, Nov. 11, 1955, Bureau of Military History, 11–12.

81. O'Brien, *Country Girl: A Memoir*, 6.

82. O'Brien, *Country Girl: A Memoir*, 126; Clair Wills, *The Best Are Leaving*, 7–8.

83. Quoted in Carlson, *Banned in Ireland*, 76. In her memoir *Mother Ireland*, O'Brien says, "Irish people do not like to be contradicted. Foiled again and again they have in them a rage that comes at you unawares like a briar jutting out of a hedge" (49), and what is a novel but contradiction on a grand scale?

84. Anne Enright, "Diary," *London Review of Books*, Mar. 21, 2013.

85. Following the publication of *The Lonely Girl*, playwright Brian Friel wrote to O'Brien to commend her writing: "While I was reading [your two novels] I kept thinking, 'I know exactly how she felt' although of course I couldn't possibly)." Friel to O'Brien, Dec. 27, 1962, Edna O'Brien Papers, Emory University, Atlanta (hereafter cited as O'Brien Papers, Emory).

86. Edna O'Brien, "What Would I Write—What Use Is It?," *Sunday Times*, Apr. 13, 1986, 52. O'Brien got to know Beckett on visits to Paris in the 1970s. The minimalism of his plays extended to his correspondence, too, with one postcard enigmatically marked, "Only if the spirit moves you." Another epistle consists of a picture of a young Beckett with the inscription: "I guess this is the young man who wrote Murphy having lived in bedsits between World's End and Clare St, Dublin." Beckett to O'Brien, n.d., box 91, folder 7, O'Brien Papers, Emory. O'Brien sent Roth at his request a copy of her 1986 article, "What Would I Write—What Use Is It?," written on Beckett's eightieth birthday.

87. Quoted in Eimear McBride, preface to *The Country Girls Trilogy*, by Edna O'Brien, x. O'Brien got a measure of revenge when she was presented with the Frank O'Connor Short Story Award in 2011. O'Connor too had Jewish influences: "The man who has influenced me most, I suppose, is really Isaac Babel . . . 'Guests of the Nation' and a couple of the other stories in that book are really imitations of Babel's stories in *The Red Calvary*." Frank O'Connor, "The Art of Fiction, No. 19."

88. Roth, quoting English critic Frank Tuohy, said, "While Joyce . . . was the first Irish Catholic to make his experience and surroundings recognizable, the world Nora Barnacle . . . had to wait for the fiction of Edna O'Brien." O'Brien, "A Conversation with Edna O'Brien," 45.

89. Joseph Heller to Jason Epstein, n.d. (1962), box 5, folder 34, O'Brien Papers, Emory; O'Brien to Malamud, Dec. 14, 1961, box 14, folder 14, Bernard Malamud Papers, Harry Ransom Center, University of Texas at Austin, reprinted by permission of Peters Fraser & Dunlop (www.petersfraserdunlop.com) on behalf of Edna O'Brien; Malamud to O'Brien, May 1, 1962, box 7, folder 49, O'Brien Papers, Emory, copyright © 1962 by Bernard Malamud, permission granted by Russell & Volkening as agents for the author's estate; Philip Davis, *Bernard Malamud: A Writer's Life*, 199. O'Brien applauded Roth's obituary of Malamud in a letter to him: "I liked your Malamud piece a lot. There were moments where it soared." O'Brien to Roth, May 23, 1986, box 26, folder 10, Roth Papers, LC. Reprinted by permission of Peters Fraser & Dunlop (www.petersfraserdunlop.com) on behalf of Edna O'Brien.

90. O'Brien to Bellow, May 17, 1965, Saul Bellow Papers, University of Chicago. Reprinted by permission of Peters Fraser & Dunlop (www.petersfraserdunlop.com) on behalf of Edna O'Brien.

91. Bellow to O'Brien, Dec. 31, 1965, in *Saul Bellow: Letters*, ed. Taylor, 254; O'Brien, *Country Girl: A Memoir*, 252; Elliot Fremont-Smith, "A Way Back to Life," review of *August Is a Wicked Month*, by Edna O'Brien, *New York Times*, June 3, 1965; Edna O'Brien,

Casualties of Peace, 38. The protagonist's abusive husband imagines himself to be Jewish: "People clung to being the thing they were not and that if brought too far was their undoing. Herod called himself a Jew but had none of a Jew's ways, and Herod's transplanted uncles, had they been Jews, would not be alive; as it was they had survived the war and then with a million others were evicted as a reprisal" (89).

92. Quoted in John Horgan, "Edna O'Brien Faces Limerick Audience," *Irish Times*, Apr. 23, 1966. Strangely for the times, O'Brien was defended at this meeting by a Catholic priest, Father Peter Connolly (a lecturer at Saint Patrick's College, Maynooth), who suggested that *The Country Girls* was "amoral rather than immoral." Quoted in O'Brien, *Country Girl: A Memoir*, 143.

93. Julia Carlson, "Edna O'Brien," 1749; Diarmaid Ferriter, *Transformation of Ireland, 1900–2000*, 609.

94. Edna O'Brien, "A Writer's Imaginative Life Commences in Childhood," interview by Rachel Cooke, *Guardian*, Feb. 6, 2011.

95. O'Brien might have taken inspiration from Joyce and Faulkner, but also from the French feminist writer Monique Wittig, whose 1964 novel *L'Opoponax* (trans. 1966) employs second-person narration to great effect. O'Brien reviewed Wittig's second novel, *Les Guérillères* (1969), for the *Observer* in 1971.

96. Edna O'Brien, "Our Edna—a Song of S.W.3," interview by Elgy Gillespie, *Irish Times*, June 10, 1972.

97. Isaac Bashevis Singer to O'Brien, Oct. 9, 1972, box 11, folder 46, O'Brien Papers, Emory; Erica Jong to O'Brien, Aug. 5, 1977, box 6, folder 19, O'Brien Papers, Emory. Copyright © Erica Jong, 2018, all rights reserved.

98. Norman Mailer to O'Brien, Dec. 21, 1983, box 7, folder 46, O'Brien Papers, Emory; O'Brien, *Country Girl: A Memoir*, 256.

99. O'Brien, *Country Girl: A Memoir*, 263. Though print media posited an intense rivalry between Roth and Mailer, they were friends and correspondents. Roth was also acquainted with Brodsky, who wrote an introduction for Yugoslavian Danilo Kiš's *A Tomb for Boris Davidovich* (1976), for Roth's "Writers from the Other Europe" series.

100. Stephen Watt, "Brendan Behan, Borscht Belt Comedian," 149.

101. Roth, foreword to *Fanatic Heart*, by O'Brien, ix, x. In this foreword Roth starkly contradicts hostile reviewers who wrote off O'Brien's prose as purple, overly lyrical, and overwrought. He named *A Fanatic Heart* one of his books of the year, writing, "On the evidence of this collection of two decades work—and its masterpiece, 'A Rose in the Heart of New York'—there is no better short story writer in English."

102. O'Brien to Roth, Aug. 16, 1984, box 26, folder 10, Roth Papers, LC. Later she would write jocularly to Roth: "I may have to get you to sign my name a few 1000 times—are you any good at forgery?" O'Brien to Roth, Oct. 9, 1984, box 26, folder 10, Roth Papers, LC. Reprinted by permission of Peters Fraser & Dunlop (www.petersfraserdunlop.com) on behalf of Edna O'Brien.

103. O'Brien to Roth, Aug. 16, 1984.

104. O'Brien, "Roth@80"; Clair Wills, "Lyrical Paraphernalia: The Novels of Edna O'Brien and *The Little Red Chairs*," *Los Angeles Review of Books*, July 17, 2016; O'Brien, "A Conversation with Edna O'Brien," 42, 45.

105. Roth, "Roth@80" (emphasis in the original).

106. O'Brien, "A Conversation with Edna O'Brien," 46 (emphasis in the original).

107. There is more evidence of this desire to return home in his letters to O'Brien around this time: "I'm so hungry for America I could even forgive the bastard who cut me off and nearly killed me on the New Jersey Turnpike. I just laughed and said, 'Ride 'em, cowboy.' England's made an American out of me. For the moment." Roth to O'Brien, June 5, 1986, box 10, folder 45, O'Brien Papers, Emory. Copyright © 1986 by Philip Roth, used by permission of The Wylie Agency LLC.

108. O'Brien to Roth, Oct. 9, 1984, box 26, folder 10, Roth Papers, LC. Reprinted by permission of Peters Fraser & Dunlop (www.petersfraserdunlop.com) on behalf of Edna O'Brien. Possibly a copy of the playwright's complete works, which Roth notes at the beginning of the interview: "On the desk . . . there's a volume of J. M. Synge's collected works open to a chapter in 'The Aran Islands.'" O'Brien, "A Conversation with Edna O'Brien," 43.

109. Peggy O'Brien, "The Silly and the Serious: An Assessment of Edna O'Brien," 474; O'Brien, "Roth@80."

110. O'Brien to Roth, Dec. 1, 1986, and June 9, 1933, box 26, folder 10, Roth Papers, LC. Reprinted by permission of Peters Fraser & Dunlop (www.petersfraserdunlop.com) on behalf of Edna O'Brien.

111. O'Brien to Roth, Oct. 19, 1990, box 26, folder 10, Roth Papers, LC. Reprinted by permission of Peters Fraser & Dunlop (www.petersfraserdunlop.com) on behalf of Edna O'Brien.

112. In the preface to *The Facts*, Zuckerman offers a critique of Roth's memoir, arguing that his creator's view of women is hopelessly one-sided and that he would have been better off writing a novel from his former wife's point of view, titled "My Life as a Woman"—a direct response to his 1974 novel *My Life as a Man*. Here is another example of Roth metatextually noting his limited perspective. Intriguingly, a perusal of O'Brien's notebooks from *Time and Tide* reveals that she toyed with the title "My Life as a Woman." Edna O'Brien, "*Time and Tide*, Notebooks," box 36, folder 1, O'Brien Papers, Emory. Reprinted by permission of Peters Fraser & Dunlop (www.petersfraserdunlop.com) on behalf of Edna O'Brien.

113. Her friend David Marcus, Jewish Irish editor of *Irish Writing*, praised the book's courage and brilliance in a letter to O'Brien.

114. O'Brien meticulously researched *Down by the River*, as evidenced by her archive at Emory. There, a copy of the "X case" ruling can be found, where the staid legal text is juxtaposed by graphic antiabortion leaflets that lie nestled in its pages.

115. Edna O'Brien, "Conversation with Edna O'Brien," 69.

116. Ronan Bennett, "The Country Girl's Home Truths," review of *In the Forest*, by Edna O'Brien, *Guardian*, May 4, 2002; Kathleen Costello-Sullivan, *Trauma and Recovery in the Twenty-First Century Irish Novel*, 16; Sinéad Mooney, "Edna O'Brien," 248.

117. O'Brien to Roth, July 30, 2003, box OB102, O'Brien Papers, University College Dublin. Reprinted by permission of Peters Fraser & Dunlop (www.petersfraserdunlop .com) on behalf of Edna O'Brien. O'Brien tells Roth that marriage and writing do not necessarily go hand in hand, to which he says she must find herself a Leonard Woolf. Her rejoinder, "I do not want a Leonard Woolf. I want Lord Byron and Leonard Woolf mixed in together." O'Brien, "A Conversation with Edna O'Brien," 47.

118. Quoted in O'Brien, "A Writer's Imaginative Life"; O'Brien, *Country Girl: A Memoir*, 277.

119. Edna O'Brien, email interview with the author, Oct. 2, 2012. Reprinted by permission of Peters Fraser & Dunlop (www.petersfraserdunlop.com) on behalf of Edna O'Brien.

120. O'Brien, "Roth@80."

121. Quoted in Edna O'Brien, "Edna O'Brien Is Stilled Gripped by Dark Moral Questions," interview by Roslyn Sulcas, *New York Times*, Mar. 25, 2016; O'Brien, "Roth@80."

122. Despite being, according to journalist Ron Rosenbaum, "rivals for the Nobel Prize." As with Mailer and Roth, this rivalry appears to be a media creation.

123. O'Brien, *Country Girl: A Memoir*, 335. This duality is one of the reasons O'Brien's fiction remains germane in 2019, as Ireland's relationship with Britain enters the crucible of Brexit. Torn apart by fears over migration, Britain would do well to listen to the testament of this old immigrant.

124. Her latest novel, *Girl*, inspired by the 2014 kidnapping of 276 schoolgirls in Nigeria by Boko Haram (which the octogenarian O'Brien researched over several months in the country), was published in 2019 and has received high praise on both sides of the Atlantic.

125. Edna O'Brien, email to the author, Oct. 10, 2018, reprinted by permission of Peters Fraser & Dunlop (www.petersfraserdunlop.com) on behalf of Edna O'Brien; Roth, *The Anatomy Lesson*, 105.

126. Edna O'Brien, purple notebook, folder OB550, O'Brien Papers, University College Dublin. Reprinted by permission of Peters Fraser & Dunlop (www.petersfraserdunlop .com) on behalf of Edna O'Brien. The quotation comes from Bellow's essay "Distractions of a Fiction Writer" in Granville Hicks collection *The Living Novel* (1957). Underneath Bellow's words, O'Brien has added her own view: "We are dwarfed by public events, public life, known to us as it was never known to the great Herodotus. We are in hiding because the only thing we can begin to understand is ourselves. The rest is too vast, too muddled, too contradictory, too confused."

127. There may have also been a class affinity between O'Brien, who grew up poor, and these Jewish writers who largely came from working-class backgrounds. Certainly, she seemed more drawn to them than to her titled country woman Elizabeth Bowen or the

upper-class Irish American Mary McCarthy. O'Brien's first American publisher, Blanche Knopf, attempted to introduce O'Brien and Bowen, but the meeting does not seem to have taken place, as O'Brien relates: "[Knopf] was very remote and very patrician and asked me did I have the same nightmare as her and. . . . Bowen—you're staying in a very grand country house and nobody brings you breakfast in the morning? 'My fear is that I'll never be invited to such a house,' I said." Edna O'Brien, "Country Matters," *Guardian*, Oct. 1, 1999.

128. Philip Roth, *American Pastoral*, 35; Edna O'Brien, "Virginia, Notes," box 67, folder 3, O'Brien Papers, Emory, reprinted by permission of Peters Fraser & Dunlop (www.petersfraserdunlop.com) on behalf of Edna O'Brien; Edna O'Brien, *Night*, 15.

2. "A Nice Catholic Irish Girl Ruined by a Dirty Foreigner"

1. McBride, preface to *The Country Girls Trilogy*, by O'Brien, x; O'Brien, preface to *Playboy of the Western World*, by Synge, x; Patricia Coughlan, "Killing the Bats: O'Brien, Abjection, and the Question of Agency," 173.

2. Marie McGonagle outlines the difference between Irish censorship and that of other nations: "During the first half of the 20th century . . . a policy of isolationism and of the development of a pure and catholic state, untainted by immoral influences from abroad, led to a degree of moral censorship unsurpassed in any other western state." McGonagle, "Ireland," 1215.

3. Quoted in Maureen O'Connor, "Girl Trouble." Writing in the *Irish Press* newspaper, Sean White praised *The Country Girls*, saying it "calls for applause and encourages bright hopes for [O'Brien's] future novels." However, the newspaper failed to give any coverage to the book's banning less than a month later. White, "Sun-Showery Land of Girlhood," *Irish Press*, May 27, 1960, 20.

4. Quoted in John Cooney, *John Charles McQuaid: Ruler of Catholic Ireland*, 348.

5. Yvonne Murphy, *Murphy Commission: Report into the Catholic Archdiocese of Dublin*, 191. In her memoir, O'Brien says of him: "[He] kept Ireland free from paganism and modern aberrations. Dublin was in thrall to him, with his distinctive aura . . . wearing the 'Borgia ring' . . . presented at his inauguration by the Knights of St Columbus. . . . His powers were primordial, what with an acquiescent government, a vast network of spies and numerous religious sodalities." O'Brien, *Country Girl: A Memoir*, 87.

6. McBride, preface to *The Country Girls Trilogy*, by O'Brien, x.

7. As this chapter is rooted in 1950s and early 1960s Irish history, later additions to the trilogy including the altered ending to *Girls in Their Married Bliss* and the 1986 epilogue fall outside its scope. See Kristine Byron's "'In the Name of the Mother . . .': Reading and Revision in Edna O'Brien's *Country Girls Trilogy and Epilogue*" for more.

8. Edna O'Brien, "Edna O'Brien," 211; Declan Kiberd, *After Ireland: Writing the Nation from Beckett to the Present*, 68.

9. Here he paraphrases the satirist Jonathan Swift, while missing the satiric pitch of O'Brien's jocose mix of biography and fiction.

10. In school Caithleen reads Henry David Thoreau's "A Winter's Walk," perhaps a sly nod to the failure of the Irish state's own (failed) program of economic independence conducted during the 1930s and 1940s.

11. Edna O'Brien, *The Country Girls*, 16.

12. O'Brien, *The Country Girls*, 27.

13. For example, in the Anglo-Irish literary tradition, the crumbling big house often represented the disintegrating power of the gentry over the nineteenth and early twentieth centuries, as in the fiction of Edgeworth and Elizabeth Bowen. Leading on from this point, the isolated, authoritarian farm household in later Irish fiction might be taken as a metaphor for the independent Irish state, as in John McGahern's *The Dark* (1965).

14. O'Brien quoted in Carlson, *Banned in Ireland*, 75; O'Brien, *The Country Girls*, 10.

15. O'Brien, *The Country Girls*, 8; Kiberd, *After Ireland*, 63.

16. Patrick Kavanagh, "The Great Hunger," in *The Great Hunger*. O'Brien and Kavanagh were not the only ones confronting this issue at this time. Jack B. Keane's play *Sive* (1959), which was first performed the year before *The Country Girls* was published, sees a young girl tragically wed to an ancient farmer for the pecuniary benefit of her aunt and the local matchmaker. Though not censored by the state, the play was turned down by the Abbey, the national theater.

17. O'Brien, *The Country Girls*, 93, 112.

18. O'Brien, *The Country Girls*, 22, 54; Kiberd, *After Ireland*, x, 64.

19. O'Brien, *The Country Girls*, 73, 77, 108, 31; quoted in Diarmaid Ferriter, *Judging Dev: A Reassessment of the Life and Legacy of Eamon de Valera*, 363; O'Brien, *The Country Girls*, 20.

20. In *Mother Ireland* O'Brien sardonically says of de Valera: "Dev was a holy man, went to Mass and the sacraments every day, and spent a holy hour besides in a chapel in Leeson Street, no doubt examining his conscience." O'Brien, *Mother Ireland*, 83.

21. O'Brien, *The Country Girls*, 13; W. B. Yeats and Lady Gregory, *Caithleen Ni Houlihan*, 11, 7; Julieann Veronica Ulin, Heather Edwards, and Sean O'Brien, eds., *Race and Immigration in the New Ireland*, 1.

22. Kiberd, *After Ireland*, 82. Like *The Country Girls*, *The Catcher in the Rye*—a book O'Brien loved.

23. O'Brien, *The Country Girls*, 105; Julia C. Obert, "Mothers and Others in Edna O'Brien's *The Country Girls*," 285.

24. John Brannigan, *Race in Modern Irish Literature and Culture*, 145; O'Brien, *The Country Girls*, 36; Edna O'Brien, "The Connor Girls," 32, 33, 35, 39.

25. Edna O'Brien, *The Lonely Girl*, 275; Declan Kiberd, "Irish Literature and Irish History," 272; Edna O'Brien, "Too Near the Bone," interview with Seamus Kelly, *Irish Times*, Oct. 8, 1965; David Marcus, *Oughtobiography: Leaves from the Diary of a Hyphenated Jew*, 29; Edna O'Brien, "Camera on Clare," *Irish Press*, Oct. 9, 1952, 6.

26. O'Brien, *The Lonely Girl*, 181; Wills, *The Best Are Leaving*, xii; Edna O'Brien, "I'd Like to Live Out There beyond the West," *Irish Press*, June 1, 1952, 3.

27. Kiberd, *After Ireland*, 81; O'Brien, *Mother Ireland*, 87; Michelle Woods, "Red, Unread, and Edna: Ernest Gébler and Edna O'Brien," 66.

28. Carlo Gébler, *The Projectionist*, 15, 2.

29. O'Brien, *Country Girl: A Memoir*, 126; Michelle Woods, "Eat or Be Eaten: Ernest Gébler's Self-Fashioning as Jewish Monster in *Shall I Eat You Now?*," 78; Michael Chanan, *From Handel to Hendrix: The Composer in the Public Sphere*, 200.

30. Laura Doyle, *Bordering on the Body: The Racial Matrix of Modern Literature and Culture*, 27.

31. Dermot Keogh, *Jews in Twentieth-Century Ireland*, 80.

32. Quoted in Kevin Rockett, *Irish Film Censorship: A Cultural Journey from Silent Cinema to Internet Pornography*, 94.

33. Kevin Rockett, "Ireland: Film, Radio, and Television," 1221.

34. O'Brien, *The Lonely Girl*, 205. Joanna's anti-Semitism appears to contradict Obert's view of her as a positive role model for Caithleen (yet as Obert's argument focuses only on *The Country Girls* it falls outside her argument's scope to consider Joanna's racial views as expressed in *The Lonely Girl*).

35. Biagini, "Minorities," 448; Keogh, *Jews in Twentieth-Century Ireland*, 126; Donal Ó Drisceoil, "Ireland: Neutrality during World War II," 1219; Marcus, *Oughtobiography*, 77. Novelist John McGahern says of his time training to be a teacher in Saint Patrick's College in the years following the war: "When we left the College, the Dean . . . gave us all a little packet of salt . . . [and] informed us that while we had our own Catholic country now, nearly all the wealth of the country was controlled by Protestants or Jews. This salt, was the one brand owned by a Catholic company." The scene's rich comedy echoes Stephen Dedalus's encounter with the dean in *Ulysses* (1922), but also bears out Biagini's point on the widespread nature of anti-Semitism in Ireland at this time. John McGahern, "The Church and Its Spire," 225.

36. Justice Department memo quoted in Ray Rivlin, *Jewish Ireland: A Social History*, 41. The inverted logic that Jews themselves create anti-Semitism is one Roth explores in "Eli, the Fanatic" in which assimilated American Jews turn against recently arrived Holocaust survivors, whose presence, it is felt, will provoke Gentile neighbors. O'Brien later spoke about the effects of wartime censorship: "I never lived through a war, and I doubt that I will now. The nearest we came to it was a little rationing and some news bulletins on the wireless. When I grew up I felt guilty about this. I wept when I read the diary of Anne Frank, I wept that others had to die on my behalf." Edna O'Brien, "Casualties All . . . ," *Hibernia*, n.d. (1965), box 84, folder 20, Edna O'Brien Papers, Emory University, Atlanta (hereafter cited as O'Brien Papers, Emory). Reprinted by permission of Peters Fraser & Dunlop (www.petersfraserdunlop.com) on behalf of Edna O'Brien.

37. O'Brien, *The Lonely Girl*, 246, 321, 299, 183, 298 (emphasis in the original).

38. O'Brien relates the actual events in *Country Girl: A Memoir*, where she and Gébler elope to the Isle of Man, pursued by her infuriated family. The housekeeper's role of savoir was in reality played by Gébler's friend, novelist J. P. Donleavy, "who had trained under outstanding boxing coaches in New York . . . and tore into [O'Brien's father and brother]." O'Brien, *Country Girl: A Memoir*, 116.

39. O'Brien outlines Joyce's own battles with censors in her biography of him: "[The publication of the "Nausicaa" chapter of *Ulysses* in the *Little Review*] was an insult to the mores and morals of America. As he heard that issues . . . were being burned, Joyce the joker said that by being burned twice on earth he would possibly be ensured a quick passage through purgatory." As with Synge, there are echoes here of O'Brien's own reception. Edna O'Brien, *James Joyce*, 117.

40. Catherine Hezser, "'Are You Protestant Jews or Roman Catholic Jews?': Literary Representations of Being Jewish in Ireland," 159; Joyce, *Ulysses*, 12.1151, 12.1158.

41. O'Brien, *The Lonely Girl*, 298, 300; Joyce, *Ulysses*, 12.1812–14.

42. O'Brien, *The Lonely Girl*, 251, 252, 297. The autobiographical fallacy that for so long afflicted the reception of O'Brien's work picks out the most O'Brien-like protagonist and argues that it is O'Brien's spokesperson. But O'Brien's novels are not some didactic tracts; rather, they are, both internally and externally, densely dialogic works. O'Brien is more than the sum of Caithleen and Baba: she is also Eugene, and James Brady, and Jack Holland. We can perhaps imagine O'Brien, paraphrasing her beloved Gustave Flaubert, exclaiming, "Eugene Gaillard, c'est moi."

43. Heather Ingman, *Twentieth-Century Fiction by Irish Women: Nation and Gender*, 42; Cooney, *John Charles McQuaid*, 70, 71. McQuaid's anti-Judaic rhetoric shares much with the tirades of Fr. Charles Coughlin, the 1930s Irish American radio priest (and bogey figure for a young Roth). It was also a common attitude in Ireland at the time, as Cormac Ó Gráda points out: "Militant Catholicism embodied or promoted anti-Semitism at various levels: some of its adherents saw Jews and Freemasons (often coupled together) as part of an anti-Catholic conspiracy, while others were convinced of the age-old smear that 'Jews killed Jesus Christ.'" Cormac Ó Gráda, *Jewish Ireland in the Age of Joyce: A Socioeconomic History*, 181.

44. Quoted in Clara Cullen and Margaret Ó hÓgartaigh, *His Grace Is Displeased: The Selected Correspondence of John Charles McQuaid, 1950–1972*, 231 (emphasis in the original). McQuaid used the Knights of Saint Columbanus to enforce literary censorship as well, with several members of the Irish Censorship Board during the 1950s belonging to the organization. Though the Knights were not officially anti-Semitic, some of Ireland's leading anti-Semites were prominent in the society, such as the Fine Gael T. D. Oliver Flanagan, who famously said that "there was no sex in Ireland before television." In his less remembered 1943 maiden speech to the Dáil, he exhorted the government to "rout the Jews out of this country." C. J. O'Reilly was a lifelong knight and served on the Censorship

Board between 1951 and 1956. There is no suggestion that he was anti-Semitic—he was an equal-opportunity censor, banning work by writers such as F. Scott Fitzgerald, Benedict Kiely, Doris Lessing, Colette, Henry Miller, and Samuel Beckett. Yet it is worth noting that on his watch Arthur Koestler's *Arrow in the Blue* (1951) and *The Age of Longing* (1951) were both banned, as was J. D. Salinger's *The Catcher in the Rye* (1951) and Saul Bellow's *The Adventures of Augie March* (1953). Oliver Flanagan quoted in Hilary Tovey and Perry Share, *A Sociology of Ireland*; and "Parliamentary Debates," *Dáil Éireann*, July 9, 1943.

45. O'Brien, *The Lonely Girl*, 353. Roth covers the McCarthy era in *I Married a Communist* (1998), a novel O'Brien read in proof form, given to her by historian Arthur Schlesinger Jr.

46. O'Brien, *The Lonely Girl*, 246.

47. O'Brien, *The Lonely Girl*, 239; O'Brien, *Country Girl: A Memoir*, 150. Explaining to Roth the pervasive presence of Joyce in her work (and somewhat spoiling the flirtatious rather than familial metaphor of influence), O'Brien says, "In the constellations of geniuses, [Joyce] is a blinding light and father of us all." O'Brien, "A Conversation with Edna O'Brien," 45.

48. O'Brien, letter to Bernard Malamud, Mar. 22, 1962, box 14, folder 14, Bernard Malamud Papers, Harry Ransom Center, University of Texas at Austin. Reprinted by permission of Peters Fraser & Dunlop (www.petersfraserdunlop.com) on behalf of Edna O'Brien. Malamud had written to O'Brien on May 11, 1961, promising her an advanced copy of *A New Life*. In their correspondence, O'Brien also speaks of her admiration for Malamud's *The Assistant* (1958), banned in Ireland in 1960, while he speaks glowingly of her *New Yorker* short story "Irish Revel": "You have a wonderful way with people." Malamud to O'Brien, Oct. 15, 1962, box 7, folder 49, O'Brien Papers, Emory. Copyright © 1962 by Bernard Malamud. Permission granted by Russell & Volkening as agents for the author's estate.

49. The quotation is taken from the "Oxen and the Sun" episode, set in a maternity ward where Bloom goes to visit an expectant friend. The sentence's archaic nature is the stylistic means by which Joyce highlights the poetic effect the Irish language and Irish artists have had on the development of the English language: "The Irish, condemned to express themselves in a language not their own, have stamped on it the mark of their own genius and compete for glory with the civilized nations. The result is called the English language." Roth describes the hybrid nature of his mentor Malamud's use of language: "English that often appeared to have . . . been clipped together from . . . the least promising stockpiles[:] . . . the locutions, inversions and diction of Jewish immigrant speech, a heap of broken verbal bones that looked [lost], until he came along . . . to make them dance to his sad tune." Malamud plays on the term "Levin," which means "lightning" but is also a common Jewish family name. Like Joyce, Malamud was the midwife for a new type of language, born out of the union of Yiddish and English. Inspired by Joyce's fusion

of English and Irish, Malamud jolts to life (as if by lightning) the dying Yiddish tongue, transplanting it into the body of American English speech. James Joyce quoted in Kiberd, *Inventing Ireland*, 35; Philip Roth, "Pictures of Malamud," 121.

50. O'Brien, *The Lonely Girl*, 286, 288, 308, 310.

51. Bernard Malamud, *A New Life*, 229, 224, 227, 224–25, 230; Malamud to O'Brien, May 1, 1962, box 7, folder 49, O'Brien Papers, Emory. Copyright © 1962 by Bernard Malamud. Permission granted by Russell & Volkening as agents for the author's estate.

52. O'Brien, *The Lonely Girl*, 372.

53. Clair Wills, *Lovers and Strangers: An Immigrant History of Post-war Britain*; "What They Think about Her," *Irish Times*, Dec. 14, 1967, 8.

54. O'Brien, *The Lonely Girl*, 179; Edna O'Brien, *Girls in Their Married Bliss*, 420. In his essay "Pasting It Together," Fitzgerald advises that "the standard cure for one who is sunk is to consider those in actual destitution of physical suffering—this is an all-weather beatitude for gloom in general and fairly salutary day-time advice for everyone. But at three o'clock in the morning . . . the cure doesn't work—and in a real dark night of the soul it is always three o'clock in the morning, day after day." F. Scott Fitzgerald, *My Lost City: Personal Essays, 1920–1940*, 145.

55. Joe Cleary, "Irish American Modernisms," 179; O'Brien, *Girls in Their Married Bliss*, 386, 395; Cleary, "Irish American Modernisms," 179; O'Brien, *Girls in Their Married Bliss*, 433.

56. F. Scott Fitzgerald, *The Great Gatsby*, 37; Helen Jones, *Health and Society in Twentieth Century Britain*, 129; O'Brien, *Girls in Their Married Bliss*, 405, 406, 525.

57. Marjorie Howes, "Public Discourse, Private Reflection, 1916–70," 929.

58. The antiquated nature of British censorship laws and the British establishment more generally is captured by Crown prosecutor Mervyn Griffith-Jones, who asked the jury without irony: "Is [this] a book . . . you would . . . wish your wife or your servants to read?" Quoted in Dominic Sandbrook, "*Lady Chatterley's Lover*—Fifty Years On," *Telegraph*, Oct. 16, 2010.

59. John Broderick, "The Essence of Edna O'Brien," *Irish Times*, Oct. 28, 1978, 6; Isobel Ross to O'Brien, Mar. 19, 1964, box 2, folder 35, O'Brien Papers, Emory; O'Brien, *Girls in Their Married Bliss*, 440; Tom Maschler to Mark Hamilton, May 5, 1964, box 2, folder 35, O'Brien Papers, Emory. Maschler received the legal advice to publish from Michael Rubenstein, who had defended Penguin in the Lawrence obscenity case.

60. According to Rebecca Pelan, *Girls in Their Married Bliss* was not widely reviewed and would not be published "in the United States until 1967," perhaps as a result of this defiance. O'Brien also, predictably, earned the loathing of American "decency" advocates, as a letter regarding the novel from the "Almy Associates" makes clear: "I have not read it; I have followed through page 8 and haphazardly glanced through the other pages. . . . How . . . can . . . Jonathan Cape . . . publish such a filthy book . . . [where] under the wrappings of a charming cover, such incredible rottenness is disseminated[?]" Pelan,

"Reflections on a Connemara Dietrich," 19; Almy Associates to Jonathan Cape Publishers, Feb. 1, 1965, box 2, folder 35, O'Brien Papers, Emory.

61. Edna O'Brien, email interview with the author, Oct. 2, 2012, reprinted by permission of Peters Fraser & Dunlop (www.petersfraserdunlop.com) on behalf of Edna O'Brien; Alfred Kazin, review of *Goodbye, Columbus*, by Philip Roth, 43; Norman MacLeod, "A Note on Philip Roth's *Goodbye, Columbus* and Fitzgerald's *The Great Gatsby*," 105; William Peden, review of *Goodbye, Columbus*, by Philip Roth, *New York Times*, May 17, 1959, BR4.

62. Philip Roth, *Goodbye, Columbus, and Five Short Stories*, 90.

63. Roth, "Writing about Jews," 219. This advice recalls Synge's opinion of the freedom granted authors writing in inaccessible Irish and exposes the shared defensiveness and inward-looking nature of both Jewish American and Irish religious authorities.

64. Before it was banned, *Goodbye, Columbus* was positively reviewed in the *Irish Times* as "a light wisp of a book, given unexpected and welcome weight by an ending rich in comic observance." Roth's book makes several references to Irish American writer Mary McCarthy, whose books inform Neil and Brenda about contraception. In particular, it alludes to the short story "Dottie Makes an Honest Woman of Herself," which later became part of her novel *The Group* (1963). McCarthy wrote this story with the stated intention of using it to defy the American postal censorship system, which until 1957 forbade the sending of information regarding contraception through the mail. BVS, "A Bunch of Wild Paradigms," review of *Goodbye, Columbus*, by Roth, *Irish Times*, Nov. 7, 1959.

65. Roth, *Goodbye, Columbus*, 100.

66. R. F. Foster, *The Irish Story: Telling Tales and Making It Up in Ireland*, 98. In a 1970 review, Derek Mahon counters what he terms Irish "cultural Savonarolas" who see "O'Brien [as] un- or even anti-Irish, when quite the reverse is true. Her fierce feminism, her passionate love-hate for the place, ring bells of memory and self-recognition for a great number of people." Mahon, review of *A Pagan Place*, by Edna O'Brien, *Listener*, Apr. 23, 1970, 556.

67. O'Brien, preface to *Playboy of the Western World*, by Synge, x.

3. "A Contrast of Explosive Nature"

1. "Times Literary Supplement," review of *Night*, by Edna O'Brien, *Times*, Oct. 6, 1972; "Beyond the (Garbage) Pale," editorial, *New York Times*, Apr. 1, 1969, 46; Bruce Williamson, "Confessions on the Couch," review of *Portnoy's Complaint*, by Philip Roth, *Irish Times*, Apr. 26, 1969, 8. Unsurprisingly, *Portnoy's Complaint* was banned in Ireland. However, it was only the paperback version banned, as the *Irish Times* points out: "The Board takes the view that only adults and those wanting the book for its literary merit would pay the hard back edition price." This anomaly meant those who could afford to buy the hard-copy edition could circumvent censorship, as one letter writer to the *Irish*

Press sarcastically reasons: "By paying 31/6 . . . I rise above temptation; I can read about the vilest of sexual perversions. . . . On the other hand, if I'm in the social class which pays a niggardly eight shillings for reading material, I'm equated with a chimpanzee who blindly imitates everything he sees." *Night* was the first of O'Brien's books not to be banned, owing to changes in censorship laws in 1967 and 1972. One 1971 commentator observed the decreasing effectiveness of the literary restrictions: "Whatever about Church censorship, State censorship is a bigger myth than ever it was in the last decade. True we still ban the muck stuff but you can buy Gore Vidal and Philip Roth and Edna O'Brien in the thickest belt of the snipe grass of Pollawaddy." "Paperback Ban on *Portnoy*," *Irish Press*, Feb. 27, 1971; Charles Runyon, letter to the editor, *Irish Press*, Feb. 13, 1971, 11; Backbencher, "Priests, Provos and Protestants," *Irish Times*, Dec. 18, 1971, 12.

2. Eilís Dillon, "Black and Blue," review of *Night*, by Edna O'Brien, *Irish Press*, Oct. 7, 1972, 14. Contradicting Dillon, Margaret Drabble wrote of *Night*, "It is not for [O'Brien] the pretence that women are unlike men, do not like [sex], do not do it," adding, "men have travelled this way often and written of it; women too have been there but few of them have recorded their journey." Alison McMahon, "Edna O'Brien," letter to the editor, *Irish Times*, Oct. 21, 1972.

3. Quoted in Pierpont, *Roth Unbound*, 14.

4. Kevin Stevens, "Everything He Hated," review of *Indignation*, by Philip Roth, *Dublin Review of Books*, Sept. 1, 2006.

5. Roth, *Portnoy's Complaint*, 3; Shostak, *Philip Roth: Countertexts, Counterlives*), 83. In Erica Jong's novel *Fear of Flying* (1973), her Jewish American protagonist ruminates on this Portnoy: "When I think of my mother I envy Alexander Portnoy. If only I had a real Jewish mother—easily pigeonholed and filed away—a real literary property." Jong herself was inspired by *Portnoy's Complaint*, seeing it as part provocation, part stimulation: "*Portnoy's Complaint* dared to take literature into the precincts of the bedroom from a man's point of view. It remained for a woman to expose female fantasy with as much frankness." *Fear of Flying* also openly flirts with O'Brien's fiction, with one of the chapter epigraphs taken from *Girls in Their Married Bliss*: "The vote, I thought, means nothing to women. We should be armed." Jong, *Fear of Flying*, 147; Jong, "*Fear of Flying* Turns Twenty," ix.

6. Cooper, *Philip Roth and the Jews*, 56; Roth, *Portnoy's Complaint*, 27; Lawrence Sterne, *The Life and Opinions of Tristram Shandy*, 5; Roth, *Portnoy's Complaint*, 50.

7. Roth, *Portnoy's Complaint*, 7, 74, 52, 193; Philip Roth, "Interview with the *London Sunday Times*," 113.

8. Roth, *Portnoy's Complaint*, 81 (emphasis in the original). Sociologists Charles S. Liebman and Steven Cohen write about this sense of Jewish difference from mainstream society (a sense often shared by Irish Americans and other ethnic groups): "Jews harboured many unflattering images both of Gentile . . . culture. These negative images were constituent elements in traditional Jewish identity, reinforcing Jewish notions of their . . .

collective superiority." As Portnoy says, "We were Jews—and we weren't ashamed to say it! We were Jews—and not only were we not inferior to the *goyim* who beat us at football, but the chances were that because we could not commit our hearts to victory in such a thuggish game, we were superior! We were Jews—*and we were superior!*" Liebman and Cohen, *Two Worlds of Judaism: The Israeli and American Experience*, 37; Roth, *Portnoy's Complaint*, 56 (emphasis in the original).

9. Roth, *Portnoy's Complaint*, 40; Joyce, *Ulysses*, 12.1809; Philip Roth, "Philip Roth's Exact Intent," 35, 36; Joyce, *Portrait*, 76.

10. Roth, *Portnoy's Complaint*, 18, 19; Joyce, *Ulysses*, 15.3909. Throughout *Ulysses*, Bloom's unorthodox eating habits are tied to his erotic appetites: "Mr Leopold Bloom ate with relish the inner organs of beasts and fowls. . . . A kidney oozed bloodgouts on the willowpatterned dish. . . . He stood by the nextdoor girl at the counter . . . His eyes rested on her vigorous hips" (3.148).

11. Roth, *Portnoy's Complaint*, 79.

12. Roth, *Portnoy's Complaint*, 83, 91, 85.

13. Roth, *Portnoy's Complaint*, 53, 60. As in *The Lonely Girl*, this tribal battle scene grew from a biographical kernel, as Roth's father relates in *Patrimony*: "My father [Roth's grandfather] had to beat my older brother Ed to prevent him from marrying a worldly woman." Roth, *Patrimony: A True Story*, 86.

14. Roth, *Portnoy's Complaint*, 34.

15. Irving Howe, "Philip Roth Reconsidered," 69.

16. Jonathan Swift, "Verses on the Death of Dr. Swift," in *The Oxford Authors: Jonathan Swift*.

17. Barry Slepian, "The Ironic Intention of Swift's Verses on His Own Death," 250, 256. As Swift did with his nemesis William Wotton—whose pedantic notations on the dean's *A Tale of a Tub* (1704) were mockingly subsumed into later editions—Roth does with Howe, transforming him into the critic Milton Appel in his 1983 novel, *The Anatomy Lesson*, a book in which the narrator describes his writerly motto: "Stand alone. Like Swift." Roth's deep engagement with Swift is apparent throughout his work, but it is at its most acute in the experimental novels that succeed *Portnoy's Complaint*. This point is evidenced in *Our Gang*, which quotes *Gulliver's Travels* in the epigraph: "The Use of Speech was to make us understand one another, and to receive Information of Facts; now if anyone said the Thing which was not, these Ends were defeated; because I cannot properly be said to understand him; and I am so far from receiving Information, that he leaves me worse than in Ignorance; for I am led to believe a Thing Black when it is White, and Short when it is Long"; in *The Breast* (1972), which sees its protagonist transformed into a giant mammary gland, exploring ideas of sexual monstrosity prompted by a scene from Brobdingnag, "I must confess that no Object ever disgusted me so much as the sight of her monstrous Breast"; and in *The Great American Novel* (1973), with its postmodern echoes of *Tale of a Tub* (a book alluded to in *My Life as a Man* [1974]).

18. Roth, *Portnoy's Complaint*, 284, 40, 235; Aidan Beatty, *Masculinity and Power in Irish Nationalism, 1884–1938*, 6; Leon Uris, *Exodus*, 55; Debra Shostak, "Roth and Gender," 114.

19. Roth, *Portnoy's Complaint*, 244; Ari Shavit, *My Promised Land: The Triumph and Tragedy of Israel*, xi; Roth, *Portnoy's Complaint*, 253, 252, 254.

20. Roth, *Portnoy's Complaint*, 254; Ian Black, *Enemies and Neighbours: Arabs and Jews in Palestine and Israel, 1917–2017*, 49; Roth, *Portnoy's Complaint*, 259; Joshua Lambert, *Unclean Lips: Jews, Obscenity, and American Culture*, 126; Roth, *Portnoy's Complaint*, 265.

21. Shostak, *Philip Roth: Countertexts, Counterlives*, 84; Bernard Avishai, *Promiscuous: Portnoy's Complaint and Our Doomed Pursuit of Happiness*, 5; Roth, *Portnoy's Complaint*, 269; Cooper, *Philip Roth*, 9.

22. Roth, *Portnoy's Complaint*, 271 (emphasis in the original), 274.

23. Isaac Bashevis Singer, letter to Edna O'Brien, Oct. 9, 1972, box 11, folder 46, Edna O'Brien Papers, Emory University, Atlanta (hereafter cited as O'Brien Papers, Emory); Edna O'Brien, interview by Mark Featherstone-Witty, 6.

24. Edna O'Brien, "The Artist and His Country," 232–33. O'Brien perhaps skims too lightly over her own negative reception in Ireland, a country that had, in her friend Robert Graves's estimation, "the fiercest literary censorship this side of the Iron Curtain." Also, while Britain may have lacked the overt persecution of, say, Czechoslovakia, for women (particularly those women seeking divorce) there existed more informal systems of control, as O'Brien explains in a recent essay: "So began a long and ugly battle for custody, in which local doctor, school headmaster and other notables attested to my unsuitability as a mother. So Ireland wasn't the only place with a big stick." Roth agrees with O'Brien's position, saying of artists in Czechoslovakia, many of whom he befriended on visits there in the 1970s: "It occurred to me that I work in a society where as a writer everything goes and nothing matter, while for [them], nothing goes and everything matters." Robert Graves quoted in Michael Adams, *Censorship: The Irish Experience*, 250; Edna O'Brien, "A Woman in Transit," 74; Roth, "Art of Fiction."

25. O'Brien, "Artist and His Country," 232–33 (emphasis added).

26. O'Brien, "Artist and His Country," 232–33; Philip Roth, "Writing American Fiction," 176. In a peculiarly Rothian coincidence, the *Irish Times* reviewer of *Reading Myself and Others*, Jack Holland, shares the name of Edna O'Brien's *The Lonely Girl*'s small-town literary scholar. Holland suggests that the title is emblematic of Roth's self-obsessed oeuvre: "Reading himself is an activity which is to creation what masturbation is to making love: a poor substitute at best and at worst, a sign of incapacity." Jack Holland, "Roth about Roth," review of *Reading Myself and Others*, by Philip Roth, *Irish Times*, Dec. 29, 1975, 8.

27. O'Brien, "Artist and His Country," 233.

28. Roth too worried over the fact that the threat facing "First World" writers was not "the repressive Eastern totalitarian nightmare" but only "the Western farce of media

stupidity and cynical commercialism—American-style philistinism run amok." Roth, "Art of Fiction."

29. Edna O'Brien, "Art of Fiction, No. 82."

30. O'Brien, "Art of Fiction" (emphasis in the original).

31. O'Brien, *Night*, 8; Helen Thompson, "Hysterical Hooliganism: O'Brien, Freud, Joyce," 36. Less flatteringly, the (now little remembered) Irish novelist John Broderick described O'Brien as a "bargain basement Molly Bloom." John Broderick, "The Essence of Edna O'Brien," *Irish Times*, Oct. 28, 1978, 6.

32. O'Brien, *Night*, 10; Joyce, *Ulysses*, 18.999.

33. O'Brien, *Night*, 13, 16, 69, 12, 15, 17.

34. O'Brien, *Night*, 49; Joyce, *Portrait*, 188, 189; O'Brien, *Night*, 47, 51; Colletta and O'Connor, introduction to *Wild Colonial Girl*, 7.

35. O'Brien, *Night*, 53; Sharon Lambert, "Irish Women's Emigration to England, 1922–60: The Lengthening of Family Ties," 154; O'Brien, *Night*, 55, 150, 50.

36. O'Brien, *Night*, 95, 104.

37. Bertrand Cardin, "Words Apart: Epigraphs in Edna O'Brien's Novels," 70; Andrew O'Hagan, "Edna O'Brien's *Night* Is All Passion, All Mind," *Guardian*, Aug. 22, 2014.

38. *North* was published in October 1972, while the Widgery Report was made public on April 18, 1972.

39. Thomas Kinsella, "Butcher's Dozen," 244.

40. O'Brien, *Country Girl: A Memoir*, 236.

41. O'Brien, *Night*, 5; O'Brien, *Country Girl: A Memoir*, 236.

42. Auden was fascinated by the war poetry of Yeats, of whom he writes, "Mad Ireland hurt you into poetry," in "In Memory of W. B. Yeats." He also befriended other Irish poets such as Louis MacNeice and acted as a literary mentor to the young Jewish American short-story writer Grace Paley.

43. Edna O'Brien, "A Reason of One's Own," *Times*, Sept. 30, 1972, 10.

44. O'Brien, *Night*, 10.

45. O'Brien, *Night*, 106.

46. This also recalls the irony that the one true friend of the purity-obsessed Citizen in *Ulysses* is his "mangy mongrel, Garryowen" (12.119).

47. O'Brien, *Night*, 9.

48. O'Brien, *Night*, 30.

49. "Ticking" might also refer to the IRA bombing campaign, which was massively ramped up during 1972, with dozens killed and hundreds injured.

50. Paul Bew and Gordon Gillespie, *Northern Ireland: A Chronology of the Troubles, 1968–1999*, 41. Derry Women's Aid saw such acts as a proof of the "failure of feminist issues to emerge as part of" the nationalist and republican movements: "This view is not surprising given the historical link between Irish Catholicism and Nationalism which

even in this day and age manifest itself [*sic*] when such organisations tar and feather women who break the 'moral code.'" Derry's Women's Aid, "Feminism and Nationalism: A View from Derry Women's Aid," 397.

51. O'Brien, *Night*, 39. O'Brien might have had the IRA member James McCann, who escaped Crumlin Prison in 1971, in mind when sketching McKann.

52. Further signs that the dean was on O'Brien's mind at this time are evident in her published work and archives. The year 1967 also saw the tercentenary of Swift's birth celebrated in Dublin. Eamon de Valera—during whose rule many of the greatest Irish writers of the twentieth century saw their work suppressed—opened the proceedings, praising Swift as a "great prose-writer and satirist." The irony would have been even greater had O'Brien been present as the organizers intended (she declined the invitation). O'Brien mentions Swift in *Mother Ireland* and includes his letters to "Vanessa" Vanhomrigh and "Stella" Johnson in *Some Irish Loving*. She later wrote of him in an unpublished article on Dublin: "It was here [in Dublin] that Dean Swift . . . wrote *Gulliver's Travels* and the *Drapier's Letters* urging the Irish to burn everything English except her coal." O'Brien, "Dublin," n.d., box 57, folder 11, O'Brien Papers, Emory. Reprinted by permission of Peters Fraser & Dunlop (www.petersfraserdunlop.com) on behalf of Edna O'Brien.

53. Quoted in Pro-Quidnunc, "An Irishman's Diary," *Irish Times*, Apr. 26, 1967, 9.

54. O'Brien, *Night*, 103, 114.

55. Much has been written about the similarities and differences between the conflicts in Israel and Palestine and in Northern Ireland. While early-twentieth-century Irish nationalists often saw parallels between their struggle and Zionism, post-1969 republicans in the North saw stronger connections between themselves and the Palestinians, and this shifting analogy is mined by critics such as Elizabeth Butler Cullingford, Joe Cleary, and Abby Bender.

56. O'Brien, *Night*, 149, 33, 11. These lines recall Gerald Stern's "livid chimneys and smoking hillsides."

57. O'Brien, "Artist and His Country," galleys, box 57, folder 1, O'Brien Papers, Emory; O'Brien, "Artist and His Country," 233.

58. Andrew Furman argues that "Roth was one of the first Jewish American authors to question the sanctity of Israel with *Portnoy's Complaint*. He did for Israel what *Goodbye, Columbus* did for the Jewish American community . . . depicted it without false idealism." He adds, "Roth deserves much credit for rescuing American Jewish fiction about Israel from the realm of the conventional Zionist propaganda novel." Andrew Furman, "A New 'Other' Emerges in American Jewish Literature: Philip Roth's Israel Fiction," 635.

59. Both thus follow Joyce's own antiheroic maxim: "Do you not think the search for heroics damn vulgar? . . . I am sure however that the whole structure of heroism is, and always was, a damned lie and that there cannot be any substitute for individual passion as the motive power of everything." Joyce quoted in introduction to *Ulysses*, x.

4. "A Harp in the Hallway"

1. O'Brien, "A Conversation with Edna O'Brien," 47. There is no little irony in Roth's question, as Gavin Keulks points out: "Numerous male writers—D. H. Lawrence, John Updike, and Philip Roth, to name a few—have received fawning admiration for their sexual frankness versus the censorship that O'Brien's work once received." Gavin Keulks, "Edna O'Brien," 5:117.

2. Darren Hughes, "The 'Written World' of Philip Roth's Nonfiction," 267; David Gooblar, *The Major Phases of Philip Roth*, 59; Roth, foreword to *Fanatic Heart*, by O'Brien, ix.

3. O'Brien, "A Conversation with Edna O'Brien," 42; Roth, *Zuckerman Unbound*, 190; Brett Ashley Kaplan, *Jewish Anxiety and the Novels of Philip Roth*, 45; Scott W. Klein, "Zuckerman as Irish Jew: James Joyce, National Difference and Roth's *The Counterlife*," 154; Roth, *Zuckerman Unbound*, 187. When speaking of Irish American identity, this chapter is primarily concerned with Irish Catholic identity. For a broader discussion of Irish Protestant American identity in literature, see Tara Stubbs's *American Literature and Irish Culture, 1910–1955: The Politics of Enchantment* (2013).

4. Roth, *Zuckerman Unbound*, 186, 189; Klein, "Zuckerman as Irish Jew," 163.

5. It is certain that Roth read O'Brien's memoir, as he refers to it at the beginning of the *New York Times* interview.

6. R. A. Stewart MacAlister, ed. and trans., *Lebor Gabála Érenn: The Book of the Taking of Ireland*, 181–83; O'Brien, *Mother Ireland*, 12.

7. Klein, "Zuckerman as Irish Jew," 163; Francis J. Byrne, *Irish Kings and High-Kings*, 9; John Carey, *The Irish National Origin-Legend: Synthetic Pseudohistory*, 4, 2.

8. Murray Pittock, *Celtic Identity and the British Image*, 81; Maureen O'Connor, "The Mythopoeic Ireland of Edna O'Brien's Fiction," 215; O'Brien, *Mother Ireland*, 11, 72.

9. O'Brien's work thus also anticipates more recent arrivals from Europe, Africa, and Asia.

10. Joyce, *Ulysses*, 2.441.

11. O'Brien, *Mother Ireland*, 35, 52.

12. Madison Grant, *The Passing of the Great Race*, 96.

13. Use of the *Book of Invasions* was widespread in racial discourse in the early twentieth century. Exemplary of this fact is the deeply anti-Irish and anti-Semitic journal *Plain English*, founded by Lord Alfred Douglas (better known as the lover of Oscar Wilde) in 1920. Historian R. M. Douglas (no relation to Lord Alfred) explains that the journal "argued . . . that the guerrilla warfare tactics of the Irish Republican Army unmistakably stamped its members" as descendants of the Fir Bolg. In the amalgamative process common to conspiracy theorists, contributors to the journal argued, "The evidence strongly favoured a biological relationship between the Irish and the Jews." R. M. Douglas, "Anglo-Saxons and Attacotti: The Racialization of Irishness in Britain between the World Wars," 46, 47.

14. Bruce Nelson corroborates this notion: "Significant numbers of Anglo American Protestants continued to resent the Catholicism, ethnic cohesion, and political clout of the American Irish. But except among an especially bigoted minority, their whiteness was no longer in question." The lingering half-life of this bigotry would surface in the 1928 anti-Catholic riots protesting Irish Catholic Al Smith's presidential campaign, with some prejudice still apparent as late as John F. Kennedy's electoral triumph in 1960. Bruce Nelson, *Irish Nationalists and the Making of the Irish Race*, 86.

15. Grant, *Passing of the Great Race*, 188.

16. Matthew Frye Jacobson, *Whiteness of a Different Color: European Immigrants and the Alchemy of Race*, 14.

17. Roth, *Zuckerman Unbound*, 136; Jacobson, *Whiteness of a Different Color*, 8. In acknowledgment of Roth's prescience regarding the protean nature of race, Jacobson opens his book *Whiteness of a Different Color* with a close reading of *The Counterlife*.

18. As Enda Leaney affirms of British imperial attitudes toward nineteenth-century Ireland: "Phrenology revealed that the Irish Catholics were sui generis a flawed and degenerate breed." Enda Leaney, "Phrenology in Nineteenth-Century Ireland," 32.

19. Karen Brodkin, *How the Jews Became White Folk and What That Says about Race in America*, 3; Roth, *Zuckerman Unbound*, 143, 291; Klein, "Zuckerman as Irish Jew," 162.

20. Roth, *Zuckerman Unbound*, 188. Both O'Brien and Roth were friends of this pioneering Jewish scholar of Irish writing. Ellmann aided Roth secure the Yeats estate's acquiescence to the inclusion of quotations from "Leda and the Swan" in *Portnoy's Complaint*.

21. Klein, "Zuckerman as Irish Jew," 163.

22. Roth, *Zuckerman Unbound*, 259. MacMurphy is not a wild invention on Roth's part, as historian J. J. Lee explains: the daughters of nineteenth-century Irish immigrants often became teachers and thus "played a potentially formative role in the education of immigrant children, presumably bringing an intriguing mixture of values to the task." J. J. Lee, "Introduction: Interpreting Irish America," 36.

23. Roth, *Zuckerman Unbound*, 249, 254. Roth has spoken of his admiration for Irish American Catholic writer James F. Powers, whose work may also have influenced Roth's depiction of these priests.

24. Roth, *Zuckerman Unbound*, 289.

25. Richard Dyer, *White*, 20, 52; Roth, *Zuckerman Unbound*, 189. Roth similarly singles out O'Brien's skin during his interview with her: "Because everything she is wearing . . . is black you cannot, of course, miss the white skin, the green eyes and the auburn hair." Roth, "A Conversation with Edna O'Brien," 49.

26. Roth, *Zuckerman Unbound*, 138; Dominic Sandbrook, *Mad as Hell: The Crisis of the 1970s and the Rise of the Populist Right*, 59–60; Timothy Parrish, "Roth and Ethnic Identity," 128; Kaplan, *Jewish Anxiety*, 54.

27. Roth, *Zuckerman Unbound*, 245, 142; Kaplan, *Jewish Anxiety*, 46; Roth, *Zuckerman Unbound*, 243, 246.

28. Roth, *Zuckerman Unbound*, 157; Jacobson, *Whiteness of a Different Color*, 7; Tresa Grauer, "Identity Matters: Contemporary Jewish American Writing," 271.

29. Roth, *Zuckerman Unbound*, 165; Brodkin, *How the Jews Became White Folk*, 26.

30. Roth, *Zuckerman Unbound*, 291, 289, 291, 285, 6.

31. O'Brien, *Mother Ireland*, 2; Sandbrook, *Mad as Hell*, 60; Lee Lourdeaux, *Italian and Irish Filmmakers in America*, 14; Peter Quinn, "The Future of Irish America," 682.

32. Roth, *Zuckerman Unbound*, 192, 259, 187.

33. Loosely appropriating Swift's metaphor of the spider spinning its story from its own insides, Irish reviewer Patrick Murray says of *The Ghost Writer*, "This latest novel strikes me as . . . spun too fine from the author's own life." Murray, review of *Zuckerman Unbound*, by Roth, *Irish Press*, Sept. 17, 1981, 6.

34. Roth, *Zuckerman Unbound*, 196. This linkage with *The Ghost Writer* was a late addition to the text. In early drafts it was in Synge's *Deirdre of the Sorrows* (1910) that Caesara got her start in theater.

35. Roth, *Zuckerman Unbound*, 271, 275, 236. Further strengthening Caesara's role as a mirror for Zuckerman, she too has a debased Peplerian copy, Gayle Gibraltar, Pepler's fantasy love object: "Look . . . she's not Miss O'Shea, not by a long shot. Miss O'Shea has style. Miss O'Shea has class. Gayle is somebody . . . without hang-ups. That's what she projects, you see" (154).

36. Roth, *Zuckerman Unbound*, 153, 154.

37. Edward Said, "Propaganda and War," 1; Louis Gordon, "Leon Uris," 355; Ira Nadel, *Leon Uris: Life of a Bestseller*, 116; Grauer, "Identity Matters," 271; Philip Roth, "Some New Jewish Stereotypes," 202.

38. Wiesel's story strongly echoes Frank O'Connor's Irish War of Independence short story "Guests of the Nation" (1931)—itself influenced by the work of the Russian Jewish short-story master Isaac Babel. In the preface to *Dawn*, Wiesel sets down some of the ethical questions that prompted it: "Does murder call for murder, despair for revenge? Can hate engender anything by hate?"

39. Roth, "Some New Jewish Stereotypes."

40. Roth, *Zuckerman Unbound*, 137; Kathleen Shine Cain, *Leon Uris: A Critical Companion*, 132.

41. Roth, *Zuckerman Unbound*, 150, 151, 235, 245.

42. Ann McGlinn, review of *Trinity*, by Leon Uris, *Saturday Evening Post*, Sept. 10, 1976, 73; Reginald Byron, *Irish America*, 259–60; Kevin Kenny, *The American Irish: A History*, 251; Nadel, *Leon Uris*, 225; Kenny, *American Irish*, 248.

43. O'Brien, *Night*, 128. In an email interview O'Brien told me, "The first book of his that I read was *Goodbye, Columbus*. The first book of mine that he read was *Night*. We

didn't really go into discussions about them. But the sense of solidarity was always there." O'Brien, email interview with the author, Oct. 2, 2012. Reprinted by permission of Peters Fraser & Dunlop (www.petersfraserdunlop.com) on behalf of Edna O'Brien.

44. O'Brien, *Mother Ireland*, 32; Roth, *Zuckerman Unbound*, 196. Caesara might at first glance seem only to parody O'Brien, just as Zuckerman parodies Roth. Indeed, on being asked about similarities between herself and Roth's character, O'Brien answered jocularly: "She recites Yeats, mistily, and is an admirer or Richard Ellmann; she's also had a burst appendix. Now some of these qualities are actually fairly true, but I have to say that one piece of the book must be based on someone else, because [she's bound] for an assignation with Fidel Castro in Havana. I did attend an eight hour marathon of Fidel's in Havana, without I assure you any amorous musings on my part." Yet O'Brien also recognized the character's complexity, continuing, "What I like about being remotely connected with Caesara is that both she and Zuckerman, God help them, are intensity afflicted." It is a hallmark of the true writer, as O'Brien tells Roth in an interview: "You, like me, are trying to make something out of nothing and the anxiety is extreme." O'Brien, "Roth@80"; O'Brien, "Conversation with Edna O'Brien."

45. Kenny explains Reagan's "Irishness": "Anxious to consolidate this new support, Ronald Reagan made a famous tour of Ireland in 1984, where he unearthed an unlikely ancestor or two, much to the skepticism of most Irish onlookers." In a letter to O'Brien that year, Roth notes he will be returning to America from London to vote in the "grim November election." Kenny, *American Irish*, 254; Roth to O'Brien, Aug. 23, 1984, copyright © 1984 by Philip Roth, used by permission of The Wylie Agency LLC.

46. Ira N. Forman, "The Politics of Minority Consciousness: The Historical Voting Behavior of American Jews," 153.

5. "Dark Knowledge"

1. O'Brien, email interview with the author, Oct. 2, 2012. Reprinted by permission of Peters Fraser & Dunlop (www.petersfraserdunlop.com) on behalf of Edna O'Brien; O'Brien, "Roth@80."

2. O'Brien quoted in *Irish Women Writers Speak Out: Voices from the Field*, ed. Helen Thompson and Catriona Moloney, 200; Roth quoted in Charles McGrath, "Zuckerman's Alter Brain," *New York Times*, May 7, 2000. The other novels in O'Brien's trilogy are *Down by the River* (1996) and *Wild Decembers* (1999); in Roth's, they are *I Married a Communist* (1998) and *The Human Stain* (2000).

3. Roth, "Philip Roth at Seventy," interview with David Remnick, *BBC4*, Mar. 19, 2003.

4. Eileen Battersby, "The Many Faces of Philip Roth," *Irish Times*, Mar. 20, 1993, A8; Eileen Battersby, "At Last: The Great American Novel?," *Irish Times*, Mar. 31, 1997, 8; Helen Meany, "Bravo, Edna," *Irish Times*, Aug. 24, 1996, 12.

5. While Roth was praised for his alleged newfound subject matter, the response to O'Brien's shift was distinctly qualified, with Arminta Wallace admiring the "ingeniously constructed" *House of Splendid Isolation* while lambasting its "highly romanticised view" and its, implicitly negative, "mixture of poetry and politics." Arminta Wallace, review of *House of Splendid Isolation*, by Edna O'Brien, *Irish Times*, May 27, 1995, 9.

6. William Faulkner, *Requiem for a Nun*, 85; Edna O'Brien, "Sex, Books and a Lifetime of Defiance," interview with Janan Ganesh, *Financial Times*, July 14, 2017; Philip Roth quoted in Christopher Lydon, "Remembering Philip Roth."

7. O'Brien, *Country Girl: A Memoir*, 309. O'Brien is also enamored with women writers of the American South, having reviewed Carson McCullers's *Clock without Hands* in 1961: "Like Chekhov, Miss McCullers's interest centers on the loose texture of life, the boring, awful, day-to-day living punctuated at times by something strange, violent." She tells Shusha Guppy that she reads "a lot of Southern writers: Carson McCullers, Eudora Welty, Flannery O'Connor." Jonathan Yardley says of her short stories, "O'Brien's Ireland is as hard and unremitting a place as O'Connor's South. Yet longings her women feel for love and peace, for a kind connection with another human being, give these stories a tenderness that is both surprising and enriching." O'Brien, "The Strange World of Carson McCullers," 32; O'Brien, "Art of Fiction"; Yardley, "The Ironies of Irish Love," review of *Fanatic Heart*, by O'Brien, *Washington Post*, Nov. 25, 1984.

8. Sandra Manoogian Pearce, "An Interview with Edna O'Brien," 5; Philip Roth quoted in Edna O'Brien, "Passion's Progress"; Edna O'Brien, "Edna O'Brien Is Compelled by the Dark Sensibility of William Faulkner," *Sunday Times*, Sept. 1, 1996, Books, 2. O'Brien makes a similar unspoken comparison to Synge in her preface to *The Playboy of the Western World*, as discussed in the introduction. Synge's plays of Irishwomen of the house threatened by exotic strangers, best exemplified in *In the Shadow of the Glen*, and their criticism of Irish isolationist arguments are pertinent to this chapter.

9. Roth, *The Counterlife*, 162.

10. O'Brien, "Compelled by the Dark Sensibility," 2. O'Brien favorably contrasts Faulkner to a writer she regards as more partisan: "He does not, as John Steinbeck does in *The Grapes of Wrath*, pit the poor against the rich." It will be recalled that in "The Artist and His Country," O'Brien upheld Steinbeck against the seeming lack of overt political engagement in writers such as Roth, suggesting that her belief in the necessity of this writer's fixed political position hardened over time. O'Brien, "Compelled by the Dark Sensibility," 2.

11. O'Brien, *Country Girl: A Memoir*, 236.

12. O'Brien, "Art of Fiction"; Sean O'Faolain, "William Faulkner: More Genius than Talent," 75; Cleanth Brooks, "The American South and Yeats's Ireland," 734; O'Brien, "Compelled by the Dark Sensibility," 2; W. B. Yeats, *Per Amica Silentia Lunae*, 29; Edna O'Brien, "The Public and the Private Self," 5.

13. Kieran Quinlan, *Strange Kin: Ireland and the American South*, 4. Yeats's poem "Valley of the Black Pig," referenced in the opening pages of *House of Splendid Isolation*, speaks of this marginal placement, with the speaker expressing a weariness of "the world's empires."

14. Kathryn Stelmach Artuso, *Transatlantic Renaissances: Literature of Ireland and the American South*, xiv, xvii; Brian Dooley, *Black and Green: The Fight for Civil Rights in Northern Ireland & Black America*, 1.

15. Josie's desperate and futile attempts to procure an illegal abortion from her local doctor—"She would talk code and he would talk code back"—recall Dewey Dell's similarly failed endeavor in *As I Lay Dying* (1930): "She looking at [the doctor], saying You could do so much for me if you just would. If you just knew. I am I and you are you and I know it and you dont know it and you could do so much for me if you just would and if you just would then I could tell you and then nobody would have to know." O'Brien has described *As I Lay Dying* as Faulkner's "most perfect novel." O'Brien, *House of Splendid Isolation*, 47; Faulkner, *As I Lay Dying*, 46–47; O'Brien, "Compelled by the Dark Sensibility," 3.

16. Her infatuation with Fr. John reminds her of an older romance from her time in America: "She had felt this restlessness once before, with a married man, a Jewish man in Brooklyn." O'Brien, *House of Splendid Isolation*, 126.

17. O'Brien, *House of Splendid Isolation*, 140, 59. Here we find something of Faulkner's women, praised by O'Brien as ones who "grapple with the terrifyingness of their near-unbearable lives, toiling, copulating, enduring, yet immeasurably separate from [the men] they have not been a day or an hour apart from." There seems a particular resonance between one of the female characters of *House of Splendid Isolation*—"a woman who personifies greyness, grey hair, a wraparound grey apron and black-grey eyes, like a periwinkle—and Martha Armstid of *Light in August*: "the grey woman with a cold, harsh, irascible face . . . the grey woman not plump nor thin, man hard, workhard, in a serviceable grey garment worn savage and brusque, her hands on her hips, her face like those of generals who have been defeated in battle." O'Brien says of him, "Faulkner is thought to be a man's writer, focusing on the male prerogatives and not on women. This is simply not the case. He saw unflinchingly into women." O'Brien, *House of Splendid Isolation*, 16; Faulkner, *Light in August*, 15; O'Brien, "Compelled by the Dark Sensibility," 2.

18. Malamud sent O'Brien a copy of *The Tenants* in 1972, and she reciprocated by sending him *Night*. Of *The Tenants*, Malamud's biographer Philip Davis has said, "[It] was written to . . . bring a greater understanding of the black and white races such as Malamud believed had only previously been achieved by William Faulkner." For Malamud it was an attempt for each side to see the other's history: "It is a great pity that two groups of people, each with an identical history of persecution, are living together with that amount of antagonism. One can only hope that eventually they will recognize each other's history and come together." Davis, *Bernard Malamud*, 267, 269.

19. John Dunne, "Terrible Things Happen," 159; Imhof Rüdiger, review of *House of Splendid Isolation*, by Edna O'Brien; *The Book of Intrusions*, by Desmond MacNamara; *The Seduction of Morality*, by Tom Murphy; and *A Goat's Song*, by Dermot Healy, 27; Ed Moloney, "Media Censorship during 'the Troubles,'" *Nieman Reports*, June 15, 2000.

20. Eve Stoddard, *Positioning Gender and Race in (Post)colonial Plantation Space: Connecting Ireland and the Caribbean*, 131.

21. O'Brien, *House of Splendid Isolation*, 57, 61; O'Brien, *Night*, 1. In one of her *House of Splendid Isolation* notebooks O'Brien has written out a list of what she describes as "Coose Phrases," apparently confirming that she was thinking of *Night*, and its created village of Coose, while writing her 1994 novel. Of Coose, Grace Eckley has said, "Using real Irish names, Miss O'Brien has now created a territory as Faulkner did with Yoknapatawpha." As Maureen O'Connor notes, "O'Brien is ever citing and rewriting her own oeuvre even as she interpolates, ventriloquizes, and interacts with other writers and traditions, and her practices of intertextuality are only recently receiving attention in critical analyses of her work." Eckley, *Edna O'Brien*, 77–78; Maureen O'Connor, review of *The Light of Evening*, by O'Brien, 887.

22. O'Brien, "Compelled by the Dark Sensibility," 2; O'Brien, "*House of Splendid Isolation*, Notebooks," box 44, folder 9, Edna O'Brien Papers, Emory University, Atlanta (hereafter cited as O'Brien Papers, Emory). Reprinted by permission of Peters Fraser & Dunlop (www.petersfraserdunlop.com) on behalf of Edna O'Brien. Fittingly, O'Brien's archives have ended up in the South, joining those of other Irish artists such as Seamus Heaney at Emory.

23. William Faulkner, *Absalom, Absalom!*, 378.

24. O'Brien, *House of Splendid Isolation*, 44; William Faulkner, *The Sound and the Fury*, 31; Diane Roberts, *Faulkner and Southern Womanhood*, 4; Faulkner, *Sound and the Fury*, 108. It is phrase also used by Joe Christmas of *Light in August*.

25. O'Brien, *House of Splendid Isolation*, 35, 36.

26. In this essay, O'Brien sets one of her own protagonists in an Irish and southern American tradition of antiheroines: "Baba came to me partly through an impatience with my own character and partly in acknowledgment of that long line of daring and invincible heroines which includes . . . Molly Bloom and Scarlett O'Hara."

27. Edna O'Brien, "Why Irish Heroines Don't Have to Be Good Any More," *New York Times*, May 11, 1986, BR13.

28. O'Brien, *House of Splendid Isolation*, 137; Danine Farquharson and Bernice Schrank, "Blurring Boundaries, Intersecting Lives: History, Gender, and Violence in Edna O'Brien's *House of Splendid Isolation*," 117; O'Brien, *House of Splendid Isolation*, 140, 123.

29. Stoddard, *Positioning Gender and Race*, 122.

30. A clear sign of the counteraction of women's rights in Ireland and black rights in the American South is evident in the political sphere. Eric Foner reveals the fact that "not until the 1990s would the number of black legislators in the South approach the level seen during Reconstruction." In Ireland the six women elected to the second Dáil

in 1921 would not be surpassed until the 1980s. Foner, *Give Me Liberty! An American History*, 691.

31. Farquharson and Schrank, "Blurring Boundaries," 117; O'Brien, "*House of Splendid Isolation*, Notebooks," box 44, folder 9, O'Brien Papers, Emory; Faulkner, *Absalom, Absalom!*, 182, 184; O'Brien, *House of Splendid Isolation*, 53.

32. O'Brien, *House of Splendid Isolation*, 37, 92, 189; O'Brien, "*House of Splendid Isolation*, Notebooks," box 44, folder 9, O'Brien Papers, Emory.

33. O'Brien, *House of Splendid Isolation*, 77, 50; Artuso, *Transatlantic Renaissances*, xv.

34. Liam Harte, *Reading the Contemporary Irish Novel, 1987–2007*, 164.

35. O'Faolain, "William Faulkner," 75.

36. O'Brien, *House of Splendid Isolation*, 77.

37. O'Brien, *House of Splendid Isolation*, 75, 87. O'Brien might also here be riffing on Paul Durcan's poem "In Memory: The Miami Showband—Massacred 31 July 1975," in which he rejects poetry reduced to the simplistic taking of sides: "His eyes glitter hate and vanity, porter and whiskey, / And I realize that he is blind to the braille connection / Between a music and a music maker."

38. O'Brien, *House of Splendid Isolation*, 13, 129.

39. As a young author, Faulkner was coy about the effects of Joyce on his fiction: "You know sometimes I think there must be a sort of pollen of ideas floating in the air, which fertilizes similarly minds here and there which have not had direct contact. I had heard of Joyce of course." However, Faulkner's evasions must be taken with the appropriate reservation, as he was also known to quote *Ulysses* at length. He would later feel confident enough to tell an interviewer, "You should approach Joyce's *Ulysses* as the illiterate Baptist preacher approaches the Old Testament: with faith." Quoted in Michael Zeitlin, "James Joyce," 209; William Faulkner, "The Art of Fiction, No. 12."

40. Joyce, *Portrait*, 146.

41. O'Brien, *House of Splendid Isolation*, 113; O'Brien, *Country Girl: A Memoir*, 241; O'Brien, *House of Splendid Isolation*, 63.

42. O'Brien, *House of Splendid Isolation*, 21, 31, 32, 51.

43. O'Brien, *House of Splendid Isolation*, 197; Faulkner, *Absalom, Absalom!*, 361. Exemplary of the paralyzing effects of history is Reverend Gail Hightower of *Light in August* (1932), who cannot stop reliving a particular instance of the Civil War (which ended before he was born), in which his grandfather, a Confederate cavalry officer, was ignobly shot while stealing chickens: "He is entering it again, the street which ran for thirty years. . . . It had made a circle and he is still inside of it. . . . he is still inside the circle. . . . But I have never got outside that circle." The obsession Faulkner's characters have with the past, and how this obsession prevents (or intentionally obscures) any attempted resolution of the racial divisions that define the southern states, clearly influenced O'Brien. In her notebook she has taken down the quotations, "He is entering it again, the street which

ran for thirty years." More recently, she has said that *Light in August* is one of the novels, along with Roth's *Sabbath's Theater* (1994), that she returns to "again and again." William Faulkner, *Light in August*, 266–67; O'Brien, "*House of Splendid Isolation,* Notebooks," box 44, folder 9, O'Brien Papers, Emory; Edna O'Brien, "Edna O'Brien: By the Book," *New York Times*, Mar. 24, 2015.

44. Faulkner, *Absalom, Absalom!*, 361; O'Brien, *House of Splendid Isolation*, 86; O'Brien, "*House of Splendid Isolation*, Notebooks," box 44, folder 9, O'Brien Papers, Emory.

45. O'Brien nevertheless had the complex interweaved racial heritage of the South in her thoughts as she was writing this passage, as on the back page of one of the *House of Splendid Isolation* notebooks, she draws the hybrid family tree of the black Turl McCaslin, whose white slave master father, Lucius Quintus Carothers McCaslin, was also his grandfather.

46. Faulkner, *Absalom, Absalom!*, 361; O'Brien, *House of Splendid Isolation*, 180.

47. Louis Menand, "The Irony and the Ecstasy: Philip Roth and the Jewish Atlantis," 94.

48. Norman Podhoretz, "The Adventures of Philip Roth," 34. Podhoretz was one of the signatories of the "Project for the New American Century" in 1997, which provided the philosophical foundation for the invasion of Iraq. George Bush awarded him the Presidential Medal of Freedom in 2004 for his intellectual prowess. If proof is needed on how radically far apart Podhoretz and Roth actually stood politically, it can be found in Roth's coded attack on the Bush administration, *The Plot against America* (2004).

49. Bill Clinton sees a connection between Roth and Faulkner in their attachment to their respective regions: "What Dublin was to Joyce, what Yoknapatawpha County was to Faulkner, Newark is to Philip Roth." Roth is three times winner of the PEN/Faulkner Award, for *Operation Shylock* in 1994, *The Human Stain* in 2001, and *Indignation* in 2007 (O'Brien was a guest speaker at the PEN/Faulkner Awards in 1994, where she read sections of *House of Splendid Isolation*). Pierpont, *Roth Unbound*, 244.

50. Roth, *American Pastoral*, 89.

51. William Carlos Williams, "At Kenneth Burke's Place," 20–21; Roth, *American Pastoral*, 189.

52. Posnock, *Philip Roth's Rude Truth*, 90. Here is the path of "Gold dinnerware" not taken by Neil Klugman after his epiphany in Saint Patrick's Cathedral.

53. Roth, *American Pastoral*, 75.

54. Roth, *American Pastoral*, 163.

55. Roth, *Zuckerman Unbound*, 163, 343, 194.

56. Jessica G. Rabin, "Requiem for a Dream: Philip Roth's *American Pastoral* and William Faulkner's *Absalom, Absalom!*," 220, 228.

57. Roth, *American Pastoral*, 398.

58. Disapproval of Jewish-Catholic intermarriage did remain strong enough in the 1970s that the popular sitcom *Bridget Loves Bernie* (1972–73)—essentially a remake of

Abie's Irish Rose—was canceled after one series because of threats from religious groups. Also running as counternarrative to the idea that tension between Jews and Irish Catholics had completely dissipated by the 1990s is Roth's exchange with Mary McCarthy, his friend and a model for his early iconoclastic attacks on pious American sensibilities (see chapter 2). McCarthy writes to Roth taking exception to his depiction of a Christmas service in *The Counterlife*, as discussed in chapter 1.

59. Roth, *American Pastoral*, 392, 400, 11.

60. David Halberstam, *The Fifties*, xi; Roth, *American Pastoral*, 309; Roth, "Preface to the Thirtieth Edition," xi; Bernard Schwartz and Stephan Lesher, *Inside the Warren Court, 1953–1969*, 87; Hannah Arendt, "Reflections on Little Rock," 236.

61. Rabin, "Requiem for a Dream," 221; Roth, *American Pastoral*, 306; Roth, *The Plot against America*, 81; Melvyn Stokes, *D. W. Griffith's "The Birth of a Nation"? A History of the Most Controversial Motion Picture of All Time*, 111. The battle over his legacy continues today with antiracist campaigners demanding Princeton reassess its largely laudatory views of this former president of the university. His relationship with the Irish is also complicated. Of Ulster-Scots stock himself, Wilson was attacked by the Irish American press for his failure to support Irish independence at Versailles. He did, however, make the Irish Catholic Joseph Patrick Tumulty his private secretary, over the protests of his anti-Catholic southern wife.

62. Roth, *American Pastoral*, 302.

63. Halberstam, *The Fifties*, 483.

64. Roth, *American Pastoral*, 68, 121, 304. Slavery was abolished in New Jersey in 1804, but incrementally so that the last slave was granted freedom only in 1865.

65. Roth, *Goodbye, Columbus*, 90.

66. Roth, *American Pastoral*, 276, 314.

67. Roth, *American Pastoral*, 268–69.

68. By having the novelist Zuckerman imagine the Swede's interiority, Roth squares a circle of Faulkner's, in which his less educated characters were often said to be more internally articulate than it was possible for them to be (an accusation that has troubling elitist implications). It is less a fault on Faulkner's part (as many critics argued at one time) than a useful reminder that consciousness, as received through literary texts, is always an artistic sleight of hand—that is to say, a fiction.

69. At the time he wrote *Goodbye, Columbus*, Roth was reading Baldwin, an author who formed part of what Roth calls his "republic of discourse." Roth did at this time criticize Baldwin's play *Blues for Mr. Charlie* (1964) for failing to live up to its stated intention of "understand[ing] [a] wretched [white] man" who has murdered his black neighbor. Roth, "Preface to the Thirtieth Edition," xi; Philip Roth, "Channel X: Two Plays on the Race Conflict."

70. James Baldwin, *The Fire Next Time*, 6, 10.

71. In Ferguson, near St. Louis, Missouri, particularly, the methodical impoverishing of minorities through unpayable fines enforced by an overwhelmingly white police to cover shortfalls in local government finances calls to mind the kleptocratic sharecropping system of the South.

72. Roth, *American Pastoral*, 193.

73. Hermione Lee summarizes these issues in her interview with Roth: "Supposing I say to you that nearly all the women in the books are there to obstruct, or to help, or to console the male characters. There's the woman who cooks and consoles and is sane and calming, or the other kind of woman, the dangerous maniac, the obstructer." Roth, "Art of Fiction."

74. Her self-inflicted silence is a form of narrative protest, akin to that of Zuckerman's lover Maria of *The Counterlife*, who in a metatextual flourish decides to leave the novel.

75. Remnick, "Into the Clear," 118.

76. Edna O'Brien, "En Route to Nowhere . . . ," letter to Philip Roth, undated (1997), box 10, folder 45, O'Brien Papers, Emory. Reprinted by permission of Peters Fraser & Dunlop (www.petersfraserdunlop.com) on behalf of Edna O'Brien.

77. Asked whether she thought her trilogy influenced Roth's "turn to history," O'Brien demurred: "As for the shift in his writing, I think it was inevitable, with a mind so capacious as his." O'Brien, email interview with the author, Oct. 2, 2012. Reprinted by permission of Peters Fraser & Dunlop (www.petersfraserdunlop.com) on behalf of Edna O'Brien.

78. Roth, *American Pastoral*, 420, 419.

79. Edna O'Brien, *Down by the River*, 2, 3; Heather Ingman, "Edna O'Brien: Stretching the Nation's Boundaries," 260; O'Brien, *Down by the River*, 2–3; O'Brien, "Passion's Progress."

80. This scene is added at some point between *American Pastoral* "Drafts, First, with Changes" (November 1995) and "Draft Fourth Copy C" (July 1996), Roth Papers, Library of Congress.

81. O'Brien, *Down by the River*, 121.

82. David Brauner, "Subverting History in *American Pastoral*," 27; Roth, *American Pastoral*, 44; Harte, *Reading the Contemporary Irish Novel*, 159.

6. "We're All in Our Own Coffins"

1. O'Brien to Roth, July 30, 2003, box OB102, Edna O'Brien Papers, University College Dublin. Reprinted by permission of Peters Fraser & Dunlop (www.petersfraserdunlop.com) on behalf of Edna O'Brien.

2. Janan Ganesh, "Older Writers Saved the Novel," *Financial Times*, June 23, 2017. Interviewing O'Brien, Ganesh wonders "if she fears being defined by her early work just as Philip Roth . . . remains tied to *Portnoy's Complaint* half a century and several superior

novels later," to which O'Brien replies: "If you are defined at all, that's something." Janan Ganesh, "Sex, Books and a Lifetime of Defiance," *Financial Times*, July 14, 2017.

3. Claire Lowdon, "The Butcher of Bosnia Holes Up in an Irish Backwater," review of *The Little Red Chairs*, by O'Brien, *Spectator*, Nov. 14, 2015; James Wood, "Stranger in Our Midst"; Edward Said, "Thoughts of Late Style," 4. Adam Zachery Newton uses Said's essay to read Roth's late work in "'I Was the Prosthesis': Roth and Late Style."

4. Banville, "Z/R"; Roth, *The Plot against America*, 10.

5. Roth, *The Plot against America*, 8–9.

6. Roth, *The Plot against America*, 7.

7. Jay P. Dolan, *The Irish Americans: A History*, 236.

8. David Nirenberg, *Anti-Judaism: The Western Tradition*, 458.

9. Roth, *The Plot against America*, 13, 4, 5, 14, 15–16.

10. Roth, *The Plot against America*, 17, 18. The Kishinev Pogrom in 1903 saw dozens of Jews killed in the Russian city of Kishinev (now Chişinău in Moldovia) and sparking even greater Jewish emigration from Russia. Irish nationalist Michael Davitt visited the area as a correspondent for the *New York Times* and reported on the massacre in his book *Within the Pale: The True Story of Anti-Semitic Persecutions in Russia* (1903).

11. Roth, *The Plot against America*, 85, 94.

12. Jennifer Glaser, "The Jew in the Canon: Reading Race and Literary History in Philip Roth's *The Human Stain*," 1465; Roth, *The Plot against America*, 23, 22.

13. Roth, *The Plot against America*, 65.

14. Ralph Ellison, in his speculative alternate history essay "What America Would Be Like without Blacks," delineates the role of minority writer as devil's advocate to complacent, misleading views of America: "Today it is the black American who puts pressure upon the nation to live up to its ideals. It is he who insists that we purify the American language by demanding that there be a closer correlation between the meaning of words and reality, between ideal and conduct, between our assertions and our actions." Roth says of Ellison, when both faced criticisms for their unadorned depictions of their respective communities, "His intellectual position was virtually identical to mine but he was presenting it as a black American, instructing through examples drawn from *Invisible Man* and the ambiguous relationship that novel had established with some vocal members of his own race." Ellison, "What American Would Be Like without Blacks," in *The Collected Essays of Ralph Ellison*, 583; Roth, "Writing about Jews," 209.

15. Roth, *The Plot against America*, 160, 210, 211, 116.

16. W. E. B. DuBois, *The Souls of Black Folk: Essays and Sketches*, 10; Roth, *The Plot against America*, 124; James Weldon Johnson, *The Autobiography of an Ex-Colored Man*, 8; Aharon Appelfeld, "Conversation in Jerusalem with Aharon Appelfeld."

17. In *The Human Stain*, Roth imagines the life of a light-skinned African American Newarker Coleman Silk, who "passes" as Jewish.

18. Roth, *The Plot against America*, 182; J. O'Neill, "Roth v. Roth v. Roth."

19. Roth, *The Plot against America*, 244.

20. Roth, *The Plot against America*, 262.

21. Roth, *The Plot against America*, 262.

22. Roth, *The Plot against America*, 261; Roth quoted in Pierpont, *Roth Unbound*, 326. Roth threads this phrase through his fiction, in *The Dying Animal*, *American Pastoral*, *The Counterlife* ("He had pretended to be dead, suppose he were at it again"), and *Sabbath's Theater*: "At it again. How he'd began was how he'd end, he who had gone gloomily around for years believing his life of adulteries and arthritis and professional embitterment to have been senselessly lived outside of conventions, without unity or purpose." O'Brien too contemplates this scene in a 2002 speech given to the American Academy of Arts and Letters that attacked literary censorship: "Joyce dismantled the human body, male and female, with the prodigality of a poet, the smut of a pornographer, and the objectivity of a mortician. When an episode from 'Nausicaa,' of *Ulysses*, appeared in *The Little Review*, all issues were confiscated and burnt. . . . The chapter centers on Gerty MacDowell, a model of Catholic girlhood, who has gone to the seaside for a bit of relaxation. She who crimsoned at rude words finds herself yielding to the lascivious glances of a mysterious stranger, none other than Leopold Bloom. And while she swings her legs in and out and watches some fireworks, she gives the gentleman a good view of her nainsook knickers, imagines him to be in deep mourning, missing perhaps a wife, while Bloom, on the point of emission, reverts to his old drollery, at it again." Edna O'Brien, "Danger Zone."

23. Roth, *The Plot against America*, 305; Harriet Beecher Stowe, *Uncle Tom's Cabin*, 45; Roth, *The Plot against America*, 274.

24. Michael Gorra, "Philip Roth's Inventions of Self," review of *The Plot against America*, by Roth, in *Times Literary Supplement*, Oct. 8, 2004.

25. Timothy Snyder, *On Tyranny: Twenty Lessons from the Twentieth Century*, 13; Madeline Albright, *Fascism*, 63. Snyder recommends *The Plot against America* as a novel that can guard against this by "enliven[ing] our ability to think about ambiguous situations and [to] judge the intentions of others." Clay Risen writes about the prevalence of the Ku Klux Klan in 1920s American society and suggests there are two ways to look at these dark aspects of American history: "One could say, great—we've met the enemy before, and defeated him. We'll do it again. Or we could realize that we've met the enemy, and he is us." Snyder, *On Tyranny*, 62; Clay Risen, "The Ku Klux Klan's Surprising History," review of *The Second Coming of the KKK*, by Linda Gordon, *New York Times*, Dec. 4, 2017.

26. Foucault, introduction to *Anti-Oedipus*, xiii.

27. Philip Roth, "The Story behind *The Plot against America*," *New York Times*, Sept. 19, 2004; Roth, "Roth@80."

28. Roth's friend David Remnick also references *The Plot against America* in his commentary on the election and read the result as a type of alternate history: "Surely

such a cruel and retrograde figure could succeed among some voters, but how could he win? . . . And yet Trump . . . recognized that he could embody and manipulate these dark forces. . . . Trump was not elected on a platform of decency, fairness, moderation, compromise, and the rule of law; he was elected, in the main, on a platform of resentment. Fascism is not our future . . . but this is surely the way fascism can begin." David Remnick, "An American Tragedy."

29. Philip Roth, "Philip Roth Emails on Trump."

30. Roth, *American Pastoral*, 86; Roth, *The Plot against America*, 114.

31. Quoted in O'Brien, "Talking with Edna O'Brien," interview by John Freeman, *Milwaukee Journal-Sentinel*, Oct. 1, 2006.

32. Julie Wheelwright, "Edna O'Brien: The Mother of Invention," review of *The Light of Evening*, by O'Brien, *Independent*, Sept. 28, 2006. When Roth asked O'Brien how much she was influenced by the rural Irish world of her childhood she answered, "There's no telling, really. If I had grown up on the steppes of Russia, or in Brooklyn—my parents lived there when they were first married—my material would have been different but my apprehension might be just the same." O'Brien, "A Conversation with Edna O'Brien," 42.

33. O'Brien, *The Light of Evening*, 24; Faulkner, *Light in August*, 62.

34. O'Brien, *The Light of Evening*, 28, 29, 31, 36.

35. John Powell, *Encyclopedia of North American Immigration*, 208–9.

36. O'Brien, *The Light of Evening*, 36, 35.

37. Sara Goek, "From Ireland to the US: A Brief Migration History," *Irish Times*, Oct. 29, 2015.

38. O'Brien, *The Light of Evening*, 41; Norman Mailer, *The Naked and the Dead*, 227, 267.

39. Walt Whitman, "Crossing Brooklyn Ferry," 132–38.

40. O'Brien, *The Light of Evening*, 51.

41. Philosopher John Dewey writes of this process in his essay "Racial Prejudice and Friction": "The phenomenon [of racial prejudice is] . . . seen in the attitude of the earlier immigrants to the United States towards later comers. The Irish were among the first to feel the effects; then as they became fairly established and the other older stock become used to them and no longer regarded them as intruders, the animosity was transferred to southern Europeans, especially to the Italians; later the immigrants from eastern and southeastern Europe become the suspected and feared party. And strikingly enough it had usually been the group which had previously been the object of hostile feelings which has been most active in opposing the new-comers." Dewey, *John Dewey: The Middle Works, 1899–1924*, 245.

42. O'Brien, *The Light of Evening*, 53.

43. O'Brien, *The Light of Evening*, 70 (emphasis added), 71, 72.

44. Gabriel takes Dilly to the beach at Coney Island. Their failed relationship mirrors that of another immigrant, the protagonist of Isaac B. Singer's short story "A Day in

Coney Island," who loses "refuge in America and a woman I really loved." O'Brien wrote to Singer in 1972 to express her admiration for the story.

45. O'Brien, *The Light of Evening*, 113, 115, 4.

46. O'Brien, *The Light of Evening*, 129, 151, 123; Ellen McWilliams, "Making It Up with the Motherland: Revision and Reconciliation in Edna O'Brien's *The Light of Evening*," 51; O'Brien, *The Light of Evening*, 129, 142.

47. O'Brien, *The Light of Evening*, 304; O'Brien, "Talking with Edna O'Brien," interview by Freeman.

48. Pia Masiero, *Philip Roth and the Zuckerman Books*, 1.

49. Marisol Morales Ladrón, "(M)Others from the Motherland in Edna O'Brien's *The Light of Evening* and Colm Tóibín's *Brooklyn*."

50. O'Brien to Roth, May 23, 1986, box 26, folder 10, Roth Papers, Library of Congress, Washington, DC. Reprinted by permission of Peters Fraser & Dunlop (www.petersfraserdunlop.com) on behalf of Edna O'Brien.

51. Roth to O'Brien, June 5, 1986, box 10, folder 45, O'Brien Papers, Emory University, Atlanta (hereafter cited as O'Brien Papers, Emory). Copyright © 1986 by Philip Roth, used by permission of The Wylie Agency LLC.

52. O'Brien, *The Light of Evening*, 167, 267; Edna O'Brien, "Friday's Appointment," box 30, folder 11, O'Brien Papers, Emory (emphasis added); Reprinted by permission of Peters Fraser & Dunlop (www.petersfraserdunlop.com) on behalf of Edna O'Brien; O'Brien, *The Light of Evening*, 267; O'Brien, "Edna O'Brien," 218.

53. O'Brien, *The Light of Evening*, 294.

54. Roth, *Patrimony: A True Story*, 177. Roth, in his acceptance speech for the Historical Society Award for *Patrimony*, said of his father: "I would not hesitate to place his encyclopedic knowledge of prewar Newark alongside James Joyce's overbrimming sense of the Dublin whose life he renders with such sensuous precision in *Ulysses*."

55. O'Brien, "Roth@80."

56. Philip Roth, foreword to *Other Men's Daughters*, by Richard Stern, xi.

57. Joyce Carol Oates, review of *The Little Red Chairs*, by O'Brien, *New York Times*, Mar. 28, 2016; Claire Messud, review of *The Little Red Chairs*, by O'Brien, *Financial Times*, Oct. 23, 2015; Patricia Craig, "Monsters in the Midst," review of *The Little Red Chairs*, by O'Brien, *Independent*, Oct. 22, 2015; O'Brien, "Mythopoeic Ireland," 215.

58. Edna O'Brien, "It's a Bad Time Out There for Emotion," *New York Times*, Feb. 14, 1993.

59. In 2015, as she was writing *The Little Red Chairs*, she praised the short stories of Kafka, which she returns to "again and again." Edna O'Brien, "Edna O'Brien: By the Book," *New York Times*, Mar. 24, 2015.

60. In 1972 O'Brien wrote to Singer praising his short story "Gimpel the Fool," set in a Polish shtetl where, according to Ben Siegel, "the real and unreal fuse . . . convincingly." Roth made his debt to Singer apparent in the character of I. E. Lonoff in *The Ghost Writer*. Ben Siegel, "Gimpel the Fool, and Other Stories."

61. John Banville, introduction to *The Love Object: Selected Stories*, by Edna O'Brien, xiii.

62. Dragan is modeled in part on Serbian leader Radovan Karadzic who hid out from international justice for years in a small Austrian village.

63. Ganesh, "Sex, Books and a Lifetime of Defiance."

64. Edna O'Brien, *The Little Red Chairs*, 3; W. B. Yeats, "Easter, 1916," 93–94. Yeats surfaces throughout the novel, and Dragan is finally arrested for his crimes against humanity on his way to read his "own poetry at the foot of Ben Bulben, in homage to Yeats." Dragan's fascination with Yeats is perhaps a sly nod at Yeats's own flirtation with fascistic ideologies. O'Brien, *The Little Red Chairs*, 123.

65. O'Brien, *The Little Red Chairs*, 8, 11, 13.

66. O'Brien, *The Little Red Chairs*, 37, 49; Messud, review of *The Little Red Chairs*, by O'Brien.

67. O'Brien, *The Little Red Chairs*, 68, 70, 119, 130.

68. Ed Vulliamy, "Bosnia's Victims Twenty Years On," *Observer*, Apr. 8, 2012. O'Brien thanks Vulliamy in the acknowledgments to *The Light of Evening*.

69. O'Brien, *The Little Red Chairs*, 146, 150; Éilís Ní Dhuibhne, review of *The Little Red Chairs*, by O'Brien, *Irish Times*, Oct. 24, 2015.

70. O'Brien, *The Little Red Chairs*, 167.

71. O'Brien, *The Little Red Chairs*, 175, 177, 192.

72. O'Brien, *The Little Red Chairs*, 204, 207, 213, 212; Maureen O'Connor, "Seeing Red," review of *The Little Red Chairs*, by O'Brien, *Irish Literary Supplement*, Oct. 1, 2017.

73. O'Brien, *The Little Red Chairs*, 239, 269, 265, 297.

74. Oates, review of *The Little Red Chairs*, by O'Brien, *New York Times*, Mar. 28, 2016; Messud, review of *The Little Red Chairs*, by O'Brien; Edna O'Brien, "In the Company of Tyrants," interview with Philip Maughan, *New Statesman*, Nov. 3, 2015. Along with places like Argentina, Ireland too provided a haven for several prominent Nazis in the postwar years, to which the book seems to call attention.

75. Morris Dickstein, "Philip Roth's New Novel—*Nemesis*."

76. Leah Hager Cohen, "Summer of '44," review of *Nemesis*, by Roth, *New York Times*, Oct. 8, 2010; Victoria Aarons, "Expelled Once Again: The Fantasy of Living the Counterlife in Roth's *Nemesis*," 55; Philip Roth, *Nemesis*, 38; Nicholas Lezard, "The Talented Mr Roth," review of *Nemesis*, by Roth, *Guardian*, Sept. 27, 2011.

77. Roth, *Nemesis*, 53, 69; Eric J. Sundquist, *Strangers in the Land: Blacks, Jews, Post-Holocaust America*, 246. Roth's interview with Appelfeld can be found in his nonfiction collection *Shop Talk*, alongside his interview with O'Brien.

78. Aharon Appelfeld, *Badenheim 1939*, 38.

79. Roth, *Nemesis*, 15, 106, 82, 163.

80. Roth, *Nemesis*, 273, 267.

81. O'Brien, "Roth@80."

Conclusion

1. Alison Flood, "Edna O'Brien Wins PEN/Nabokov Lifetime Award," *Guardian*, Feb. 7, 2018.

2. Hannah Arendt, "'A Daughter of Our People': A Response to Gershom Scholem," 162.

3. Quoted in Cheryl Miller, "Why Malamud Faded"; quoted in Nathaniel Rich, "Roth Agonistes"; Roth, *Zuckerman Unbound*, 154.

4. J. O'Neill, "Roth v. Roth v. Roth"; John Banville, "Grave Thoughts from a Master," review of *Everyman*, by Philip Roth, *Guardian*, Apr. 29, 2006. Banville follows in Roth's footsteps by providing a preface for O'Brien's short-story anthology *The Love Object: Selected Stories* (2013), seeing traces of Henry James in her "exile's measuring eye." Banville, introduction to *Love Object*, by O'Brien, ix.

5. Kevin Barry, "Jumping Off a Cliff."

6. O'Brien's friend Colum McCann, who frequently addresses Jewish themes in his fiction, is also inspired by Doctorow's work: "The best writers attempt to become alternative historians. . . . My sense of the Great Depression is guided by the works of Doctorow, for instance." McCann quoted in Joel Lovell, "Colum McCann's Radical Empathy," *New York Times Magazine*, May 30, 2013. McCann's colleague at Hunter College the Jewish American writer Nathan Englander tells him of their shared endeavor: "All of us who write are sick with the same disease. We've been infected by books, and now we must infect others." Looking further afield, Anne Enright—who continues the trope of the Irish-Jewish love affair in *The Forgotten Waltz* (2011)—speaks of her Jewish influences: "I keep going back to 'The Sin of Jesus,' by Isaac Babel. . . . The way Babel writes fragments reminds me of Grace Paley and Clarice Lispector, two amazing short-story writers who share his Ukrainian Jewish heritage." Nathan Englander quoted in Julia Jackson, "Nathan Englander's Serious Moral Act"; Anne Enright, "Anne Enright on Writing from Life."

7. Erica Jong to O'Brien, Aug. 5, 1977, box 6, folder 19, Edna O'Brien Papers, Emory University, Atlanta. Copyright © Erica Jong, 2018, all rights reserved.

8. O'Brien, *Country Girls: A Memoir*, 268.

9. Jules Melvin Bukiet, "A Tithe of Irish Sorrows," review of *Down by the River*, by O'Brien, *Fort Lauderdale Sun-Sentinel*, May 25, 1997.

10. Joshua Cohen, "Bloody Hell," review of *A Girl Is a Half-Formed Thing*, by Eimear McBride, *New York Times*, Sept. 21, 2014, BR12.

Bibliography

Works by Edna O'Brien

"The Artist and His Country." *Vogue*, Sept. 1, 1971.

"Art of Fiction, No. 82." Interview with Shusha Guppy. *Paris Review* 92 (1984).

August Is a Wicked Month. London: Penguin, 1967.

Byron in Love. London: Weidenfeld & Nicolson, 2009.

Casualties of Peace. London: Penguin, 1966.

"The Connor Girls." In *The Love Object: Selected Stories*. New York: Little, Brown, 2013.

"Conversation with Edna O'Brien." Interview with Glenn Patterson. In *Conversations with Edna O'Brien*, edited by Alice Hughes Kersnowski, 69–71. Jackson: Univ. Press of Mississippi, 2014.

"A Conversation with Edna O'Brien." Interview with Philip Roth. *New York Times*, Nov. 18, 1984. In *Conversations with Edna O'Brien*, edited by Alice Hughes Kersnowski, 40–48. Jackson: Univ. Press of Mississippi, 2014.

Country Girl: A Memoir. London: Faber, 2012.

The Country Girls. In *Country Girls Trilogy*. London: Penguin, 1987.

The Country Girls Trilogy and Epilogue. London: Penguin, 1987.

"Danger Zone." *New Yorker*, June 3, 2002.

Down by the River. London: Phoenix, 2000.

"Edna O'Brien." Interview with Mike Murphy. In *Reading the Future: Irish Writers in Conversation with Mike Murphy*, edited by Clíodhna Ní Anluain, 211–18. Dublin: Lilliput Press, 2000.

A Fanatic Heart: Selected Stories. Harmondsworth, Middlesex: Penguin, 1984.

Girl. London: Faber, 2019.

Girls in Their Married Bliss. In *Country Girls Trilogy*. London: Penguin, 1987.

House of Splendid Isolation. London: Weidenfeld & Nicolson, 1994.

Interview with Mark Featherstone-Witty. *Palatinate,* Oct. 1971.

"In the Company of Tyrants." Interview with Philip Maughan. *New Statesman,* Nov. 3, 2015.

In the Forest. London: Weidenfeld & Nicolson, 2002.

"Irish Revel." In *A Fanatic Heart: Selected Stories,* by Edna O'Brien, 177–98. Harmondsworth, Middlesex: Penguin, 1984.

James Joyce. London: Paperview UK, 2006.

Johnny, I Hardly Knew You. London: Weidenfeld & Nicolson, 1977.

The Light of Evening. London: Houghton Mifflin Harcourt, 2006.

The Little Red Chairs. London: Faber, 2015.

The Lonely Girl. In *Country Girls Trilogy and Epilogue.* London: Penguin, 1987.

"Manhattan Medley." In *Saints and Sinners.* London: Faber, 2011.

Mother Ireland. London: Weidenfeld and Nicolson, 1976.

Mrs Reinhardt, and Other Stories. London: Penguin, 1978.

Night. New York: Alfred A. Knopf, 1972.

"Passion's Progress." Interview with Katie Bolick. *Atlantic,* Apr. 20, 2000.

Preface to *Dubliners,* by James Joyce. New York: Signet Classics, 2007.

Preface to *The Playboy of the Western World,* by J. M. Synge. New York: Signet Classics, 2006.

"Roth@80: The Life and Work of Philip Roth." Newark Public Library, Newark, NJ, Mar. 19, 2013.

A Scandalous Woman, and Other Stories. London: Penguin, 1974.

Some Irish Loving. London: Penguin, 1987.

"The Strange World of Carson McCullers." Review of *Clock without Hands,* by Carson McCullers. *Bookman,* Jan. 30, 1962.

Triptych. In *Triptych and Iphigenia: Two Plays.* New York: Grove Press, 2003.

"Who's Afraid of Edna O'Brien?" Interview with Mary Maher. *Irish Times,* Dec. 14, 1967. In *Conversations with Edna O'Brien,* edited by Alice Hughes Kersnowski, 3–7. Jackson: Univ. Press of Mississippi, 2014.

Wild Decembers. London: Hachette, 2000.

"A Woman in Transit." *Stinging Fly* 31, no. 2 (2015): 74–77.

Works by Philip Roth

Afterword to *The Book of Laughter and Forgetting,* by Milan Kundera. Penguin: London, 1983.

American Pastoral. London: Vintage, 1998.

The Anatomy Lesson. In *Zuckerman Bound: A Trilogy and Epilogue.* London: Vintage, 1998.

"Art of Fiction, No. 84." Interview with Hermione Lee. *Paris Review* 93 (1984).

The Breast. New York: Houghton Mifflin, 1972.

"Channel X: Two Plays on the Race Conflict." *New York Review of Books,* May 28, 1964.

"A Confusion of Realms." Interview with Ian Hamilton. *Nation,* June 1, 1985. In *Conversations with Philip Roth,* edited by George J. Searles, 192–97. Jackson: Univ. Press of Mississippi, 1992.

"Conversation with Philip Roth." Interview with Hermione Lee. In *Conversations with Philip Roth,* edited by George J. Searles. Jackson: Univ. Press of Mississippi, 1992.

"A Conversation with Philip Roth." Interview with Joyce Carol Oates. *Ontario Review* (1974). In *Conversations with Philip Roth,* edited by George J. Searles, 89–99. Jackson: Univ. Press of Mississippi, 1992.

"The Conversion of the Jews." In *Goodbye, Columbus, and Five Short Stories,* by Philip Roth, 137–58. London: Houghton Mifflin Harcourt, 1989.

The Counterlife. London: Vintage, 2011.

Deception. London: Vintage, 1990.

The Dying Animal. London: Houghton Mifflin Harcourt, 2001.

Everyman. London: Random House, 2006.

"An Exchange with Mary McCarthy." In *Shop Talk,* edited by Philip Roth, 113–19. London: Jonathan Cape, 2001.

Exit Ghost. London: Random House, 2007.

The Facts: A Novelist's Autobiography. London: Random House, 1988.

Foreword to *A Fanatic Heart: Selected Stories,* by Edna O'Brien, ix–x. Harmondsworth, Middlesex: Penguin, 1984.

Foreword to *Other Men's Daughters,* by Richard Stern, i–xiii. New York: New York Review of Books Classics, 2017.

"The Ghosts of Roth." Interview with Alain Finkielkraut. In *Conversations with Philip Roth,* edited by George J. Searles, 120–30. Jackson: Univ. Press of Mississippi, 1992.

The Ghost Writer. In *Zuckerman Bound: A Trilogy and Epilogue.* London: Vintage, 1998.

Goodbye, Columbus, and Five Short Stories. London: Houghton Mifflin Harcourt, 1989.

The Human Stain. London: Random House, 2010.

The Humbling. London: Jonathan Cape, 2009.

"'I Always Wanted You to Admire My Fasting'; or, Looking at Kafka." In *Reading Myself and Others*, edited by Philip Roth, 303–26. London: Penguin, 1985.

"Imagining Jews." In *Reading Myself and Others*, edited by Philip Roth, 251–80. London: Penguin, 1985.

I Married a Communist. New York: Houghton Mifflin, 1998.

Indignation. London: Random House, 2008.

"In Response to Those Who Have Asked Me: 'How Did You Come to Write That Book Anyway?'" In *Reading Myself and Others*, edited by Philip Roth, 29–36. London: Penguin, 1985.

"Interview with the *London Sunday Times*." In *Reading Myself and Others*, edited by Philip Roth, 111–18. London: Penguin, 1985.

Introduction to *Laughable Loves*, by Milan Kundera. In *Reading Myself and Others*, edited by Philip Roth, 251–70. London: Penguin, 1985.

Letting Go. London: Random House, 1962.

My Life as a Man. London: Penguin, 1985.

Nemesis. London: Random House, 2010.

"On Satirizing Presidents." Interview with Alan Lelchuk. In *Reading Myself and Others*, edited by Philip Roth. New York: Viking Penguin, 1985.

"On *The Breast*." Interview with Alan Lelchuk. In *Reading Myself and Others*, edited by Philip Roth, 65–74. London: Penguin, 1985.

"On *The Great American Novel*." Interview with Philip Roth. In *Reading Myself and Others*, edited by Philip Roth, 75–92. London: Penguin, 1985.

Operation Shylock: A Confession. New York: Simon & Schuster, 1993.

Patrimony: A True Story. London: Vintage, 2010.

"Philip Roth at Seventy." Interview with David Remnick. BBC4, Mar. 19, 2003.

"Philip Roth Emails on Trump." Interview with Judith Thurman. *New Yorker*, Jan. 30, 2017.

"Philip Roth's Exact Intent." Interview with George Plimpton. In *Conversations with Philip Roth*. Jackson: Univ. Press of Mississippi, 1992.

"Pictures of Malamud." In *Shop Talk*, edited by Philip Roth, 113–19. London: Jonathan Cape, 2001.

The Plot against America. Boston: Houghton Mifflin, 2004.

Portnoy's Complaint. New York: Vintage, 1994.

"Preface to the Thirtieth Edition." In *Goodbye, Columbus, and Five Short Stories*. London: Houghton Mifflin Harcourt, 1989.

The Professor of Desire. New York: Farrar, Straus and Giroux, 1977.

Reading Myself and Others. New York: Viking Penguin, 1985.
"Roth@80: The Life and Work of Philip Roth." Newark Public Library, Newark, NJ, Mar. 19, 2013.
Sabbath's Theater. London: Vintage, 1996.
Shop Talk. London: Jonathan Cape, 2001.
"Some New Jewish Stereotypes." In *Reading Myself and Others*, edited by Philip Roth, 173–93. London: Penguin, 1985.
"Writers Have a Third Eye." Interview with Alvin P. Sanoff, 1987. In *Conversations with Philip Roth*, edited by George J. Searles, 209–13. Jackson: Univ. Press of Mississippi, 1992.
"Writing about Jews." In *Reading Myself and Others*, edited by Philip Roth, 205–26. London: Penguin, 1985.
"Writing American Fiction." In *Conversations with Philip Roth*, edited by George J. Searles, 173–92. Jackson: Univ. Press of Mississippi, 1992.
Zuckerman Unbound. In *Zuckerman Bound: A Trilogy and Epilogue*. London: Vintage, 1998.

Archives

Bellow, Saul. Papers. Univ. of Chicago.
Malamud, Bernard. Papers. Harry Ransom Center, Univ. of Texas, Austin.
O'Brien, Edna. Papers. Emory Univ., Atlanta.
———. University College Dublin.
Roth, Philip. Papers. Library of Congress, Washington, DC.

Other Sources

Aarons, Victoria. "Expelled Once Again: The Fantasy of Living the Counterlife in Roth's *Nemesis*." *Philip Roth Studies* 9, no. 1 (2013): 51–63.
Adams, Michael. *Censorship: The Irish Experience*. Dublin: Sceptre Books, 1968.
Albright, Madeline. *Fascism*. London: HarperCollins, 2018.
Appelfeld, Aharon. *Badenheim 1939*. Boston: David R. Godine, 1980.
———. "Conversation in Jerusalem with Aharon Appelfeld." In *Shop Talk*, edited by Philip Roth, 18–39. London: Jonathan Cape, 2001.
Arendt, Hannah. "'A Daughter of Our People': A Response to Gershom Scholem." In *The Portable Hannah Arendt*, edited by Peter Baehr, 391–96. New York: Penguin, 2000.
———. "Reflections on Little Rock." *Dissent* 6, no. 1 (1959). In *The Portable Hannah Arendt*, edited by Peter Baehr, 231–46. New York: Penguin, 2000.

Artuso, Kathryn Stelmach. *Transatlantic Renaissances: Literature of Ireland and the American South*. Newark, NJ: Univ. of Delaware Press, 2013.

Auden, W. H. "September 1, 1939." In *W. H. Auden: Selected Poems*, 95–98. London: Vintage, 2007.

Avishai, Bernard. *Promiscuous: Portnoy's Complaint and Our Doomed Pursuit of Happiness*. New Haven, CT: Yale Univ. Press, 2012.

Baldwin, James. *The Fire Next Time*. New York: Modern Library, 1995.

Banville, John. Introduction to *The Love Object: Selected Stories*, by Edna O'Brien. New York: Little, Brown, 2013.

———. "Z/R." Review of *Exit Ghost*, by Philip Roth. *London Review of Books*, Oct. 4, 2007.

Baron, Scarlett. *"Strandentwining Cable": Joyce, Flaubert, and Intertextuality*. Oxford: Oxford Univ. Press, 2011.

Barry, Kevin. "Jumping Off a Cliff." Interview with Jonathan Lee. *Paris Review*, Nov. 12, 2013.

Barthes, Roland. "The Death of an Author." In *Image–Music–Text*, by Roland Barthes. Translated by Stephen Heath. London: Fontana, 1987.

———. *The Pleasure of the Text*. Translated by Richard Miller. New York: Hill and Wang, 2000.

Beatty, Aidan. *Masculinity and Power in Irish Nationalism, 1884–1938*. London: Palgrave, 2016.

Bellow, Saul. *The Adventures of Augie March*. London: Viking, 2003.

———. "Distractions of a Fiction Writer." In *The Living Novel*, edited by Granville Hicks, 1–20. New York: Macmillan, 1957.

———. *Saul Bellow: Letters*. Edited by Benjamin Taylor. New York: Viking, 2010.

———. "The Swamp of Prosperity." Review of *Goodbye, Columbus*, by Philip Roth. *Commentary*, July 1, 1959.

Bender, Abby. *Israelites in Erin: Exodus, Revolution, and the Irish Revival*. Syracuse, NY: Syracuse Univ. Press, 2015.

Bew, Paul, and Gordon Gillespie. *Northern Ireland: A Chronology of the Troubles, 1968–1999*. Lanham, MD: Scarecrow, 1999.

Biagini, Eugenio. "Minorities." In *The Cambridge Social History of Modern Ireland*, edited by Eugenio Biagini and Mary Daly. Cambridge: Cambridge Univ. Press, 2017.

Black, Ian. *Enemies and Neighbours: Arabs and Jews in Palestine and Israel, 1917–2017*. London: Allen Lane, 2017.

Bloom, Harold. *The Anxiety of Influence: A Theory of Poetry*. New York: Oxford Univ. Press, 1997.

———. "Harold Bloom Interview." *RTE*, Oct. 16, 2015.

———. *A Map of Misreading*. Oxford: Oxford Univ. Press, 1975.

Bornstein, George. *The Colors of Zion: Blacks, Jews, and Irish from 1845 to 1945*. Cambridge, MA: Harvard Univ. Press, 2011.

———. "Hybrid Identities." In *Irish Questions and Jewish Questions: Crossovers in Culture*, edited by Aidan Beatty and Dan O'Brien, 127–39. Syracuse, NY: Syracuse Univ. Press, 2018.

Bourke, Angela, and Seamus Deane. *The Field Day Anthology of Irish Writing*. Vols. 4–5, *Irish Women's Writing and Traditions*. Cork: Cork Univ. Press, 2002.

Brannigan, John. *Race in Modern Irish Literature and Culture*. Edinburgh: Edinburgh Univ. Press, 2009.

Brauner, David. *Philip Roth*. Manchester: Manchester Univ. Press, 2007.

———. "Subverting History in *American Pastoral*." In *Philip Roth: "American Pastoral," "The Human Stain," "The Plot against America,"* edited by Debra Shostak. London: Continuum Black, 2011.

Brodkin, Karen. *How the Jews Became White Folk and What That Says about Race in America*. New Brunswick, NJ: Rutgers Univ. Press, 1998.

Brody, Richard. "The Frightening Lessons of Philip Roth's *The Plot against America*." *New Yorker*, Feb. 1, 2017.

Brooks, Cleanth. "The American South and Yeats's Ireland." In *Literary Theory and Criticism Festschrift Presented to René Wellek in Honor of His Eightieth Birthday*, edited by Joseph P. Strelka, 729–40. Bern: Peter Lang, 1984.

Burns, John. "If the Aim of Literature Is to Spark Debate, Philip Roth Has Succeeded." *PopMatters*, Nov. 4, 2017.

Byrne, Francis J. *Irish Kings and High-Kings*. Dublin: Four Courts Press, 2001.

Byron, Kristine. "'In the Name of the Mother . . . ': Reading and Revision in Edna O'Brien's *Country Girls Trilogy and Epilogue*." Introduction to *Wild Colonial Girl: Essays on Edna O'Brien*, edited by Lisa Colletta and Maureen O'Connor. Madison: Univ. of Wisconsin Press, 2006.

Byron, Reginald. *Irish America*. Oxford: Oxford Univ. Press, 1999.

Cain, Kathleen Shine. *Leon Uris: A Critical Companion*. Westport, CT: Greenwood Press, 1998.

Cardin, Bertrand. "Words Apart: Epigraphs in Edna O'Brien's Novels." In *Edna O'Brien: New Critical Perspectives*, edited by Kathryn Laing, Sinead Mooney, and Maureen O'Connor, 68–82. Dublin: Carysfort, 2006.

Carey, John. *The Irish National Origin-Legend: Synthetic Pseudohistory*. Cambridge: Department of Anglo-Saxon, Norse, and Celtic, Univ. of Cambridge, 1994.

Carlson, Julia. *Banned in Ireland: Censorship and the Irish Writer*. Athens: Univ. of Georgia Press, 1990.

———. "Edna O'Brien." In *Censorship: A World Encyclopaedia*, edited by Derek Jones, 1749–50. London: Routledge, 2001.

Chanan, Michael. *From Handel to Hendrix: The Composer in the Public Sphere*. London: Verso, 1999.

Cheyette, Bryan. *Constructions of "the Jew" in English Literature and Society: Racial Representations, 1875–1945*. Cambridge: Cambridge Univ. Press, 1995.

Clayton, Jay, and Eric Rothstein. "Figures in the Corpus: Theories in Intertextuality and Influence." In *Influence and Intertextuality in Literary History*, edited by Jay Clayton and Eric Rothstein, 3–36. Madison: Univ. of Wisconsin Press, 1991.

Cleary, Joe. "Irish American Modernisms." In *The Cambridge Companion to Irish Modernism*, edited by Joe Cleary. Cambridge: Cambridge Univ. Press, 2014.

———. *Literature, Partition and the Nation-State: Culture and Conflict in Ireland, Israel and Palestine*. Cambridge: Cambridge Univ. Press, 2002.

Coetzee, J. M. "What Philip Knew." Review of *The Plot against America*, by Philip Roth. *New York Review of Books*, Nov. 18, 2004.

Cole, Robert. *Propaganda, Censorship and Irish Neutrality in the Second World War*. Edinburgh: Edinburgh Univ. Press, 2006.

Colletta, Lisa, and Maureen O'Connor. Introduction to *Wild Colonial Girl: Essays on Edna O'Brien*. Madison: Univ. of Wisconsin Press, 2006.

Cooney, John. *John Charles McQuaid: Ruler of Catholic Ireland*. Syracuse, NY: Syracuse Univ. Press, 1999.

Cooper, Alan. *Philip Roth and the Jews*. Albany: State Univ. of New York Press, 1996.

Costello-Sullivan, Kathleen. *Trauma and Recovery in the Twenty-First Century Irish Novel*. Syracuse, NY: Syracuse Univ. Press, 2018.

Coughlan, Patricia. "Irish Literature: Feminist Perspectives." In *Irish Literature: Feminist Perspectives*, edited by Patricia Coughlan and Tina O'Toole, 1–16. Dublin: Carysfort Press, 2008.

———. "Killing the Bats: O'Brien, Abjection, and the Question of Agency." In *Edna O'Brien: New Critical Perspectives*, edited by Kathryn Laing, Sinead Mooney, and Maureen O'Connor, 171–95. Dublin: Carysfort Press, 2006.

Coughlan, Patricia, and Tina O'Toole, eds. *Irish Literature: Feminist Perspectives.* Dublin: Carysfort Press, 2008.

Cronin, Michael G. *Impure Thoughts: Sexuality, Catholicism and Literature in Twentieth Century Ireland.* Manchester: Manchester Univ. Press, 2012.

Cullen, Clara, and Margaret Ó hÓgartaigh. *His Grace Is Displeased: The Selected Correspondence of John Charles McQuaid, 1950–1972.* Dublin: Merrion, 2012.

Cullingford, Elizabeth Butler. *Ireland's Others: Gender and Ethnicity in Irish Literature and Popular Culture.* Cork: Cork Univ. Press, 2001.

Davis, Philip. *Bernard Malamud: A Writer's Life.* Oxford: Oxford Univ. Press, 2007.

Davitt, Michael. *Within the Pale: The True Story of Anti-Semitic Persecution in Russia.* New York: Jewish Publication Society of America, 1903.

Dawson, Graham. *Making Peace with the Past? Memory, Trauma and the Irish Troubles.* Manchester: Manchester Univ. Press, 2011.

Deleuze, Gilles, and Félix Guattari. *A Thousand Plateaus: Capitalism and Schizophrenia.* Translated by Brian Massumi. Minneapolis: Univ. of Minnesota Press, 1987.

Derry's Women's Aid. "Feminism and Nationalism: A View from Derry Women's Aid." In *The Field Day Anthology of Irish Writing.* Vols. 4–5, *Irish Women's Writing and Traditions*, edited by Angela Bourke and Seamus Deane, 397–98. Cork: Cork Univ. Press, 2002.

Dewey, John. *John Dewey: The Middle Works, 1899–1924.* Edited by Jo Ann Boydston. Carbondale: Southern Illinois Univ. Press, 1983.

Dickstein, Morris. "Philip Roth's New Novel—*Nemesis.*" *Daily Beast*, Oct. 3, 2010.

Doctorow, E. L. *Ragtime.* New York: Random House, 2007.

Dolan, Jay P. *The Irish Americans: A History.* New York: Bloomsbury, 2010.

Dooley, Brian. *Black and Green: The Fight for Civil Rights in Northern Ireland & Black America.* London: Pluto Press, 1998.

Douglas, R. M. "Anglo-Saxons and Attacotti: The Racialization of Irishness in Britain between the World Wars." *Ethnic and Racial Studies* 25, no. 1 (2002): 40–63.

Douglass, Frederick. *The Life and Times of Frederick Douglass.* Mineola, NY: Dover, 2012.

Doyle, Laura. *Bordering on the Body: The Racial Matrix of Modern Literature and Culture.* New York: Oxford Univ. Press, 1994.

DuBois, W. E. B. *The Souls of Black Folk: Essays and Sketches.* New York: Floating Press, 2010.

Duncan, Dawn. "Edna O'Brien and Virginia." *Canadian Journal of Irish Studies* 22, no. 2 (1996): 99.

Dunne, John. "Terrible Things Happen." Review of *A Goat's Song*, by Dermot Healy; *House of Splendid Isolation*, by Edna O'Brien; *The Fish in the Stone*, by Eamonn McGrath; *A Marked Woman*, by Jeremy Leland; and *The Maid's Tale*, by Kathleen Ferguson. *Books Ireland* 178 (1994): 159–60.

Dyer, Richard. *White*. London: Routledge, 1997.

Eckley, Grace. *Edna O'Brien*. Lewisburg, PA: Bucknell Univ. Press, 1974.

Ellison, Ralph. *The Collected Essays of Ralph Ellison*. New York: Modern Library Classics, 2011.

Enright, Anne. "Anne Enright on Writing from Life." Interview with Deborah Treisman. *New Yorker*, Mar. 6, 2017.

Fargnoli, Nicholas. *Critical Companion to James Joyce: A Literary Reference to His Life and Work*. New York: Infobase, 2014.

Farquharson, Danine, and Bernice Schrank. "Blurring Boundaries, Intersecting Lives: History, Gender, and Violence in Edna O'Brien's *House of Splendid Isolation*." In *Wild Colonial Girl: Essays on Edna O'Brien*, edited by Lisa Colletta and Maureen O'Connor, 110–42. Madison: Univ. of Wisconsin Press, 2006.

Farrell, James T. *Studs Lonigan*. New York: Penguin, 2001.

Faulkner, William. *Absalom, Absalom!* London: Vintage, 2005.

———. "The Art of Fiction, No. 12." Interview by Jean Stein. *Paris Review* 12 (1956).

———. *As I Lay Dying*. London: Vintage, 2004.

———. *Light in August*. London Vintage, 2008.

———. *Requiem for a Nun*. London: Vintage, 2015.

———. *The Sound and the Fury*. London: Vintage, 1995.

Felsenthal, Julia. "Sophie Portnoy." *New Yorker*, May 7, 2009.

Ferriter, Diarmaid. *Judging Dev: A Reassessment of the Life and Legacy of Eamon de Valera*. Dublin: Royal Irish Academy, 2007.

———. *The Transformation of Ireland, 1900–2000*. London: Profile, 2005.

Fitzgerald, F. Scott. *The Great Gatsby*. New York: Simon and Schuster, 2013.

———. *My Lost City: Personal Essays, 1920–1940*. Edited by James L. W. West. Cambridge: Cambridge Univ. Press, 2005.

Foner, Eric. *Give Me Liberty! An American History*. Vol. 2. New York: W. W. Norton, 2011.

Forman, Ira N. "The Politics of Minority Consciousness: The Historical Voting Behavior of American Jews." In *Jews in American Politics: Essays*, edited by

L. Sandy Maisel and Ira N. Forman. Lanham, MD: Rowman & Littlefield, 2004.

Foster, John Wilson. "Irish Fiction, 1965–1990." In *The Field Day Anthology of Irish Writing*, edited by Seamus Deane, 3:938–43. Derry: Field Day, 1991.

Foster, R. F. *The Irish Story: Telling Tales and Making It Up in Ireland*. Oxford: Oxford Univ. Press, 2002.

———. *W. B. Yeats: A Life*. Vol. 2, *The Arch-Poet*. Oxford: Oxford Univ. Press, 2005.

Foucault, Michel. Introduction to *Anti-Oedipus: Capitalism and Schizophrenia*, by Gilles Deleuze and Félix Guattari. Translated by Robert Hurley, Mark Seem, and Helen R. Lane. Minneapolis: Univ. of Minnesota Press, 1983.

Freud, Sigmund. *Civilization and Its Discontents*. Edited by Todd Dufresne. Translated by Gregory C. Richter. Peterborough, ON: Broadview Press, 2016.

Furman, Andrew. "A New 'Other' Emerges in American Jewish Literature: Philip Roth's Israel Fiction." *Contemporary Fiction* 36, no. 4 (1995): 633–53.

Gébler, Carlo. *Father and I: A Memoir*. London: Abacus, 2001.

———. *The Glass Curtain: Inside an Ulster Community*. London: Abacus, 1992.

———. *The Projectionist*. Dublin: New Island, 2015.

Genette, Gerard. "Introduction to the Paratext." Translated by Marie Maclean. *New Literary History* 22, no. 2 (1991): 261–72.

Giemza, Bryan Albin. *Rethinking the Irish in the American South: Beyond Rounders and Reelers*. Jackson: Univ. Press of Mississippi, 2013.

Giles, Paul. *The Global Remapping of American Literature*. Princeton, NJ: Princeton Univ. Press, 2011.

Gillespie, Michael Patrick. "Edna O'Brien and the Lives of James Joyce." In *Wild Colonial Girl: Essays on Edna O'Brien*, edited by Lisa Colletta and Maureen O'Connor, 78–91. Madison: Univ. of Wisconsin Press, 2006.

Gilroy, Paul. *The Black Atlantic: Modernity and Double Consciousness*. London: Verso, 1993.

Glaser, Jennifer. "The Jew in the Canon: Reading Race and Literary History in Philip Roth's *The Human Stain*." *PMLA* 123, no. 5 (2008): 1465–78.

Gooblar, David. *The Major Phases of Philip Roth*. London: Continuum, 2011.

Gordon, Louis. "Leon Uris." In *Encyclopedia of American Popular Fiction*, edited by Geoff Hamilton and Brian Jones, 354–55. New York: Infobase, 2009.

Grant, Madison. *The Passing of the Great Race*. Indianapolis: Palingenesis Project, 2012.

Grauer, Tresa. "Identity Matters: Contemporary Jewish American Writing." In *The Cambridge Companion to Jewish American Literature*, edited by Hana

Wirth-Nesher and Michael P. Kramer, 269–85. Cambridge: Cambridge Univ. Press,.

Gray, Breda. *Women and the Irish Diaspora*. London: Routledge, 2004.

Greenwood, Amanda. *Edna O'Brien*. London: Northcote House, 2003.

Halberstam, David. *The Fifties*. New York: Villard, 1993.

Harte, Liam. *Reading the Contemporary Irish Novel, 1987–2007*. Oxford: Wiley, 2013.

Hezser, Catherine. "'Are You Protestant Jews or Roman Catholic Jews?': Literary Representations of Being Jewish in Ireland." *Modern Judaism* 25, no. 2 (2005): 159–88.

Howe, Irving. "Philip Roth Reconsidered." *Commentary* 54, no. 6 (1972): 69–72.

Howes, Marjorie. Introduction to *The Cambridge Companion to W. B. Yeats*, edited by Marjorie Howes. Cambridge: Cambridge Univ. Press, 2006.

———. "Public Discourse, Private Reflection, 1916–70." In *The Field Day Anthology of Irish Writing*. Vols. 4–5, *Irish Women's Writing and Traditions*, edited by Angela Bourke and Seamus Deane, 923–30. Cork: Cork Univ. Press, 2002.

Hughes, Darren. "The 'Written World' of Philip Roth's Nonfiction." In *Philip Roth: New Perspectives on an American Author*, edited by Derek Parker Royal, 255–70. Westport, CT: Greenwood Press, 2005.

Ingman, Heather. "Edna O'Brien: Stretching the Nation's Boundaries." *Irish Studies Review* 10, no. 3 (2002): 253–65.

———. *Twentieth-Century Fiction by Irish Women: Nation and Gender*. Burlington, VT: Ashgate, 2007.

Ivanova, Velichka. Introduction to *Philip Roth and World Literature: Transatlantic Perspectives and Uneasy Passages*, edited by Velichka Ivanova. London: Cambria Press, 2014.

Jackson, Julia. "Nathan Englander's Serious Moral Act." *Electric Lit*, Feb. 10, 2012.

Jacobson, Matthew Frye. *Whiteness of a Different Color: European Immigrants and the Alchemy of Race*. Cambridge, MA: Harvard Univ. Press, 1998.

Jaher, Frederic Cople. "The Quest for the Ultimate." *American Quarterly* 35, no. 5 (1983): 518–42.

Johnson, James Weldon. *The Autobiography of an Ex-Colored Man*. New York: Dover, 2012.

Jones, Derek. *Censorship: A World Encyclopaedia*. London: Routledge, 2001.

Jones, Helen. *Health and Society in Twentieth Century Britain*. London: Routledge, 2013.

Jong, Erica. *Fear of Flying*. New York: HarperCollins, 1998.

———. "*Fear of Flying* Turns Twenty." Introduction to *Fear of Flying*, viii–x. New York: HarperCollins, 1998.

Joyce, James. "Ireland, Island of Saints and Sages." In *The Critical Writings of James Joyce*, edited by Ellsworth Mason and Richard Ellmann. London: Viking, 1964.

———. *Letters of James Joyce*. Edited by Richard Ellmann. Vol. 1. London: Faber, 1966.

———. *A Portrait of the Artist as a Young Man*. New York: Penguin, 2003.

———. *Ulysses*. Edited by Declan Kiberd. London: Penguin, 2000.

Kaplan, Brett Ashley. *Jewish Anxiety and the Novels of Philip Roth*. New York: Bloomsbury, 2015.

Karel, William, and Livia Manera. *Philip Roth: Unmasked*. PBS, American Masters Series, 2013.

Kavanagh, Patrick. *The Great Hunger*. London: Penguin, 2018.

Kazin, Alfred. Introduction to *Call It Sleep*, by Henry Roth. New York: Picador, 1990.

———. Review of *Goodbye, Columbus*, by Philip Roth. *Reporter* 1, no. 20 (1959): 42–43.

Keating, Geoffrey. *The History of Ireland*. Edited and translated by Patrick S. Dinneen. Vol. 2. London: Irish Texts Society, 1908.

Kenny, Kevin. *The American Irish: A History*. New York: Pearson, 2000.

Keogh, Dermot. *Jews in Twentieth-Century Ireland*. Cork: Cork Univ. Press, 1998.

Kersnowski, Alice Hughes, ed. *Conversations with Edna O'Brien*. Jackson: Univ. Press of Mississippi, 2014.

Keulks, Gavin. "Edna O'Brien." In *The Oxford Encyclopedia of British Literature*, edited by David Scott Kastan, 5:117–20. Oxford: Oxford Univ. Press, 2006.

Kiberd, Declan. *After Ireland: Writing the Nation from Beckett to the Present*. London: Head of Zeus, 2017.

———. *Inventing Ireland: The Literature of a Modern Nation*. London: Random House, 2009.

———. "Irish Literature and Irish History." In *The Oxford History of Ireland*, edited by R. F. Foster. Oxford: Oxford Univ. Press, 1992.

Kibler, M. Alison. *Censoring Racial Ridicule: Irish, Jewish, and African American Struggles over Race and Representation, 1890–1930*. Chapel Hill: Univ. of North Carolina Press, 2015.

Kiernan, Frances. *Seeing Mary Plain: A Life of Mary McCarthy*. New York: W. W. Norton, 2002.

Kinsella, Thomas. "Butcher's Dozen." In *An Anthology of Modern Irish Poetry*, edited by Wes Davis, 244–50. Cambridge, MA: Belknap Press, 2013.

Klein, Scott W. "Zuckerman as Irish Jew: James Joyce, National Difference and Roth's *The Counterlife*." *Philip Roth Studies* 4, no. 2 (2008): 153–69.

Krauss, Nicole. "The Presence of Philip Roth." *New Yorker*, May 24, 2018.

Kristeva, Julia. "Word, Dialogue, and Novel." In *Desire in Language*, edited by Leon Roudiez, translated by Thomas Gora. New York: Colombia Univ. Press, 1990.

Ladrón, Marisol Morales. "(M)Others from the Motherland in Edna O'Brien's *The Light of Evening* and Colm Tóibín's *Brooklyn*." *Journal of Irish Studies* 3 (2013).

Laing, Kathryn, Sinéad Mooney, and Maureen O'Connor, eds. *Edna O'Brien: New Critical Perspectives*. Dublin: Carysfort Press, 2006.

Lambert, Joshua. *Unclean Lips: Jews, Obscenity, and American Culture*. New York: New York Univ. Press, 2013.

Lambert, Sharon. "Irish Women's Emigration to England, 1922–60: The Lengthening of Family Ties." In *Irish Women's History*, edited by Alan Hayes and Diane Urquhart. Dublin: Irish Academic Press, 2004.

Leaney, Enda. "Phrenology in Nineteenth-Century Ireland." *New Hibernia Review/Iris Éireannach Nua* 10, no. 3 (2006): 24–42.

Lee, J. J. "Introduction: Interpreting Irish America." In *Making the Irish American*, edited by J. J. Lee and Marion R. Casey, 1–62. New York: New York Univ. Press, 2006.

Lentin, Alana, and Ronit Lentin, eds. Introduction to *Race and State*, edited by Alana Lentin and Ronit Lentin, 1–14. Newcastle, UK: Cambridge Scholars Press, 2009.

Liebman, Charles S., and Steve Cohen. *Two Worlds of Judaism: The Israeli and American Experience*. New Haven, CT: Yale Univ. Press, 1990.

Lourdeaux, Lee. *Italian and Irish Filmmakers in America*. Philadelphia: Temple Univ. Press, 1990.

Lydon, Christopher. "Remembering Philip Roth." Radio Open Source, May 21, 2018.

MacAlister, R. A. Stewart, ed. and trans. *Lebor Gabála Érenn: The Book of the Taking of Ireland*. Dublin: Education Company of Ireland, 1938.

MacLeod, Norman. "A Note on Philip Roth's *Goodbye, Columbus* and Fitzgerald's *The Great Gatsby*." *International Fiction Review* 12, no. 2 (1985): 104–7.

Mahon, Derek. Review of *A Pagan Place*, by Edna O'Brien. *Listener*, Apr. 23, 1970.

Mailer, Norman. *The Naked and the Dead*. New York: Picador, 2000.

Malamud, Bernard. *A New Life*. London: Chatto & Windus, 1980.

Maloney, Ed. "Media Censorship during 'the Troubles.'" *Nieman Reports*, June 15, 2000.

Marcus, David. *Oughtobiography: Leaves from the Diary of a Hyphenated Jew*. Dublin: Gill & Macmillan, 2001.

Masiero, Pia. *Philip Roth and the Zuckerman Books*. Amherst, NY: Cambria Press, 2011.

McBride, Eimear. Preface to *The Country Girls Trilogy*, by Edna O'Brien. London: Faber, 2017.

McCain, John. "McCain on Israel, Iran and the Holocaust." Interviewed by Jeffrey Goldberg. *Atlantic*, May 30, 2008.

McCarthy, Mary. *The Group*. New York: Houghton Mifflin, 1986.

———. *Memories of a Catholic Girlhood*. London: Random House, 2006.

McGahern, John. "The Church and Its Spire." In *Love of the World: Essays*, edited by John McGahern, 220–45. London: Faber, 2013.

McGlinn, Ann. Review of *Trinity*, by Leon Uris. *Saturday Evening Post*, Sept. 15, 1976.

McGonagle, Marie. "Ireland." In *Censorship: A World Encyclopaedia*, edited by Derek Jones, 1215–18. London: Routledge, 2001.

McWilliams, Ellen. "Making It Up with the Motherland: Revision and Reconciliation in Edna O'Brien's *The Light of Evening*." *Women: A Cultural Review* 22, no. 1 (2011): 50–68.

———. *Women and Exile in Contemporary Irish Fiction*. New York: Palgrave Macmillan, 2013.

Meagher, Timothy. "Abie's Irish Enemy: Irish and Jews, Social and Political Realities and Media Representations." In *Screening Irish-America*, edited by Ruth Barton, 45–58. Dublin: Irish Academic Press, 2009.

Menand, Louis. "The Irony and the Ecstasy: Philip Roth and the Jewish Atlantis." *New Yorker*, May 19, 1997.

Metcalf, Allan A. *Predicting New Words: The Secrets of Their Success*. New York: Houghton Mifflin Harcourt, 2004.

Miller, Cheryl. "Why Malamud Faded." *Commentary*, June 1, 2008.

Mishkin, Tracy. *The Harlem and Irish Renaissances: Language, Identity and Representation*. Gainesville: Univ. Press of Florida, 1998.

Mooney, Sinéad. "Edna O'Brien." In *A History of Modern Irish Women's Literature*, edited by Heather Ingman and Clíona Ó Gallchoir, 244–56. Cambridge: Cambridge Univ. Press, 2018.

Murphy, Yvonne. *Murphy Commission: Report into the Catholic Archdiocese of Dublin*. 2009.

Murray, Tony. *London Irish Fictions: Narrative, Diaspora and Identity*. Liverpool: Liverpool Univ. Press, 2012.

Nadel, Ira. *Joyce and the Jews: Cultures and Texts*. London: Macmillan Press, 1989.

———. *Leon Uris: Life of a Bestseller*. Austin: Univ. of Texas Press, 2010.

Nelson, Bruce. *Irish Nationalists and the Making of the Irish Race*. Princeton, NJ: Princeton Univ. Press, 2012.

Newton, Adam Zachery. "'I Was the Prosthesis': Roth and Late Style." In *Roth after Eighty: Philip Roth and the American Literary Imagination*, ed. David Gooblar and Aimee Pozorski, 127–48. Lanham, MD: Rowman and Littlefield, 2016.

Nirenberg, David. *Anti-Judaism: The Western Tradition*. New York: W. W. Norton, 2014.

Obert, Julia C. "Mothers and Others in Edna O'Brien's *The Country Girls*." *Irish Studies Review* 20, no. 3 (2012): 283–97.

O'Brien, Peggy. "The Silly and the Serious: An Assessment of Edna O'Brien." *Massachusetts Review* 28, no. 3 (1987): 474–88.

O'Connor, Frank. "The Art of Fiction, No. 19." Interview with Anthony Whittier. *Paris Review* 17 (1957).

O'Connor, Maureen. "Edna O'Brien, Irish Dandy." In *Edna O'Brien: New Critical Perspectives*, edited by Kathryn Laing, Sinead Mooney, and Maureen O'Connor, 38–53. Dublin: Carysfort Press, 2006.

———. "Girl Trouble." *Dublin Review of Books*, May 6, 2014.

———. "The Mythopoeic Ireland of Edna O'Brien's Fiction." In *Blackwell Companion to Irish Literature*, edited by Julia M. Wright, 209–23. Chichester, West Sussex: Wiley-Blackwell, 2010.

———. Review of *The Light of Evening*, by Edna O'Brien. *Women's Studies: An Interdisciplinary Journal* 37, no. 7 (2008): 885–91.

———. "Seeing Red." Review of *The Little Red Chairs*, by Edna O'Brien. *Irish Literary Supplement*, Oct. 1, 2017.

Ó Drisceoil, Donal. "Ireland: Neutrality during World War II." In *Censorship: A World Encyclopaedia*, edited by Derek Jones, 1219–21. London: Routledge, 2001.

O'Faolain, Sean. "William Faulkner: More Genius than Talent." In *The Vanishing Hero: Studies in Novelists of the Twenties*, by Sean O'Faolain, 73–111. Boston: Little, Brown, 1957.

Ó Gráda, Cormac. *Jewish Ireland in the Age of Joyce: A Socioeconomic History*. Princeton, NJ: Princeton Univ. Press, 2016.

O'Neill, Joseph. "Roth v. Roth v. Roth." *Atlantic*, Apr. 2012.

O'Neill, Peter D., and David Lloyd. *The Black and Green Atlantic: Cross-Currents of the African and Irish Diasporas*. London: Palgrave Macmillan UK, 2009.

Parrish, Timothy, ed. *The Cambridge Companion to Philip Roth*. Cambridge: Cambridge Univ. Press, 2007.

———. "Introduction: Roth at Mid-Career." In *Cambridge Companion to Philip Roth*, edited by Timothy Parrish, 1–7. Cambridge: Cambridge Univ. Press, 2007.

———. "Roth and Ethnic Identity." In *Cambridge Companion to Philip Roth*, edited by Timothy Parrish, 127–41. Cambridge: Cambridge Univ. Press, 2007.

Pearce, Sandra Manoogian. "An Interview with Edna O'Brien." *Canadian Journal of Irish Studies* 22, no. 2 (1996): 5–8.

Pease, Donald E., John Carlos Rowe, and Winfried Fluck, eds. *Re-framing the Transnational Turn in American Studies*. Hanover, NH: Dartmouth College Press, 2011.

Pelan, Rebecca. "Reflections on a Connemara Dietrich." In *Edna O'Brien: New Critical Perspectives*, edited by Kathryn Laing, Sinead Mooney, and Maureen O'Connor, 12–37. Dublin: Carysfort Press, 2006.

Phillips, Adam. *On Flirtation*. Cambridge, MA: Harvard Univ. Press, 1994.

Pierpont, Claudia Roth. *Roth Unbound*. London: Jonathan Cape, 2013.

Pinter, Harold. *Collected Poems and Prose*, London: Methuen, 1986.

Pittock, Murray. *Celtic Identity and the British Image*. Manchester: Manchester Univ. Press, 1999.

Plante, David. "Conversations with Philip: Diary of a Friendship" (1984). In *Reading Myself and Others*, edited by Philip Roth, 150–61. London: Viking, 1985.

Podhoretz, Norman. "The Adventures of Philip Roth." *Commentary*, Oct. 1998.

Posnock, Ross. *Philip Roth's Rude Truth: The Art of Immaturity*. Princeton, NJ: Princeton Univ. Press, 2006.

Powell, John. *Encyclopedia of North American Immigration*. New York: Infobase, 2009.

Pozorski, Aimee. *Roth and Trauma: The Problem of History in the Later Works (1995–2010)*. London: Bloomsbury, 2013.

Price, Stanley. *James Joyce and Italo Svevo: The Story of a Friendship*. Dublin: Somerville, 2016.

Quinlan, Kieran. *Strange Kin: Ireland and the American South*. Baton Rouge: Louisiana State Univ. Press, 2005.

Quinn, Peter. "The Future of Irish America." In *Making the Irish American*, edited by J. J. Lee and Marion R. Casey, 680–85. New York: New York Univ. Press, 2006.

Rabin, Jessica G. "Requiem for a Dream: Philip Roth's *American Pastoral* and William Faulkner's *Absalom, Absalom!*" In *Reading Philip Roth's American Pastoral*, edited by Velichka D. Ivanova, 219–30. Toulouse: Presses Universitaires du Mirail, 2011.

Reizbaum, Marilyn. *James Joyce's Judaic Other*. Stanford, CA: Stanford Univ. Press, 1999.

Remnick, David. "An American Tragedy." *New Yorker*, Nov. 9, 2016.

———. "Into the Clear: Philip Roth." *New Yorker*, May 8, 2000. In *Reporting: Writing from the "New Yorker."* London: Macmillan, 2008.

Rich, Nathaniel. "Roth Agonistes." Review of *Why Write?*, by Philip Roth. *New York Review of Books*, Mar. 2018.

Rivlin, Ray. *Jewish Ireland: A Social History*. Dublin: History Press, 2011.

Roberts, Diane. *Faulkner and Southern Womanhood*. Athens: Univ. of Georgia Press, 1994.

Rockett, Kevin. "Ireland: Film, Radio, and Television." In *Censorship: A World Encyclopaedia*, edited by Derek Jones, 1221–23. London: Routledge, 2001.

———. *Irish Film Censorship: A Cultural Journey from Silent Cinema to Internet Pornography*. Dublin: Four Courts Press, 2004.

Rosenbaum, Ron. "Novelist Edna O'Brien Explores the True Nature of Evil." *Smithsonian*, July 2016.

Roth, Henry. *Call It Sleep*. New York: Picador, 1990.

Royal, Derek Parker. "Roth, Literary Influence, and Postmodernism." In *Cambridge Companion to Philip Roth*, edited by Timothy Parrish, 22–34. Cambridge: Cambridge Univ. Press, 2007.

Rüdiger, Imhof. Review of *House of Splendid Isolation*, by Edna O'Brien; *The Book of Intrusions*, by Desmond MacNamara; *The Seduction of Morality*, by Tom Murphy; and *A Goat's Song*, by Dermot Healy. *Linen Hall Review* 11, no. 2 (1994): 26–29.

Russell, Dick. *The Life and Ideas of James Hillman*. New York: Skyhorse, 2013.

Safer, Elaine B. "The Double, Comic Irony, and Postmodernism in Philip Roth's *Operation Shylock*." In *Philip Roth: Bloom's Modern Critical Views*. Broomall, PA: Chelsea, 2003.

Said, Edward. "Propaganda and War." *Al-Ahram Weekly*, Aug. 30, 2001.

———. "Thoughts of Late Style." *London Review of Books*, Aug. 5, 2004.

Sampson, Steven. *Corpus Rothi: Tome 2, le Philip Roth tardif, de pastorale américaine à némésis*. Paris: CNL, 2012.

Sandbrook, Dominic. *Mad as Hell: The Crisis of the 1970s and the Rise of the Populist Right*. New York: Anchor, 2011.

Schreier, Benjamin. "The End of Promiscuity." Review of *Promiscuity*, by Bernard Avishai. *American Literary History* 27, no. 1 (2015): 162–71.

Schwartz, Bernard, and Stephan Lesher. *Inside the Warren Court, 1953–1969*. New York: Doubleday, 1983.

Searles, George J., ed. *Conversations with Philip Roth*. Jackson: Univ. Press of Mississippi, 1992.

Shakespeare, William. *Merchant of Venice*. In *Norton Shakespeare*, edited by Stephen Greenblatt, Walter Cohen, Jean E. Howard, and Katharine Eisaman Maus, 1111–76. New York: W. W. Norton, 2008.

Shavit, Ari. *My Promised Land: The Triumph and Tragedy of Israel*. New York: Random House. 2013.

Shechner, Mark. *Up Society's Ass, Copper: Rereading Philip Roth*. Madison: Univ. of Wisconsin Press, 2003.

Shostak, Debra B. *Philip Roth: Countertexts, Counterlives*. Columbia: Univ. of South Carolina Press, 2004.

———. "Roth and Gender." In *Cambridge Companion to Philip Roth*, edited by Timothy Parrish, 111–26. Cambridge: Cambridge Univ. Press, 2007.

Showalter, Elaine. "Many Feminists Find Philip Roth's Work Off-Putting." Interview with Christopher Shea. *Vox*, May 26, 2018.

Siegel, Ben. "Gimpel the Fool, and Other Stories." In *Encyclopaedia of Jewish American Literature*, edited by Gloria L. Cronin and Alan L. Berger, 99–100. New York: Facts on File, 2009.

Singer, Isaac B. *Collected Stories*. London: Penguin, 2003.

Slepian, Barry. "The Ironic Intention of Swift's Verses on His Own Death." *Review of English Studies* 14, no. 55 (1963): 249–56.

Smith, Zadie. "Zadie Smith Remembers Philip Roth." *New Yorker*, May 23, 2018.

Snyder, Timothy. *On Tyranny: Twenty Lessons from the Twentieth Century.* London: Bodley Head, 2017.

Sollors, Werner. *The Invention of Ethnicity.* New York: Oxford Univ. Press, 1989.

Stern, Gerald. "Sixteen Minutes." In *Jewish American Literature: A Norton Anthology*, edited by Jules Chametzky et al., 828–31. New York: W. W. Norton, 2001.

Sterne, Lawrence. *The Life and Opinions of Tristram Shandy.* London: Wordsworth, 1996.

Stevens, Kevin. "Everything He Hated." Review of *Indignation*, by Philip Roth. *Dublin Review of Books*, Sept. 2006.

Stoddard, Eve. *Positioning Gender and Race in (Post)colonial Plantation Space: Connecting Ireland and the Caribbean.* New York: Palgrave Macmillan, 2012.

———. "Sexuality, Nation and Land in the Postcolonial Novels of Edna O'Brien and Jamaica Kincaid." In *Edna O'Brien: New Critical Perspectives*, edited by Kathryn Laing, Sinead Mooney, and Maureen O'Connor, 104–21. Dublin: Carysfort, 2006.

Stokes, Melvyn. *D. W. Griffith's "The Birth of a Nation"? A History of the Most Controversial Motion Picture of All Time.* Oxford: Oxford Univ. Press, 2007.

Stowe, Harriet Beecher. *Uncle Tom's Cabin.* New York: Dover, 2005.

Stubbs, Tara. *American Literature and Irish Culture, 1910–1955: The Politics of Enchantment.* Manchester: Manchester Univ. Press, 2013.

Styron, William. *Selected Letters of William Styron.* Edited by Rose Styron and R. Blakeslee Gilpin. New York: Random House, 2012.

Sullivan, Moynagh. "Raising the Veil: Mystery, Myth, and Melancholia in Irish Studies." In *Irish Literature: Feminist Perspectives*, edited by Patricia Coughlan and Tina O'Toole, 245–77. Dublin: Carysfort Press, 2008.

Sundquist, Eric J. *Strangers in the Land: Blacks, Jews, Post-Holocaust America.* Cambridge, MA: Harvard Univ. Press, 2009.

Swift, Jonathan. *The Oxford Authors: Jonathan Swift.* Edited by Angus Ross and David Woolley. Oxford: Oxford Univ. Press, 1984.

Thompson, Helen. "Hysterical Hooliganism: O'Brien, Freud, Joyce." In *Wild Colonial Girl: Essays on Edna O'Brien*, edited by Lisa Colletta and Maureen O'Connor, 31–57. Madison: Univ. of Wisconsin Press, 2006.

Thompson, Helen, and Catriona Moloney, eds. *Irish Women Writers Speak Out: Voices from the Field.* Syracuse, NY: Syracuse Univ. Press, 2003.

Tovey, Hilary, and Perry Share. *A Sociology of Ireland.* Dublin: Gill & Macmillan, 2000.

Ulin, Julieann Veronica, Heather Edwards, and Sean O'Brien, eds. *Race and Immigration in the New Ireland.* Notre Dame, IN: Univ. of Notre Dame Press, 2013.

Uris, Leon. *Exodus.* New York: Random House, 2000.

Varadharajan, Asha. "The Unsettling Legacy of Harold Bloom's *Anxiety of Influence.*" *Modern Language Quarterly* 69, no. 4 (2008): 461–80.

Watt, Stephen. "Brendan Behan, Borscht Belt Comedian." *Irish University Review* 44, no. 1 (2014): 149–64.

———. *"Something Dreadful and Grand": American Literature and the Irish-Jewish Unconscious.* Oxford: Oxford Univ. Press, 2015.

Whitman, Walt. "Crossing Brooklyn Ferry." In *Portable Walt Whitman.* New York: Penguin, 2003.

———. "Song of Myself." In *The Portable Walt Whitman.* New York: Penguin, 2003.

Wiesel, Elie. Preface to *Dawn.* New York: Hill and Wang, 2006.

Wilde, Oscar. "The Decay of Lying." In *Oscar Wilde: Plays, Prose Writings and Poems,* edited by David Campbell, 71–99. London: Everyman's Library, 1991.

———. "De Profundis." In *Oscar Wilde: Plays, Prose Writings and Poems,* edited by David Campbell, 543–650. London: Everyman's Library, 1991.

———. *Oscar Wilde: Plays, Prose Writings and Poems.* Edited by David Campbell. London: Everyman's Library, 1991.

———. "The Truth of Masks." In *Oscar Wilde: Plays, Prose Writings and Poems,* edited by David Campbell, 101–26. London: Everyman's Library, 1991.

Williams, William Carlos. "At Kenneth Burke's Place." In *The Collected Poems of William Carlos Williams, 1939–1962,* edited by Walton Litz and Christopher MacGowan. New York: New Directions, 1991.

Wills, Clair. *The Best Are Leaving.* New York: Cambridge Univ. Press, 2015.

———. *Lovers and Strangers: An Immigrant History of Post-war Britain.* London: Allen Lane, 2017.

Wood, James. "Stranger in Our Midst." Review of *The Little Red Chairs,* by Edna O'Brien. *New Yorker,* Apr. 25, 2016.

Woods, Michelle. "Eat or Be Eaten: Ernest Gébler's Self-Fashioning as Jewish Monster in *Shall I Eat You Now?*" *Journal of Jewish Identities* 3, no. 2 (2010): 77–92.

———. "Red, Unread, and Edna: Ernest Gébler and Edna O'Brien." In *Edna O'Brien: New Critical Perspectives,* edited by Kathryn Laing, Sinead Mooney, and Maureen O'Connor, 54–97. Dublin: Carysfort Press, 2006.

Yeats, W. B. "Easter, 1916." In *Selected Poetry*, edited by Norman Jeffares. London: Macmillan, 1970.

———. "The Lake Isle of Innisfree." In *Selected Poetry*, edited by Norman Jeffares, 16. London: Macmillan, 1970.

———. *Per Amica Silentia Lunae*. Norwood, MA: Norwood Press, 1918.

———. "The Valley of the Black Pig." In *Selected Poetry*, edited by Norman Jeffares, 32. London: Macmillan, 1970.

Yeats, W. B., and Lady Gregory. *Caithleen Ni Houlihan*. In *Modern and Contemporary Irish Drama*, edited by John P. Harrington, 3–11. New York: W. W. Norton, 2009.

Zax, Tayla. "Why Zadie Smith Thinks Philip Roth, and Alexander Portnoy, Changed the World." *Forward*, Oct. 28, 2016.

Zeitlin, Michael. "James Joyce." In *A William Faulkner Encyclopaedia*, edited by Robert W. Hamblin and Charles A. Peek. Westport, CT: Greenwood, 1999.

Index

Dan O'Brien is an Irish Research Council postdoctoral fellow at University College Dublin, where he received the inaugural Maurice J. Bric Postdoctoral Medal for Excellence in the Humanities. He is coeditor of *Irish Questions and Jewish Questions: Crossovers in Culture* and *New Voices: Contemporary Jewish-American Literature* and has written for a range of publications, including *Breac, Philip Roth Studies, Irish Studies Review, Irish Times, Dublin Review of Books*, and *RTÉ*. His chapter on Philip Roth's literary conversations is forthcoming in *Philip Roth in Context*, part of Cambridge University Press's Literature in Context series.

Select Titles in Irish Studies

Irish Questions and Jewish Questions: Crossovers in Culture
Aidan Beatty and Dan O'Brien, eds.

J. M. Synge and Travel Writing of the Irish Revival
Giulia Bruna

Kate O'Brien and Spanish Literary Culture
Jane Davison

Laying Out the Bones: Death and Dying in the Modern Irish Novel
Bridget English

The Rebels and Other Short Fiction
Richard Power; James MacKillop, ed.

Respectability and Reform: Irish American Women's Activism, 1880–1920
Tara M. McCarthy

Science, Technology, and Irish Modernism
Kathryn Conrad, Cóilín Parsons, and Julie McCormick Weng, eds.

Trauma and Recovery in the Twenty-First-Century Irish Novel
Kathleen Costello-Sullivan

For a full list of titles in this series,
visit https://press.syr.edu/supressbook-series
/irish-studies/.